Matthias Grotkopp
Cinematic Poetics of Guilt

Cinepoetics

—

Edited by
Hermann Kappelhoff and Michael Wedel

Volume 9

Matthias Grotkopp

Cinematic Poetics of Guilt

Audiovisual Accusation as a Mode of Commonality

Translated by
Daniel Hendrickson

DE GRUYTER

ISBN 978-3-11-108779-5
e-ISBN (PDF) 978-3-11-061211-0
e-ISBN (EPUB) 978-3-11-061129-8
ISSN 2569-4294

Library of Congress Control Number: 2020947019

Bibliographic information published by the Deutsche Nationalbibliothek
The Deutsche Nationalbibliothek lists this publication in the Deutsche Nationalbibliografie;
detailed bibliographic data are available on the Internet at http://dnb.dnb.de.

Author's Note

This is the abridged translation of my PhD-thesis that I submitted in 2014 and which studies the feeling of guilt not as a state of individual persons but as an aesthetic modality that connects film viewers to a sense of commonality and a shared past, present and future.

First of all, I would like to thank Hermann Kappelhoff and Michael Wedel for their support and the opportunity to present this book to the English-speaking public and I would like to thank Daniel Hendrickson for his faithful translation. Many thanks also to Christina Schmitt, Kaspar Aebi, Maximilian Grenz and Maja Roth for their diligent and thorough support in getting this manuscript into the printing press.

To keep this book lean and handy, I had to cut one of the cases studies in each of the three thematic chapters: For the German post-war cinema I have dropped the chapter on DIE MÖRDER SIND UNTER UNS (THE MURDERERS ARE AMONG US, 1946, Wolfgang Staudte) since it is discussed in practically every book on the topic. For the part on Hollywood genre cinema I have dispensed with the chapter on CASUALTIES OF WAR (1989, Brian De Palma) because the war film is already well represented in the Cinepoetics book series. For the part on climate change documentaries I chose the opposite argument and cut the chapter on THE AGE OF STUPID (2009, Franny Armstrong) and kept AN INCONVENIENT TRUTH (2006, Davis Guggenheim) in order to make the case for a study of affect rhetoric even stronger by applying it to one of the most prominent examples within the field of cinema and ecology, climate change and the Anthropocene.

I have resisted the urge to rewrite larger passages, only smaller expendable digressions have been left out and I added a handful of bibliographic references that have appeared in the meantime and that I find to be especially meaningful connections that are worth being made.

I dedicate this edition to Josephine and Benjamin. May they never become victims of our comfort.

https://doi.org/10.1515/9783110612110-202

Contents

Introduction

At some point western societies gave up building triumphal arches and victory columns and started putting up memorials and monuments. The confrontation with the horrible crimes of the past – not only in Germany, but in almost all the states of Europe and North America, which look back at a history of exploitation, slavery, colonialism, and eradication of other human groups – has become a fundamental principle of self-legitimation and identity formation: "Regret is the emblem of our times."[1]

Even a theorist like Richard Rorty, for whom histories of one's own past are always at the same time part of representing hopes for the future, and who postulates an identity[2] based in pride and other positive feelings as the requirement for political thinking and acting, admits that our past and present can hardly give us any utopian feelings: "I do not think that we liberals *can* now imagine a future of 'human dignity, freedom and peace.' That is, we cannot tell ourselves a story about how to get from the actual present to such a future."[3]

Also, the thinking of possibility in art is more than ever concerned with recounting suffering, putting thought and memory things[4] into the world that allow us to understand the fact that *such things* are possible in the world in which we live. At the latest after the break in civilization created by the Shoah, according to Hannah Arendt, the "fear of the inescapable guilt of the human race," and of what "men are capable of bringing about," is an unavoidable "precondition of any modern political thinking."[5] Remembering an injustice that has been perpetrated marks a dimension of the social, political, and cultural reality as an unavoidable component of our legacy. Any question of morality and ethics is thus inseparably bound to processes of power and violence and appears to us – as to Friedrich Nietzsche – as something that has "really never quite lost a certain odour of blood and torture."[6]

---

1 Jeffrey K. Olick: *The Politics of Regret. On Collective Memory and Historical Responsibility.* New York / London 2007, 14.

2 Cf. Richard Rorty: *Achieving our Country. Leftist Thought in Twentieth-Century America.* Cambridge 1999, 3–5.

3 Richard Rorty: *Contingency, Irony, and Solidarity.* Cambridge 1998, 181–182.

4 Cf. Hannah Arendt: *The Human Condition.* Chicago 1958, 168–174.

5 Hannah Arendt: Organized Guilt and Universal Responsibility [1946]. In: id.: *Essays in Understanding. 1930–1954: Formation, Exile, and Totalitarianism.* New York 1994, 121–132, here 132.

6 Friedrich Nietzsche: *On the Genealogy of Morality* [1887]. Cambridge 2016, 43.

https://doi.org/10.1515/9783110612110-001

Time periods are, according to Siegfried Kracauer, a "precarious conglomerate of tendencies, aspirations, and activities"[7] and form their own non-chronological configurations. They develop physiognomies from events and dispositions which are never homogenous, yet they interact and in their own way establish that particular temporality named history.[8] The time period of the twentieth and the early twenty-first centuries can now be described, among other things, as a connection between certain events and a disposition that I would propose calling a collective sense of guilt. This sense of guilt neither signifies human sinfulness in an eschatological or depth psychology perspective, not does it signify an attribute that can defined concretely, spatially, temporally, and numerically, but a structure in which we today experience the relationship between I and we, between past, present, and future.

Cinema also has its share, perhaps even a privileged one, in the physiognomy of this time period. The goal of the present work is to determine the degree to which films can shape the disposition of the sense of guilt, in terms of both film theory and a theory of feeling, and the degree to which they attend to the affective foundations of historicity and a shared sense of values in view of experiences of injustice and suffering, which go beyond the realm of personal morality.

The sense of guilt here will be addressed as one of the forms in which people experience themselves as politically, socially, and historically located beings. It is therefore to be aligned with its counterpart, absolution, but also and in particular with the sense of responsibility and duty, which stands behind the capacity to promise. The human being is – according to Hannah Arendt – embedded in the irreversibility of time in a dual mode by the sense of guilt and by the promise, and at the same time stands open in unpredictability through absolution and the endless, creative possibilities of the new, of natality.[9]

As an affective structuring of time and public sphere, both the sense of guilt as well as absolution and promise only make sense when they are borne by the presence and recognition of others.[10] The retrospection of crime justifies a political community, which is committed to preserving the memory, the compensation, and the anticipated promise to ward off any future return of the injustice. The declaration of universal human rights and its liberal-ironic counterpart in Rorty, the call to expand solidarity and the avoidance of cruelty,[11] are historically grounded in the genesis and stabilization of this register of feelings in relation to

---

7 Siegfried Kracauer: *History. The Last Things Before the Last* [1969]. New York 1995, 66.

8 Cf. Kracauer: *History*, 146–159.

9 Cf. Arendt: *The Human Condition*, 236–247.

10 Cf. Arendt: *The Human Condition*, 237.

11 Cf. Rorty: *Contingency, Irony, and Solidarity*.

the community.[12] Due to it being integrated into historically contingent processes of politics, history, and feelings, the sense of guilt, as a crisis-laden formation of temporality and memory, is, in a converse argument, also tied to concrete forms and practices, that is, to aesthetic processes. What follows is meant to show how films – as perfect examples of such forms and practices in the arts and media – shape and model how the sense of guilt is experienced. The modalities of aesthetic experience cannot any more afford a final justification of morality and responsibility than can the philosophical argument, jurisprudence, or religious revelation, but they can confront us with an unconditional claim to morality and responsibility:

> I would therefore like to say a word about Dostoevsky's *Crime and Punishment*, which plays through the idea that neither by reflecting on, discussing, or even disputing the Enlightenment can any reason by found why a person should not be killed. This reason is impossible. And then Raskolnikov commits this murder and discovers in the concrete confrontation with a concrete person what this is – guilt. And he does not allow this guilt to be taken away, not by any court in the world.[13]

This work is not concerned with the guilty conscience of having eaten the last cookie, of crossing against a red light, or cheating at Monopoly. Rather, it will analyze a form by which we experience that being a person in a community means that one is always already a Raskolnikov among Raskolnikovs, that one recognizes history and community as a sequence of monstrosities, and that one cannot simply shake off this burden, but instead must add it into the affective fabric of moral and political identity. By emphasizing an affective link, I am drawing on an understanding of community that is neither defined as ethnic, genealogical, or territorial, nor by a fixed ensemble of cultural qualities and convictions, etc. as substantial, actual, and intrinsic. The term community here means a manifestation of individual sensation and not census. It is, like in Benedict Anderson, a matter of *Imagined Communities*,[14] although in comparison to Anderson I would put more emphasis on the fact that the ideas of moving boundaries between 'us' and 'those others,' of sovereignty, and of "deep horizontal comradeship"[15] represent processes based in feelings. Using the term sense of guilt is meant to make visible precisely the relation between

---

12 Cf. Olick: *The Politics of Regret*, 123–126.

13 Contribution by Dietmar Kamper to a discussion panel with Claus H. Bachmann and Gerburg Treusch-Dieter: Schuld und Geschichte – Aufs Spiel gesetzt. In: Gerburg Treusch-Dieter, Dietmar Kamper, Bernd Ternes (eds.): *Kursbuch 37. Schuld.* Tübingen 1999, 21–32, here 32 [trans. DH].

14 Benedict Anderson: *Imagined Communities. Reflections on the Origin and Spread of Nationalism* [1983]. London / New York 2006.

15 Anderson: *Imagined Communities*, 7.

individual feeling, perception, and thinking and a community in the sense of a field of stress conditions, unclear boundaries, and internal differentiations.

The collective sense of guilt serves here as a starting point from which to get a grasp on how to think the political and the historical after Hannah Arendt and Stanley Cavell, based on the operations on the concrete sensibilities of a shared approach to reality and to a structure of recognition and refusals of self-articulation. It is exactly in this understanding that the worldview of the sense of guilt is linked to the Cavellian idea of film as a way of thinking in "world projections."[16]

I am borrowing from Cavell to name my starting position, which I would like to expand to include a perspective according to which film is not only the world as it is seen, the *World Viewed*, but also the world as a structure of feeling, the world as an event of expression, of which every movement, shade, and hue is expressive.[17] Film, according to Cavell, creates a world that is similar to our own, that is like ours and at the same time not like ours, a world that features us and from which we are radically excluded. The fact that we are excluded from this world and haunt it as perceiving beings is what makes it possible in the first place that we can use it to fulfill the wish for possession and knowledge of the world, that the laws of this world unfold completely and utterly in our perception:

> Film is a moving image of skepticism: not only is there a reasonable possibility, it is a fact that here our normal senses are satisfied of reality while reality does not exist – even, alarmingly, because it does not exist, because viewing is all it takes. [...] The basis of film's drama [...] lies in its persistent demonstration that we do not know what our conviction in reality turns upon.[18]

Cinema taps into the uncanny idea that the state of our existence is somehow impossible and faulty, and that we are only spectators in our lives, haunting our own existence.[19] It thus makes it possible, by restricting the visual surface and banishing the viewer from the world viewed, to conceive the conditions and limitations of human existence, namely that how we physically are to the world and to one another always already goes beyond what our individual senses provide to us, and we can nonetheless engage with the world and with each other,[20] that we have access to something that we can call, along with

---

16 Stanley Cavell: *The World Viewed. Reflections on the Ontology of Film* [1971]. Cambridge / London 1979, 72.

17 Cf. Daniel Yacavone: *Film Worlds. A Philosophical Aesthetics of Cinema*, New York 2015.

18 Cavell: *The World Viewed*, 188–189.

19 Cf. Cavell: *The World Viewed*, 160.

20 Cf. Stanley Cavell: What Becomes of Things on Film. In: id: *Themes out of School. Effects and Causes*. Chicago / London 1984, 173–183, here 175.

Immanuel Kant and Arendt: "an extra sense – like an extra mental capability (German: *Menschenverstand*) – that fits us into a community."[21]

The world-views of the cinema therefore also include making evident that the conditions of this world consist in the fact that it can always only appear from particular angles, from limited standpoints, and that others, just as good, are always possible. Without the contingency of limitations and standpoints, without fragmenting perception there is simply no world,[22] at least no world as something that occurs between people, that can be collectively cared for: "Without being talked about by men and without housing them, the world would not be a human artifice but a heap of unrelated things."[23] At the same time, for Hermann Kappelhoff the connection between contingency and political reality is one of the possibilities of cinema, its utopian potential, "an opportunity to take the historical, social, and media conditions that establish the space of everyday perception, and thus the possibility of experiencing with the senses, and to make them sensually graspable, viewable, evident."[24]

Cinema makes it possible to experience the degree to which the world is no object, but a structure of relationships that is newly calibrated as a whole with every word, every look, and every movement. This structure is never neutral. It is always already permeated with projections, that is, with dramatizations and fictionalizations of everyday processes of perception, feeling, and thinking: "I suppose that the ease with which we accepted film reality came from our having already taken reality dramatically."[25]

Film thus thinks what it means to recognize the conditions and limitations of our existence, what it means that we are visible to one another[26] and that the problem of the self and the other is not a problem of knowledge, but of recognizing contingency and incomplete expression: "But movies also promise us happiness exactly not because we are rich or beautiful or perfectly expressive, but because we can tolerate individuality, separateness, and inexpressiveness."[27]

---

21 Hannah Arendt: *Lectures on Kant's Political Philosophy* [1982], ed. Ronald Beiner. Chicago 1992, 70.

22 Cf. Cavell: *The World Viewed*, 156.

23 Arendt: *The Human Condition*, 204.

24 Hermann Kappelhoff: *The Politics and Poetics of Cinematic Realism* [2008]. New York 2015, 15.

25 Cavell: *The World Viewed*, 90.

26 Cf. Stanley Cavell: What Photography Calls Thinking [1985]. In: William Rothman (ed.): *Cavell on Film*. Albany 2005, 115–133.

27 Cavell: *The World Viewed*, 213.

As concrete sensual interventions in the contingent orders of perception and taste,[28] cinema makes visible these orders as changing and constantly open to shifts in their inclusions and exclusions. The aspiration of thinking and compassion is not manifest through any abstract insight, but by facing one's own visibility. Precisely because human beings have very few 'natural' modes of expression, we have the task of constantly, but always only provisionally, giving ourselves our modes of putting ourselves in space, time, and corporality: "What happens is that they [people, MG] have become (always already) victims of expression – readable in every sound and gesture [...] as if we are expression machines, and virtually never turned off."[29]

The unlimited range of expression is ultimately not restricted to the bodies that appear in the world projections of films. The specific law of the world that becomes visible preordains the lines of the spectator's movements of perception and sensation with every frame, every movement. In a certain dimension of film aesthetics this connection is then so obviously the focal point that the spectator's feelings are "the direct obverse, the continuation of cinematic movement images"[30] and the image "directly clamps down on the spectator's affect movement, realizing itself uniquely in the time of his or her perception."[31] In this regard, films are processes of transmitting temporal structures of cultural, historical, and medial patterns of subjectivity and expressivity to individual spectator bodies. Being in the community is immanent to the rhythms and dynamics of the film as a specific feeling in each case, as an aesthetic phenomenon, the actual context of which is the perception of one's own being-affected-by-something. As such, films do not 'treat' problems of politics and history, but construct them in the first place as orders of perception, thought, and feeling, as structures of recognizing contingency and the restriction of human self-articulation.

The aim of this work is to propose a relationship between individually embodied perception and culturally formed practices of meaning, with regard to both political philosophy and film theory, and to ground that relationship in a

---

28 The judgment of taste assumes a special place in Arendt and Cavell and describes the basic structure of balancing human cooperation and the conditions of the political. Cf. Arendt: *Kant's Political Philosophy*; Stanley Cavell: Aesthetic Problems of Modern Philosophy [1976]. In: id.: *Must We Mean What We Say?* Cambridge 2002, 73–96.

29 Stanley Cavell: Performative and Passionate Utterance. In: id.: *Philosophy the Day after Tomorrow*. Cambridge / London 2005, 155–191, here 186–187.

30 Hermann Kappelhoff: *Matrix der Gefühle. Das Kino, das Melodrama und das Theater der Empfindsamkeit*. Berlin 2004, 17 [trans. DH].

31 Hermann Kappelhoff: *Matrix der Gefühle*, 19 [trans. DH].

theory of feelings as well as the context of morality and aesthetic experience, bringing this into the realm of film analysis. How do films evoke the moral sense of guilt as an experience of shared values and shared history?

This also covers the central purpose that I am addressing here in terms of film studies. The work targets a gap between two dominant research directions. On one hand there are various approaches to the relationship between audiovisuality and affect, in which examining moral attitudes, however, only plays a subordinate role and in many cases is merely named at the level of the cognitive evaluation of the characters and actions represented.[32] On the other there are theories of the morality of aesthetic paradigms and questions according to a morality of positioning the spectator, in which, however, the aspect of concrete physical sensations remains secondary.[33]

This gap is precarious because the potential for being affected by film and other audiovisual media, as well as their social, political, and historical efficacy, has increasingly been the focus of psychology, historiography, and the social sciences. All too often their interest is characterized by the fact that the genuinely aesthetic dimensions of film do not play any role at all, or only quantifiable content analyses and character identification that can be described psychologistically are taken into account.[34]

Such a reduction can also be seen in the only relevant approach to analyzing the modulation of a feeling of guilt in film. In Carl Plantinga's work this is limited to the congruency between the characters' wishes and those of the spectators, who are drawn to them in sympathy.[35] This should be contrasted with a model that makes the moving dimension of film comprehensible as a way of structuring the spectator's feeling as the sense of guilt.

Aside from the work mentioned by Plantinga, there is no other noteworthy research literature on the specific conjunction of the sense of guilt and audiovisual

---

32 In particular, this would include the works of Tan, Grodal and Plantinga. Ed S. Tan: *Emotion and the Structure of Narrative Film. Film as an Emotion Machine.* Mahwah 1996; cf. Torben Grodal: *Embodied Visions. Evolution, Emotion, Culture and Film.* Oxford 2009 and Carl Plantinga: *Moving Viewers. American Film and the Spectator's Experience.* Berkeley 2009.

33 See for instance the analyses in Catherine Wheatley: *Michael Haneke's Cinema. The Ethic of the Image.* New York / Oxford 2009.

34 For a critique of this tendency, see: Hermann Kappelhoff, Jan-Hendrik Bakels: Das Zuschauergefühl. Möglichkeiten qualitativer Medienanalyse. In: *Zeitschrift für Medienwissenschaft* (2011), Vol. 5, No. 2, 78–96.

35 Cf. Carl Plantinga: Synästhetische Affekte. Szenarios von Schuld und Scham in Hitchcocks Filmen. In: Anne Bartsch, Jens Eder, Kathrin Fahlenbrach (eds.): *Audiovisuelle Emotionen. Emotionsdarstellung und Emotionsvermittlung durch audiovisuelle Medienangebote.* Cologne 2007, 350–361.

presentation. The situation with research on the related feeling of shame is somewhat different, which partly has to do with the fact that shame has been inseparably identified with visual structures at least since Jean-Paul Sartre's phenomenological analysis of consciousness in *Being and Nothingness*.[36] Shame is then also interpreted by Tarja Laine as a particular form of analogizing and interrupting the gazes of the camera, the character, and the spectator.[37]

The decisive point in closing the gap mentioned above seems to me to be taking up an understanding of morality that not only covers cognitive evaluation,[38] but also and primarily the aesthetic modulation of affectivity. Moral feelings should be understood as processes of unlocking the self, the world, and values. The validity of norms in this concept is based on the authority of feelings and not the other way around.[39] The 'rationality'[40] and morality of feelings would thus be located not in the singular feeling, but in a comprehensive network made up of repetitions, reflections, ambivalences, interactions, displacements, and revisions. Furthermore, I assume that aesthetic feelings in this alliance are embedded in felt evaluations and participate as specific forms of experience[41] in the individual and the cultural constitution of identity by means of structures of responsibility and capacities to judge.[42]

Following these theoretical assumptions, I follow here the hypothesis that the evocation of moral feelings by films results from the fact that expressive patterns and temporal structures, which are congruent with the processuality of the physical sensing of specific feelings, are linked to a perspective on constellations of plot and character that may conform to the formal criteria of the corresponding feeling. Current cognitive theories on film and emotion only

---

36 Jean-Paul Sartre: *Being and Nothingness* [1943]. New York 1993, cf. Hilge Landweer: *Scham und Macht. Phänomenologische Untersuchungen zur Sozialität eines Gefühls*. Tübingen 1999, 103–107.

37 Cf. Tarja Laine: *Shame and Desire. Emotion, Intersubjectivity, Cinema*. Brussels 2007.

38 For an overview of the various philosophical theories of feeling, cf. Christoph Demmerling, Hilge Landweer: *Philosophie der Gefühle. Von Achtung bis Zorn*. Stuttgart 2007 and Sabine Döring (ed.): *Philosophie der Gefühle*. Frankfurt a. M. 2009.

39 Cf. Hermann Schmitz: *Das Reich der Normen*. Freiburg i. Br. 2012; Jan Slaby: Möglichkeitsraum und Möglichkeitssinn. Bausteine einer phänomenologischen Gefühlstheorie. In: Kerstin Andermann, Undine Eberlein (eds.): *Gefühle als Atmosphären. Neue Phänomenologie und philosophische Emotionstheorie*. Berlin 2011, 125–138.

40 Cf. the book title that has become almost proverbial: Ronald de Sousa: *The Rationality of Emotion*. Cambridge 1987.

41 Cf. John Dewey: *Art as Experience* [1934]. New York 1980.

42 Cf. Maria-Sibylla Lotter: *Scham, Schuld, Verantwortung. Über die kulturellen Grundlagen der Moral*. Frankfurt a. M. 2012.

tend to take the second half of this equation into account, at the risk of neglecting the material dimension of film and its perception, embodied by the spectator. They thus lead into the theoretical dead end of a separation of narrative and formal, audiovisual presentation. Here, however, I will be taking a phenomenological approach in which the levels of fiction and of understanding are only shaped in the first place by the temporal unfolding of the embodied experience of patterns of perceiving and affecting.[43] Even the most complex sense and value constructions of moral norms and political belonging are based on the operations and connections of such patterns over the duration of the film. These constructions and meaning-makings should be traced back in their genesis into micro-events of perceiving, feeling, and thinking. It is therefore not a matter of basic emotions, but of forms of treating temporality as complex feelings. The sense of guilt should be regarded as a specific temporal structure. Film and spectator feeling are not in a relation of cause and effect, they are a cohesive theoretical dimension, an expressive tense, which is to be conceived as directly realized in embodied processes.

Ultimately, the concrete question of the sense of guilt should be a contribution to a wider understanding of the specific media conditions of organizing social and moral feelings. We are not dealing with isolated shapes and evaluating object relations. Instead, it is a matter of complex operations and connections, aimed at creating the experience of participating out of a shared relationship, to the self and to the world. The sense of guilt and other so-called "negative affects"[44] are therefore to be seen in the context of a principle of aesthetic experience oriented to affective self-pleasure, for which it is primarily a question of the experience of being integrated into a shared horizon of values.

Beyond the problems of film and media studies, the reflections here are also meant to affect the question of the place of feelings in contemporary political theory, in which – apart from certain exceptions[45]– feelings are largely viewed as input to be managed for decisions or output of the executive and legislature.[46] I intend to show how media and cultural practices, as specific relations to the self and the world and an associate affective integration into a political community,

---

43 I consider the pioneering work in such an approach to be Vivian Sobchack: *The Address of the Eye. A Phenomenology of Film Experience*. Princeton 1992.

44 Chris Tedjasukmana: Wie schlecht sind die schlechten Gefühle im Kino? Politische Emotionen, negative Affekte und ästhetische Erfahrung. In: *montage AV* (2012), Vol. 21, No. 2, 11–27.

45 For instance, Sara Ahmed: *The Cultural Politics of Emotion*. New York 2004.

46 Cf. Gary S. Schaal and Felix Heidenreich: Zur Rolle von Emotionen in der Demokratie. In: *Aus Politik und Zeitgeschichte* (2013), Vol. 63, No. 32/33, 3–11, here 9.

not only secondarily administer, manipulate, or suppress, but also create the conditions for the possibility of the political.

The following work is divided into two parts. In the first part it is argued that the connection between audiovisual image and moral feelings is based in the aesthetic modulation of the affect self-reflection of the spectator. Starting from a phenomenological theory of feeling and the normativity of feelings, and following a descriptive film analytical method, it will be derived how the sense of guilt proceeds as a relation to the self and to the world by treating the embodied perception of the spectator through formal audiovisual structures. In this regard the operation is exploratory and is aimed at comparing such structures and their embeddedness in specific historical and political contexts. The analytical descriptions of the films and the qualification of their expressive structures, as modellings of emotional processes, are thus not statements about empirically verifiable spectator reactions – which would also be a questionable undertaking due to historical distance and the impossibility of taking into account subjective requirements and reception situations – but about how affecting is calculated in the specific films, which is immanent to these structures.

The variety in the poetics and historical constellations analyzed in the second part will thus serve as an instrument to dissect the similarities and differences, the specific qualities of the media reference to sense of commonality in the various ways of presentation. Different strategies of creating a shared horizon of values and meaning can be seen in the three thematic focal points. First there are the aesthetic forms of separating the guilty from the innocent accomplices in German post-war cinema, second of Hollywood genre cinema and the constant revision of its poetic model, and third of the principles of rhetoric as a basic structure for addressing the spectator in documentaries on climate change. If we wish to express the relationship of the three objects of study here systematically, the relationship experienced in the films between feelings and cultural, historical identities appears in each case as a problem of the present, the past, or the future.

In German post-war film the distinction between attributions of guilt or the dramaturgical transformation of feelings of guilt, shame, and other affects becomes a form to position spectators in the political present. The historical context of post-war Germany is the paradigmatic case for questions of collective responsibility: "The confrontation with German guilt has raised issues that, in many ways, have defined an age."[47] The fact that this confrontation did not play out in public discourse and in aesthetic forms directly and unambiguously, but was

---

47 Jeffrey K. Olick: *In the House of the Hangman. The Agonies of German Defeat. 1943–1949.* Chicago / London 2005, xiii.

marked by contradictions and lapses, which to this day are talked about as a second guilt,[48] should also be worked out in the films, in their audiovisual dynamics and in how they structure the spectator's sensations.

A film that is paradigmatic for the ideological presentation of affect-dramaturgical engagements with history and identity is DER RAT DER GÖTTER (COUNCIL OF THE GODS, 1950, Kurt Maetzig), a DEFA production that was made at the time of the founding of the GDR. By embedding an analysis of the film in the context of contemporary debates, and in particular the discussion around Karl Jaspers's *The Question of German Guilt*,[49] it can be shown that there is a specific concept of communality inherent in cinematic affect dramaturgy – without degenerating into a fixed division into cultures of shame or guilt.[50] To what degree does the processual interaction of feelings itself point to whether community is conceived of in each case as contingent and variable, or essentialist and left to fate? A leading hypothesis in this question runs that the latter is true for immediate post-war German cinema, and that the former is the case for Hollywood genre poetics.

One of the starting points for the question posed by this work as a whole was an observation in later Westerns starting in the 1960s – from CHEYENNE AUTUMN (1964, John Ford) to UNFORGIVEN (1992, Clint Eastwood) – and in the relationship of Vietnam war films to classical war films about the Second World War. They are characterized by moralizing revisions of genre poetics and are understood as critiques of the self-images and actions of the American nation, which at the same time aims to reshape the affective fabric of the community. Following the relevant works about the cultural self-image of the USA that is expressed in the western genre, the myth of the *frontier*,[51] and Hermann Kappelhoff's affect-poetic concept of genre, the context created by revising the genre-poetic model and modulating feelings of guilt will be presented. In doing so I will be drawing on a

---

48 Cf. Holger Schmale: Ein Präsident, der gerne mehr tun würde. Gauck bekennt das Vergessen als zweite deutsche Schuld. Reparationsforderungen wird er in Berlin ansprechen. In: *Berliner Zeitung* (8 March 2014). Cf. Olick: *In the House of the Hangman*, 4 and Ralph Giordano: *Die zweite Schuld – oder Von der Last Deutscher zu sein.* Hamburg 1987.

49 Karl Jaspers: *Die Schuldfrage. Zur politischen Haftung Deutschlands* [1946]. Munich 1987.

50 Cf. the classic study of Ruth Benedict: *The Chrysanthemum and the Sword. Patterns of Japanese Culture* [1946]. London 1967. See also Claudia Benthien: *Tribunal der Blicke. Kulturtheorien von Scham und Schuld und die Tragödie um 1800.* Cologne / Weimar / Vienna 2011.

51 Cf. Richard Slotkin: *Gunfighter Nation. The Myth of the Frontier in Twentieth-Century America.* New York 1992; John G. Cawelti: *The Six Gun Mystique.* Bowling Green 1971; John G. Cawelti: The Frontier and the Native American. In: Joshua C. Taylor: *America as Art.* Washington D. C. 1976, 135–183.

concept of genre as a system of different modes of dynamically arranging modalities of aesthetic experience.[52] The film selected – LITTLE BIG MAN (1970, Arthur Penn) – is characterized by how it links the variation of genre-poetic models with the presentation and failure and powerlessness against one's own cultural self-images and communalization processes.

While post-war German cinema addresses a destroyed reality of the political community and American genre cinema refers to a sense for the communal that has to be configured anew over and over again, the documentaries about the causes and consequences of global climate change work by means of techniques of medial witnessing, by which spectators can be constituted in the first place as a community of those who bear responsibility for the future. The anticipated feelings of guilt for the coming destruction are meant to be viewed as a building block in translating the data from the natural sciences into cultural contexts of meaning and affect, moral attitudes. In addition, the films are meant to be viewed within the framework of rhetoric as a cultural practice of dealing with evidence and normativity[53] as well as with respect to the idea of rhetoric as conceptualizing convincing 'speech,' to be shown in concrete audiovisual dynamics of movement.[54] It is also necessary to take into account questions of the representability of climate change and its cultural-historical and media theoretical requirements.[55]

In selecting films for this topic there is no way around AN INCONVENIENT TRUTH (2006, Davis Guggenheim), which has not only had the greatest worldwide distribution, in part due to its prominent casting of former US presidential candidate Albert Arnold "Al" Gore, but which, because it is a film of a lecture in front of an audience, is eminently suitable to examine the connection between classical rhetoric and film presentation.

---

52 Cf. Christine Gledhill: Rethinking Genre. In: id., Linda Williams (eds.): *Reinventing Film Studies*. London 2000, 221–243.

53 Cf. Aristotle: *The "Art" of Rhetoric*, trans. John Henry Freese. London 1926; cf. Blumenberg, Hans: An Anthropological Approach to the Contemporary Significance of Rhetoric. In: Kenneth Baynes, James Bohman, Thomas McCarthy (eds.): *After Philosophy. End or Transformation.* Cambridge 1987, 429–438; cf. Hilge Landweer: Normativität, Moral und Gefühle. In: id. (ed.): *Gefühle. Struktur und Funktion.* Berlin 2007, 237–254.

54 Cf. Hermann Kappelhoff, Cornelia Müller: Embodied Meaning Construction. Multimodal Metaphor and Expressive Movement in Speech, Gesture, and Feature Film. In: *Metaphor and the Social World* (2011), Vol. 1, No. 2, 121–153. Cf. For an initial overview: Gesche Joost: *Bild-Sprache. Die audio-visuelle Rhetorik des Films.* Bielefeld 2008.

55 Cf. Paul J. Crutzen, Michael D. Mastrandrea, Stephen H. Schneider, Mike Davis, Peter Sloterdijk (eds.): *Das Raumschiff Erde hat keinen Notausgang.* Frankfurt a. M. 2011 and Joachim Radkau: *The Age of Ecology* [2011]. Cambridge 2014.

What are the crimes of the concentration and extermination camps? What is life in the ruins? What is war? What is history? What is climate change? The possible answers to these questions are diverse, but they are all shot through with feelings as social realities. I am not concerned here with representing the sense of guilt in the individual contexts as the (more) correct or (more) desirable feeling, and also not with impressing a categorizing concept on certain phenomena with the sense of guilt. Rather, basic qualities, ambivalences, and relations are meant to be made visible through the effect that the question of feelings of guilt has on the analysis of films and their aesthetics, poetic, and rhetorical concepts.

For in the end the focus is on the way feelings per se take part in the intersubjective cultivation of a shared sensual access to reality, of a shared structure of recognition – and less this or that feeling. The object should not be individual judgments and affective evaluations, but the structures in which we experience the standards and modes according to which it becomes visible whether there is something there to be judged or evaluated at all, and in which these are transformed in the experience. The idea is to examine what part feelings have in structuring the contingent standpoints of judgment, in the claims to justification, agreement, and consent, in the possibilities and limits of community.[56]

---

56 Cf. Stanley Cavell: *Cities of Words. Pedagogical Letters on a Register of the Moral Life.* Cambridge / London 2004, 24–27, and passim.

Part 1: **Theoretical Positions**

1 Feeling and Morality in the Cinema

My investigations in the present work are aimed as a whole at whether and how it is possible for films to shape, evoke, and treat a feeling of guilt. To put it more generally the question is how an aesthetic modulation, not only of feelings, but of decidedly moral feelings, can be understood and described. The answer to this question should in turn serve to analyze and evaluate the historical and political meaning of treating the feelings of collective guilt and collective responsibility in various film historical constellations and in a variety of film poetics.

Before I can attempt the latter in the three thematic analytic chapters, I must first deduce the theoretical requirements of an aesthetic modulation of moral feelings. It is also necessary to define the three key terms and how they relate to one another. That means presenting and accounting for which theory of feeling I am referring to in the following, which concept of morality I am using as a basis, and which understanding of aesthetics, or aesthetic experience my remarks apply to. This, however, cannot amount to – or at least it would far exceed the claims of this work – proposing a general and all-encompassing theory of feeling, morality, and aesthetics in each case, and deploying this once again in all its possible interferences and dissonances, overlappings, and connections. Neither, I would claim, would this ideal impartiality be at all conceivable. There is simply a difference depending on whether one starts from a concept of feeling that looks for its meaning in morality, or in reverse from an idea of right living and living together that looks for the role of feeling in this idea, etc.

Since this is a work in film studies, the primacy of media aesthetics is initially clear. Aside from this, however, it should be justified on its own terms and in the interests of the research laid out in the introduction. For if film and other audiovisual media are increasingly the focus of both history and the social sciences as well as psychology, this has been motivated by the fact that their potential for emotionalizing and their social, political, and historical – that is, also even moral – efficiency has been registered. On the other hand it is also the case that this interest is all too often characterized by the fact that the genuinely aesthetic dimensions of film often only play a supporting role to questions of quantifiable content and character identification, described in psychologistic terms.[1]

---

[1] For a critique of the situation of media analysis in an interdisciplinary context and on the approaches within film and media studies that work with a theory of emotions, cf. Hermann Kappelhoff, Jan-Hendrik Bakels: Das Zuschauergefühl. Möglichkeiten qualitativer Medienanalyse. In: *Zeitschrift für Medienwissenschaft* (2011), Vol. 5, No. 2, 78–96.

https://doi.org/10.1515/9783110612110-002

My reflections here on feeling and morality should thus decisively be worked out in view of a complex understanding of the film image as a form of aesthetic experience. This might indeed have recourse to innate and learned mechanisms, but as an aesthetic experience this is far from the whole story. "Spectator feeling"[2] consists much more in realizing audiovisual images over the duration of the film as acts of perception performed by the spectator, as acts of perception in which all spatial and temporal order in and of the images proceeds simultaneously as the unfolding of forces and vectors of a world as a whole, of a way of viewing the world[3] in the spectators embodied experience.[4] The locations and characters of the film should always be understood as atmospheres, movements, and forces that refer to the faculty of the spectator and that unfold in him or her. These forces are also where spectators experience their own powers of sensation, enjoying themselves as perceiving, thinking, and feeling. The first step of this work should thus be to interrogate the theories of feelings to find a model that would be in the position to correspond to this idea. That is, a theory of feelings should be sought out that understands them as holistic forms of being integrated into a world, taking them as forms of positioning oneself and behaving in a world with the senses and the body – be it the everyday world that we live in or the world of the duration of the film.

A further principle in the internal logic of this work, that of feeling in the face of morality, will be worked out more precisely in the following and theoretically grounded, although it can be formulated succinctly as follows: Without a concrete, affective concern for justice and injustice, for concern and care, for the well-being and woes of others, no morality and no bond to norms is possible, or is so only as an ideal duty, which is not of this world.[5] This, however, is not about some naïve 'hurrah for feelings and empathy,' but about the descriptive value of such a course of action. The fact that I am concerned here with the sense of guilt already suggests that it is always about the experience that our feelings fail us as a moral compass, that the 'right' feelings can come 'too late'!

---

2 Kappelhoff, Bakels: *Das Zuschauergefühl.*

3 Cf. Stanley Cavell: *The World Viewed. Reflections on the Ontology of Film* [1971]. Cambridge / London 1979.

4 Cf. Hermann Kappelhoff: Die vierte Dimension des Bewegungsbildes. Das filmische Bild im Übergang zwischen individueller Leiblichkeit und kultureller Fantasie. In: Anne Bartsch, Jens Eder, Kathrin Fahlenbrach (eds.): *Audiovisuelle Emotionen. Emotionsdarstellung und Emotionsvermittlung durch audiovisuelle Medienangebote.* Cologne 2007, 297–311.

5 Cf. Hermann Schmitz: *Das Reich der Normen.* Freiburg i. Br. 2012; Hilge Landweer: Normativität, Moral und Gefühle. In: id. (ed.): *Gefühle. Struktur und Funktion.* Berlin 2007, 237–254.

It is decidedly not – and this is also what is meant by the primacy of the aesthetic experience – about feelings that would be completely identical with individual psychological emotions. Instead I mean affective processes and dynamics that could be designated as feelings of guilt due to their somatic qualities and the shape of their course, when they would be encountered 'in relation to' an individual person. They are congruent as forms, similar as dynamic patterns, but not identical. Films take on a "family resemblance"[6] with this personal feeling in order to shape a certain form of cultural, interpersonal experience of the guilty conscience, which is realized by individual embodied spectators. They thus generate feelings of guilt as forms of creating cultural meaning, which do not simply remain at the level of personal, individual attitudes, but are turned, as I would like to claim, into a historically emergent mode of forming community.

When speaking of feelings of guilt in the following, this means feeling what it is like to have feelings of guilt, it means sensing the "feeling tone,"[7] as Carl Plantinga puts it. Only that this 'what it is like' decidedly does not refer strictly to 'what it is like for the character' – as is the case in Plantinga's work. It is in fact much more about certain procedural forms of affects and semantics, which spectators themselves realize as the experience of a world that finds them guilty, that addresses them as responsible. In other words: At first I feel the lump in my throat, at first I sense the finger pointing in my direction, only then do I understand an event as injustice. In this way we are met by a physically sensed 'response' within the aesthetic modulation of feelings, which only then seeks out its 'stimulus,' that is, something to evaluate – narrative, personal, character-based, historical – constructing it as an experience of community and history under the sign of the guilty conscience.

What Schiller says about his own creative process can also stand for the affective experience of the spectator here:

> The preparations for so intricate a work as a Drama is, set the mind in motion in a very extraordinary manner. [...] With me the conception has at first no decided or distinct body: this forms itself only later. A certain musical mood arises first in my mind, and only after this follows the poetical idea.[8]

---

6 Ludwig Wittgenstein: *Philosophical Investigations* [1953], trans. G. E. M. Anscombe. Oxford 1958, 32.

7 Carl Plantinga: *Moving Viewers. American Film and the Spectator's Experience*. Berkeley 2009, 166.

8 Schiller's letter to Goethe, Jena (18 March 1796). In: *Correspondence Between Schiller and Goethe from 1794 to 1805,* ed. George H. Calvert. New York 1845, 136.

The aesthetic modulation of spectator sensation, the 'musical mood,' precedes understanding and judgment, indeed not only in terms of time – for instance as in Jenefer Robinson's model[9]– but also of logic. Understanding and judgment is led by this modulation of feelings, and only by means of these do we even know that there is something to understand and to judge.

One model for this renunciation of the stimulus-response one-way street, alongside the model of the expressive movement,[10] which is central to my work here, are the works of the New Phenomenology by and following Hermann Schmitz. These works attempt to find models to describe feelings as atmospheres, as dynamic volumes of the body, and as suggestions of movement, through which it becomes evident that it is not feelings that are subjective, but the specific realization of feelings in the personal situation.[11] From the perspective of film studies, such reflections have a certain appeal for analyzing a physicality and resonance that spans across bodies. Working Schmitz's system out into analytical models is still a valuable goal, but it cannot be carried out here in any complete sense. A similar attempt, which can be traced back to the developmental psychologist Daniel Stern, is Raymond Bellour's suggestion to position emotions in the wealth of forms of film movement, and to derive them from an amodal perception – as possibilities of rhythm, form, and intensity.[12]

For me, however, it is not a matter of flatly rejecting theories of cognitive appraisal. I still believe, though, and precisely in view of its dominance in international research on the object 'film and feeling,' that it is important to develop and try out models that position emotional sensations, moral thinking and acting more strongly in the aesthetic experience, which should be described in concrete, phenomenological terms. For only in the wake of empirical research on embodiment has it become clear that what we once believed we could isolate as rational, sign-based thinking, is in fact inseparable from embodied perception and the concrete ways that the body moves.[13] The possible inferences

---

9 Cf. Jenefer Robinson: *Deeper Than Reason. Emotion and its Role in Literature, Music, and Art.* Oxford 2005.

10 Cf. Kappelhoff: *Matrix der Gefühle. Das Kino, das Melodrama und das Theater der Empfindsamkeit.* Berlin 2004, 152–155.

11 Cf. Hermann Schmitz: *New Phenomenology. A Brief Introduction* [2009]. Milan 2019.

12 Cf. Raymond Bellour: Going to the Cinema with Guattari and Stern. In: Eric Alliez, Andrew Goffey (eds.): *The Guattari Effect.* London 2011, 220–234; cf. Raymond Bellour: *Le Corps du Cinéma. Hypnoses, Émotions, Animalités.* Paris 2009, 101–221.

13 According to the thesis that we can call the strongest version of the embodiment paradigm. Cf. Margaret Wilson: Six Views of Embodied Cognition. In: *Psychonomic Bulletin & Review* (2002), Vol. 9, No. 4, 625–636; cf. also Lotte Meteyard, Gabriella Vigliocco: The Role of Sensory and Motor Information in Semantic Representation. A Review. In: Paco Calvo, Toni Gomila

on the role of a basal sensation for our process of understanding present a particular challenge for any theories that would postulate exclusively cognitive judgments and propositions – that is, units of information in the form of statements – as the causes, or at least as the sufficient and necessary criteria for feelings. Also, a phenomenological approach to feeling, morality, and aesthetics does not in the same way produce paradoxes where there are none. Neither the 'paradox of negative feelings' nor the 'paradox of fiction'[14] have much weight if we assume that spectators first and foremost experience themselves as enjoying their own responsiveness. Aesthetically modulated feelings concern one's own activity in constructing a world and not the circumstances – positive or negative – within this world. Indeed, these are only created as objects of a certain feeling in the first place by the 'mood.'

1.1 Feeling

The debates carried out in the 1980s over a philosophy of feeling that would be appropriate to its object centered around the question of the *rationality of emotions*,[15] precisely because the focus was on the relationship between feeling and correct action on the one hand, and between feeling and thinking – as an outcome of new methods of empirical research – on the other. My investigations of feelings of guilt and their relation to social and historical 'knowledge,' to collective self-image, in part also aim at describing a specific rationality and reflexivity in our emotional life. In this endeavor it is important to emphasize that it cannot be a matter of completely joining, and therefore identifying, feelings with other manifestations of human reason, but of comprehending them as their own form of reflexivity. And this can only work – one of the central re-

---

(eds.): *Handbook of Cognitive Science. An Embodied Approach.* Amsterdam / Oxford / San Diego 2008, 293–312, here 294: "to achieve representation, semantic content *necessarily* and *directly* recruits the sensory and motor systems used during experience."

14 For approaches that work on this as a conceptual problem, cf. for instance Noël Carroll: *The Philosophy of Horror or Paradoxes of the Heart.* New York 1990; cf. Minet de Wied, Dolf Zillmann, Virginia Ordman: The Role of Empathic Distress in the Enjoyment of Cinematic Tragedy. In: *Poetics* (1995), Vol. 23, No. 1/2, 91–106; cf. Holger Schramm, Werner Wirth: Exploring the Paradox of Sad-Film Enjoyment. The Role of Multiple Appraisals and Meta-Appraisals. In: *Poetics* (2010), Vol. 38, No. 3, 319–335; cf. Robert J. Yanal: *Paradoxes of Emotion and Fiction.* University Park 1999.

15 Cf. Ronald de Sousa: *The Rationality of Emotion.* Cambridge 1987.

quirements here – if we understand feelings as embodied, dynamic, and relational processes.

Before I continue to present various positions, as well as verifying their suitability, one preliminary terminological remark is necessary. In the German-language literature there are two often parallel possibilities used to deal with the term 'feeling.'[16] On the one hand it is seen as a synonym for a "terminus technicus,"[17] an understanding of emotion that is generally quite narrow in scope, such as we find also and in particular in the natural sciences from Anglo-Saxon theory. On the other hand it has become an umbrella term for the entire range of human affectivity, which also encompasses, along with more or less clearly attributed emotions, 'nameless' affects, diffuse moods, and complex sensibilities.

My usage of the term feeling is ultimately aimed precisely at the space between these two meanings. On the one hand I assume that the dimension of feeling that I am concerned with here is related in a strict sense to processes in the world, to processes between organism and environment. On the other hand I do not see anything to gain by taking this relation to overestimate evaluative aspects in relation to the physical dimension of sensing, thus sweeping under the rug the extreme differences between various emotions in relation to the spectrum of intensity, the motivation for acting, expression, the faculty of representation, rationalization, etc. This is why I follow those positions that are based on the assumption that "no clear boundaries can be drawn between feelings in the strict sense (emotions) and moods, and transitional phenomena can often be observed."[18]

In addition to this kind of broad concept of feelings, I will also make use of the terminologies of affect and affection in order to point to the contact zone between the dynamic micro-events of medial forms and the capacity of the individual body to be moved by them. While processes of affection, following Gilles Deleuze and Félix Guattari[19] as well as Brian Massumi,[20] mean quasi anonymous, pre-subjective rhythms and intensities, I conceive feelings then as the realization

---

16 On this see Christoph Demmerling, Hilge Landweer: *Philosophie der Gefühle. Von Achtung bis Zorn.* Stuttgart 2007, 1–7; Sabine A. Döring: Allgemeine Einleitung. Philosophie der Gefühle heute. In: id. (ed.): *Philosophie der Gefühle.* Frankfurt a. M. 2009, 12–65.
17 Döring: *Allgemeine Einleitung. Philosophie der Gefühle heute,* 13 [trans. DH].
18 Demmerling, Landweer: *Philosophie der Gefühle,* 5 [trans. DH].
19 Cf. Gilles Deleuze and Félix Guattari: *What is Philosophy?* [1991], trans. Graham Burchell, Hugh Tomlinson. London 1994, 163, and passim.
20 Cf. Brian Massumi: Of Microperception and Micropolitics. Interview by Joel McKim. In: id.: *Politics of Affect.* Cambridge 2015, 47–82.

of affects as experiences, as physically sensed relationships to the self and to the world.

Speaking of feelings seems to me then to capture better the potential complexity of affect relations to world and self, their role in intersubjective, social, and cultural processes, their cultivatability and historicity, than speaking of emotions. Furthermore, the central dimension of dynamic, physically-grounded meaning construction is more clearly represented in this usage. I therefore also decide against the cognitive paradigm that is prevalent in analytical philosophy and psychology, which clearly prefers a narrower idea of emotion, equated with subjective value judgments.

Feeling as embodied appraisal

Cognitive theories on feeling can be traced back to two different lines, which intersect but which at the same time can also be differentiated into differing model formations. The first is the philosophical critique of the neglect of emotion in the philosophy of mind from an existentialist (Robert C. Solomon[21]) or neo-Stoic, neo-Aristotelian perspective (Martha Nussbaum[22]) and the other is the psychological appraisal theories that were first developed by Magda Arnold and Richard Lazarus.[23] The point of intersection is the hypothesis that feelings or emotions can be adequately and completely grasped as appraisals or judgments of persons, things, and events in our surroundings. The differences within these theories stems from the disagreement about whether these appraisals or judgments can be understood as cognitive activities in the sense of higher activities of reason, or whether they merely represent a way that neuronal activity works, which can also run its course completely automatically and unconsciously.[24]

As a rule the psychological models are characterized by the attempt to control the phenomenon of emotions by making discrete or dimensional subdivisions, by

---

21 Cf. Robert C. Solomon: *The Passions. Emotions and the Meaning of Life*. Indianapolis / Cambridge 1976 and Robert C. Solomon: *True to Our Feelings. What Our Emotions Are Really Telling Us*. Oxford 2006.

22 Cf. Martha Nussbaum: *Love's Knowledge. Essays on Philosophy and Literature*. Oxford 1990 and Martha Nussbaum: *Upheavals of Thought. The Intelligence of Emotions*. Cambridge 2001.

23 Cf. Magda Arnold: *Emotion and Personality*. New York 1960; Richard Lazarus: *Emotion and Adaptation*. New York 1991.

24 Cf. Amy Coplan: Feeling without Thinking. Lessons from the Ancients on Emotion and Virtue-Acquisition. In: *Metaphilosophy* (2010), Vol. 41, No. 1/2, 132–151, here 138.

developing component theories – the model by Klaus Scherer can be mentioned at this point as one of the most ingenious and well-known examples.[25] While these attempts of *divide et impera* certainly have their value within the constraints of empirical counting and measuring, their conceptual disadvantage is indeed significant, since they either cannot explain emotions as a synthesis of individual components, or they must understand their interaction so narrowly that a division into components is no longer meaningful.[26]

The problems of cognitive theories from philosophy, however, are positioned differently. Starting from the impulse to defend the intrinsic meaningfulness and functional rationality of emotions, they go on to argue that these are essentially determined through higher cognitive processes. Some of the most prominent spokespersons, such as Solomon and Nussbaum, even go so far as to claim that emotions can only be defined in the form of assessments. Emotions then, as value judgments, would stand in a close connection to our convictions and attitudes, they would be conceptually competent and thus accessible and congenial to reasoned argumentation.[27] The cognitivist attempt to elevate feelings to the rank of a conceptual action of judgment unduly intellectualizes them and equates them with thinking in propositions, by which their specific quality as bodily meaning making is precisely marginalized. In other words: these theories demand too much and too little of the emotions at the same moment, they position them too high as cognitive processes and at the same time divest them of one of their central qualities. What is lacking is the fact of affection or being physically affected[28] as the way that emotions or feelings insert us into the world in a way that creates meaning. The reasonability of feelings should not be established by aligning them with thinking in propositions and attitudes, but with the capacity to produce complex value judgments, relations to world and self as a multimodal modeling of physical feeling.

Some positions in this field attempt to start from the paradigm of cognitive theory while at the same time breaking away from it by clearly not equating feelings and judgments, nonetheless seeing emotions explicitly oriented toward complex cognitions to such a degree that they see their function as the creation

---

25 Cf. Klaus Scherer: What Are Emotions? And How Can They Be Measured? In: *Social Science Information* (2005), Vol. 44, No. 4, 693–727.

26 Cf. Döring: *Allgemeine Einleitung. Philosophie der Gefühle heute*, 31; Demmerling, Landweer: *Philosophie der Gefühle*, 32.

27 Cf. Martha Nussbaum: Emotions as Judgments of Value and Importance. In: Robert C. Solomon (ed.): *Thinking About Feeling. Contemporary Philosophers on Emotions*. New York 2004, 183–199, here 196; cf. Solomon: *True to Our Feelings*, 203–218, and passim.

28 Cf. Demmerling, Landweer: *Philosophie der Gefühle*, 20–24.

of the framing conditions for thinking and acting: feelings as programs of overcoming contingency, as "salient patterns,"[29] which submit something to the faculty of judgment, which tells desire where it is worth turning. For Ronald de Sousa, for instance, feelings have a semantics that is not identical with that of propositions, of units of information that would form statements, but that can be derived from learned *paradigm scenarios*.[30] Nonetheless, not only is the simple ontogenetic explanatory model in de Sousa too one-sided and too vague, it also grants no place to the fundamentally physical dimension of feelings.

With respect to the latter, Christiane Voss has taken an approach, working from the viewpoint of the philosophy of language, to develop an emotional consciousness from the narrative structuring of physical and mental processes. This approach is equally only convincing to a certain degree.[31] She also criticizes the rigid attempts within cognitive theory that erase the differences between feelings and other forms of intentionality, and in particular neglect the specific temporality of emotions.[32] She claims that a narrative integration of thoughts, memories, and physical sensations is what structures conscious experience in the first place. As with the component theories from psychology mentioned above, however, here there is also a problem in an unexplained relationship between the parts and their synthesis. And even if I take the position that feelings can only be meaningfully described in the first place in a holistic model, and that, second, they can be worked out quite resolutely by analyzing temporal dynamics, the term narrative is nonetheless insufficient to conceptualize this.

A completely different attempt to historicize feelings individually as a form of memory is the approach by the philosophizing neuroscientist Antonio R. Damasio.[33] For him emotions designate the quality of the brain that registers currently elapsing processes of perception and attention as somatic changes and aligns them with similar 'body states,' the 'somatic markers.' In this respect emotions are 'warning signals,' which themselves are not processes of decision-making or passing judgment, but frame or adjoin them.[34] Furthermore, Damasio distinguishes emotions, the unconscious alignment of current physical states

---

29 De Sousa: *The Rationality of Emotion*, 296.

30 Cf. De Sousa: *The Rationality of Emotion*, 181–184.

31 Cf. Christiane Voss: *Narrative Emotionen. Eine Untersuchung über Möglichkeiten und Grenzen philosophischer Emotionstheorien*. Berlin 2004.

32 Cf. Voss: *Narrative Emotionen*, 181–184.

33 Cf. Antonio R. Damasio: *Descartes' Error. Emotion, Reason and the Human Brain*. New York 2006 and Antonio R. Damasio: *Looking for Spinoza. Joy, Sorrow and the Feeling Brain*. Orlando 2003.

34 Cf. Damasio: *Descartes' Error*, 165–204.

with other possible somatic states, from feelings as the self-perception of this alignment and the physical adaptation processes that emerge from it.[35] In forming a theoretical model on the connection between feelings and aesthetic processes, it is therefore not uninteresting that for Damasio the relationships between the actual physical state and the self-mapping of the image of the body in the brain, which can be manipulated from a variety of sides, plays a central role.[36] Damasio's approach does, however, ultimately present difficulties because the neurobiological temporal structure of what he calls emotions remains in the area of the millisecond, and the sensation of feeling based on this ultimately does not experience any attention of its own.

Damasio's model belongs to a tradition of theory formation that, building on the so-called James Lange theory, claims the primacy of physical feeling over cognitive appraisal. William James, for instance, argues that feelings can be described as perceptions of physical changes:

> [The] more rational statement is that we feel sorry because we cry, angry because we strike, afraid because we tremble, and not that we cry, strike, or tremble, because we are sorry, angry, or fearful, as the case may be. Without the bodily states following on the perception, the latter would be purely cognitive in form, pale, colourless, destitute of emotional warmth.[37]

Even if the direct causal nexus of this thesis is no longer followed, many theories and empirical research nonetheless rely on the idea that the body can meaningfully evaluate its surroundings without utilizing complex processes of thinking and judging. Jenefer Robinson, for instance, working directly from the research of Damasio and Joseph LeDoux,[38] attempts to transfer the millisecond response of emotions in the strict natural sciences sense with the slower feedback phenomena of feeling and understanding into a coherent process model, using it for a theory of emotionalization through literary forms.[39] If neither the evaluative nor the physiological reaction alone characterize an emotion, and if it can also not be consolidated through simple addition, then emotions must, according to Robinson's simple conclusion, consist of their continual, mutual influence:

> [Emotion] is not a thing or a response or a state or a disposition; it is a process, a sequence of events. An affective appraisal draws attention to something in the environment

---

35 Cf. Damasio: *Looking for Spinoza*, 29–38 and 83–93.

36 Cf. Damasio: *Looking for Spinoza*, 112–118.

37 William James: What Is an Emotion? In: *Mind* (1884), Vol. 9, No. 34, 188–205, here 190.

38 Cf. Joseph LeDoux: *The Emotional Brain. The Mysterious Underpinnings of Emotional Life.* New York 1996.

39 Cf. Robinson: *Deeper than Reason.*

significant to me or mine and gets my body ready for appropriate action. Then immediately cognitive evaluation kicks in, checks the affective appraisal to see if it is appropriate, modifies autonomic activity, and monitors behaviour.[40]

What exact relationship there is, however, between the coarse non-cognitive appraisals and the specific cognitive evaluations and self-control, what forms of sequence formation and what typifications of processes might be proposed, remains unexplained for Robinson.[41] And so the close interaction proposed here into a coherent, continual process once again runs the risk of breaking apart into the different, independently proceeding aspects.

The theory of emotions as embodied appraisals by Jesse Prinz[42] circumvents exactly this problem by simply realizing that the evaluating dimension lies directly in the somatic changes of the body itself, that the intentionality of emotion, its relations to self and world are in a strong sense directly embodied: "Emotions are states that appraise by registering bodily changes."[43] For Prinz emotions precisely do not have any terminological content and no propositional structure. They are contingent ways that bodies discover relevant aspects of the interaction between organism and surroundings as affecting-the-body, without explicitly describing them.[44] There is, however, a gap in Prinz's presentation, since he neglects the role of the dimension of the subjective experience of feelings in favor of what they mean.[45]

---

40 Robinson: *Deeper than Reason*, 59.

41 Cf. Robinson: *Deeper than Reason*, 76.

42 Cf. Jesse Prinz: *Gut Reactions. A Perceptual Theory of Emotion*. New York 2004.

43 Prinz: *Gut Reactions*, 78.

44 Cf. Jesse Prinz: *The Emotional Construction of Morals*. New York 2007, 63. Against this approach, the argument has been leveled that there can be no sufficient differentiation and adequacy criteria for feelings without stable cognitive contents. This, however, is only valid under the precondition that the relationship between the physical patterns and the various emotions be absolutely unambiguous and that at the same time the feelings not only deliver the particular affective mode of the situation, but also and at the same time extensive knowledge about the objects and facts found in this situation. This means, however, breaking what feelings can achieve away from the interaction with the other capacities of the mind. As a rule, such objections contain an all too quick reduction of physical patterns into things like pulse rates and skin conductance, as if it were possible to claim that loud music and airplanes starting up were indistinguishable because of the similarity in their decibel measurement. For such an objection, cf. David Pugmire: Emotion and Emotion Science. In: *European Journal of Analytic Philosophy* (2006), Vol. 2, No. 1, 7–27.

45 Cf. Jan Slaby: Affective Intentionality and the Feeling Body. In: *Phenomenology and the Cognitive Sciences* (2008), Vol. 7, No. 4, 429–444, here 443.

Many approaches attempt to cope with this aspect, such as Peter Goldie's concept of (world) targeted "feelings towards"[46] or Bennett Helm's thesis that emotions, as 'felt evaluations,' are rational containments of pleasure and pain, which should not be judged for their rationality or suitability in isolation, but only in the overall view of the faculty of sensation.[47] In a similar vein there are also attempts to intensify the similarity of feelings and perceptions into an absolute analogy, and, in the tradition of Max Scheler's ethics of value, to claim that "emotions are perceptions of values."[48] All the approaches mentioned here, however, fall short with regard to the physical dynamic of feelings. A detailed phenomenological description of the specific forms of physical feeling in each case, however, should be in the position to lead to a sufficient differentiation of feelings without explicit propositional contexts, as presented in the following.

Phenomenology of physical sensation

What can it mean, though, to base on understanding of feelings on the physicality of the sensed body in its temporal, intensive, and dynamic dimension? The body as physicality neither indicates a measurable factum of psychological processes, nor a machine for symptomatologically transforming *stimuli* into *responses*: "The use a man is to make of his body is transcendent in relation to that body as a mere biological entity."[49] This is why it is a matter of the structures of physical experience and the occurrence of feelings, which are only uncircumventable from the point of view of the first person singular, "the subject-pole that can no longer be objectified or put into the object position"[50] This means physical traces and sensations as "whatever someone feels in the vicinity (not always within the boundaries) of their material body as belonging to themselves and without drawing on the senses."[51]

At this point I cannot take on the task of consolidating the three varieties of phenomenology cited here, of Maurice Merleau-Ponty, Helmuth Plessner, and Hermann Schmitz and possible other positions, nor do I have the space here to

---

46 Peter Goldie: *The Emotions. A Philosophical Exploration.* Oxford 2000.
47 Cf. Bennett Helm: *Emotional Reason. Deliberation, Motivation, and the Nature of Value.* Cambridge 2001.
48 Christine Tappolet: Emotionen und die Wahrnehmung von Werten. In: Sabine A. Döring (ed): *Philosophie der Gefühle.* Frankfurt a. M. 2009, 439–461, here 455 [trans. DH].
49 Maurice Merleau-Ponty: *Phenomenology of Perception* [1945]. London 2002, 220.
50 Helmuth Plessner: *Levels of Organic Life and the Human. An Introduction to Philosophical Anthropology* [1929], trans. Millay Hyatt. New York 2019, 270.
51 Schmitz: *New Phenomenology,* 65.

present and assess the various differences in detail. Instead, with regard to my approach to how audiovisual forms modulate feelings, it is important that these phenomenological positions each provide a way to account for the fact that feelings can be described in the physicality of feeling as "dynamical volume with suggestions of motion and directions"[52] "Every feeling has a certain shape to its process, which distinguishes it physically in a characteristic way from other affects."[53]

The fact that we can claim a dynamic congruence between motor attitudes and physical-affective feeling, and that feelings can be conceived as shapes of a process, represents the central dimension in which feelings answer to events in the world and coordinate with expression and action.[54] Describing them as constellations of forces, spatial and temporal dynamics, furthermore also shows how they relate to one another, are reciprocally constituted and formed: "that the impulse for one emotion can always serve for another emotion."[55]

The physical foundation of feelings is thus the indispensable requirement for any theory of feelings for two reasons. First it is what creates the conditions in the first place for a matrix of describing feelings that can capture their accessibility to relational and aesthetic processes, and second, it clarifies the existential dimension of the feeling-oneself of a feeling being, the affective grounding for every form of relation to the self and to the world.

With regard to the latter, it should once again be stressed that whole ways of being are fulfilled in feelings,[56] that feelings describe the style and the rhythm of the relationship between an organism and its surroundings and are not – as John

---

52 Schmitz: *New Phenomenology*, 92. Cf. Schmitz: *New Phenomenology*, 35–39 and 75–92. Treated more thoroughly in: Hermann Schmitz: Der Gefühlsraum. In: id.: *System der Philosophie*. Vol. III,2. Bonn 1969.

53 Hilge Landweer: *Scham und Macht. Phänomenologische Untersuchungen zur Sozialität eines Gefühls*. Tübingen 1999, 42 [trans. DH].

54 Cf. Maxine Sheets-Johnstone: Getting to the Heart of Emotions and Consciousness. In: Paco Calvo, Toni Gomila (eds.): *Handbook of Cognitive Science. An Embodied Approach*. Amsterdam / Oxford / San Diego 2008, 453–465.

55 Robert Musil: *The Man Without Qualities*. Vol. II [1932]. New York 1995, 1307. On Musil's theory of the processual character of emotions, cf. Musil: *The Man Without Qualities*, 1222–1311; and Demmerling, Landweer: *Philosophie der Gefühle*, 18–20.

56 Cf. Jan Slaby: Möglichkeitsraum und Möglichkeitssinn. Bausteine einer phänomenologischen Gefühlstheorie. In: Kerstin Andermann, Undine Eberlein (eds.): *Gefühle als Atmosphären. Neue Phänomenologie und philosophische Emotionstheorie*. Berlin 2011, 125–138, here 126; cf. Jan Slaby: Emotionaler Weltbezug. Ein Strukturschema im Anschluss an Heidegger. In: Hilge Landweer (ed.): *Gefühle. Struktur und Funktion*. Berlin 2007, 93–112.

Dewey criticized in William James and Charles Darwin[57] – merely passive perceptions and causal chains. Rather, they encompass and 'color' a person's entire relation to the world, since they directly tap into the affective aspects of one's own existence.[58]

From this perspective it will perhaps once again become plausible, and to an increased degree, how much we must speak of the fact that while feelings can indeed be dismantled heuristically into their elements, we cannot transform this dismantling into a simple causal chain, into a model of *stimulus-response*. Countering this "psychological fallacy," and undercutting its favorite example, Dewey states:

> The "bear" is, psychologically, just as much a discrimination of certain values, within this total pulse or coordination of action, as is the feeling of "fear." The "bear" is constituted by the excitations of eye and coordinated touch centres, just as the "terror" is by the disturbances of muscular and glandular systems. The reality, the co-ordination of these partial activities, is that whole activity which may be described equally well as "that terrible bear," or "Oh, how frightened I am." It is precisely and identically the same actual concrete experience; and the "bear" considered as one experience, and the "fright" as another, are distinctions introduced in reflection upon this experience, not separate experience.[59]

Fear creates the bear at least as much as the bear creates fear. This is even more so when we leave the woods and enter into phenomena of intersubjectively, socially and culturally, historically, and medially configured interactions. Feelings are not simply the private, internal evaluation of external processes. In their subjectively experienced physicality they are always already active, dynamic, and interpersonal. Only through the individual and cultural processes of taking form, only through the returning rhythms, temporalities, intensities of sensed physicality does something like personal and cultural identity emerge. The other way around, processes of meaning only unfold the levels of their cultural, social, and political effects, as well as their historical changeability, by being realized in individually sensed physicality. For a human being can behave in relation to his or her feelings, instead of only discharging them, letting them loose on the environment, like the emotions of animals.[60] he or she can form them, give them rhythm and character, can make them visible to him or herself and others through resistance and tensions.

---

57 Cf. John Dewey: The Theory of Emotion I. Emotional Attitudes. In: *The Psychological Review* (1894), Vol. 1, No. 6, 553–569 and John Dewey: The Theory of Emotion II. The Significance of Emotions. In: *The Psychological Review* (1895), Vol. 2, No. 1, 13–32.
58 Cf. Slaby: *Möglichkeitsraum und Möglichkeitssinn*, 131–135.
59 Dewey: *The Theory of Emotion II*, 20–21.
60 Cf. Dewey: *Art as Experience*, 162.

Feelings as relational practices

A theory of feelings that anchors them in the experience of a living, sensitive body – one that does not simply suffer through experiences but is engaged in the world –, makes it possible to understand feelings as forms of interaction, as cultivatable practices that also structure social and cultural interconnectedness at the micro and macro levels by modulating specific rhythms, intensities, and dynamics. The phenomena of expressive events in Plessner's sense[61] and of experience in Dewey's sense,[62] the forms of vitality in Stern,[63] the antagonistic encorporation [*Einleibung*] according to Schmitz[64]– these are just some of the descriptions attempting to capture the degree to which expression and emotional sensation are interactive organizational modes between bodies, the degree to which the human being perceives, thinks, feels, and acts with his or her complete being-in-the-situation, and how we contribute in each case to embodying the expressivity and responsiveness of others.

What we call language, culture, and media is then – not only, but possibly first and foremost – characterized by the fact that it is a matter of bringing forth, modeling, and suspending processes of physically being affected, of shaping forms of bodily resonance, consonance, and dissonance. And if we then take this a step further, then we can even claim that certain forms of identity formation, and in particular collective, political forms of subjectivization, are only generated and completed at all performatively through feelings as practices,[65] by addressing physical sensation in specific contexts:

> Emotions create the very effect of the surfaces and boundaries that allow us to distinguish an inside and an outside in the first place. So emotions are not simply something 'I' or 'we' have. Rather it is through emotions, or how we respond to objects and others, that

---

61 Cf. Helmuth Plessner: *Die Stufen des Organischen und der Mensch*; Helmuth Plessner: *Laughing and Crying. A Study of the Limits of Human Behaviour* [1941]. Evanston 1970 and Helmuth Plessner: Zur Hermeneutik nichtsprachlichen Ausdrucks [1967]. In: id.: *Gesammelte Schriften. Vol. VII: Ausdruck und menschliche Natur*. Frankfurt a. M. 1982, 459–477.

62 Cf. John Dewey: *Art as Experience* [1934]. New York 1980.

63 Cf. Daniel Stern: *Forms of Vitality. Exploring Dynamic Experience in Psychology, the Arts, Psychotherapy, and Development*. Oxford 2010.

64 Cf. Schmitz: *New Phenomenology*, 68–69.

65 Cf. Monique Scheer: Are Emotions a Kind of Practice (and Is that What Makes Them Have a History)? A Bourdieuian Approach to Understanding Emotion. In: *History and Theory* (2012), Vol. 51, No. 2, 193–220, here 200. Scheer cites four basic categories of such emotional practices: Mobilizing, Naming, Communicating, and Regulating.

surfaces or boundaries are made: the 'I' and the 'we' are shaped by, and even take the shape of, contact with others.[66]

Since cultural signs and emotional sensation can never depict one another in their entirety, since feelings themselves, as meaning-making practices, are furthermore in the position to construct events and other signifying materials as their objects, since we regulate sensing processes of feelings alone through naming and communication styles, there arises a human capacity to change the affective structure of the realm of their social and cultural experience.[67]

And within these practices of feelings, in turn, media and the arts take on a privileged role in the mutual transformation of the contexts of cultural meaning into physically grounded relations to self and world and vice versa. In this respect, this work is also a contribution to a history of feelings. A certain way of feeling guilty, culturally, collectively, and historically, which cannot be separated from concrete naming practices and concrete modelings of aesthetic experience, should be joined to the historical emergences and submergences of the practices of feeling.[68]

1.2 Feeling and Morality

In the history of philosophy, but also that of anthropology, sociology, and psychology, the relation between feelings and the moral have been described in many different ways, ranging from considering any affective impulse as absolutely detrimental for right thinking and acting on the one hand to making feelings the indispensable basis for the development of having morality at all. For a long time the former was supported by a tradition of thought that viewed the faculty of reason as an entity to set norms, furnishing it with a claim to exclusivity. The latter was supported by the idea that reason might indeed establish what was right and wrong, but it is only feelings that can tell us what is actually important in this distinction, and that without them we would not do anything at all, neither for the good nor for the bad.

---

66 Sara Ahmed: *The Cultural Politics of Emotion*. New York 2004, 10.
67 Cf. Birgitt Röttger-Rössler: Emotion und Kultur. Einige Grundfragen. In: *Zeitschrift für Ethnologie* (2002), Vol. 127, No. 2, 147–162, here 157.
68 Cf. Ute Frevert: *Emotions in History. Lost and Found*. Budapest / New York 2011.

It is surely no surprise then if at this point I clearly position myself in the spectrum that tends towards the second of the two extreme positions, without committing to a naïve sentimentalism. The fact that feelings can also be cruel, hurtful, and immoral is the very reason that it makes any sense at all to look into the relationship between them and morality. In the words of a philosophical-political theorist whose texts usually emphasize the capacity of clear thinking and judging:

> Absence of emotion neither causes nor promotes rationality. "Detachment and equanimity" in view of "unbearable tragedy," can indeed by "terrifying" [...] In order to respond reasonably one must first of all be 'moved' and the opposite of emotional is not "rational," whatever that may mean, but either the inability to be moved, usually a pathological phenomenon, or sentimentality, which is a perversion of feeling.[69]

In the following, starting from the understanding of feelings sketched out above as a physical feeling and sensing of relations to world and self, I will therefore attempt to capture a certain area within this as moral feelings. These are feelings that quite concretely concern one's own social behavior and that of others with respect to their adequacy for norms and values, rights and duties.

And here is where the difficulties begin. They lie in the ambiguity between a subjectivity and an objectivity of the adequate, they lie in the historical and culturally specific variations of norms, they lie in the imprecision between emergent feelings in specific situations and stabile dispositions, between being affected physically and emotionally as an individual and cultural value systems with their claim to generalization, etc.

I am working here with an understanding of morality that does not begin from general rules, but from the concrete concern of normativity in a specific situation, from which the possibility of an affective foundation of norms as more general can be viewed in the first place. The intersubjective concepts of norms and shared values are the result of complex, historically emergent processes of interaction, of communication, and of the mobilization of individually embodied sensations of value. Perhaps the actual level where we need to look for the significance in moral feelings is in intersubjective cultivation, in the oscillating relationship between the physical traces of justice and injustice on the one hand and the meta-situation 'What do we share?' on the other. This, for

---

69 Hannah Arendt: *On Violence.* New York 1969, 64.

instance, can be seen where moral feelings do not simply convey judgments, but become *passionate utterances*, which confront, which can be owed and demanded.[70]

Lines of tradition

It cannot be my goal at this point to treat morality and feeling in its historical and systematic diversity in a way that would give rise to a coherent, much less complete, narrative within the history of ideas. Nonetheless, it is necessary briefly to mention those lines of tradition without which any representation of the problem at hand would be more than simply incomplete.

For those current positions that endeavor to prove the power of judgment and rationality of feelings, one of the central references in particular is Aristotle's idea of using reason to deal with feelings.[71] Here morality is an opportunity for a balance between feeling and reason, for building a character that is in a position "so as to enjoy and be pained by the things we should."[72]

The question of the role of feelings in morality is therefore a difficult – or simple – one for Aristotle, since he announces it as no particular problem. He assumes that feelings – and indeed always the whole palette of them[73]– are utterly essential and immanent to human life in all areas, and therefore only dealing with them correctly in the here and now distinguishes whether a feeling in a certain situation represents a virtue or a vice. For Aristotle, correct dealing does not consist in suppressing feelings. Instead, he decidedly assigns pleasure a place in the virtuous life, which is quite explicitly not subordinated to any universal law or calculating reason, but to the law of the specific situation and to the pragmatic intelligence of the individual.

Feelings, however, need not be reasonable at all if we assume, as did the Scottish philosophers of *moral sense* in the eighteenth century, that the motivating power of feelings is the actual source of morality, as is expressed by

---

70 Cf. Stanley Cavell: Performative and Passionate Utterance. In: id.: *Philosophy the Day after Tomorrow*. Cambridge / London 2005, 155–191, 187.

71 Cf. for instance Amélie O. Rorty (ed.): *Explaining Emotions*. Berkeley 1980; cf. Amélie O. Rorty (ed.): *Essays on Aristotle's Ethics*. Berkeley 1980; cf. Martha Nussbaum: *The Fragility of Goodness. Luck and Ethics in Greek Tragedy and Philosophy*. Cambridge 1986.

72 Aristotle: *Nicomachean Ethics*, trans. C D. C Reeve. Indianapolis 2014, 23.

73 Cf. Christoph Rapp: Aristoteles. Bausteine für eine Theorie der Emotionen. In: Hilge Landweer, Ursula Renz (eds.): *Klassische Emotionstheorien. Von Platon bis Wittgenstein*. Berlin 2008, 47–67.

David Hume's famous statement: "Reason is, and ought only to be the slave of the passions, and can never pretend to any other office than to serve and obey them."[74] Any question of moral judgment would then have to obey no other standard than that of the reactions of feelings. It is in fact only feelings themselves that justify morality, indeed without accounting for any principles or derivations, but merely because in human sociality morality and feelings are found in line with one another, because we sympathize with others, conveying our inclinations and sensations to them and thus sharing them.[75]

This train of thought, unlike with Aristotle, initially identifies and emphasizes a section from the spectrum of feelings that contains the specifically moral feelings, namely, sympathy, charity, or benevolence.[76] There are therefore certain feelings that produce moral consciousness in the first place by motivating us to behaviors in relation to the other, allowing us to perceive others as valuable. By emphasizing the directly sensed evidence of the happiness of others – "the pleasure of seeing it"[77]– for the phenomenon of the feeling of sympathy in Adam Smith, there is also an indication of the not exactly desirable preconception of pure charity for one's own kind over those outside, distorting the sensation of justice and injustice.[78]

While one reaction to this imbalance would be to prefer a different class of feelings to the actually moral ones, namely those of condemnation and admonishment – related to the self and to others[79]– there is another possible conclusion, that the feeling of sympathy should be restricted by a strongly deontological ethics. Adam Smith's extremely significant contribution to the philosophy of moral sense was then also what supplemented the immediacy of empathy with a conscious effort of the imagination, providing further validation for the trope of an *impartial observer*.

---

74 David Hume: *A Treatise of Human Nature* [1739], ed. David Fate Norton, Mary J. Norton. Oxford 2000, 264.

75 Cf. Christoph Demmerling and Hilge Landweer: Hume. Natur und soziale Gestalt der Affekte. In: Hilge Landweer, Ursula Renz (eds.): *Klassische Emotionstheorien. Von Platon bis Wittgenstein.* Berlin 2008, 395–412, here 409.; cf. Aaron V. Garrett: Leidenschaften und Moral Sense. In: Hilge Landweer, Ursula Renz (eds.): *Klassische Emotionstheorien. Von Platon bis Wittgenstein.* Berlin 2008, 373–391 as well as Christian Strub: Sympathie, moralisches Urteil und Interesselosigkeit. In: Hilge Landweer, Ursula Renz (eds.): *Klassische Emotionstheorien. Von Platon bis Wittgenstein.* Berlin 2008, 415–434.

76 Cf. Frevert: *Emotions in History*, 149–162.

77 Adam Smith: *The Theory of Moral Sentiments* [1759], ed. Knud Haakonsen. Cambridge 2002, 11.

78 Cf. Frevert: *Emotions in History*, 182–184; Brian Massumi: Navigating Movements. Interview by Mary Zournazi. In: id.: *Politics of Affect*. Cambridge 2015, 1–46.

79 Cf. Prinz: *Emotional Construction of Morals*, 105.

The paradigmatic representative of a deontological ethics is certainly Immanuel Kant, not least because he understood his reason-based theory of morality in the *Critique of Practical Reason* as an explicit counter-proposal to the philosophy of *common sense*. The precise role of feelings in this reason-based theory of morality ultimately depends on which Kant is at question. For instance, in the *Groundwork on the Metaphysics of Morals* we read that actual moral and valuable action occurs "not from inclination ... but from duty"[80] and in the *Anthropology from a Pragmatic Point of View* we read: "To be subject to affects and passions is probably always an illness of the mind, because both affect and passion shut out the sovereignty of reason."[81] On the other hand, in the second part of the *Metaphysics of Morals* moral feeling, the conscience, philanthropy as a duty to benevolence, esteem and self-esteem as "conditions of receptiveness to the concept of duty"[82] become pivotal: "No human being is entirely without moral feeling, for were he completely lacking in receptivity to it he would be morally dead."[83]

What holds these two poles together seems at first glance to behave in a way similar to the Aristotelian dictum of the proper way to deal with feelings. It is different from this, however, in its aim to universalize and above all in not permitting feelings to endanger the control of reason, the self-determination of the human being as a rational being. Feelings should thus be 'cultivated' in such a way that they are precisely "induced most intensely ... by a merely rational representation."[84] What becomes particularly central, therefore, is the feeling of esteem [*Achtung*] for moral law as the only subjective 'mainsprings' of moral action.[85] In contrast to Hume's sympathy feelings, esteem is a thus a matter of a moral feeling the object of which is not *the* other, but *all* others, the idea of humanity.

The *other* has a completely different function in theories of empathy, such as have been developed from the late nineteenth century and up to present-day developmental psychology and neurosciences, namely the function of the concrete, embodied counterpart. The precise meaning of the term empathy, however, the extent of its affectivity and its moral capacity sometimes differs massively within the individual disciplines and paradigms. Furthermore, the

---

80 Immanuel Kant: *Groundwork of the Metaphysics of Morals* [1785/1786]. Cambridge 1998, 11.

81 Immanuel Kant: *Anthropology from a Pragmatic Point of View* [1798/1800]. Cambridge 2006, 149.

82 Kant: *The Metaphysics of Morals* [1797]. Cambridge 1991, 201.

83 Kant: *The Metaphysics of Morals*, 201.

84 Kant: *The Metaphysics of Morals*, 201.

85 Cf. Immanuel Kant: *Critique of Practical Reason* [1788]. Cambridge 1997, 62–75.

boundaries between synonym and systematic distinction with terms such as empathy and sympathy are not always clearly drawn. Discord reigns, for example, over whether empathy, as a process of understanding the feelings of others, is conceivable without any actual feelings, whether understanding is a direct requirement of empathizing with others, or whether it is even a matter of separate phenomena,[86] but also over how similar the feelings of others and those of oneself must be, whether "vicarious feelings"[87] such as embarrassment for others or empathy with fictional characters belong in this class or not, whether processes of involuntary contagion and mimicry count as full-blooded empathy, or merely preliminary stages of it, etc.

Empathy retrieves a particularly strong thesis on the ties between feeling and morality when empathetic feelings are in fact aimed at the feeling of others and the affective affliction of others becomes the object of one's own feeling.[88] Such an idea is also the focus of the historical formation of the term empathy, which, as a translation of the German '*Einfühlung*,' goes back to the writings of Friedrich Theodor Vischer and especially Theodor Lipps.[89] Very early on, the concept of empathy posed by Lipps, as one of melding, as *feeling as one*, was criticized. Nonetheless, his idea of physical resonance due to movement and expressivity, set a direction, precisely for theories of aesthetic experience, which I will come back to at a later point. One of the most convincing explanations of this is the work of Edith Stein, who develops a concept of empathy that need no conclusion by analogy or higher mental activities, but is conveyed directly by means of physical expression and which at the same time sustains the I/other distinction: "In my non-primordial experience I feel, as it were, led by a primordial one not experienced by me but still there, manifesting itself in my non-primordial experience. Thus empathy is a kind of act of perceiving sui generis."[90]

Unfortunately a large part of Stein's dissertation is lost, including the part on *Empathy in the Ethical Sphere*, and we can only speculate about the relationship between empathy and values in her work.[91] From those parts that remain,

---

86 One argument is that the understanding of suffering by sadists and torturers, in gladiator battles and executions is anything but a direct path to empathy. Cf. Demmerling, Landweer: *Philosophie der Gefühle*, 169.

87 Demmerling, Landweer: *Philosophie der Gefühle*, 188–190 [trans. DH].

88 Cf. Demmerling, Landweer: *Philosophie der Gefühle*, 167–185.

89 Cf. Theodor Lipps: *Ästhetik, Psychologie des Schönen und der Kunst I. Grundlegung der Ästhetik*. Hamburg 1903.

90 Edith Stein: *On the Problem of Empathy* [1917], trans. Waltraut Stein. Washington, D. C. 1989, 11.

91 Cf. Maria A. Sondermann: Einführung. In: Edith Stein: *Gesamtausgabe. Vol. V: Zum Problem der Einfühlung*, ed. Maria A. Sondermann. Freiburg 2008, xi–xxvi.

however, it is already permissible to conclude that it is at least possible with Stein to develop a way to account for the close link between feeling and morality, according to which empathy would play a key role in the "constitution of the person in emotional experiences,"[92] by understanding through empathy not only others, but also by feeling ourselves layer for layer.

Ultimately, however, there is validity to any critique that finds empathy – due to that fact that it is value neutral on the one hand and manipulatable on the other – insufficient as a basis for the faculty of moral judgment.[93] Historically the response to this in the eighteenth century was an overriding cultivation of the capacity for compassion as a social norm, the extension of which is effective to this day as sentimental culture, and which gave the Age of Sentimentalism its name.[94] Forms of culture, especially literature and theater, were the media of a comprehensive cultural technology of sensitizing to compassion, which served to create what was meant to be one of the most effective inventions of all time: humanity.[95]

No other figure protested against the cult of the sensitive soul so much as Friedrich Nietzsche, and no other contributed so much to a knowledge, which can no longer be dismissed from today's humanities, about the historicity of feelings and morality. And no other produced so many – self-inflicted as well as not – misunderstandings.

Nietzsche's polemics are less directed at compassion as an affect in relation to the suffering person, and much more "against the cultivation of affect as a central virtue and against elevating compassion to a principle of moral action."[96] For him, compassion is suspect on the one hand as a form of power. He views it as a form of cruelty in relation to the suffering person, an exercise of superiority, which is inherent to any ability to be compassionate, for one is not suffering oneself. But compassion for him is also a crime against the idea of human life when it negates the constitutive role of suffering:

> You want, if possible (and no "if possible" is crazier) *to abolish suffering*. And us? – it looks as though *we* would prefer it to be heightened and made even worse than it has ever been! Well-being as you understand it – that is no goal; it looks to us like an *end*! – a condition that immediately renders people ridiculous and despicable – that makes their

---

92 Stein: *On the Problem of Empathy*, 98–108.

93 Cf. Jesse Prinz: Is Empathy Necessary for Morality? In: Amy Coplan, Peter Goldie (eds.): *Empathy. Philosophical and Psychological Perspectives*. Oxford 2011, 211–229.

94 Cf. Kappelhoff: *Matrix der Gefühle*.

95 Cf. Frevert: *Emotions in History*, 163–170.

96 Wilhelm Roskamm: Mitleid. In: Henning Ottmann (ed.): *Nietzsche Handbuch. Leben – Werk – Wirkung*. Stuttgart / Weimar 2011, 283–284, here 283 [trans. DH].

decline into something *desirable*! The discipline of suffering, of great suffering – don't you know that this discipline has been the sole cause of every enhancement in humanity so far?[97]

Even if it may sound different here, Nietzsche is not lauding blind violence, causing suffering, but admonishing the denial of violence, closing one's eye to the connection between suffering and culture as a denial of life. Suppressing suffering means suppressing life – or at least a certain idea of life that has brought forth Greek tragedy or the philosophy of Dionysus.[98]

Nietzsche teaches that values and morality are not based on natural and universal connections: "There are absolutely no moral phenomena, only a moral interpretation of the phenomena ..."[99] and "in short, even morality is just a *sign language of the affects*!"[100] Values and the sense of value have a history, and this history, all of human society, is based on crime and the shedding of blood. The value systems that appear so evident today are built on power struggles and base motives or are simply internalized command structures.[101]

In the *Genealogy of Morality* there is an attempt to get to a critique of values by reconstructing the emergence of the morality of compassion: "The value of these values should itself, for once, be examined."[102] In brief, for Nietzsche the Christian morality of compassion is the result of reinterpreting factual, sociological distinctions into a question of morality, reinterpreting the 'good and strong' into the 'evil' and the 'bad and weak' into the 'good.' The process by which cultural and social values are created, according to Nietzsche, was thus radically altered. Instead of a "pathos of distance,"[103] it is now *ressentiment* that measures the value of human beings and of actions:

> Whereas all noble morality grows out of a triumphant saying 'yes' to itself, slave morality says 'no' on principle to everything that is 'outside,' 'other,' 'non-self': and this 'no' is its creative deed. This reversal of the evaluating glance – this *essential* orientation to

---

97 Friedrich Nietzsche: *Beyond Good and Evil: Prelude to a Philosophy of the Future* [1886], ed. Rolf-Peter Horstmann, Judith Norman, trans. Judith Norman. Cambridge 2002, 116–117.

98 Cf. Giorgio Colli: Afterword. In: Friedrich Nietzsche: *The complete works of Friedrich Nietzsche. Vol. VIII: Beyond Good and Evil / On the Genealogy of Morality.* Stanford 2014, 423–430, here 429.

99 Nietzsche: *Beyond Good and Evil*, 64.

100 Nietzsche: *Beyond Good and Evil*, 77.

101 Cf. Nietzsche: *Beyond Good and Evil*, 86–87; cf. Prinz: *Emotional Construction of Morals*, 217.

102 Friedrich Nietzsche: *On the Genealogy of Morality* [1887]. Cambridge 2016, 7.

103 Nietzsche: *On the Genealogy of Morality*, 11.

the outside instead of back onto itself – is a feature of *ressentiment*: in order to come about, slave morality first has to have an opposing, external world, it needs, physiologically speaking, external stimuli in order to act at all, – its action is basically a reaction.[104]

At the latest at this point it is indispensable to introduce the oscillation of 'with Nietzsche against Nietzsche,' for it cannot be a matter of retracing a justification for 'master morality,' but of soberly viewing the hidden connections in the polemics. For it seems that not much more is being said here than that there is in fact *one* possibility to define morality and values that cannot be dissociated from a sensitivity, from a responsiveness. And this feeling-based form of creating morality and values has a direct effect on processes of community building. Moral judgments and feeling-based responses give rise to something like unions in the first place, and these in turn are never absolutely inclusive, but are always also defined in relation to an outside.[105]

In Nietzsche's analysis of the sense of guilt, if it is formulated more neutrally, there are also theses to be discovered that can provide direction and above all connection. These include the meaning of guilt and assurance as the conditions for the human being as a political being,[106] the not at all altruistic function of morality to make the individual calculable for the community, as well as pain as a medium to develop something like cultural memory.[107] Guilt, conscience, and duty are then no longer the opposite of violence and suffering, but these things themselves in an altered form: "The categorical imperative smells of cruelty."[108] The history of morality is also the history of instrumentalizing suffering.

The authority of feelings

The resigning attitude contained in Nietzsche's polemic, precisely if we compare it to Kant's emphasis on reason and Hume's on sympathy, has garnered support from recent empirical research in the neurosciences and evolutionary psychology in two respects. They disenchant altruistic feeling as egotistical

---

104 Nietzsche: *On the Genealogy of Morality*, 20.
105 Cf. Nietzsche: *Beyond Good and Evil*, 119.
106 Cf. Hannah Arendt: *The Human Condition*. Chicago 1958, 245.
107 Cf. Nietzsche: *On the Genealogy of Morality*, 37–40.
108 Nietzsche: *On the Genealogy of Morality*, 43.

distress avoidance and reduce rational thinking to just the cherry on top of the cream cake of unconscious and automatic neuronal processes.[109]

For me at this point, however, it is not a matter of salvaging or discarding the term reason. Instead I wish to develop an understanding of morality and feeling that anchors the validity of norms in the "authority of feelings"[110] and the "forfeiting of affective involvement."[111] Such an understanding, and this also indicates a particular interpretation of the *Genealogy of Morality*, must therefore in fact more strongly emphasize the reactive, painful, debilitating feelings over the so-called 'positive' ones – not least also from mnemonic arguments:

> This suggests a general asymmetry between positive and negative emotions in morality. Desirable behavior is more likely to be shaped through negative emotions than positive, and, as a result we are more generous with blame than praise. [...] It's not entirely clear why punishment should be more effective than praise. It may be a brute fact about us that good feelings are fleeting (especially in the face of bad temptation), while bad feelings are more likely to leave an enduring mark on memory and motivation.[112]

The possibility of morality is based on feelings – which is not the same thing as to say that feelings *alone* can motivate them, but merely that the validation of any form of right or wrong, of desirable or forbidden, of praiseworthy or blameworthy, rests on *my* being affectively involved. At this point I want to substantiate this thesis with two completely different but mutually complementary ways of describing, the one being the (neo)phenomenological description of Hermann Schmitz[113] and Hilge Landweer,[114] the other from the highly interdisciplinary approach of Jesse Prinz.[115] These two positions have completely different terminologies and levels of argumentation, so that the following amounts much less to a homogenizing formation of theory than to a montage of their compatible elements, with which it should be possible to present a basic understanding of morality and feelings that would be open to a wide variety of disciplinary junctions from media analysis, philosophy, and the life sciences.

---

109 Cf. Carla Bagnoli: Introduction. In: id. (ed.): *Morality and the Emotions*. Oxford 2011, 1–36.

110 Schmitz: *Das Reich der Normen*, 18 [trans. DH].

111 Schmitz: *Das Reich der Normen*, 11 [trans. DH].

112 Prinz: *Emotional Construction of Morals*, 79–80.

113 Cf. Schmitz: *Das Reich der Normen*.

114 Cf. Landweer: *Normativität, Moral und Gefühle*; cf. Hilge Landweer: Der Sinn für Angemessenheit als Quelle von Normativität in Ethik und Ästhetik. In: Kerstin Andermann, Undine Eberlein (eds.): *Gefühle als Atmosphären. Neue Phänomenologie und philosophische Emotionstheorie*. Berlin 2011, 57–78.

115 Cf. Prinz: *Emotional Construction of Morals*.

Moral feelings, praising and blaming, therefore appear as culturally processed, ontogenetically and phylogenetically verified and trained modulations of basal affects, which are enriched and refined in and through the physical experience of situations and contexts.[116] The foundation of this is the experience of injustice, of transgression. Every formulation of moral rules or ethical or legal principles is only a secondary behavior towards an "injustice initially sensed as pressing"[117] or towards a threat to a diffusely present order. The feeling indicates a transgression, the transgression shows the norm – not in reverse.[118]

The source of the validity of justice and moral judgments are feelings, and they are to a certain degree self-sufficient. The sense of justice indicates that an injustice has occurred – without it being possible to use the feelings themselves to define what counts as a norm at a certain time in a certain place.[119] And in this respect they are self-justifying: "The emotions that we experience when we grasp those judgments are also responsible for making the judgments true: moral facts are consequences of our emotional reactions."[120]

Both Schmitz as well as Prinz set great value on the fact that this emphasis on the role of feelings and individual, physical concern and the correspondingly un-circumventable relativistic and subjective validity of norm does not lead to moral feelings and the question of justice and injustice being a purely private matter and thus completely non-binding. In the first place, a norm for the individual remains binding, except that this bond is not the cause, but the result of the authority of feelings.[121] And second, what is subjective is not remotely private and idiosyncratic, but insists on recognition and publicness in order to realize its claim.[122]

The reality or objectivity of norms and values, which our feelings bear witness to, and whose validity imposes feelings subjectively on us, describes the presence of *a* morality, and never of *the* morality.[123] Its effectiveness is relative, dependent on intersubjective practices and reactions, and at the same time is real in a way that Prinz compares with the objectivity of monetary value. Once they are in the world as social constructions and treatments of originary affects

---

116 Cf. Prinz: *Emotional Construction of Morals*, 67.

117 Schmitz: *Das Reich der Normen*, 60 [trans. DH].

118 Cf. Landweer: *Der Sinn für Angemessenheit als Quelle von Normativität in Ethik und Ästhetik*, 59.

119 Cf. Schmitz: *Das Reich der Normen*, 48.

120 Prinz: *Emotional Construction of Morals*, 88.

121 Cf. Schmitz: *New Phenomenology*, 104.

122 Cf. Landweer: *Normativität, Moral und Gefühle*, 244; cf. Prinz: *Emotional Construction of Morals*, 164; cf. Schmitz: *Das Reich der Normen*, 59–60; cf. Stanley Cavell: *Cities of Words. Pedagogical Letters on a Register of the Moral Life*. Cambridge (MA) / London 2004.

123 Cf. Landweer: *Normativität, Moral und Gefühle*, 246.

of injustice, they are reliably perceived, developed by our feelings. Only then is there any justification for speaking of a perception of values by feelings.[124]

What can once again be seen as a problem at this point is the question of intersubjective, cultural treatment of subjective involvement in relation to the ability to rationalize feelings, to the question of their appropriateness. For if on the one hand it is correct that feelings and moral values are free of the burden of certain forms of justification and reason – "basic values provide reasons, but they are not based on reasons"[125]– then this must not and cannot mean that there is no way to find criteria for the rationality and appropriateness of feelings in individual, specific situations and in the spatio-temporally conceived situation of a socio-cultural realm of experience.

One possibility arises, and to a certain degree this corresponds to the educational impetus of Aristotle, if we do not simply take feelings to be ersatz rationality, but turn them into the object of interrogation itself, if we examine the values and facts that they disclose, the actions and attitudes that they lead to, with precise descriptions and with respect to their mutual ability to fit. "It is precisely those feelings that determine the authority of the conscience that press for articulation."[126]

Furthermore, feelings are not only passively registered receivers, they are themselves ways of transmitting knowledge, they disclose complex situations to be integral, physical experiences, thus contributing to the fact that the individual meanings and perceptions, which at first hang together only diffusely, then differentiate and unfold into communicable facts.[127] What is significant here is that it is not only one's own feelings that belong to any particular situation, but also the sanctioning power of the praising and blaming feelings of others, which in turn only contribute to an authority of moral feelings when they are accompanied by a sense – of course not immune to deception – for the commonality of the norm, by a feeling of belonging: "a positive feeling for living in accord with oneself and others."[128]

A further way to judge the appropriateness and ability to rationalize moral feelings is to verify them for their stability and reciprocity. No single feeling is in a position to describe a norm completely. But feelings – and especially moral feelings – can be classified in a meaningful way and represent a systematic

---

124 Cf. Prinz: *Emotional Construction of Morals*, 167–169.
125 Prinz: *Emotional Construction of Morals*, 32.
126 Landweer: *Normativität, Moral und Gefühle*, 248 [trans. DH].
127 Cf. Landweer: *Normativität, Moral und Gefühle*, 251.
128 Landweer: *Der Sinn für Angemessenheit als Quelle von Normativität in Ethik und Ästhetik*, 65 [trans. DH].

context in which reciprocity is the first and most important condition. We are ashamed of something or feel guilty in a morally relevant sense only when we would be appalled by a similar transgression on the part of others.[129] We then only feel morally relevant gratification for a good deed when we would in fact have a sense of gratitude in a reverse case.[130]

This is why we should emphasize once more that anchoring morality in the subjective physical senses does indeed contain a healthy skepticism and assumption of fallibility, but does not contain any nihilistic devaluation of all sense of values. This means:

> [representing] a perspectival relativism of morality, not to make a case for laisser faire, but in reverse, to defend the absolute gravity of the moral claim that entails its most personal character against any attempts at arbitrariness.[131]

The validity or transgression of a norm is directly linked to confirming or questioning our culturally and socially formed self-understanding, stabilizing or threatening the value that I am in the position to attach to my own person, my own identity.[132]

These ways of justifying moral feelings through feelings themselves lead to the fact that the degree of stability in a feeling is an indicator of the degree to which the situation is in fact determined, the degree to which the validity of the norm in question is certain or uncertain. Whenever we are not sure about the validity of a norm, closer inspection reveals ambivalences, nuances, or even other feelings, perhaps even contrary feelings, with which previously undiscovered elements of the situation being experienced can be newly contoured in a gestalt-like manner.[133] Reasonable objections to a feeling have factual influence on this feeling when and only when they are borne by another affective grounding of one's own. To quote Nietzsche here: "The will to overcome an affect is, in the end, istelf only the will of another, or several other, affects."[134]

---

129 Cf. Landweer: *Der Sinn für Angemessenheit als Quelle von Normativität in Ethik und Ästhetik*, 59–66; Landweer: *Normativität, Moral und Gefühle*, 244–247; Prinz: *Emotional Construction of Morals*, 76–79.

130 Cf. Prinz: *Emotional Construction of Morals*, 81.

131 Schmitz: *Das Reich der Normen*, 144 [trans. DH].

132 Cf. Maria-Sibylla Lotter: *Scham, Schuld, Verantwortung. Über die kulturellen Grundlagen der Moral*. Frankfurt a. M. 2012, 55–64; Prinz: *Emotional Construction of Morals*, 120–121.

133 Cf. Landweer: *Normativität, Moral und Gefühle*, 250.

134 Nietzsche: *Beyond Good and Evil*, 65.

Precisely in this process of mutually providing nuance and perspective to the morally relevant and non-relevant feelings, to the emotions in a stricted sense, and to complex, mixed, diffuse moods and affects lies the stake of rhetoric and aesthetics for the moral structure of our physically grounded, affective experiential realm: "All psychotherapeutic operations and all clever political strategies of influencing public opinion are based on such feeling-based rational processes of transforming the realm of feeling."[135] What such aesthetic and rhetorical operations might look like in detail will be presented in the film analytical chapters of this book. At this point I would just like to make a few brief suggestions. On the one hand there are by now enough indications in the empirical research that some of the feelings that have an influence on moral attitudes are brought about by completely external, irrelevant factors. We can join Jesse Prinz in concisely summarizing: "And, of course, emotions can be altered by drugs, sex, and rock and roll."[136]

Further forms of 'transforming the realm of feelings' are those that extend existing emotional evidence to new examples, new relevant cases, which evoke compassion with people or outrage over injustice where previously detachment or indifference had reigned.[137] In this, however, it is not always a matter of merely quantitatively expanding a feeling's realm of validity, but we can also argue that feelings also qualitatively change with every such extension.

Lastly we can still assume, on the basis of describing feelings as physical dynamics with their own operational shape, that a direct affective treatment of such physicality in its intensities and directions can be morally relevant to the process of creating value.[138] In this temporal opening and closing of an affective realm of possibility[139] of acting and suffering there is a further form of transformation in which permitting or refusing the operational shape is reflected on feeling as a temporal dynamic.[140] There are the aesthetic strategies of film to bring forth such experiences of feelings as operational shapes, as completed figures of expressive movement, which will be foregrounded in the analyses here and verified for their moral relevance.

---

135 Landweer: *Normativität, Moral und Gefühle*, 252 [trans. DH].

136 Prinz: *Emotional Construction of Morals*, 57.

137 Cf. Prinz: *Emotional Construction of Morals*, 307.

138 Cf. Schmitz: *Das Reich der Normen*, 63–73.

139 Cf. Slaby: *Möglichkeitsraum und Möglichkeitssinn*.

140 Cf. Hilge Landweer: Die Macht der Erinnerung. Gewissensgefühle in Khaled Hosseinis Drachenläufer. In: Ingrid Kasten (ed.): *Machtvolle Gefühle*. Berlin 2010, 297–311.

1.3 Aesthetic Experience, Moral Feelings, and Common Sense

The reflections above on anchoring morality in subjective physical sensations as dynamics with their own processes, which reciprocally affect one another with their nuances and perspectives, ultimately come close to Nietzsche's position, where morality turns out to be a question of aesthetics, a question of perceiving gestalt-like processes and of moods and atmospheres evoked by the senses.[141] In order to investigate this more thoroughly, I will supplement this here with perspectives that see in the combination of aesthetics and morality a quite specific, feeling-based relation to community, and develop implications from this for the relationship between politics and aesthetics.

Moral feelings in general and the sense of guilt in particular, which will be the focus of the remainder of this work, are not addressed here as individual psychological mental states, but as affective processes that represent a cultural, interpersonal form of experience and meaning-making. As dynamics shaped by media, they are indeed embodied in the reception of individuals, but it is precisely because of this that these individual bodies show themselves to be directly socialized, related to the life of the community in their perceiving, thinking, and feeling, engaged in a commonly shared world, empathizing. It is a matter of experiencing a community and common values, which are grounded in processes of affective resonance. First, this does not mean that the 'I' is dissolved, but that it is always preserved in the 'we.'[142] And second, alongside resonances and communal ecstasy, such experiences also always include interruptions and dissonances, unheard of affects, new collectives, and new demarcations.

The meaning of aesthetics for morality should not be sought in spelling out consequences and principles, but in the fact that it is a matter of training the ability to behave in a playful way toward moral conflicts and the ambivalent or incoherent blend of feelings in specific situations.[143]

This means we need a conception of aesthetics that includes the various dimensions of physical feelings, of reason, and of knowledge as well as the practices and forms of interaction, without however negating the differences.[144]

---

141 Cf. Henry Kerger: Moral. In: Henning Ottmann (ed.): *Nietzsche Handbuch. Leben – Werk – Wirkung*. Stuttgart / Weimar 2011, 284–286.

142 Cf. Edith Stein: *On the Problem of Empathy* [1917]. Washington D. C. 1989, 16–18.

143 Cf. Landweer: *Der Sinn für Angemessenheit als Quelle von Normativität in Ethik und Ästhetik*, 69–70.

144 Cf. Josef Früchtl: *Ästhetische Erfahrung und moralisches Urteil. Eine Rehabilitierung*. Frankfurt a. M. 1996, 12–31.

The "sense of appropriateness"[145] is configured aesthetically to the degree that this is meant as concrete shaping phenomena that do not arise from abstractly deduced cross-sections, but in fact produce a "sense for the specific,"[146] which unfolds over the duration of the experience. For this reason I will develop a model here based on Dewey, attempting to explain the concept of experience starting from aesthetic experience and its potential to affect morality.

Dewey: Unity and experience

What makes Dewey's approach so relevant at this point is not only that he assumes a fundamental continuity between aesthetic experiences as "refined and intensified forms of experience that are works of art" and "everyday events, doings, and sufferings."[147] It is above all the way in which he does not position the continuity and the difference in some sort of objective qualities of artworks, but in the special kind of affective, physical realization of their qualities in the act of reception. The possibility of something like art is essentially grounded in certain everyday production methods and experiential contents, namely in their potential not simply to happen to us, not simply to be a contingent result of perceptions and actions, but sometimes also to be in accord:

> A piece of work is finished in a way that is satisfactory; a problem receives its solution; a game is played through; a situation [...] is so rounded out that its close is a consummation and not a cessation. Such an experience is a whole and carries with it its own individualizing quality and self-sufficiency. It is *an* experience.[148]

Two fundamental characteristics of ordinary interaction participate here in a very special way: on the one hand the dimension of temporality made up of rhythm[149] and duration,[150] and on the other of feeling as the moment in which the bodily realization of the rhythm of disturbing and recreating the "interaction of organism and environment"[151] in turn becomes accessible to reflection. Making the aesthetic experience the experience of experiencing

---

145 Landweer: *Der Sinn für Angemessenheit als Quelle von Normativität in Ethik und Ästhetik*, 66–69 [trans. DH].

146 Landweer: *Der Sinn für Angemessenheit*, 70 [trans. DH].

147 Dewey: *Art as Experience*, 2.

148 Dewey: *Art as Experience*, 37.

149 Cf. Dewey: *Art as Experience*, 12–16, 58 and 158.

150 Cf. Dewey: *Art as Experience*, 24–25.

151 Dewey: *Art as Experience*, 22.

does not simply designate a state or a certain content of experience, but a heightened vitality and an increased self-pleasure in dealing with the world.[152] Ultimately this lies in the fact that the affective qualities of the rhythmic-dynamic interaction of an I and its surroundings takes on a special meaning in relation to the practical and the intellectual interaction: "Emotion is the moving and cementing force. It selects what is congruous and dyes what is selected with its color, thereby giving qualitative unity to materials externally disparate and dissimilar. It thus provides unity in and through the varied parts of an experience."[153]

With genuine aesthetic experiences, as opposed to everyday experiences with an aesthetic character, the ego as a feeling is indeed implicated and involved in a harmonic cooperation between human being and world, but at the same time it impersonally depends on objects, constructions, and organizations that link this experience to socially shared forms of experience.[154] It is precisely here that the exemplary value of the aesthetic experience lies, namely the successful interaction of human being and world, and thus to demonstrate the possibility of improving the experience, the possibility of enriching the relationships and activities between people. This is why moral effect is not direct for Dewey, but

> by disclosure, through imaginative vision addressed to imaginative experience (not to set judgment) of possibilities that contrast with actual conditions. A sense of possibilities that are unrealized and that might be realized are when they are put in contrast with actual conditions, the most penetrating 'criticism' of the latter that can be made.[155]

The decisive difference to conceptions such as those of Martha Nussbaum[156] or Noël Carroll[157] is that the role of the moral feeling is not that of a product of the process of understanding, that moral feeling does not get added to the aesthetic

---

152 Cf. Dewey: *Art as Experience*, 18–19.

153 Dewey: *Art as Experience*, 44.

154 Cf. Dewey: *Art as Experience*, 6–9 and 193.

155 Dewey: *Art as Experience*, 360.

156 Cf. Nussbaum: *Love's Knowledge*; Martha Nussbaum: *Poetic Justice. The Literary Imagination and Public Life*. Boston 1995.

157 Cf. Noël Carroll: Art, Narrative, and Moral Understanding. In: *Beyond Aesthetics. Philosophical Essays*. Cambridge 2001, 270–293; Noël Carroll: Art, Narrative & Emotion. In: *Beyond Aesthetics. Philosophical Essays*. Cambridge 2001, 215–235; Noël Carroll: Aesthetic Experience. A Question of Content. In: *Art in Three Dimensions*. Oxford / New York 2010, 77–108.

experience as a didactic intention or propositional knowledge, but that it is aesthetically relevant wherever it itself defines the experience:

> We are repelled by the intrusion of a moral design in literature while we esthetically accept any amount of moral content if it is held together by a sincere emotion that controls the material. A white flame of pity or indignation may find material that feeds it and it may fuse everything assembled into a vital whole.[158]

The moral feeling as a unifying power of the aesthetic experience is what turns intellectually expressible moral principles into an "aspect of value that is shared in experience"[159] and also contributes to the fact that this is a mode that "enables one to participate more richly in the worthwhile experiences of others."[160] The aesthetic experience thus becomes an exemplary form of being human, of social being, that is, "the process of associating in such ways that experiences, ideas, emotions, values are transmitted and made common."[161]

In this fundamental sociality of human beings lies the parallel between Dewey's usage of experience and that of common sense [*Gemeinsinn*] in Kant, which is to be examined in the following – with the distinction that in Dewey this does not designate any inherent faculty of judgment nor any a priori subjective necessity, but exists only in and through the implementation experienced. Morality is the successful coordination of activity, and the function of art is to make, maintain, and propagate the forms of this coordination, which are what defines the community in its everyday relation to activity, as aesthetically, that is, emotionally experienceable.[162]

Unfortunately, what is not at all unproblematic for a political theory of the aesthetic experience in Dewey is the all too light suspension of the individual in the common coordination of experience. Communication for him always already anticipates agreement. Possibilities of ambivalence, dissent, conflict, and misunderstandings are barely taken into account. Instead, we should emphasize the multiplication of forms of experience with a simultaneous assurance of the possibilities of their compatibility in the sense of Dewey's writings on democratic theory. Unity of experience therefore means being able to take part in the experience of the most possible others in the most possible areas. It is the

---

158 Dewey: *Art as Experience*, 71.

159 Dewey: *Art as Experience*, 362.

160 John Dewey: *The Middle Works, 1899–1924, Vol. IX: 1916. Democracy and Education.* Carbondale 2008, 127.

161 John Dewey: *Reconstruction in Philosophy* [1919]. New York 1920, 207.

162 Cf. Dewey: *Reconstruction in Philosophy*, 94; Dewey: *Democracy and Education*, 12; Dewey: *Art as Experience*, 84 and 360.

realization of such participation as a contingent process that always and anew creates a common sense as an experience of community.[163]

Kant, Arendt, and Rorty: Taste, the power of judgment, and solidarity

Dewey's work thus speaks to a level of aesthetic experience in which the feelings of the individually embodied reception process join up with the life of the community, in which sensing and going through an experience is put into relation to the faculties of others to sense and to experience, just as my moral feelings in their "highly personal character"[164] also articulate that I am in a community of people. This a priori sociability of human beings, rooted in the aesthetic, their common sense, was first spelled out in such clarity by Kant in his *Critique of Judgment*, and later interpreted by Hannah Arendt as the basis of the political.[165]

The common sense evident in the judgment of taste is characterized, according to Kant, by the fact that it can neither be defined by the causal constraints and qualities of the world of objects and appearances and of the human sense apparatus, nor by the laws of reason that would be equally valid in all possible universes.

> If judgments of taste had (as cognitive judgments do) a determinate objective principle, then anyone making them in accordance with that principle would claim that his judgment is unconditionally necessary. If they had no principle at all, like judgments of the mere taste of sense, then the thought that they have a necessity would not occur to us at all. So they must have a subjective principle, which determines only by feeling rather than by concepts, though nonetheless with universal validity, what is liked or disliked. Such a principle, however, could only be regarded as a common sense. This common sense is essentially distinct from the common understanding that is something also called common sense (*sensus communis*); for the latter judges not by feeling but always by concepts, even though these concepts are usually only principles conceived obscurely.[166]

It is not reason, but being-in-community here that is the pivot point. To say that something is beautiful only makes sense if one is not alone in the world. The sought after 'subjective principle' is freed of any restriction by thinking in concepts and logical conclusions. But at the same time it is not unregulated.

---

163 Cf. Dewey: *Reconstruction in Philosophy*, 188 and 207.

164 Schmitz: *Das Reich der Normen*, 144 [trans. DH].

165 Cf. Hannah Arendt: *Lectures on Kant's Political Philosophy* [1982], ed. Ronald Beiner. Chicago 1992.

166 Immanuel Kant: *Critique of Judgment*. Cambridge 1987, § 20, A63, 87.

The power of judgment aligns itself with the imaginative power of reason by provoking this to take account of judgments of others, "not so much with the actual as rather with the merely possible"[167] judgments. It makes the lawless connections between the general and the particular, which the power of imagination creates, at least conceivable as objectively valid connections, and realizes this conceivability as a subjective sensation, a sense for the fact that we are in the world with other human beings.[168]

It is well known that the assertion that the aesthetic judgment as pleasure, "without all interest,"[169] is not a judgment about the agreeable, the good, the useful, or the true. This does not, however, mean that there is no connection between the aesthetic and other, practical or moral judgments. The judgment of taste serves cognition not by conveying truths about things or terms, but by exercising the condition of cognition, the sense of aligning the cognitive faculties in a free play, and by realizing the principle of common sense in subjective sensation.[170] The judgment of taste is the motivation to moral action because it shows, by making it conceivable, that practical reason – despite all disappointments in practical reality – can achieve what it is supposed to in moral orientation because the world is potentially in the position to be reasonable.

Here we can recognize the breaking point at which Kant clearly sets himself apart from Dewey's position. Indeed, the latter precisely emphasizes the necessity of factually fulfilled, contingent experiences and the concrete communication of the participants for any possibility of sharing the forms of experience, while Kant's presentation of the aesthetic judgment tends toward self-abstraction, which then does abandon the subjective-physical experience, the question of desire and pleasure, as well as the forces of cohesion of particular, oppositional judgments of taste without any claim to general validity.

It was Kant's particular innovation to separate taste and the faculty of judgment from the competition both with rule-based cognitive faculty and with the ideas and bodies of knowledge called common sense that are only shared in the first place by being acquired in practice, turning subjective sensation into the faculty with which every individual is provided access to communality in his or her physical-sensual existence. For Hannah Arendt, Kant's description of common sense, understood as a sense of reality, is at the same time the condition for the

---

167 Kant: *Critique of Judgment*, §40, A155, 160.
168 Cf. Kant: *Critique of Judgment*, §9, A31, 62.
169 Kant: *Critique of Judgment*, §2, A5, 166.
170 Cf. Kant: *Critique of Judgment*, §59, A257, 226–228.

possibility of the political: "We find here [...] sociability as the very origin, not the goal, of man's humanity."[171]

The political does not begin with factual problems and differences, nor with the necessities of surviving and living together, but with the capacity of living together at all, of setting ourselves up in a common world. Only on this basis do those other phenomena come in, do economic activities come into play. The core of the political thus does not lie in action, but in the public realm that that action is related to, that provides this action with a sense, a space, in which it can appear at all:

> The public realm is constituted by the critics and the spectators, not by the actors or the makers. And this critic and spectator sits in every actor and fabricator; [...] Spectators exist only in the plural. The spectator is not involved in the act, but he is always involved with fellow spectators. He does not share the faculty of genius, originality, with the maker or the faculty of novelty with the actor; the faculty they have in common is the faculty of judgment.[172]

The position of spectators is the standard of the events, the standard of speaking and acting in the space of the political. Spectators relate the events to one another and decide whether they are appropriate to be taken as an example. The political is thus not only as general as possible, but it is also fragile and can be usurped at any time by the realm of the (seeming) necessities – ultimately Arendt is writing from the bitter experience that the possibility of totalitarianism is very real, that the capacity to judgment can either be choked by a retreat into the ego or by the ideological fixations of reality.[173]

The actual overlapping of the spheres of morality, aesthetics, and politics is the unfolding of the individual faculty of judgment as the *ratio* of living together, a *ratio* whose chances to be realized are restricted by the historical and political frame in each case, which in turn – here we can see the historical meaning of the experiential modalities of media publics – is accessible to aesthetic modulation. Art and literature teach us that it is possible to deal with 'things as they are,' to transfigure it via the power of judgment, and not only to imagine the boundaries of the changeable and non-changeable, but to place them like things before ourselves, to position them in the form of works in the common world.[174] Here we can also see the fact that for Arendt the historical

---

171 Arendt: *Lectures on Kant's Political Philosophy*, 73–74; cf. Hannah Arendt: *Was ist Politik? Fragmente aus dem Nachlaß*, ed. Ursula Lud. Munich 1993.

172 Arendt: *Lectures on Kant's Political Philosophy*, 63.

173 Cf. Hannah Arendt: *The Promise of Politics*, ed. Jerome Kohn. New York 2005.

174 Cf. Hannah Arendt: Truth and Politics [1969]. In: id.: *Between Past and Future. Eight Exercises in Political Thought*. New York 2006, 223–259, here 257–258.

emergence of a philosophical theory of common sense cannot be separated from its context, that is, from the decidedly modern appearance of a medial public realm, even one that encompasses the globe, through which we as spectators are connected to other spectators in a way that is evident to the senses.

Feelings seem not to have any explicit role in this, so that we might accuse Arendt of making her categories of thinking and judging too intellectual: "Rather than endorse the entry of feelings into ethics or, for that matter, politics, Arendt sees it as crucial that feelings be precluded from the exercise of moral as well as political judgment."[175] This conclusion, however, is premature. It is correct that for Arendt compassion and love disrupt the space of the political as highly private feelings[176] and that concrete compassion in the sense of empathetic commiseration does not fall under the qualities of judgment:

> I must warn you here of a very common and easy misunderstanding. The trick of critical thought does not consist in an enormously enlarged empathy through which one can know what actually goes on in the mind of others. To think, according to Kant's understanding of enlightenment, means Selbstdenken, to think for oneself.[177]

But this does not mean abstracting away the particularity of what is judged in the greatest possible generality of the viewpoints taken into account in the judgment, nor does it mean that we cannot be moved and even highly personally affected by our judgments in our quality as uninvolved spectator, that is, as members of the public. This being involved not only assumes the shape of private emotional states, but presents us with the challenge of practicing and developing a mode of genuinely public and political emotional states. As I have already noted, Arendt is no advocate of emotional callousness.[178] But she does insist that in public feelings even their public coming-into-appearance must be incorporated, and that they are thus defined by a recognition of the claim to equality and a capacity to distinguish between what can and cannot be changed:

> Rage is by no means an automatic reaction to misery and suffering as such; no one reacts with rage to an incurable disease or to an earthquake or, for that matter, to social conditions that seem to be unchangeable. [...] Only when our sense of justice is offended do we act with rage, and this reaction by no means necessarily reflects personal injury.[179]

---

175 Arne J. Vetlesen: *Perception, Empathy, and Judgment. An Inquiry into the Preconditions of Moral Performance.* University Park 1994, 115.

176 Cf. Arendt: *The Human Condition*, 51 and 243.

177 Arendt: *Lectures on Kant's Political Philosophy*, 43.

178 Cf. Arendt: *On Violence*, 64.

179 Arendt: *On Violence*, 63.

It is therefore about a kind of thinking that claims to be able to assume a public position – in addition to private rights and duties, in addition to the personal use of one's own reason – and furthermore sees this possibility as directly determined by the subjective faculty. That these two forms of private and public can be strictly separated from one another in their realms of validity is the conclusion where Arendt meets Richard Rorty and both go beyond Dewey's understanding of community.

Rorty's ideal of democracy is the "free consensus between *as diverse a variety of citizens as can possible be produced*"[180] as a historical process of expanding solidarity and accord among non-similar modes of life. He makes a case for abandoning any hierarchy between philosophical, aesthetic, scientific, political, and other forms of describing reality, instead retaining only one border: that between the public realm, solidarity, justice, and morality on the one side and privacy, ironic self-creation, freedom, and ethics on the other.[181] A connection between the two only exists where art and literature, which actually serve the production of solidarity and community, that is, of the public sphere, at the same time present the possibility of freedom to eccentric self-projection in exemplary ways.[182]

The ways that individuals freely unfold and propose their selves thus have no claim to generality whatsoever. Ethics, philosophies, religions are absolutely private – but at the same time they are bound up in the utopia that is supposed to make this freedom possible for everyone, albeit with an extremely general claim, namely that freedom and justice represent the first and last goals of the political. For Rorty, the utopia of liberalism consists, and here Arendt is in agreement, in the fact that living together is not defined by regulated necessities, no matter how reasonable, and also not by some sort of ethnic or metaphysical justifications of community, but only by an appeal that points to the future: "We need a redescription of liberalism as the hope that culture as a whole can be 'poeticized' rather than as the Enlightenment hope that it can be 'rationalized' or 'scientized.'"[183]

In this poetic-experimental conception a community, a 'we,' is the unforeseeable assemblage of those who potentially agree on a historically contingent description of the world – a description of what was, is or what should be – at the moment of its usage.[184] Outside such concrete articulation, its aesthetic

---

180 Richard Rorty: *Achieving our Country. Leftist Thought in Twentieth-Century America.* Cambridge 1999, 30 [emphasis MG].

181 Cf. Richard Rorty: *Contingency, Irony, and Solidarity.* Cambridge 1998.

182 Cf. Rorty: *Achieving our Country*, 122.

183 Rorty: *Contingency, Irony, and Solidarity*, 53.

184 Cf. Rorty: *Contingency, Irony, and Solidarity*, 118–121 and 190–192.

evidence, communities have no 'being,' no 'existence.' It is the level of these descriptions that leads the conflicting communities to a competition over their members, in which they promise and evoke the strongest possible emotional connections by envisioning a common present and a possible future, promising those who agree and thereafter act the best possible temporary outcomes of history among those that are in the process of being reached.[185]

The pragmatic criterion for such a best possible outcome is what Rorty calls the production of solidarity, which, positively formulated, means the maximum agreement of the various, but which can also be described negatively as the avoidance of avoidable pain, cruelty, and humiliation.[186] The political community is thus constantly exposed to the pressure of having to justify itself, without being able to point to ahistorical standards of an external, deeper, higher, or ulterior dimension. Only by pointing to positive communal feelings and alleviated suffering can the community affirm itself. Moral right and good can only be measured by this production of solidarity. And yet, what can be considered successfully produced solidarity at all can be decided by nothing other than the agreement of the community itself. And this in turn is "achieved not by inquiry but by imagination."[187] It is the descriptive forms of art and literature that play a privileged role in the production of a "moral identity"[188] by providing the greatest clarity and variety of form to the appeals to solidarity and the avoidance of cruelty and indignity. Indeed, art cannot justify morality with final truths any more than can philosophy or lawgiving politics, but it can, through detailed descriptions of unnecessary suffering, require the creation of more solidarity. Rorty believes that sensibility is responsible for 90 percent of the work of moral progress, with the "abstract insight"[189] of moral philosophy catching up later.

What is important for Rorty in all this is to emphasize the creating, producing, or making of solidarity, since a similarity between ways of existing is not sitting somewhere in the waiting room of history, waiting to be called up, but

---

185 Cf. Rorty: *Contingency, Irony, and Solidarity*, xvi. Richard Rorty: Solidarity or Objectivity? In: id.: *Objectivity, Relativism, and Truth. Philosophical Papers.* Cambridge 1991, 21–34, here 33; Rorty: *Achieving our Country*, 10–27. Rorty assumes that these descriptions are never aimed at including all people. Cf. Rorty: *Contingency, Irony, and Solidarity*, 190: "I claim that the force of 'us' is, typically, contrastive in the sense that it contrasts with a 'they' which is also made up of human being – the wrong sort of human beings."
186 Cf. Rorty: *Contingency, Irony, and Solidarity*, 192.
187 Rorty: *Contingency, Irony, and Solidarity*, xvi.
188 Rorty: *Achieving our Country*, 13.
189 Richard Rorty: Erwiderung auf Hauke Brunkhorst. In: Thomas Schäfer, Udo Tietz, Rüdiger Zill (eds.): *Hinter den Spiegeln. Beiträge zur Philosophie Richard Rortys mit Erwiderungen von Richard Rorty.* Frankfurt a. M. 2001, 162–165, here 165 [trans. DH].

only emerges in the first place through the description of this similiarity.[190] He insists on a moral sensibility that is based on a stabilized communal feeling and at the same time is motivated, through the description of exclusions and indignities that actually discredit this community to itself, to redraw the borders of this community's solidarity over and over again. As such, despite pointing out hope and trust as the positive binding forces of community, we should not overlook the fact that liberal utopia emerges from a history that "really never quite lost a certain odour of blood and torture"[191] and thus is more solace and self-assurance than a self-conscious program for the future.[192]

Cavell: Perfectionism and acknowledgement

In the search for the connection between moral feelings and the aesthetic experience, therefore, it turns out that this can only be formulated as a theory of the political, since it has been shown that the aesthetically and morally judging subject takes on a public position as he or she is individually physically involved. While Arendt and Rorty – the one by using topographic metaphors, the other with reference to vocabularies and descriptions – attempt to separate the forms of private and public appearing, speaking, and feeling from one another, I would here like to make a case for Stanley Cavell's *moral perfectionism*, which in contrast does not treat the public as a separate sphere, but as a particular modulation of one's own voice.[193]

The subject of Kantian judgment, and potentially also that of Arendt, always tends to self-abstraction in that thinking for oneself places extreme emphasis on considering other positions. Cavell's approach is to counter this with another premise as a corrective, namely something that one might call speaking for oneself. Before considering other positions, it is necessary to make understandable, both to oneself and to others, what one's own position is, whether it is a position, whether one wants to defend or justify it, whether one is prepared to make more than just impersonal statements, and whether one in

---

190 Cf. Rorty: *Contingency, Irony, and Solidarity*, xiv and 196–197; cf. also Richard Rorty: The Priority of Democracy to Philosophy. In: id.: *Objectivity, Relativism, and Truth. Philosophical Papers*. Cambridge 1991, 175–198, here 198.

191 Nietzsche: *On the Genealogy of Morality*, 43.

192 Cf. Rorty: *Contingency, Irony, and Solidarity*, 182.

193 Cf. Andrew Norris: Political Revisions. Stanley Cavell and Political Philosophy. In: id. (ed.): *The Claim to Community. Essays on Stanley Cavell and Political Philosophy*. Stanford 2006, 80–97, here 82.

fact wants to speak and be spoken to from one's standpoint.[194] Before taking account of other standpoints, it is necessary to invite others to the articulation of these standpoints in the first place.[195]

Behind this is an inflection of the principle of the judgment of taste in Kant. For by making oneself a part of a community with one's subjective faculty, one becomes socially visible oneself in a new way: "My judgments are ineluctable grounds for judgments against me."[196] That is, while it is completely unclear in Rorty what approval should actually be, what agreement in judgment should look like, this cannot be separated from actually communicating and especially from articulating one's own 'communal feeling,' that is, the emotional state of happiness or disappointment that one develops in relation to one's community.[197]

We therefore once again have a completely new version of the register of public, political feelings, which are not meant to replace the dimension of the sense of judgment of rage and shame, of the ethics of compassion and respect for the law, but to reframe it. With happiness and unhappiness, comedy and tragedy, laughing and crying, hedonistic-aesthetic qualities decidedly become the indicator of moral and political agreement: "In a democracy, happiness is a political emotion, as depression is; each is a contribution, oppositely, to the general mood in which our joint faith in our enterprise is maintained, the one to its possibilities, the other, perhaps, to its present obstacles to its possibilities."[198]

In Cavell, therefore, the scope of applying the political is as unlimited as that of the private – without them being indistinguishable or even identical. Both are mutually related aspects of moral perfectionism. While the private asks what kind of person one wishes to be, with what moral decisions one can remain true to an achievable but not quite achieved self, the political looks into whether the conditions under which I can communicate this self are established, and whether I can accept and account for what happens in the name of community, whether I can lend it my voice.[199]

Instead of separating the spheres, it is a question of multiplying and updating the passages between the private and the public as a process of mutual

---

194 Cf. Andrew Norris: Introduction. Stanley Cavell and the Claim to Community. In: id. (ed.) *The Claim to Community. Essays on Stanley Cavell and Political Philosophy.* Stanford 2006, 1–18, here 11–12.
195 Cf. Espen Hammer: *Stanley Cavell. Skepticism, Subjectivity, and the Ordinary.* Cambridge 2002, 36.
196 Cavell: *Cities of Words*, 333.
197 Cf. Cavell: *Cities of Words*, 183–189.
198 Cavell: *Cities of Words*, 185.
199 Cf. Cavell: *Cities of Words*, 11.

stabilization and destabilization. Such passages are called language, taste, and norms, or institutions like marriage and money. Such passages, however, are also the forms of thinking and the media of the aesthetic experience and feelings, wishes, and desires. Understood as such passages, aesthetics and morality become questions for democratic theory: Where do I get the powers of imagination to explore constitutionally given potentials and at the same time to understand the scope of others? Both morality and aesthetics are thus singled out from the modes of human communication as those in which differences of opinion – in contrast for instance to logic, science, or even in contrast to religious dogmas – cannot be explained and completed on the level of facts, rules, or competence. Being in disagreement over a judgment of taste or a moral judgment is not a sign that one of the participants is incompetent or does not know all the relevant facts. Consensus and dissent are equally reasonable. The exchange about criteria, how judgments should be passed, that is, about norms and ideals, is only possible on the basis of already an existing, if diffuse, willingness to agree in the judgment.[200] Uttering such a judgment means the same thing as interrogating the degree of communality and, in case of doubt, risking the experience of separateness.[201] The discovery of a difference of opinion, however, precisely does not set the limits of the community, but its beginning. The community is then not the authority to appeal to in case of conflict – 'But that's just how *we* judge!' – but can only be presumed through the fact that we are in discussion, that we are in the process of discovering our positions, our voices – 'Is this way of judging *mine*, that is, is it *ours*?'[202]

A variety of what one might call common sense or a sense for the communal is therefore based on differences of opinion, the failure of perfect equity, the failure to perceive the perfect self, and cannot be articulated as an end, but as the expression of a common longing, a common claim, calling for argument and objection:

> The right to speak not only takes precedence over social power, it takes precedence over any particular form of accomplishment, no amount of contribution is more valuable to the formation and preservation of community than the willingness to contribute and the occasion to be heard.[203]

---

200 Cf. Cavell: *Cities of Words*, 30.

201 Cf. Hammer: *Stanley Cavell*, 93–101.

202 Cf. Sandra Laugier: Wittgenstein and Cavell. Anthropology, Skepticism, and Politics. In: Andrew Norris (ed.): *The Claim to Community. Essays on Stanley Cavell and Political Philosophy*. Stanford 2006, 19–37, here 30–35. Cf. Stanley Cavell: *The Claim of Reason. Wittgenstein, Skepticism, Morality, and Tragedy* [1979]. New York / Oxford 1999.

203 Stanley Cavell: What Photography Calls Thinking [1985]. In: William Rothman (ed.): *Cavell on Film*. Albany 2005, 115–133, here 133.

The forms of arts and media – and the voices of philosophy, that is, the voices of philosophers – as well as the judgment processes that they contain and shape, thus have the task of showing how private facts and experiences are to be transformed into public ones.[204] The first step in unfolding the power of judgment turns up not in the judgment, but already in the question of whether there is something to be judged here, whether a moral issue should be raised, whether my taste is being questioned, whether I am allowed to speak for others here and now, whether I have to account for the speech of others or not. And the fundamental difficulty of morality is not the conflict between duties or between desire and duty, and also not the deliberation between utilitarianism and deontology. The difficulties of morality begin with making oneself understandable to oneself and to others, with confronting oneself and others with the insecurity of not knowing what and how one should actually desire, of acknowledging one another in insecurity.[205]

It is a matter of respecting the claims of others in a sense that not only considers others' positions in the clandestine dialogue between the self and the ego, but in a way that addresses others, that requires an answer from them, invites them to further exchange and remains quick to reply to their positions, prepared to have one's own morality unsettled by them: "an invitation to improvisation in the disorders of desire."[206]

Feeling and commonality

By locating aesthetic experience, the judgment of taste, and the understanding of community in relation to Dewey, Kant, Arendt, Rorty, and Cavell, I am trying to get to a specific form of speaking (to) feelings that sees them as an aspect of public life, of the "world of appearances."[207] The claim of morality is a claim to understandability, that is, to a will to understand and to make oneself understood. How this is to be achieved is not given, and like in the case of the judgment of taste it is not subject to any rules, but it is achievable. And feelings are one aspect of this, precisely when they point out understanding, lack of under-

---

204 Cf. Cavell: *Cities of Words*, 29.

205 Cf. Cavell: *Cities of Words*, 42.

206 Cavell: *Performative and Passionate Utterance*, 185. Cf. also Cavell: *Performative and Passionate Utterance*, 176 and 184–186.

207 Arendt: *On Violence*, 66.

standing, or a misunderstanding, when there is praise or blame, when there is an expression of happiness or despair.[208]

Feelings, as elements of the aesthetic experience, are not simply understood here as references to issues in the world. Rather, the modes of referencing themselves are at play in them. Can I explain these feelings? Can I share them and generalize them? Can I take on different, reciprocal positions in relation to them? Can I require them of others, can I require a reaction to these feelings from others? The answer to these questions is given not only by the judgments of reason and of moral argumentation, but also by the judgment of taste, common sense, the authority of feeling to be added into a shared world of values, symbols, and judgments.

This feeling of being affectively embedded in a community therefore does not describe an emotion in itself, but a dimension of feelings that allows us to sense the fact that we, as feeling beings, not only stand in relation to the world, but also to others who are feeling. These other feeling persons do not represent any homogenous, enclosed, and accountable belonging. Rather, belonging encompasses precisely the sense for inclusion and exclusion in conflict over how to constitute a shared past, present, and future.

The judgment of taste in aesthetic matters is thus not only a metaphor for a political common sense, but is its basis in the production and embodiment of positions through projections and explanations of immediately pressing feelings. No universal idea of human subjectivity should be achieved in the generalization of the judgment. Instead it is a matter first of becoming engaged in determining a position, of making oneself visible and accountable,[209] and second of relating positively to the possibility of difference wherever judgments differ, by affirming how judgments are achieved without rules, without concepts and conclusions.[210] In this understanding, common sense, the feeling for the communal, is not a homogenizing sense of resonance, but always only a work-in-progress with fractures, interference, frictional loss, always only the promise of the possibility of recognition.[211] It constantly oscillates between the abstract 'we' of the judgment of taste and the concrete sociality that the judgment is exposed to, which frustrates, contradicts, and challenges it over and over again.

---

208 Cf. Cavell: *Cities of Words*, 25–26.
209 Cf. Ludger Schwarte: *Vom Urteilen. Gesetzlosigkeit, Geschmack, Gerechtigkeit*. Berlin 2012, 174.
210 Cf. Massumi: *Of Microperception and Micropolitics*.
211 Cf. Joseph Vogl: Einleitung. In: id. (ed.): *Gemeinschaften. Positionen zu einer Philosophie des Politischen*. Frankfurt a. M. 1994, 7–27.

The world projections of film make it possible to perceive the plurality and the necessity of the contingency and restriction of positions from which it would be possible to say 'I' or 'we.' The different modalities of the aesthetic experience of film do not *represent* the emotional register of an empirical community, but *project* it, modulating and shaping sensibilities and forms of subjectivity. Feelings in them are ways to create meaning, to behave toward the possibility of community. This is why it is ultimately not particularly informative to establish *whether* a film targets a dimension of a moral sense of values. Rather one must ask *what kind of* idea of morality and community is presented. For even – to corroborate this with extreme examples – films like TRIUMPH DES WILLENS (TRIUMPH OF THE WILL, 1935, Leni Riefenstahl) or JUD SÜß (1940, Veit Harlan) address a social and motivational value orientation in their spectators, affectively embedding them in contexts of responsibility and duty.

The examination of the relations between aesthetics, feelings, and morality must therefore also confront the fact that racism, hate, and indifference represent one of the possible forms of unfolding specific ideas of community and politics, of processes of feeling and judging. Cavell's answer is that the moral evil in aesthetic forms of intolerance and preparation for cruelty consists in succumbing to the temptation of skepticism, in wanting to own the world as an object, and in avoiding the human community: "This takes moral evil as the will to exempt oneself, to isolate oneself, from the human community. It is a choice of inhumanity, of monstrousness."[212] Moral evil is not a characteristic of deeds or intentions, but of indifference, that is, the "negation of subjective claims to happiness"[213] and thus the negation of the condition of perfectionism: "It is an awful, an awesome truth that the acknowledgment of the otherness of others, of ineluctable separation, is the condition of human happiness. Indifference is the denial of this condition."[214]

It is in the forms of aesthetic experience themselves that it must be possible to analyze the distinction between recognizing the contingency of positions and judgments of taste on the one hand and its negation on the other. Not every incident of feelings being addressed by audiovisual forms is therefore equally manipulative or emancipatory. And this must be seen at the level of the temporal unfolding of the images themselves, in the specific mode of perceiving, feeling,

---

212 Stanley Cavell: *Pursuits of Happiness. The Hollywood Comedy of Remarriage.* Cambridge / London 1981, 80.
213 Hermann Kappelhoff: Politik der Gefühle. Veit Harlan, Detlef Sierck und das Melodrama des NS-Kinos. In: Harro Segeberg (ed.): *Mediale Mobilmachung I. Das Dritte Reich und der Film.* Munich 2004, 248–265, here 265 [trans. DH].
214 Cavell: *Cities of Words*, 381.

and thinking that is staged and realized by the spectators as embodied experience in their own perceptive, affective, and cognitive faculties.

And when it is a matter of articulating my agreement, my happiness about or my despair over the state of the community, the experiences that I have in the aesthetic forms are for the public moral imagination what words are for a conversation,[215] namely seemingly general, rule-based forms whose meaning, however, can never be detached from their expression in the here and now, in this context, in this conversation between the others and myself, in this novel, in this film at this point. They show that morality and feelings are political and related to the community not despite, but because of their highly personal character, for "in each moral decision of our lives, our sense of ourselves, and of what, and whom, we are prepared to consent to, are at stake."[216]

1.4 Film and Feeling

Film, or rather cinema[217] can be considered the paradigmatic object for focusing on the relationship between mediality and emotions, and the evidence for this is legion:

> Since its inception, the cinema has been considered an affective medium that leads to particularly strong emotional reactions, which affect the spectator somatically. Fear and rage, somatic, often involuntary reactions such as laughing or crying may not be the exclusive to the cinema, but they are privileged zones there – not to mention the thrill(er) of goose bumps.[218]

---

215 "Words for a Conversation" is the subheading of the introduction in Cavell's *Pursuits of Happiness*.

216 Cavell: *Cities of Words*, 39.

217 The developments in media technology over the last few decades has made it necessary to differentiate in principle between the forms of audiovisual moving images and cinematic situations. The cinema, the "succession of automatic world projections" (Cavell: *The World Viewed*, 72) as the theoretical dimension of a particular, corporeal space of experience of the big screen, of the dark room, and of the comfortable seat – which can also be approximated today in an ordinary living room – remains crucial for me here not only because the objects of later analyses are positioned in the form of reception by media history, but because they still represent a certain logic of how audiovisual forms are staged and presented. Cf. Francesco Casetti: *The Lumière Galaxy. Seven Keywords for the Cinema to come.* New York 2015.

218 Gertrud Koch: Zu Tränen gerührt. Zur Erschütterung im Kino. In: Klaus Herding, Bernhard Stumpfhaus (eds.): *Pathos, Affekt, Gefühl. Die Emotionen in den Künsten.* Berlin 2004, 562–574, here 563.

What largely marks current interdisciplinary attempts to research this connection, however, is the reduction of such somatic effectivity to the representative contents, to characters or events that get this or that emotional property ascribed to them. In contrast, the power of audiovisual strategies themselves to be funny, sad, frightening, etc. is less often examined.[219] A brief summary of the theses so far should serve to clarify the framework for a theory of how the audiovisual shapes feelings.

First, the focus in understanding feelings, and thus also medial feelings, must be on physicality as the sensed body in its temporal and dynamic dimension.

Second, a theory of how the audiovisual shapes feelings must assume that it is not simply a matter of passively processing spectators, but that their corporeality actively relates to the film image, realizing the rhythms and intensities of the film image.

Third, on this basis the concrete operation of a medial modeling of feelings should be analyzed as the direct evocation and control of the experiential gestalt of subjective feeling through the temporal shaping process of the film image, through the rhythms, through the duration and intensity of the atmospheres and moods, through movement vectors and synaesthesia.

Forth, even complex feelings and moral feelings should be described on the basis of such audiovisual operational shapes as unity-forming, shape-giving principles of the aesthetic experience. The concrete rhetorical and aesthetic processes point to an affectively rooted dimension of the shared relation to value and thus at the same time address physically grounded, culturally and socially formed self-understandings.

Fifth, the challenge of a cultural studies analysis then consists in conceptualizing the forms of the audiovisual modulation of feelings as modes of developing genuinely public, social, and political emotional states and practices, that is, as forms that do not address feelings as individual mental states, but as affective processes that represent a formed and formable cultural, interpersonal form of experience. The fact that affective dynamics shaped by media in the process of reception are each individually embodied can thus be understood as the process in which these individual physicalities are socialized and related to

---

219 Cf. Kappelhoff, Bakels: *Das Zuschauergefühl*, 78–79. Added to this is the tendency of an "extensive separation between media studies on the one hand, oriented toward cultural studies, and the empirically oriented media psychology and communication studies on the other" (Kappelhoff, Bakels: *Das Zuschauergefühl*, 79 [trans. DH]), with which the questions of the cultural significance of medially modulated emotional processes and the questions of how processes of reception are concretely guided by media strategies can only be represented by each other to a limited degree.

the life of the community in their scope of experience, their perceiving, thinking, and feeling.

Beyond cognition and empathy

A large part of the new interest in feelings, also in film and media studies, comes from the area of cognitive theory – directly in the wake of cognitive psychology and cognitive philosophical theories of feeling. This includes the increasing attempts to transfer terms and models over from the neurosciences and evolutionary psychology. These approaches are to be credited, among other things, with the fact that they stand for a tendency – in a shift away from the semiotic and psychoanalytical film theories of the 1960s to 1980s – to revalue individual film perception in their models. It should not, however, be overlooked that, in their basic tendencies, they neglect the physical and sensual dimension in favor of character-based and narrative informational processes.

Representatives of cognitive approaches such as Ed S. Tan,[220] Torben Grodal,[221] Carl Plantinga,[222] or Murray Smith[223] assume a functionalist understanding of emotions, in which, by analogy to living individual interests and needs, the characters' states and options to act, as well as the meanings of their situations, are mentally construed and projected on narrative processes. Grodal, for instance, postulates that film emotions can be completely explained as universal evolutionary adaptations of programs for coping with situations.[224]

Within cognitive approaches we can distinguish two separate foci. On the one hand there are attempts to arrange information and events in narratives as ways to structure the process of understanding and thus of emotional reaction. The various states of foreshadowing or withholding information and the associated perceived control over the narrative events is meant to form the basis for

---

220 Cf. Ed S. Tan: *Emotion and the Structure of Narrative Film. Film as an Emotion Machine*. Mahwah 1996.

221 Cf. Torben Grodal: *Moving Pictures. A New Theory of Genres, Feelings and Cognition*. Oxford 1997; cf. Torben Grodal: *Embodied Visions. Evolution, Emotion, Culture and Film*. Oxford 2009.

222 Cf. Plantinga: *Moving Viewers*.

223 Cf. Murray Smith: *Engaging Characters. Fiction, Emotion, and the Cinema*. Oxford 1995.

224 Cf. Torben Grodal: Emotions, Cognitions, and Narrative Patterns in Films. In: Carl Plantinga, Greg M. Smith (eds.): *Passionate Views. Film, Cognition, and Emotion*. Baltimore 1999, 127–145, here 129.

any emotionalization of the spectator.[225] Grodal goes so far as to equate the structuring of narrative processes of understanding directly with universal qualities in the architecture of the human brain, attempting to describe them as shaping a 'flow' of perception, emotion, cognition, movement.[226]

On the other hand, there is a focus on the relationship of the spectator to the fictional characters. For Tan the general emotional benefit is determined from assuming narrative "concerns" from out of the spectator's position as witness, structured by the postponed fulfillment of the expected narrative courses.[227] Murray Smith or Margrethe Bruun Vaage also describe structures of sympathy (Smith[228]) or empathy (Bruun Vaage[229]) with film characters as the basic structure of emotionalizing the spectator, sometimes more, sometimes less complex, but always subordinating the physical-affective to narrative understanding and not granting it any experiential dimension of its own.

The problems of cognitive film theories do not simply consist in the fact that they hardly go beyond the strict coupling of the feelings of the spectator and the characters and narrative structures. This is much more the effect of a conception of emotion that allows for no aesthetic dynamic of its own and that makes its concept of the spectator follow the utilitarian rationality of a process of understanding based in evolutionary psychology.[230] This includes the tendency to reduce

---

225 For instance Peter Wuss: Konflikt und Emotion im Filmerleben. In: Matthias Brütsch, Vinzenz Hediger, Ursula von Keitz, Alexandra Schneider, Margrit Tröhler (eds.): *Kinogefühle. Emotionalität und Film*. Marburg 2005, 205–224. Earlier examples include William F. Brewer and Edward H. Lichtenstein: Stories Are to Entertain. A Structural-Affect Theory of Stories. In: *Journal of Pragmatics* (1982), Vol. 6, 473–486.

226 Cf. Grodal: *Embodied Visions*, 145–157. In contrast to Grodal, however, recent neuroscientific research suggests less of a unidirectional flow of neuronal processing than a network of simultaneous, mutually regulating processes, so that affective defaults and movement impulses already contribute to structuring the perception of the environment. Cf. Lisa Feldman Barrett and Moshe Bar: See it with Feeling. Affective Predictions during Object Perceptions. In: *Philosophical Transactions of the Royal Society* (2009), Vol. 364, 1325–1334.

Another cross-sectional study has pointed out that even basic visual perceptions are not free of cultural influences. This can lead us to conclude that the binary distinction of variable-universal is deceptive. Cf. Joseph Henrich, Stephen J. Heine, Ara Norenzayan: The Weirdest People in the World? In: *Behavioral and Brain Sciences* (2010), Vol 33, 61–135.

227 Cf. Ed S. Tan: Film-Induced Affect as a Witness Emotion. In: *Poetics* (1995), Vol. 23, No. 1/2, 7–32; Tan: *Emotion and the Structure of Narrative Film*.

228 Cf. Smith: *Engaging Characters*, 73–106.

229 Cf. Margrethe Bruun Vaage: Fiction Film and the Varieties of Empathic Engagement. In: *Midwest Studies in Philosophy* (2010), Vol. 34, 158–179.

230 Cf. Kappelhoff, Bakels: *Das Zuschauergefühl*, 81; Thomas Morsch: *Medienästhetik des Films. Verkörperte Wahrnehmung und ästhetische Erfahrung im Kino*. Munich 2011, 106–109.

something like mental states in general and the states of the characters in particular to a special case of 'objects' to be deciphered cognitively, instead of understanding them as expressive relations. The consequence is that neither the physically affective dimension of embodied perception in the spectator nor the expressive perceptual performance of audiovisual forms comes into view.

A variation of the cognitive approach is delivered by Greg M. Smith,[231] who assumes the same cognitive structures, but does not see them as aimed at characters and narrative, but at objectless diffuse states, moods, which are set through mood cues and evoke an emotional reaction to narrative structures. He assumes that emotions are triggered and can be implemented as "multidimensional response syndromes"[232] by a wide variety of systems, which merge into an associative network of physiological, cognitive, and expressive components. Since there are so many different forms of arousing an emotion, the redundancy and coherence of the various forms becomes the decisive factor for the emotionalization.[233] A mood is thus created through the summation of individual formal creative qualities – such as music, montage, lighting, dialogue, facial expression, atmospheres, etc. – each of which, taken in itself, is insufficient for a full-fledged emotionalization, but that are cognitively registered as mood cues and, if coherent, lead to a stable orientation in the direction of an emotion: "Redundant cues collaborate to indicate to the viewer which emotional mood is called for."[234] But Smith too ultimately aligns the creation of mood as signal processes solely to narrative understanding, to the sensation of emotions justified by the narrative.[235] In addition he tends to adhere to a quantitatively conceived coherence of independent creative elements, instead of seeing this interplay as the expressive quality of the shape of a process of the audiovisual experience itself.[236]

With Noël Carroll as well there is a clear restriction of the term mood in cognitivist approaches, which always only conceives feelings as the results of chains of stimulus-response.[237] This reduction is particularly evident when

---

231 Cf. Greg M. Smith: *Film Structure and the Emotion System*. Cambridge 2003. A further variation is represented by the term "artefact emotions" in Ed Tan's work, which means a level of emotional evaluation of a film's aesthetic qualities that is clearly separate from narrative emotions. This, however, in no way means reflecting on one's own enjoyment, but of judging 'what is done well or badly' concerning the constructedness and object qualities of films that is being foregrounded. Cf. Tan: *Emotion and the Structure of Narrative Film*, 64–83.

232 Smith: *Film Structure and the Emotion System*, 23.

233 Cf. Smith: *Film Structure and the Emotion System*, 29.

234 Smith: *Film Structure and the Emotion System*, 43.

235 Cf. Smith: *Film Structure and the Emotion System*, 42–64.

236 Cf. Kappelhoff, Bakels: *Das Zuschauergefühl*, 85.

237 Cf. Noël Carroll: Art and Mood. In: *Art in Three Dimensions*. Oxford / New York 2010, 301–328.

Carroll points out, quite rightly, that films shape a perception that is not neutral – whatever that is supposed to mean – but pre-focussed. Nonetheless, he does not manage to understand this as anything more than a mere subsumption under categories: "The descriptions and depictions of the object of our attention in the text will activate our subsumption of the relevant characters and events under the categories that are criterially apposite to the emotional state in question."[238] Such an idea always postulates a primacy of the "relevant sorts of cognitive states"[239] over "rhythmic or atmospheric effects,"[240] so that even the expressive effects of music are described as a detached "bring[ing] to mind"[241] of feelings and movements.

In this work I am not so much interested in rejecting the idea of transferring ideas from cognitive psychology to media studies per se, but in starting from where they come up short in their emphasis of understanding characters and actions, and where it becomes necessary to describe audiovisual creations as complex, temporal-dynamic processes in terms of visual theory and not merely as information to be processed. A strong conception of the film experience therefore seems to me to be the condition for grasping each specific spectator perception in its historical, cultural, and social situatedness, as well as cinema itself in its historicity, as a type of aesthetic experience. We must therefore get to an idea of audiovisual affect, which makes it possible to conceive how concrete media practices in general and historically variable audiovisual strategies in particular modulate relations to the self and the world grounded in embodied experience, thus bringing forth forms of subjectivation, social ties, and cultural contexts of meaning.

The change in the direction of thought that is brought into play here should then briefly be clarified in relation to the term empathy. In the psychologizing aesthetics of narrative, empathy is understood as a theoretical problem of a lack of knowledge of the interiority of others. I would instead suggest leaning more on Edith Stein's theses, seeing empathy as a process through which one can gain an additional "layer of sensation"[242] by feeling oneself in others, thus modifying one's own view of the world and physical sensations.[243] In this sense we might say that the primary empathic process in cinema does not concern

---

238 Noël Carroll: Film, Emotion, and Genre. In: Carl Plantinga, Greg M. Smith (eds.): *Passionate Views. Film, Cognition, and Emotion.* Baltimore 1999, 21–47, here 30.

239 Carroll: *Art and Mood*, 313.

240 Carroll: *Art and Mood*, 313.

241 Carroll: *Art and Mood*, 325.

242 Stein: *On the Problem of Empathy*, 60.

243 Cf. Stein: *On the Problem of Empathy*, 63.

the individual character, but the fact that we, "when we look at the images in a film, have an aesthetic experience of the other, in which this other is the film world, construed through the expressive and figurative components of film language and images."[244]

On this basis alone we can then analyze something like empathy with characters as a process of attribution through which a feeling character is construed starting from one's own being-moved. First come feelings, thoughts, and intentions, then comes the character they are meant to belong to.[245] Empathy therefore appears as a mode of externalizing and verbalizing one's own physical being-moved as the mental and affective processes of a character. In other words: Spectators explain and structure their somatic affects along contexts of meaning and narrative events that themselves are still grounded in spectator feelings.[246] In the aesthetic experience as a dynamic of processes of perceiving, feeling, and thinking that unfolds in time, the spectator's own sensation and the sensation that something would feel in a certain way for a character are at the very most conceptual distinctions that address the various levels of describing this process.[247]

The question of feelings in the cinema must therefore look beyond the feeling of characters – which is represented by the film – to a specific form of expressivity. This should be positioned between the two corporalities of the film and the spectators as a dynamic, affective connection in the figuration of time and movement, rhythm and intensities.[248] We must therefore think of this expressivity as a prelinguistic, non-representative form, blurring inside and outside, of "bodily-empathic identifications with objecthood, the abstract, the material."[249]

---

244 Adriano D'Aloia: Edith Stein geht ins Kino. Empathie als Filmtheorie. in: *montage AV* (2010), Vol. 19, No. 1, 79–100, here 80–81 [trans. DH].
245 Cf. Susan L Feagin: Empathizing as Simulating. In: Amy Coplan, Peter Goldie (eds.): *Empathy. Philosophical and Psychological Perspectives*. Oxford 2011, 149–161, here 150.
246 Cf. Christiane Voss: Narration, Emotion und kinematografische Illusion aus philosophischer Sicht. In: Anne Bartsch, Jens Eder, Kathrin Fahlenbrach (eds.): *Audiovisuelle Emotionen. Emotionsdarstellung und Emotionsvermittlung durch audiovisuelle Medienangebote*. Cologne 2007, 312–329, here 326.
247 Cf. Katja Mellmann: Gefühlsübertragung? Zur Psychologie emotionaler Textwirkungen. In: Ingrid Kasten (ed.): *Machtvolle Gefühle*. Berlin 2010, 107–119, here 117.
248 Cf. D'Aloia: *Edith Stein geht ins Kino*, 84–85. Tarja Laine: *Feeling Cinema. Emotional Dynamics in Film Studies*. New York 2011, 1. Cf. Kappelhoff, Bakels: *Das Zuschauergefühl*, 84.
249 Morsch: *Medienästhetik des Films*, 55 [trans. DH]; cf. also 46–58. Drawing on Stein clearly allows for the possibility of empathy with objects and dynamic effects of spaces, forms, and colors. Cf. Morsch: *Medienästhetik des Films*, 201. D'Aloia: *Edith Stein geht ins Kino*, 81.

Here I am following the works of Hermann Kappelhoff, according to whom there are three basic cornerstones in question above all others: first the examinations throughout the history of theory of the concept of expression and expressive movement and its reception in the early film theory of Béla Balázs and Sergei M. Eisenstein, second the concepts of body and perception within phenomenology, and third the Deleuzian theories on cinematic thinking in movement and time images and their central concept of the affection image. Audiovisual images, and this is the common core of these three paradigms, are conceptualized here as the realization of complex meanings in concretely and individually embodied sensibility:

> Moving images were always also perceived as images that move, images that always perceive emotion as the flip side of external action. It appears that the emotion, the emotional being-moved on the part of the spectator, is not a simple reaction to the events represented, but is directly the flip side, the continuation of the cinematic movement image in the spectator's perception, affection.[250]

Historical positions

Looking to the beginnings of film theory, it is clear that many of the central problems, from the viewpoint of psychology, film practice, and aesthetic theory, lead directly to the question of emotionalizing by means of audiovisual forms. Hugo Münsterberg, for instance, starts from the general assumption that the functional mechanisms of the technical means for creating film and of mental processes are analogous and concludes: "To picture emotions must be the central aim of the photoplay."[251] And although the feelings of characters are an important reference point for reception for him as well, he still draws the decisive conclusion that 'to picture' does not in fact mean putting characters with feelings into the image, representing them, but that feelings themselves are brought forth as visual forms: "Not the portrait of the man but the picture as a whole has to be filled with emotional exuberance."[252]

In just this sense the representatives of the historical avant-garde, and first and foremost the Russian theorists of montage, each in their own way sought to understand film as a medium of technologically manipulating the shaping of feelings. While Vsevolod Pudovkin,[253] like Münsterberg, still strongly assumed an

---

250 Kappelhoff: *Matrix der Gefühle*, 17 [trans. DH].
251 Hugo Münsterberg: *The Photoplay. A Psychological Study*. New York / London 1916, 112.
252 Münsterberg: *The Photoplay*, 122.
253 Cf. Vsevolod Pudovkin: *Selected Essays*, ed. Richard Taylor. Chicago 2006.

antecedent analogy of cinematic processes and mental processes, aiming for an emotional optimization of narrative processes, Dziga Vertov's[254] theses tended to see film as a radical alteration of human perceptual potential. But it was Sergei M. Eisenstein in particular who saw the shaping of feelings in film as making a contribution to the historical and political work on the bodies of spectators, and for whom montage went from being a film technique to an idea of directly working on affective and intellectual processes, to the idea of working on the collective world view.[255] In other words: The possibilities of film to shape ways of thinking and feeling are not solely given by the mental processes of individual psychology. The temporal gestalts of moving images and sounds facilitate new forms of thinking and feeling, conveying novel movements and affects to the spectator. The conspicuous characteristic here is the idea of a continuum from the shaping of fundamental physiological meters and rhythms, past complex compositional principles of the organic and the pathos-oriented, to semantic operations described as abstract.[256] For Eisenstein what is intellectual in film is not the purity of understanding, but precisely the synthesis of biophysics, feeling, and reason.[257]

While Eisenstein understands the modeling of affect in cinema starting from the body in movement – the legacy of Meyerhold's biomechanics[258]– Béla Balázs starts with a theory of physiognomic expression, taking the image as the medial realization of the expressivity of the human face.[259] We are dealing here with two sides of the same coin, two forms of one theoretical paradigm that had developed in the late nineteenth and early twentieth centuries in psychology, linguistics, aesthetics, and philosophical anthropology under the term expressive movement.[260] The body in movement, the gestural moving of

---

254 Cf. Dziga Vertov: *Kino-Eye. The Writings of Dziga Vertov*, ed. Annette Michelson. Los Angeles / Berkeley 1984.

255 Cf. Sergei M. Eisenstein: The Montage of Film Attractions [1924]. In: id.: *Sergei Eisenstein. Selected Works, Vol. I: Writings, 1922–1934*, ed. Richard Taylor. London 1988, 39–58.

256 Cf. Sergei M. Eisenstein: The Fourth Dimension in Cinema [1929]. In: id.: *Sergei Eisenstein. Selected Works, Volume 1, Writings, 1922–1934*, ed. Richard Taylor. London 1988, 181–194 and Sergei M. Eisenstein: Organic Unity and Pathos in the Composition of Potemkin [1939]. In: id.: *Problems of Film Direction*. Honolulu 2004, 1–9.

257 Cf. Sergei M. Eisenstein: Perspectives [1929]. In: *Sergei Eisenstein. Selected Works, Vol. I: Writings, 1922–1934*, ed. Richard Taylor. London 1988, 151–160, here 156.

258 Cf. Vsevolod Meyerhold: Biomechanics [1922]. In: id.: *Meyerhold on Theatre*. London / New York 1998, 197–203.

259 Cf. Béla Balázs: Visible Man or the Culture of Film [1924]. In: id.: *Early Film Theory. Visible Man and The Spirit of Film*. New York 2010, 1–90.

260 Cf. Kappelhoff, Bakels: *Das Zuschauergefühl*, 84–85 and Kappelhoff: *Matrix der Gefühle*. Prominent examples are Wilhelm Wundt, Georg Simmel, Karl Bühler, and Helmuth Plessner.

the face, and the moving of the film image get a common denominator here, meaning a specific dimension of movement that not only can be seen as a change of place, or gestural pointing, and not only as a succession of states. This other dimension of movement can be understood, as Plessner does, as a complete form of movement, which realizes a process of change as bodily sensation:

> Wherever movements appear in the realm of the organic, they run according to a rhythm of their own, showing a dynamic shape that is also experimentally verifiable. They do no unwind piecemeal, as if the succession of the phases had been associated from individual elements, nor do they form any temporal mosaic. Rather, they assume a certain entity, within which the individual movement curves are variable. These entities belong to the organism through is relation to its environment, its morphology, its typal instincts as motor categories.[261]

In Balázs this process is called a "chord of feeling"[262] and means an artificial vitality, the historic and socially effective emergence of the possibility of producing feelings as the "rhythm of our inner turbulence"[263] through the cinematic shaping of movement and time. In Eisenstein it is called 'conflict': "Cinema begins where the collision between different cinematic measures of movement and vibration begins."[264] The following will trace the effectivity and further development of this idea of expressive movement in current paradigms within film and media studies, and will present the film analytical concept that Hermann Kappelhoff has developed from it.

Film, phenomenology, and physicality

Embodiment as the condition for all perception and the *primacy of perception*[265] for any construction of meaning are the focal points of a phenomenology of film following Maurice Merleau-Ponty, which is dedicated to the concrete temporal and audiovisual unfolding of perceptual modulations. The spectator's action is not to understand events and characters, but to realize the cinematic rhythms and movements as a structure of things, a "modulation of

---

261 Helmuth Plessner: Die Deutung des mimischen Ausdrucks. Ein Beitrag zur Lehre vom Bewußtsein des anderen Ichs [1925]. In: *Gesammelte Schriften. Bd. 7: Ausdruck und menschliche Natur*. Frankfurt a. M. 1982, 67–130, here 77 [trans. DH].
262 Balázs: *Early Film Theory*, 34.
263 Balázs: *Early Film Theory*, 35.
264 Eisenstein: *The Fourth Dimension*, 192.
265 Cf. Maurice Merleau-Ponty: *The Primacy of Perception* [1946]. Evanston 1964; Merleau-Ponty: *Phenomenology of Perception*.

existence,"[266] a temporally unfolding modulation of relations between bodies and one's own being-in-the-world:

> The meaning of a film is incorporated into its rhythm just as the meaning of a gesture may immediately be read in that gesture: the film does not mean anything but itself. [...] The joy of art lies in its showing how something takes on meaning – not be referring to already established and acquired ideas but by the temporal or spatial arrangement of elements. [...] A movie is not thought, it is perceived.[267]

The spectator's emotional sensation can be understood as a resonance, a materialization of the audiovisual moving images in his or her own body, the "object that is *sensitive* to all the rest."[268] The rhythm of this resonance should be analyzed in the images, in their temporal gestalt, and should be described as qualitatively patterning embodied feeling as "how they use their bodies, the simultaneous patterning of body and world in emotion."[269]

Within film theory this phenomenological approach – aside from a few, usually somewhat psychologistic, empirical works of filmology from the 1940s and 1950s[270] and some that tend to propose that film itself exercises phenomenology[271] – has only been made vital and systematically developed through the conception of embodiment. Vivian Sobchack consistently formulates the idea that the emotional sensations of spectators consist in realizing in one's own body an external perceptual experience that has become expressive, that has its own behavioral patterns and intentionalities:

> In a search for rules and principles governing cinematic expression, most of the descriptions and reflections of classical and contemporary film theory have not fully addressed the cinema as life expressing life, as experience expressing experience. Nor have they

---

266 Merleau-Ponty: *Phenomenology of Perception*, 225.

267 Merleau-Ponty: The Film and the New Psychology [1947]. In: id.: *Sense and Non-Sense*. Evanston 1964, 48–62, here 57–58.

268 Merleau-Ponty: *Phenomenology of Perception*, 275.

269 Merleau-Ponty: *Phenomenology of Perception*, 219.

270 Cf. Albert Michotte van den Berck: The Character of 'Reality' of Cinematographic Projections [1948]. In: Georges Thinès, Alan Costall, George Butterworth (eds.): *Michotte's Experimental Phenomenology of Perception*. Abingdon 2013, 197–208; Albert Michotte van den Berck: The Emotional Involvement of the Spectator in the Action Represented in a Film. Toward a Theory [1953]. In: Georges Thinès, Alan Costall, George Butterworth (eds.): *Michotte's Experimental Phenomenology of Perception*. Abingdon 2013, 209–218.

271 We can also read André Bazin's concept of realism as well as passages in Merleau-Ponty in this directions (*The Film and the New Psychology*). This tendency is also represented by Edgar Morin: *The Cinema, or the Imaginary Man* [1956]. Minneapolis 2005.

explored the mutual possession of this experience of perception and its expression by filmmaker, film, and spectator – all *viewers viewing*, engaged as participants in dynamically and directionally reversible acts that reflexively and reflectively constitute *the perception of expression* and the *expression of perception*. Indeed, it is this mutual capacity for and possession of experience through common structures of embodied existence, through similar modes of being-in-the-world, that provide the *intersubjective* basis of objective cinematic communication.[272]

The film that we see is not simply a visible object in itself and also not just an aggregation, a sequence of things and bodies made visible, but is itself a perception, made perceivable by means of projection, of a film body that is capable of movement and of bestowing meaning. The spectator's experience therefore describes a dialogical interweaving of the spectator's physical capacity to sense and the activity of the film body, meant in an entirely non-metaphoric sense:

> The film experience is predicated, therefore, on the *significance of movement*, on its activity of choice-making, which is lived through the bodies of both the spectator and the film. [...] We understand that world we see projected before and for us as present *to* and *for* (not merely *in*) an embodied and conscious subject other than ourselves. [...] We recognize the moving picture as the work of an anonymous and sign-producing body-subject intentionally marking visible choices with the very behavior of its bodily being.[273]

A critique of Sobchack and other neo-phenomenological film theories within media theory sees them as anthropomorphizing film perception, and thus positioning it as normative. Even if Sobchack herself denies this,[274] her descriptions of the cinematographic apparatus tend to amount to describing it in its historical emergence as if it had developed teleologically according to an image of the

---

272 Sobchack: *The Address of the Eye*, 5.

273 Sobchack: *The Address of the Eye*, 277–278. One weak point in Sobchack's systematic elaboration is fact that her view of the intentionality of movement is always very close to a reconstruction of the behavior of the film camera, and less to the expressive spatial and temporal intensities of the film image, in contrast to her film analyses that describe a dimension of affectively associating the image with appreciable surfaces, synesthesia, and atmospheres. See Vivian Sobchak: What My Fingers Knew. The Cinesthetic Subject, or Vision in the Flesh. In: id.: *Carnal Thoughts. Embodiment and Moving Image Culture.* Berkeley / Los Angeles / London 2004, 53–84. This emphasis on the haptic and tactile in Sobchack is also continued in other works: cf. Laura Marks: *The Skin of the Film. Intercultural Cinema, Embodiment, and the Senses.* Durham 2000; Jennifer Barker: *The Tactile Eye. Touch and the Cinematic Experience.* Berkeley 2009.

274 Cf. Sobchack: *What My Fingers Knew*, 66, fn. 48.

living, human body as a norm.[275] Certain works in fact even go so far as to conceive the relation of film aesthetics to the everyday faculties and structure of perception, thinking, and feeling not in terms of aesthetic modalities of experience, but instead postulating film as already completely adapted, directed film corporality. Jennifer Barker claims, for instance: "The film's body models itself on human styles of bodily comportment, and the viewer's body in turn mirrors the muscular behavior of the film's body."[276]

The Deleuzian critique of phenomology and Merleau-Ponty also takes a similar direction. Gilles Deleuze accuses phenomenology of making 'natural perception' the norm and of seeing the moving shapes of film only in the sense of conformity or deviation.[277] He is referring here to a passage in the *Phenomenology of Perception*, which is certainly problematic in its understanding of film.[278] On the other hand, one can also argue, in the sense of Merleau-Ponty, that the thesis that embodied perception is the starting point of accessing the world and film is not fixed to any natural or ordinary dimension.[279]

This is the sense in which I will here make the case for the relationship between the technological perception of film and that of ordinary human life having no stable, psychological, or anthropological coordinates. Rather, they are realized in different ways in the individual aesthetic strategies of the films. For on the one hand, just as the aesthetic experience stands in continuity to ordinary experience, the perceiving body in the cinema is none other than the same ordinary body, which has "a real sense experience [...] in a sensual continuum of image, subject, and world."[280] On the other hand, the aesthetic modalities of these real sensual experiences should be examined for their historical, cultural constructedness, their additional quality of technological-machinic ahumanity outside of ordinary, pragmatic perceptual patterns. The perceptions and sensations in the cinema, being transformations and reconstructions, are related to the experiential potential of embodied spectators, they transform audiovisual structures into forms of physical being-in-the-world.

At the same time, we must take care not to be too hasty in equating the description of the corporality of the cinema experience with a utopian imagination

---

275 Cf. Sobchack: *The Address of the Eye*, 251. Cf. Drehli Robnik: Körper-Erfahrung und Film-Phänomenologie. In: Jürgen Felix (ed.): *Moderne Film Theorie*. Mainz 2002, 246–280, here 261.

276 Barker: *The Tactile Eye*, 77.

277 Gilles Deleuze: *Cinema I. The Movement-Image* [1983]. Minneapolis 1986, 84.

278 Cf. Merleau-Ponty: *Phenomenology of Perception*, 96.

279 Cf. Merleau-Ponty: *Phenomenology of Perception*, 230; Sobchack: *The Address of the Eye*, 30–32.

280 Morsch: *Medienästhetik des Films*, 186 [trans. DH].

of a subversive, emancipated body. Such utopias celebrate the negation of fixed linguistic and symbolic subjectivity through aesthetic forms of bodily overpowering, of loss of control and the liberation of physical subjectivity from cultural-historical overlay:[281] "The impression sometimes arises here that a (cinema) culture of wanting-to-sense-oneself-intensely-again, of wanting to be confident about the intact capacity for enjoyment and physical wholeness, becomes theoretically consecrated."[282] These tendencies omit that performances of the body – even beyond symbolic inscriptions – are also the scene of social demarcations and conditioning. The dynamic rhythms and intensities of the film image do not encounter a coherent spectator subject that precedes these, but the subjectivity experiencing the film *is* the realization of the audiovisual temporalities and affective processes. A phenomenological film analysis aims to unfold the genesis of complex processes of making meaning and media specific subjectivizations from the dynamic rhythms and intensities of film as an expressive form: "how something takes on meaning [...] by the temporal or spatial arrangement of elements."[283]

It is thus proposing an idea of body, image, and movement for which the starting point in the question of the conditions of the possibility of experience are the affect-economic forces themselves, which work in the realm of the senses. Deleuze and Guattari's sensualism attempts to avoid any individualized reference to objects or cognition in order to get directly to the contingent and particular intensities, the eventful connections within the realm of the senses:

> Percepts are no longer perceptions; they are independent of a state of those who experience them. Affects are no longer feelings or affections; they go beyond the strength of those who undergo them. Sensations, percepts, and affects are beings whose validity lies in themselves and exceeds any lived. They could be said to exist in the absence of man because man, as he is caught in stone, on the canvas, or by words, is himself a compound of percepts and affects.[284]

In Deleuze, expression,[285] sensation,[286] and the affection-image[287] are signs that are given by the events of affecting and being-affected, and thus exceed any subjective carrier, any narrativization.

---

281 One particular representative of this is Steven Shaviro: *The Cinematic Body*. Minneapolis 1993. Cf. Morsch: *Medienästhetik des Films*, 40–46.

282 Robnik: *Körper-Erfahrung und Film-Phänomenologie*, 261 [trans. DH].

283 Merleau-Ponty: *The Film and the New Psychology*, 57–58.

284 Gilles Deleuze and Félix Guattari: *What is Philosophy?* [1991] trans. Graham Burchell, Hugh Tomlinson. London 1994, 163–164.

285 Cf. Gilles Deleuze: *Expressionism in Philosophy. Spinoza* [1968]. New York 1992.

286 Cf. Gilles Deleuze: *Francis Bacon. The Logic of Sensation* [1981]. London 2003.

287 Cf. Deleuze: *Cinema I*, 71–122.

The film image is thus not only processed by subjects and bodies. It itself poses ontological questions: How does a body emerge? What does thinking in images and movements mean? The histories of its forms do not correspond to any succession of forms of representing reality, but to an unfolding of signs as relations. Their possible combinations each result in different forms of thinking space, material, and time, which can be derived from one another:

> And in each case, the thoughts are inseparable from the images; they are completely immanent to the images. There are no abstract thoughts realized indifferently in one image or another, but concrete images that only exist through these images and their means.[288]

In Deleuze, the concreteness of thoughts includes the fact that, as mental processes, they cannot be separated from an affective dimension. The symbolic quality of film images is identical to their faculty to affect bodies. The moving quality and temporality of images as processual forms becomes a practice, a "psychomechanics,"[289] with which experiences, affects, and percepts beyond subjectivity and objectivity can be realized, can unfold as relational beings and entities:[290] "Emotion does not say 'I'."[291] That is, feelings are set into the temporal structure of film as potencies, they are emotional qualities that cannot yet be split into their components of 'felt by whom' and 'felt in relation to what,' which capture the spectrum of possibilities of the spectators' ability to be affected: "Crying, or causing tears to flow, and provoking laughter are the functions of certain images. [...] How could you not cry at Griffith's BROKEN BLOSSOMS?"[292] The perceptions, thoughts, and feelings of the spectators are direct functions of the images, and film, like painting, music, and literature, gives us the world as a continual modulation and energy variation of movement and time, of bodies and forces.

At this point I would like to introduce two further references very briefly, which can be affiliated to such a conception of the audiovisual modulation of feelings as an unfolding of affects in the temporal shaping of intensities and rhythms, providing it with additional perspectives.

---

288 Gilles Deleuze: Cinema-1, Premiere [1983]. In: id.: *Two Regimes of Madness. Texts and Interviews 1975–1995*. New York 2006, 210–212, here 210.

289 Gilles Deleuze: *Cinema II. The Time-Image* [1985]. Minneapolis 1989, 262.

290 Cf. Deleuze: *Cinema I*, 95–101.

291 Gilles Deleuze: Painting Sets Writing Ablaze [1981]. In: id.: *Two Regimes of Madness. Texts and Interviews 1975–1995*. New York 2006, 181–187, here 187.

292 Gilles Deleuze: Portrait of the Philosopher as a Moviegoer [1983]. In: id.: *Two Regimes of Madness. Texts and Interviews 1975–1995*. New York 2006, 213–221, here 216.

On the one hand there is the theory of the vitality affects or vitality forms by the developmental psychologist Daniel Stern, which Raymond Bellour brought into play, explicitly in continuation from or supplementation to the Deleuzian theses.[293] Affects in Stern are applied as self-contained temporal gestalts of movement, of rhythm, and of intensity, which are not linked to individual modalities of perception or forms of interaction. It is a matter of synesthetic patterns, such as the creeping, the bulging, the explosion-like, or the fading, which can each occur as specific experiences, both in perception and in action as well as in feeling and in thinking. These are derived from primordial forms of intersubjective, cross-modal interaction, of the affective reflection of an infant's facial expression in the voice of the mother. The cinema, according to Bellour, can also be thought of as a similar interaction of constantly translating perceptions into feelings:

> in the variety of its components (the image and the modalities of the soundtrack incorporated in it) it produces – from the simple reality of the world to its fictionalization – the constant illusion of a sensory attunement between the elements of the world, just as it does between the bodies that are deployed in it.[294]

Unfortunately, both in Stern[295] and in Bellour[296] there is a tendency to equate the vitality forms as brief moments in the present with the film shot, and thus to fall back behind the complexity of the movement modulations of audiovisual forms, which they actually have won precisely by emphasizing amodal rhythms and intensities.

The second reference is the New Phenomenology following Hermann Schmitz, which aims at a dimension of amodal being-affected that is quite similar to those found in Stern and Bellour. Both with Deleuze and Schmitz, the connection between aesthetic processes and feelings can be traced back to an unavoidable synaesthetic temporal variation of the dynamic volume of the body. In Deleuze, writing about the *Logic of Sensation*, it would be an operation that:

> stands in direct contact with a vital power that exceeds every domain and traverses them all. This power is rhythm, which is more profound than vision, hearing, etc. [...] This

---

293 Bellour: Going to the Cinema with Guattari and Stern. In: Eric Alliez, Andrew Goffey (eds.): *The Guattari Effect*. London 2011, 220–234; Daniel Stern: *The Interpersonal World of the Infant*. New York 1985; Daniel Stern: *Forms of Vitality. Exploring Dynamic Experience in Psychology, the Arts, Psychotherapy, and Development*. Oxford 2010.

294 Bellour: *Going to the Cinema with Guattari and Stern*, 229.

295 Cf. Stern: *Forms of Vitality*, 94.

296 Cf. Bellour: *Daniel Stern, encore*.

rhythm runs through a painting just as it runs through a piece of music. It is diastole-systole: the world that seizes me by closing in around me, the self that opens to the world and opens the world itself.[297]

What Deleuze relates to the activity of the heart muscle, in Schmitz appears exemplified in the expansion and contraction of breathing.[298] The shaping processes of art – Schmitz above all views larger time frames in architecture and the visual arts – are for him physically perceived emotional dispositions.[299] Surpassing the impression of movement in buildings and portraits, in the audiovisual forms it is about complex shaping processes of the movements themselves that unfold over time. The communication between film image and the spectator's body can be classified in Schmitz's terminology as a one-sided "antagonistic encorporation," in which the perceived "bridge qualities" of the audiovisual "movement suggestions" and of the "synaesthetic qualities"[300] are sensed at the same time on one's own body.

The atmospheres and moods unfolding in works of art are objectivized, generalized physical base moods, which form, transform, and supplement the physical traces of the recipients so that ultimately the arts, architectures, and media practices not only have a history or are in history, but become historically effective themselves and appear as the completed "history of human physicality."[301]

The possibilities of systematically working out the "categorial analysis of physicality"[302] of contraction and expansion, tension and swelling, direction and rhythm into a model of film analysis can unfortunately not be fully fathomed here. I will, however, attempt to come back to this in the individual film analyses, and to point out the potential achievements of this vocabulary.

Film feeling as the temporal structure of moving images

Examining the audiovisual modulation of feelings is not solely about the impact of film on the spectator, not about activating and distributing feelings that the film would already find as a cultural or biological repertoire of feelings, but

297 Deleuze: *Francis Bacon*, 42–43.

298 Cf. Schmitz: *New Phenomenology*, 92.

299 Cf. Hermann Schmitz: *Der Leib im Spiegel der Kunst. System der Philosophie*. Vol. II,1. Bonn 1966, X, 44, 83, and passim.

300 Schmitz: *New Phenomenology*, 68.

301 Schmitz: *Der Leib im Spiegel der Kunst*, X [trans. DH].

302 Schmitz: *Der Leib im Spiegel der Kunst*, 19–36 [trans. DH].

quite concretely about the creation of affects as forms of being-in-the-world and of behaving, about the creation of affectivity and subjectivity, which would not exist without the interaction of film and spectator body. This can be described, following Dewey, as the idea that the structures of film are precisely not to be understood as stimuli that are completely self-constituted, and that would call up a particular response in the spectator that is only explainable through biology of psychology.[303] Instead, audiovisual expressivity already constitutes the spectator's feelings as embodied acts of perception to be completed, in the sense of a specific mode of aesthetic experience in each case. There is no ready-made tuned and tempered keyboard of feelings, no spectrum of basic film emotions. Affects can only be qualified and determined when other socio-cultural, linguistic, and speech-like registers and practices come to play, when affects are integrated into rhetorics and poetics, for instance as in the affect poetics of genre cinema.

The goal is to describe audiovisual structures in a way that makes clear how the treatment of space and time itself represents a complex feeling, and how film feelings consist in processing, interrelating different time structures. To implement such a concept of an audiovisual modulation of feelings, I will be drawing on the theoretical work and film analytical models of Hermann Kappelhoff[304] on the melodrama and on the relationship between individual corporality and the work on cultural imagination. The moving quality of images, characters, and things, their temporal structure can be grasped as the objective, external flip side of an emotional movement that on the one hand is a media construct, and on the other can be seen as affective, perceptive, and cognitive processes passed through by the spectator-subject.[305]

The movements, synaesthetic intensities, rhythms that appear and are understood as the shaping of characters, things, and settings are at the same time related, as forces and vectors, to the spectator's physicality, where they are realized as a constantly modulating, changing idea of the entirety of the film world:

> The whole of the film is the concrete duration in which forces are opened up for the spectator that prevail throughout the film world. The whole of the film is above all a specific way of hearing and seeing.

---

303 Dewey: *The Theory of Emotion* II, 26: "This distinction of stimulus and response is one of interpretation, and of interpretation from the standpoint of the value of some act considered as an accomplished end."

304 Cf. Kappelhoff: *Matrix der Gefühle.*

305 Cf. Kappelhoff: *Matrix der Gefühle,* 16–24.

> [...] In the same individual act of how each spectator perceives the film world in his or her own seeing and hearing, the spatial figurations are realized as a specific way of sensing. Over the duration of the film the spectator realizes its sense order as an emerging, growing feeling taking hold of him or her.[306]

The term expressive movement, which was put into operation following these theoretical reflections in a film analytical method, now serves to synthesize and schematize these emotionalizing forms of time and patterns of presentation, without creating universal essences and stereotypes in the process:

> A method aimed at such analytical description must make the compositional shaping of audiovisual moving images understandable as a temporal perceptual sense while making it evident and verifiable in its function for the processes of the spectator developing affect and constructing meaning. In this sense the method developed by us is not aimed at isolating individual compositional elements of specific affective value (mood cues), but at the movement figurations of audiovisual compositions themselves, at their temporal shape.[307]

In practice this method seeks to identifying three fundamental levels of temporally segmenting audiovisual forms, the middle level of which is directly accessible to a naive general understanding of film: the unit of the scene. The upper level then designates "the arrangement of scenic units themselves as the dramaturgical macrostructure of a shaped process of spectator feeling."[308] This "affect dramaturgy"[309] does not mean any simple succession of affect qualities, no simple revue of discrete emotional addresses. It means the structured, permanent modulation, and processual interaction of feelings over the duration of the film.[310] The lower lever, in contrast, aims at microstructural unity, which, as a dynamic pattern, provides a scene with its specific compositional shape: "These movement figurations designated as units of expressive movement provide us with the possibility of describing the audiovisual composition of a scene as a dynamic joining of its temporal segments."[311]

A leading hypothesis that arises from this method of temporally segmenting film and of continually and dynamically modulating spectator feeling by

---

306 Kappelhoff: *Die vierte Dimension des Bewegungsbildes*, 310–311 [trans. DH].
307 Kappelhoff, Bakels: *Das Zuschauergefühl*, 87 [trans. DH].
308 Kappelhoff, Bakels: *Das Zuschauergefühl*, 88 [trans. DH].
309 Kappelhoff, Bakels: *Das Zuschauergefühl*, 89 [trans. DH].
310 Following Tarja Laine, one could also call this continuous spectator feeling the 'emotional core' of the film. Cf. Tarja Laine: *Feeling cinema*, 3: "An emotional core is not a quality 'attached' to the film externally. Rather it is an 'affective quality' [...] that is immanent to the film and inseparable from the spectator's aesthetic experience."
311 Kappelhoff, Bakels: *Das Zuschauergefühl*, 90 [trans. DH].

the patterns of segments is that audiovisual forms are never about clearly outlined, unambiguously classifiable feelings, but always only about the specific mixtures, courses, and linkings in each case. In addition these patterns can never be unambiguously traced back to individual levels of film composition, such as the frequency of cuts or the field sizes of shots. It is therefore not possible to set up general, prediction-generating rules for the relationship between simple aesthetic qualities and their expressive, affecting qualities:

> The reason that we cannot formulate the laws underlying expression is not because they do not exist, but rather because there are too many of them. [...] Every distinct work of art instantiates different laws of expression.[312]

What constitutes the individual film as an affective aesthetic experience is the experience of the interplay of various complex and diffuse feelings, their relation to a sense of unity in multiplicity.

1.5 Feelings of Guilt as an Aesthetic Modality

As a starting point, I will take the film analytical concept in which the feelings of spectators are understood as the duration of the unfolding of the film image realized in their own physical sensations. Audiovisually modulated feelings are processes of interrelating spatialities and temporalities. This is in line with the thesis that the symbolic and linguistic, normative and political registers of cultural world construction is also linked to the affectivity of individual corporality.

In the following I will be claiming that certain audiovisual stagings have the aim of calling up a somatic realization on the part of the spectator, which is suitable for constructing the relationship of the spectator to what is represented in the sense of something to be evaluated normatively. Specific sensomotory excitations lead to indignation, the duration of a gaze instills shame, a solemn rhythm makes us proud. I would therefore like to examine certain audiovisual dynamics and temporal relations as a form of such morally relevant affective addresses for how they modulate the spectator's sensation of self as the sense of guilt. I will be considering this as a particular manifestation of cultural work on the temporal structures of the physical relation to the self and the world. Feelings are both the processes themselves as well as the materials with which films shape aesthetic experience of shared values and norms, perceptible and

---

312 Derek Matravers: *Art and Emotion.* Oxford 1998, 212–213.

traceable structures of the social world. Films confirm, modulate, or destabilize the physically grounded coordinates of our cultural self-positionings. In this respect feelings are not states of private interior worlds, but are produced, circulated, and create relations between the physically and affectively structured self-reflections and the dynamic forms of cultural patterns of interpretation and identity: "Emotions work by working through signs and on bodies to materialise the surfaces and boundaries that are lived as worlds."[313]

And this is the case, also and above all, when we understand that our desires and self-images are embedded in processes of power and violence, of inclusion and exclusion, of justice and injustice. The work of feelings consists in making it possible to trace dysfunctionalities, of making it possible to experience inherited, culturally established patterns and their changeability as a treatment of one's own physical self:

> The emotional struggles against injustice are not about finding good or bad feelings, and then expressing them. Rather, they are about how we are moved by feelings into a different relation to the norms that we wish to contest, or the wounds we wish to heal. Moving here is not about 'moving on', or about 'using' emotions to move away, but moving and being moved as a form of labour or work, which opens up different kinds of attachments to others, in part through the recognition of this work *as* work.[314]

In the following I am not interested in evaluatively comparing the sense of guilt with other moral affects, in arguing for or against the sense of guilt, or in deriving or refuting its appropriateness or desirability in specific situations and contexts. Instead I want to describe which forms of subjectivization, normativity, and historicity are at stake when such a feeling can be analytically grounded as a modality of addressing the spectator in forms of aesthetic experience. The sense of guilt is to be understood as a modality of aesthetic experience, with which spectators experience themselves as embedded in a communally shared world of perceiving, feelings, and thinking, and which shapes this embeddedness as a treatment of historicity in the mode of the temporality of an affective bind to irreversible suffering and injustice.

---

313 Ahmed: *The Cultural Politics of Emotion*, 191. Cf. also Jack Katz: *How Emotions Work*. Chicago 1999. A completely different way to formulate this conceptually – as the share of affects and wishes in the production of production – can be found in Gilles Deleuze, Félix Guattari: *Anti-Oedipus. Capitalism and Schizophrenia* [1972]. Minneapolis 1983 and Gilles Deleuze, Félix Guattari: *A Thousand Plateaus. Capitalism and Schizophrenia* [1980], trans. Brian Massumi. Minneapolis 1987. On recent reception see also: Brian Massumi: *Ontopower. War, Powers, and the State of Perception*. Durham 2015.
314 Ahmed: *The Cultural Politics of Emotion*, 201.

It is first necessary to sketch out, in the appropriate brevity and by means of a few main points, how guilt and the sense of guilt have been treated as cultural categories in history.

In a second step, the sense of guilt is to be analyzed and described in the basic characteristics of how it is seen in the sensations of subjects in the living world. To this end I will be borrowing from phenomenological descriptions, by means of which it will then be possible for me to treat the sense of guilt, in the sense of shaping processes physically experienced by individuals, as the flip side of shaping processes of aesthetic experience. What structures of physical sensations, what dynamic relationships to other domains of feeling, what subject and object relations, and above all what structures of temporality can be determined for the sense of guilt? In this work, therefore, the question of feelings of guilt is not identical to the question of theoretically ascertainable and argumentatively derived, objective, moral guilt. From the perspective represented here it is not the case that the sense of guilt could be *caused* by the reaction to a transgressed law or to a punishing authority, but that certain painful experiences of the self, pangs of conscience, can allow us to sense a transgression, a breach in normative matter of course.[315]

Finally, I will theoretically define certain basic traits of audiovisual staging patterns, through which the somatic qualities of the sense of guilt can be shaped as spectator sensation. The film analytical task of the next part of this work will thus be to identify these audiovisual patterns as structures of time and movement, and to describe them as a cultural production of meaning. The fact that our understanding of genocide, war, racism, and destruction is interwoven with feelings, that reflecting and talking about them is affectively grounded, is to be documented. This thesis is then to be taken further, that the sense of guilt is an affective modality of communal binding and collective processes of memory.

When I am speaking here of feelings of guilt as a modality of aesthetic experience, I explicitly do not mean by this so-called guilty pleasures, from camp to trash. Such reception processes, in which spectators reflect themselves as consumers of a socially disdained or ostracized entertainment form, or of certain artifacts that exceed the borders of 'good taste', will not be addressed in this work.[316] In addition I will not be dealing with the question of whether one can notice in a film that its makers had had this or that feeling in relation to the

---

315 Cf. Vladimir Jankélévitch: *The Bad Conscience* [1951]. Chicago 2014, 37; Cf. Lotter: *Scham, Schuld, Verantwortung*, 142–145. Demmerling, Landweer: *Philosophie der Gefühle*, 239–242.
316 For such an examination within cultural studies, cf. Marc Jancovich, Antonio Lázaro Reboll, Julian Stringer and Andy Willis (eds.): *Defining Cult Movies. The Cultural Politics of Oppositional Taste*. Manchester 2004.

objects and contexts filmed. And finally I am not taking up any moral evaluation of films and their producers – we might think, for instance, of the famous camera pan in Gillo Pontecorvo's KAPO (1960), with which the character played by Emmanuelle Riva was reframed after her suicide, and which Jacques Rivette took for a sign of abjection.[317] I am not dealing with the question of whether there can be an ethical stance inherent to aesthetic means per se, whether it is permissible or objectionable to apply classic ideals of beauty, balance, and composition in relation to certain objects, or whether it is permissible or objectionable to want to represent certain objects at all and whether, accordingly, spectators who accept this ethical-aesthetic norm and perceive its transgression, would react with feelings of guilt.

The sense of guilt in the following is to be seen as a fundamental form of social, cultural, historical processes, which shape morally connotated subjectivization effects. As modalities of aesthetic experience, the sense of guilt shapes a rhetoric of the self and the 'we,' with which responsibility is assumed and contingent communities are constituted in the affect of being affected.

Cultivating guilt

The enormous amount of cultural forms of a 'knowledge about guilt,' from religion and legal philosophy to psychology and psychoanalysis, cannot be comprehensively reconstructed in this work, nor should they be. They should simply be outlined here as areas of resonance, and later be brought to fruition in individual analyses, in as much as the models and metaphors that were developed in the extremely diverse contexts also in fact relate to processes of feeling and furthermore turn out to be descriptions of aesthetic strategies. I will therefore intentionally forgo proceeding chronologically, since one of the most telling qualities of the various discourses on the sense of guilt seems to be its recursivity. Both modern existential philosophy in Søren Kierkegaard and the phenomenology of values in Scheler fall back on the theological term of sin, while Sigmund Freud finds "a universal model of human (male) consciousness of guilt"[318] for the

---

317 Cf. Jacques Rivette: *On Abjection* [1961]. URL: http://www.dvdbeaver.com/rivette/ok/abjection.html (last accessed: 8 May 2020). Cf. also: Serge Daney: Le travelling de Kapo. In: *Trafic* (1992), No. 4, 5–19.
318 Claudia Benthien: Antikes 'Schuldbewußtsein' und psychoanalytische Mythologie. In: Claudia Benthien, Hartmut Böhme, Inge Stephan (eds.): *Freud und Antike*. Göttingen 2011, 241–267, here 255 [trans. DH].

psychic connection of culture and drive in the material of Oedipus, the crucifixion of Christ, and in the imagination of an archaic collective murder.

The trait that I consider central to follow through the individual contexts would be the shaping and thematizing of guilt and feelings of guilt as practicing humility, fallibility, and the painful recognition of the separateness of human beings:

> The truth here is that we *are* separate, but not necessarily *separated* (*by* something); that we are, each of us, bodies, i.e., embodied; each is this one and not that; each here and not there, each now and not then. If something separates us, comes between us, that can only be a particular aspect or stance of the mind itself, a particular way in which we relate, or are related (by birth, by law, by force, in love) to one another – our positions, our attitudes, with reference to one another. Call this our history. It is our present.[319]

It is guilt and the sense of guilt that indicate whenever the processes of violent inclusions and exclusions between us and others turn up, whenever possible recognition and solidarity is rejected.

From the Old Testament sacrificial guilt, which is closely tied to the idea of a punishing god, to the New Testament rhetoric of absolution and the *Confessiones* of Augustine: metaphysical-religious terms like sin and original sin take the affective faculty of guilt as the starting point or the prerequisite of the relationship between the individual and the species with the sphere of the divine.[320] Even as late as the twentieth century, Max Scheler writes that all guilt is a separation from God, that behind the sense of guilt as painful repentance for an act we can always sense a repentance of being and of conversion, with which the soul is saved and returns to God, even with which we would become attentive to the idea of God at all.[321]

In later modernity the meaning of guilt and sin transformed out of the relation to God's rage and chastisement into an idea of the self as a moral identity, which creates itself as a relation between the freedom and bondage of actions and principles, in a relation made of unity and estrangement. While in Ricœur[322] the fallibility of the human being denotes the bondage and myths of evil, in

---

319 Cavell: *The Claim of Reason*, 369.

320 Cf. Martin Ritter: Schuld II. 1. Hebräische Bibel und Frühjudentum. In: Joachim Ritter, Karlfried Gründer (eds.): *Historisches Wörterbuch der Philosophie*. Vol. VIII. Darmstadt 1995, 1446–1447; Matthias Laarmann: Schuld. II. 2. Neues Testament und Patristik. In: Joachim Ritter, Karlfried Gründer (eds.): *Historisches Wörterbuch der Philosophie*. Vol. VIII. Darmstadt 1995, 1448–1450.

321 Cf. Max Scheler: Repentance and Rebirth [1917]. In: id.: *On the Eternal in Man*. London 1960, 33–66.

322 Cf. Paul Ricœur: *Fallible Man* [1960], trans. Charles A. Kelbley. New York 1986.

Kierkegaard it is grounded in freedom as a possibility of choice, of the task of the human being to relate to the self as an assemblage of differences and syntheses, and of the endlessness of possible guilt that lies dormant in it.[323] Kierkegaard therefore replaces a feeling of guilt for concrete finite guilt – the concerns of the police and the courts – with fear as the feeling for the possibility of possibility.[324]

While Kierkegaard treats guilt and our human being-ensnared in relationships in which we always fail ourselves as the starting point for the transition from ethics into belief, for Freud this relation of irresolvable contradictions always contains the principle of 'culture.' Fear, despair, and the sense of guilt for him are derived from the adaptation of the individual and his or her instinctive needs to the cultural commands of the suppression of those instincts.[325] Culture deactivates the instinct for aggression and turns it against the ego. The suppression of aggression is thus not the result of an insight into good and evil, but the consequence of experiences of the loss of love, of the sense of guilt induced from the outside.[326] This becomes so internalized that even the suppression of instinct weighs on the conscience, since its prerequisite is a desire for aggression. So the sense of guilt, a constant inner tension, is unavoidable, "for guilt is an expression of the conflict due to ambivalence, of the eternal struggle between Eros and the instinct of destruction or death. This conflict is set going as soon as men are faced with the task of living together."[327]

While in Kierkegaard sin, guilt, and the sense of guilt elude direct communicability as relationships between individuals and God, and in Freud they remain first "completely unconscious"[328] and second ahistorical as a biologically grounded dialectic of instincts, the burning question here is how one might actually analyze such an awareness of guilt in concrete historical, cultural practices. And the paradigmatic case for the aesthetic experience of community and aggression is the Attic tragedy. Here the fundamental conflicts and contradictions of culture force their way into communicability. In ancient tragedy between Aeschylus and Euripides the experience is expressed that the life of the community is also dependent on the fact that "the responsibilities we have to

---

323 Søren Kierkegaard: The Sickness unto Death [1849]. In: id.: *Fear and Trembling and The Sickness unto Death*. Princeton 2013, 235–478.

324 Cf. Søren Kierkegaard: *The Concept of Anxiety* [1844]. Princeton 1980, 61.

325 Cf. Sigmund Freud: *Civilization and Its Discontents* [1930]. New York 1989.

326 This causal role of the superego and the image of the punishing parent is the central topos of psychoanalytic theory on feelings and guilt and shame. Cf. Gerhart Piers, Milton B. Singer: *Shame and Guilt. A Psychoanalytic and a Cultural Study* [1953]. New York 1971, 15–30.

327 Freud: *Civilization and Its Discontents*, 79.

328 Freud: *Civilization and Its Discontents*, 82.

recognise extend in many ways beyond our normal purposes and what we intentionally do."[329]

Guilt in tragedy points out the breaking points in communal life, shows how values and ideals are constitutively linked to aggression and terror. Over and over again tragedy stages the catastrophes, the excesses, and the transgressions that the community cannot get rid of, that it cannot come to grips with. And precisely this performing-over-and-over can be understood, following Léon Wurmser, as the endless loop of the dialectic of shame and feelings of guilt.[330] However we translate and interpret *katharsis*, *eleos* and *phobos*,[331] they are the affective effects of an encounter with our own non-identity, with the disturbance and dissolution of aesthetic operations of political self-staging: "The accomplishment of tragedy is to make it possible to imagine what is actually unthinkable, unbearable: the conflict between the civility of human order and its limitation; the awareness of the lability of the rational."[332]

The term catharsis refers to the fact that tragedy allows us to live out virulent social fears and potentials for animalistic agitation in a common act. Catharsis does not heal, it provides relief. It purifies us from damaging excesses of affect and brings the feelings that make up living together into temporary balance: "By temporarily releasing virulent fears the theatre shows its inherent effect, which is what makes it useful for the body politic."[333] In this respect 'moaning and shuddering' or 'fear and pity' are elements of a mode of aesthetic experience as a temporal structure, as the affect-dynamic, embodied flip side of tragedy as a continuous form, as the joining together of "shaping principles"[334] (and not of 'contents').

When I position myself in the following within a cultural history of the sense of guilt as an aesthetic category, I mean exactly those ideas of integrating individuals into the communal being according to which feelings are the site of reciprocally working on soma, aesthetics, and sociality. Neither human sinfulness nor an existential attunement or an intrapersonal relation of the psychic apparatus to the self are meant here as ahistorical categories, but historically and culturally positioned practices of the treatment of individually embodied

---

329 Bernard Williams: *Shame and Necessity*. Berkeley 2000, 74.

330 Cf. Léon Wurmser: *Die Maske der Scham. Die Psychoanalyse von Schamaffekten und Schamkonflikten* [1981]. Berlin / Heidelberg 1990, 112–117.

331 Cf. Aristotle: *Poetics*, trans. George Whalley. Montreal 1997, 69.

332 Theresia Birkenhauer: Tragödie. Arbeit an der Demokratie. Auslotung eines Abstandes. In: *Theater der Zeit* (2004), No. 11, 27–28, here 28 [trans. DH].

333 Theo Girshausen: Katharsis. In: Erika Fischer-Lichte, Doris Kolesch, Matthias Warstat (eds.): *Metzler Lexikon Theatertheorie*. Stuttgart 2005, 163–170, here 168 [trans. DH].

334 Aristotle: *Poetics*, 93.

beings, which on the one hand rely on such ideas and on the other hand feed on concrete violent processes of communalization.

Feelings of guilt (and shame [and rage and fear and sorrow])

In order to analyze the sense of guilt as an aesthetic modality of treating individual physicality in cultural practices, we must clarify which qualities are the basis for considering certain forms and dynamic patterns. To this end I am referring to the phenomenological descriptive approach laid out above, which understands feelings as shaping phenomena with a specific course of intensities in each case, thus allowing us to see the transitional zones between individual feeling and the temporal gestalt of art, especially of the temporal experiential forms of film. The task of film analysis will then later be to identify and describe audiovisual structures that create exactly such somatic qualities as spectator sensation, as structures of time and movement. We must also keep in mind that the audiovisual forms are not transfer pictures of the sensations of subjects from the everyday lifeworld, but their artificial treatment as aesthetic experience. The sense of guilt in the cinema is itself an affective relationship to feelings of guilt and other ordinary, common emotional registers.

If, following Hermann Schmitz, we describe the sense of guilt as a gestalt phenomenon, then we must first inquire into the anchoring point and the consolidation area of feeling. The first designates the 'where from' of the feeling, the 'site' from which is it built up. For the sense of guilt, this means the moment of misconduct, the moment in which a norm is breached, in which the moral taken-for-grantedness is interrupted. The latter designates the 'where to,' the 'site' where the feeling assumes its characteristic shape for those feeling it, in this case the wounded others. The sense of guilt is the feeling of a bond requiring balance – completely in the sense of a ribbon that can be imagined as physical, but flexible – between the misconduct and someone who is harmed by this misconduct.[335]

For the transition from acting and feeling in the lived environment to the aesthetic experience, the decisive idea is that my misconduct and the damage to others is not conceived as a primary, objective fact that I then subjectively turn into a feeling. Instead I am directly subjectively affected by the bind between my responsibility and the suffering of others through processes of perception – and can objectify suffering and guilt from this position. This is why

---

335 Cf. Demmerling, Landweer: *Philosophie der Gefühle*, 222–223. Cf. Schmitz: *Das Reich der Normen*, 49–73.

the cognitive judgment that the sense of guilt is caused by a breach of abstract norms, rights, or duties is only the secondary interpretation. It is a form of creating the possibility to communicate the primary disregard for the vulnerability of others in the discourse of moral argumentation.[336]

The question now is which concrete qualities of sensation and temporal dynamics of the sense of guilt can be derived from this first definition. One can describe the bond to the suffering of others as a physically appreciable pressure: "But even if effective compensation is impossible, this changes nothing about the fact that in the sense of guilt there are impulses, namely wishes for such a compensation, or at least *an experience of pressure* or a call for it."[337] It is the experience of taking distance to oneself, "the guilty agent is assumed to be emotionally at odds with himself,"[338] since the consolidation in others also involves a tension or division between one's own perspective and the standpoint of the wounded others. This division and interruption is experienced as painful-piercing and burdensome: "Feeling guilty, we feel weighted down [...] by a feelings [sic!] of obligation."[339] The atmosphere of the sense of guilt can also be characterized as "piercing tension"[340] and as a, heavy, pressing and strained weight.[341] This physical sensation of the sense of guilt can be distinguished through a certain slow and long-term temporality, which pressure and weight gradually build up.[342] This slow build up is interrupted over and over again, distracted, is sidestepped, so that this as a whole amounts to oscillating between the operating tendency of activity and passivity, of escape and compensation.[343] As a quality of movement and direction, the sense of guilt fluctuates between a short impulse of escape, impulses of rapprochement and compensation, and prolonged inhibition, downward squirming, yielding to the weight of responsibility.[344]

---

336 Cf. Lotter: *Scham, Schuld, Verantwortung*, 140.

337 Andreas Wildt: Die Moralspezifizität von Affekten und der Moralbegriff. In: Hinrich Fink-Eitel, Georg Lohmann (eds.): *Zur Philosophie der Gefühle*. Frankfurt a. M. 1993, 188–217, here 210, [emphasis MG, trans. DH].

338 Patricia Greenspan: *Practical Guilt. Moral Dilemmas, Emotions, and Social Norms.* New York / Oxford 1995, 130.

339 Herbert Morris: Nonmoral Guilt. In: Ferdinand Schoeman (ed.): *Responsibility, Character, and the Emotions. New Essays in Moral Psychology*. Cambridge 1987, 220–240, here 226.

340 Demmerling, Landweer: *Philosophie der Gefühle*, 222 [trans. DH].

341 Cf. Schmitz: *New Phenomenology*, 106–107; Schmitz: *Das Reich der Normen*, 140.

342 Cf. Landweer: *Scham und Macht*, 50.

343 Cf. Jankélévitch: *The Bad Conscience*, 11.

344 Cf. Jankélévitch: *The Bad Conscience*, 11; cf. Demmerling, Landweer: *Philosophie der Gefühle*, 22.

The sense of guilt is centrifugal in this sense, it constantly seeks out new directions. We attempt to stretch the bond between the moment of misconduct and the suffering of others through escape, until it rebounds even more forcibly back on us. We attempt to evade the pressure of this bond by approaching others, attempting to balance out the damages through compensation. Through the contradictory or oscillating opposing vectors, the sense of guilt tends toward repetition. The ego that feels guilty projects the offense and confronts itself over and over again with imaginary repetition and visual representation of the offense: "everywhere things reflect back to it to its own image."[345]

The relations between the sense of guilt and other feelings are already inherent to it as a relation to the self and the world, as a gestalt-like phenomenon. They can be derived from their corporeal dynamics, their tendencies of movement and action as forms of possibility for narration and affect dramaturgies. It is thus no accident that feelings of guilt are also called pangs of conscience[346] and the rage of conscience[347] or offender's regret.[348] For these designations clarify specific moments of the operating shape of feelings of guilt and above all their transition to other feelings.

Pangs of conscience emphasize the moment of the physically painful contrition. In contrast, the rage of conscience refers to the fact that the painful gnawing experience of the sense of guilt is already a form of self-punishment, as a variation of self-targeted indignation.[349] At the same time the tendency to aggressively act out, to escape from the context of guilt is inherent to it. Regret ultimately refers to the moment of passivity, the resigning retreat, in which it is not the ego that is assigned the guilt for the impossibility of changing the past, but time itself.[350] The unpredictable change between stabbing pain, bodily outbreaks and incursions, as well as the oppressive mourning of the ego's lost innocence describe the embodied dimension of the sense of guilt.[351] In this sense it is no single emotion in the individual psychological understanding "but a tendency to take on various different identificatory emotions involving a negative self-evaluation."[352]

---

345 Jankélévitch: *The Bad Conscience*, 11.

346 Cf. Claudia Benthien: *Tribunal der Blicke. Kulturtheorien von Scham und Schuld und die Tragödie um 1800*. Cologne / Weimar / Vienna 2011, 44.

347 Cf. Landweer: *Die Macht der Erinnerung*.

348 Cf. Lotter: *Scham, Schuld, Verantwortung*, 144.

349 Cf. Greenspan: *Practical Guilt*, 133; cf. Jankélévitch: *The Bad Conscience*, 39–41.

350 Cf. Jankélévitch: *The Bad Conscience*, 41–47.

351 Cf. Prinz: *The Emotional Construction of Morals*, 59.

352 Greenspan: *Practical Guilt*, 27.

Alongside fear, rage, and mourning, the sense of guilt has a particularly close link to that other feeling that judges the self to be faulty, namely shame. Here I can only cursorily and selectively go into the relationships between the feelings of shame and guilt, instead referring to the fact that within the academic examination of moral feelings in recent decades this is one of the topics that has produced the most comprehensive literature.[353]

From the perspective of feelings as phenomena of shaping and perception, the distinction consists in the fact that shame is characterized by aggregation in the socially sanctioned self as well as by absolute abruptness, while the sense of guilt is marked by the relation to the other, to the impulse to compensate and the gradual buildup of an oppressive heaviness.[354] Shame is built up in being seen, it is the feeling of an unbearable spatio-corporal co-presence.[355] The sense of guilt, by contrast, is attributed with a strong acoustic dimension, since it involves a plea by the victim and the accusing, judging, proverbial voice of conscience. While shame tends to be related to space, and inherent to it is the wish to disappear from just this space and to sink into the ground, the sense of guilt is an affective relation to temporality, which isolates the one who feels – between the retrospectively realized misconduct and the yet to arrive compensation – in or from its own present.[356] While we can therefore escape shame by changing location and with the passing of time, guilt reminds us: "Go where thou wilt, there wilt thou find thy conscience."[357]

These distinctions have been used – above all by differentiating between self-worth and the responsibility for each individual action and its relation to the other – to develop the idea of cultures of guilt and cultures of shame, first

---

353 At this point I can only mention individual texts from a variety of disciplinary backgrounds that cannot be extensively treated in this work, texts that can be posited as significantly contributing to this trend; any attempt to representatively cover the field would require several pages: Herbert Morris (ed.): *Guilt and Shame.* Belmont 1971; Jean Delumeau: *Sin and Fear. The Emergence of a Western Guilt Culture, 13th–18th Centuries* [1983]. New York 1990; Gabriele Taylor: *Pride, Shame, and Guilt. Emotions of Self-Assessment.* Oxford 1985; Jessica Tracy, June P. Tangney, Kurt W. Fischer (eds.): *The Self-Conscious Emotions. The Psychology of Shame, Guilt, Embarrassment, and Pride.* New York 1995; Silvan Tomkins: *Shame and Its Sisters. A Silvan Tomkins Reader,* ed. Eve Sedgwick, Frank Adam. Durham 1995; Martha C. Nussbaum: *Hiding from Humanity. Disgust, Shame, and the Law.* Princeton 2004; John Deigh: *Emotions, Values, and the Law.* Oxford 2008.

354 Cf. Landweer: *Scham und Macht,* 46–50.

355 Cf. Landweer: *Scham und Macht;* cf. Sartre: *Being and Nothingness.*

356 Cf. Benthien: *Tribunal der Blicke,* 57–59.

357 Denis Diderot: Conversation of a Father with His Children [1771]. In: id.: *This Is Not a Story and Other Stories.* London 1993, 126–160 here 143.

in comparative ethnology and then also in the area of cultural history.[358] It has been pointed out that shame tends to rely on external, public, social sanctions in its genesis – "ostracism is more dreaded than violence"[359]– while the sense of guilt has been linked to the internalized voice of conscience. At the same time, it is argued that the structures are socially homogeneous in the former and socially heterogeneous – with tendencies to a morally political universalism – in the latter.[360] At this point, however, I will not delve any further into this distinction, instead taking up the position that it is of course not a matter of exclusionary traits, but of a formation of dominance in each interpretive culture of morality and feeling.[361] In real life guilt and shame are ultimately often blended or follow each other in succession.[362]

The affect of the irrevocable

If the sense of guilt can be described as an affect of temporality that effectuates a tendency of imaginary repetition and representation, this lies in the fact that the realms of possibility for action[363] imposed in this feeling simultaneously are also cut off from one another, contradict each other. It is a back and forth between the wish to evade and the wish to come together in compensatory harmony:

> The sense of guilt does not block by means of stabilizing centripetal directions like shame, but is characterized by a piercing tension that arises from the oscillation between the activation aimed at compensating and the passivation of horror at one's own culpability.[364]

This horror does not, however, appear suddenly, but builds up gradually in these loops of repetition,[365] until the feeling takes up the totality of existence as an invasive extension of the past.[366] The sense of guilt, as a gnawing pain,

---

358 First in Benedict: *The Chrysanthemum and the Sword*, 156; cf. Benthien: *Tribunal der Blicke*, 33–46.

359 Benedict: *The Chrysanthemum and the Sword*, 201.

360 Cf. Jeffrey K. Olick: *The Politics of Regret. On Collective Memory and Historical Responsibility*. New York / London 2007, 133.

361 Cf. Lotter: *Scham, Schuld, Verantwortung*, 105–106 [trans. DH].

362 Cf. Landweer: *Scham und Macht*, 48; cf. Greenspan: *Practical Guilt*, 126.

363 Cf. Slaby: *Möglichkeitsraum und Möglichkeitssinn*, 128.

364 Demmerling, Landweer: *Philosophie der Gefühle*, 222.

365 Cf. Demmerling, Landweer: *Philosophie der Gefühle*, 222.

366 Cf. Jankélévitch: *The Bad Conscience*, 44–45.

becomes the most concrete and most total appearance of memory as lived and embodied memory.[367] Becoming conscious of the "bad use of our freedom"[368] occurs through flashbacks in excruciating slow motion. The sense of guilt makes it physically possible to sense the link between time and consciousness in a painful way, in which we are confronted with the fact that the possibilities of our freedom, what freedom is capable of, simultaneously encompasses the possibility of guilt. Consciousness is always already a bad conscience in stand-by mode.[369]

In this respect Vladimir Jankélévitch's thesis is central for me, according to which we can distinguish between two pathos forms of the irreversability of time. On the one hand there is regretting the irretrievability of past happiness and lost opportunities; and on the other there is the painful bad conscience in view of irrevocable acts. There is the impossibility of repeating and the impossibility of making something undone.[370] The sense of guilt coagulates the irreversible flow of time, blocking the present and the future, displacing the realms of possibility for action. For the sense of guilt, the past is not past – "the past is never dead, it's not even past,"[371] as a famous citation from Faulkner puts it – but imposes itself time and again.

While we can only regret the truly past, grieve for it, the sense of guilt, due to the constant repetition and representation of the misconduct, simultaneously contains a fear of the future, a fear of repeating the mistake. In this respect the sense of guilt – from the perspective of the individual and his or her social competence, the motivation to compensate – can be counterproductive in that it is compulsively brought into this self-representation and is thus sealed off from social reality, from acting.[372]

---

367 Cf. Jankélévitch: *The Bad Conscience*, 46–47.

368 Jankélévitch: *The Bad Conscience*, 56.

369 Cf. Jankélévitch: *The Bad Conscience*, 39; cf. also Kierkegaard: *The Concept of Anxiety*.

370 Cf. Jankélévitch: *The Bad Conscience*, 54. Another distinction that runs in parallel here between the complex emotional registers of nostalgia and melancholy can be indicated in this respect. In this view the sense of guilt, much like melancholy, would be a form of experiencing the time of transience, with the addition of violating moral equilibrium. On the cultural theory of melancholy, cf.: Sigmund Freud: Mourning and Melancholia [1917]. In: id.: *On Murder, Mourning and Melancholia*. London 2005, 201–218; Walter Benjamin: *The Origin of German Tragic Drama* [1928]. London 1998; Raymond Klibansky, Erwin Panofsky, and Fritz Saxl: *Saturn and Melancholy. Studies in the History of Natural Philosophy, Religion and Art*. New York 1964.

371 William Faulkner: *Requiem for a Nun* [1951]. New York 2011, 73.

372 Cf. Greenspan: *Practical Guilt*, 133–134.

> Like all feelings, this [the sense of justice, MG] also has its own *gestalt* as it proceeds. If this gestalt (in the sense of gestalt psychology) cannot 'close,' these feelings force their way into the present life of afflicted persons, who also only indicate distant relations to the past situation in which they originally arose.[373]

Feelings of guilt persist and recur until they are warded off through destructive aggression as a rejection of guilt, completed as ritually conducted self-punishment through gestures of absolution or until the disturbed state of equilibrium is restored through compensation. This closure of gestalt as the recreation of a state of balance, of taken-for-grantedness consists in a certain objectivizing separation or excision of the wounding of the other from the self that feels guilty.[374] With the confession one puts the mistake in full view, one acknowledges it, thus creating a space between self and infraction. Remorse indicates the possibility of a future, places the self once again into the flow of time as a possibility of future action: "Freedom, as soon as guilt is posited, returns as repentance."[375]

It is exactly this process of repeating, of slowly building up pressure and gnawing tension on the one hand and the return of balance, closure of gestalt, and objectivizing the infraction on the other that is to be analyzed as a pattern for staging and the affect-dramaturgical operations, which occur over the duration of the unfolding of the cinematic images to the spectators. It is a matter of an affective script that makes it possible to have a certain experience of temporality as irreversibility and of a certain dimension of life in plurality, namely the vulnerability and inherently violent processes of community and culture. We could describe the ideal form of this script of aesthetically experiencing the sense of guilt as follows: the reanimation of a moral identity in the process of retrospectively realizing its failure.

Feelings of guilt and audiovisual expressivity

Here, therefore, we are not talking about a sense of guilt as an individual psychological emotion, but of an affective process, a cultural, interpersonal form of experience and a form of communalization. With this form the cinema shall be described as a site of experience, which is interwoven, so to speak, with a worldview in which the spectator experiences him or herself as one who feels

---

373 Landweer: *Die Macht der Erinnerung*, 297 [trans. DH].

374 Cf. Jankélévitch: *The Bad Conscience*, 128–131.

375 Kierkegaard: *The Concept of Anxiety*, 109; cf. Jankélévitch: *The Bad Conscience*, 84–86 and Scheler: *Repentance and Rebirth*.

guilty. It is about aesthetic, "synaesthetic feelings of guilt"[376] as a sensation that holds the world of the film together over the course of its duration and cannot be reduced to the representation of one character's feelings, which one is empathetically drawn to. The term 'synaesthetic affects' comes from one of the few explicit examinations of the question of film and the sense of guilt. Using the example of Alfred Hitchcock's films, Carl Plantinga attempts to argue for the idea "that narrative scenarios of guilt and shame usually do not trigger shame and guilt, but rather associated affects that are congruent with shame and guilt or that are in line with them."[377]

Starting from an individual psychological, cognitivist paradigm, he examines narrative scenarios and relations of empathy between characters and spectators, in which spectators wish that characters would act in such and such a way, and in which a subsequent meta-emotional evaluation of this wish gives rise to a cross-modal, synaesthetic affective reaction: "a 'mix' of sensations that [...] are affectively congruent with those of a character, about whom it can be assumed that they are sensing shame or guilt."[378]

I agree with the basic direction of this assessment in as much as it is not about evoking a real-life, individual sense of guilt, but a register of aesthetic affect, which is congruent in its dynamic qualities, in its temporal gestalt. I would contrast this, however, with another derivation and another film theoretical and analytical conception of what 'congruence' means in this concept: namely not the congruence between a character's feeling and the spectator's feelings, but the congruence between the temporal unfolding of a pattern of film expressivity and the way that it physically feels to have feelings of guilt. Plantinga denies the possibility that spectators sense the paradigmatic emotion of shame of guilt that are in effect in everyday life, with the following rationale:

> As a rule, the psychic relation between a spectator and a character is not marked by the fact that the spectator feels responsible for the character's behavior or that he or she relates the guilt or the contempt associated with the character's behavior or wishes to him or herself. With regard to a character's shame and guilt, the spectator may have compassion or it might provoke tension. But normally he or she does not feel guilty or shamed *only* through the behavior, motives and wishes of this character.[379]

---

376 Carl Plantinga: Synästhetische Affekte. Szenarios von Schuld und Scham in Hitchcocks Filmen. In: Anne Bartsch, Jens Eder, Kathrin Fahlenbrach (eds.): *Audiovisuelle Emotionen. Emotionsdarstellung und Emotionsvermittlung durch audiovisuelle Medienangebote*. Cologne 2007, 350–361, here 351 [trans. DH].
377 Plantinga: *Synästhetische Affekte*, 351 [trans. DH].
378 Plantinga: *Synästhetische Affekte*, 359 [trans. DH].
379 Plantinga: *Synästhetische Affekte*, 355, [emphasis MG, trans. DH].

The starting point for my new perspective of the 'synaesthetic sense of guilt' in fact lies in the 'only.' For it makes clear that it cannot be a question solely of a relation of empathy to understanding the character, but of a specific sensation of the self and the world, realized by the spectator and staged by the perceptual performance of the film. Wherever the film image takes on the expression of a face pronouncing a guilt verdict, feelings of guilt are more than an object of the narrative.[380]

In the following, an affect poetics of the sense of guilt is meant to be understood as the process by which aesthetic modes of the affective relation to the self and the world shape their own reworking as forms of cultural identity patterns, and not simply the production and aesthetic question "of forms that narrate about affects."[381]

The sense of guilt thus functions as a heuristic search function. An audiovisually shaped relation to the self and the world in the sense of a feeling of guilt should be understood here, following Charles S. Pierce,[382] as an abductive conclusion, as a speculative rule for certain film structures and for the relationship to history and community in which it places its spectators.

If we look for the 'real reality' of the sense of guilt, then we can assume that in the moment of watching a film this does not cause any serious breach of norms and impairment of the other.[383] If we nonetheless claim such a feeling as a calculation on the part of the film, it is then about a very particular transposition of the sense of guilt, namely as a deep pleasure in one's own moral affectability.[384]

In the history of theory, what most often gets spelled out for the anxiety-pleasure of the horror film and the sentimental enjoyment of pity in the melodrama can be transferred to the entire breadth of human affectivity, namely that they are amenable to being made aesthetically enjoyable, that there is a disgust-pleasure, a shame-pleasure and even an enjoyment of the sense of guilt. Spectators are not simply accused of an actual, objective guilt in the

---

380 Cf. Kappelhoff: *Matrix der Gefühle*, 261.

381 Burkhard Meyer-Sickendiek: *Affektpoetik. Eine Kulturgeschichte literarischer Emotionen.* Würzburg 2005, 9 [trans. DH].

382 Cf. Charles S. Peirce: Lectures on Pragmatism [1903]. In: id.: *Collected Papers. Vol. V: Pragmatism and Pragmaticism*, ed. Charles Hartshorne, Paul Weiss. Cambridge 1934, 14–212.

383 Cf. Plantinga: *Synästhetische Affekte*, 358.

384 Cf. Chris Tedjasukmana: Wie schlecht sind die schlechten Gefühle im Kino? Politische Emotionen, negative Affekte und ästhetische Erfahrung. In: *montage AV* (2012), Vol. 21, No. 2, 11–27, here 12.

space outside the cinema, but they find themselves, in their embodied perception, placed into a particular, dynamic relation to responsibility.

The sense of guilt must therefore be sought out in such dynamics as an audiovisual structure that shapes a gradually constructed blockade of time, operating by means of excessive repetitions, as if the flow of images were getting bogged down time and again. In this way, the impression develops of an irrevocable belatedness, of an endless projection of imagined re-enactments swept outwards. The sense of guilt must be analyzed in its audiovisual shaping processes, which make the film image a material of sensing a corporality contorted in on itself, which over time form an atmosphere of gnawing tension[385] and oppressive and pressing weight,[386] which infiltrate the image with oscillating and contradictory qualities of movement and direction. The synaesthetic sense of guilt would correspond to the dimension of expressive movement, a visual dynamic that consists of the alternation between the visual space in its quality as volumes and the opening and closing realms of possibility of movement vectors.

The sense of guilt appears in its temporal dynamic as a retrospectively realized disturbance of the state of equilibrium. The fall from grace is to be taken literally. Also the reworkings of the sense of guilt, the search for the conditions of the possibility of being-able-to-act-again, must also be described directly by means of audiovisual and affect-dramaturgical structures: How do images work at getting back on their feet? How do the gestalt processes of repetition, the interactions with the emotional registers of shame, anger, fear, and mourning come to a close? Where do they break up, time and again?

In closing I would at this point like once again to expressly sharpen the heuristic function of the sense of guilt so that it is not a question of the spectator being released from the cinema at the end of the film with feelings of guilt. It is also not about solely identifying a moralizing intention or a mere 'what the story is about.' Rather, it is about the "moving and cementing force"[387] of the emotion "that controls the material."[388] The sense of guilt is a constitutive, dynamic structural element in the complex emotion of the spectator, which the film shapes in the amalgam of affective positionings that one has to go through over the duration of the film.[389]

---

385 Cf. Demmerling, Landweer: *Philosophie der Gefühle*, 222.
386 Cf. Schmitz: *New Phenomenology*, 106–107.
387 Dewey: *Art as Experience*, 44.
388 Dewey: *Art as Experience*, 71.
389 Cf. Kappelhoff, Bakels: *Das Zuschauergefühl*.

A modality of communal sensation

Shaping feelings of guilt through media – and this would also apply to shame, pride, or outrage and other similarly complex affect states – is not conceived in this work as a process in which a medially transported object would be supplied to an existing individual faculty – the disposition to a feeling. Instead I assume a dynamic process in which the faculty of the spectator's sensation is directly treated. For the suffering of an other and my guilty implication in this suffering are not objective facts that I then subjectively, just for myself, turn into a feeling, but in the sense of guilt I am physically affected by others and by my responsibility.

The films that I will be addressing in the following produce a 'bad conscience' as a form of experience and meaning-making made culturally and interpersonally accessible. This intersubjective form of experience is indeed realized by individually embodied spectators as a sensation, but it is aimed at the experience of being burdened in a certain way, which cannot be absorbed on the level of private morality. Rather, the feelings of guilt evoked by film are always meant to be understood here in their temporal gestalts and affect dramaturgies, as affective experiences of community, as a particular quality of experiencing commonly shared histories and value systems. Behind this lies the thesis that publicness and communality should only be conceived as products of concrete, individually embodied experience, and that this experience cannot be separated from media processes of producing spatialities and temporalities, that is, from aesthetic phenomena and complex feelings.

It was Nietzsche who was particularly insistent in his analysis of the idea that the sense of guilt and bad conscience can be understood as techniques of integrating a person into a community: "I take bad conscience to be the deep sickness into which man had to fall under the pressure of that most fundamental of all changes he ever experienced – the change of finding himself enclosed once and for all within the sway of society and peace."[390] This can in turn be evaluated differently than he did himself, namely by assessing the "sway of society" and the pride of weakness, askesis, and heteronomy as the suppression of strength, freedom, pleasure, and aristocratic self-governing. The new revaluation of the 'revaluation of values' is possible under the condition that one can imagine a democratic ethos that does not persist in the dichotomy of master-slave morality, but produces the "connection between mere passive utilitarianism and

---

390 Nietzsche: *On the Genealogy of Morality*, 56.

purely self-sufficient creativity"[391] or, to use Richard Rorty's terms, between solidarity and liberal irony.[392]

With this condition it is completely possible to simply state initially that the sense of guilt and bad conscience cannot be separated from the genesis of the person as a political being, from the idea of politics as the restraint of the potential for violence, from the task of breeding "an animal that is permitted to promise."[393] This then also includes a clear consciousness for the fact that the value of values does not designate any angelic quality, but has something to do with coming to terms with contingency and with deescalation in everyday cooperation:

> The enormous work of what I have called "the morality of custom" [...] the true work of man on himself for the longest part of the duration of the human race, his entire prehistoric work, has in this its meaning, its great justification – however much hardness, tyranny, mindlessness, and idiocy may be inherent in it: with the help of the morality of custom and the social straitjacket man was made truly calculable.[394]

What is postulated in empirical studies in psychology, namely that feelings of guilt are registered particularly often and intensely precisely in contexts of close communal ties,[395] can also be reversed in its causal logic. The cultural, aesthetic modulation of feelings of guilt would then be capable of creating social cohesion. That is, there would be a creation of communality from out of the affective experience of its violation.

But there is also another respect in which Nietzsche recognized an important aspect of feelings of guilt as forms of being integrated into a community. For, as has already been shown, these cannot be separated from a self-punishing, painful, contrite quality.[396] And precisely this painful quality of the

---

391 Stephan Günzel: Herrenmoral – Sklavenmoral. In: Henning Ottmann (ed.): *Nietzsche Handbuch. Leben – Werk – Wirkung*. Stuttgart / Weimar 2011, 253–255, here 255 [trans. DH].
392 Cf. Rorty: *Contingency, Irony, Solidarity*.
393 Nietzsche: *On the Genealogy of Morality*, 35; cf. Arendt: *The Human Condition*, 35.
394 Nietzsche: *On the Genealogy of Morality*, 36.
395 Cf. Jonathan Haidt: The Moral Emotions. In: Richard Davidson, Klaus Scherer, Hill Goldsmith (eds.): *Handbook of Affective Sciences*. Oxford 2003, 852–870, here. 861: "Guilt feelings occur overwhelmingly in the context of communal relationships [...] in which one believes one has caused harm, loss, or distress to a relationship partner. Guilt is not just triggered by the appraisal that one has caused harm; it is triggered most powerfully if one's harmful action also creates a threat to one's communion with or relatedness to the victim."
396 Cf. Nietzsche: *On the Genealogy of Morality*, 39.

sense of guilt as a form of "self-punishment on behalf of others"[397] becomes a sign of collective memory formation for Nietzsche. For him there is

> Nothing more terrible and strange in man's prehistory than his *technique of mnemonics*. 'A thing must be burnt in so that it stays in the memory: only something that continues *to hurt* stays in the memory' – that is a proposition from the oldest (and unfortunately the longest-lived) psychology on earth. You almost want to add that wherever on earth you still find ceremonial, solemnity, mystery, gloomy shades in the lives of men and peoples, something of the dread which everyone, everywhere, used to make promises, give pledges and commendation, is *still working*: the past, the most prolonged, deepest, hardest past, breathes on us and rises up in us when we become 'solemn'. When man decided he had to make a memory for himself, it never happened without blood, torments and sacrifices.[398]

What Nietzsche primarily means by memory at this point is initially the mastery of affects for the benefit of society, the reminder always already to be tied into the structures of promises, duties, and contracts. However, I would also like to refer these to actual processes of 'making a memory for oneself.' When painful experiences are had in films (and enjoyed as such), then, or so goes the thesis, it is not that the films want to remind us of pain and suffering, but that they bring forth the spectator's being-affected in the first place as mnemo-techniques, as a reminder of past injustice and suffering, and shift spectators, in their perception and physical sensation, into a position that contains a commonly shared responsibility.

Feelings of guilt in the films analyzed here are therefore collective feelings in a specific sense, collective feelings of guilt. This neither means that they are dispersed among a community of feeling persons as diffuse, pre-existing feelings, nor that a pre-existing collective can be identified that would then feel this or that way for this or that reason. It is the feeling, realized in each case by individual spectators in their own physicality, that binds them with a commonly shared past, present, and future, that allows them to experience themselves as interwoven in the moral network of a community.

Against such a collective sense of guilt it is sometimes objected that it does not fulfill the condition of the causal link between behavior and suffering and is thus utterly mistaken:

> If people manifest feelings of guilt for the action of other members of a collective, although they have not violated any duties with respect to this action, they are mistaken in

---

397 Greenspan: *Practical Guilt*, 130.
398 Nietzsche: *On the Genealogy of Morality*, 38.

the appropriate designation of their feeling. In reality they would not be experiencing guilt, but grief or horror.[399]

Without postulating subjective self-disclosure as infallible, it should indeed be questionable whether the logic starting from an abstract moral theory is in fact antecedent to emotional processes that do indeed imply their own forms of 'truth' and their own criteria for the conditions of responsibility. If, in contrast, one follows Patricia Greenspan and does not assume a false judgment, but an "identificatory mechanism"[400] that produces the agonizing sense of guilt in the first place, which only then can be judged as rational or irrational, then we can understand how such vicarious feelings do not react to chains of causation and attributions of identity and responsibility, but produce these in the first place.

The decisive question is then no longer whether – from a conceptual viewpoint – it is meaningful or not to speak of collective feelings of guilt. Rather, we must examine what aesthetic, poetic, or rhetorical mechanisms participate in the creation of affective collectivity, what social and cultural, historically contingent practices of assuming guilt and responsibility there are, and what identities and subject positions they form. The case studies in the remaining parts of this book are meant to answer exactly these questions.

The relation between the sense of guilt and history is not simply disclosed in concrete forms and practices, but is produced as a change in the faculty of sensation, as working on a collective affective network. Spectators are positioned in an affective relationship to a particular contingent community by means of feelings of guilt as an "aspect of value that is shared in experience,"[401] and through their feelings of guilt they experience particular dynamics of their communalization and their historicity anew. They experience them anew as broken dynamics, the affective sensation of solidarity in the retrospective realization of their violation, their vulnerability: "Memory and regret are not the result of the integration of the collectivity but the impossibility of this in an age of competing claims, multiple histories, and plural perceptions."[402]

---

399 Michael Schefczyk: *Verantwortung für historisches Unrecht. Eine philosophische Untersuchung.* Berlin / New York 2012, 176 [trans. DH]; cf. also: Taylor: *Pride, Shame, and Guilt*, 91–92.
400 Greenspan: *Practical Guilt*, 162–163.
401 Dewey: *Art as Experience*, 362.
402 Olick: *The Politics of Regret*, 137.

Part 2: **Affective Dramaturgies of the Sense
of Guilt**

2 The Present: German Post-War Cinema and Guilt Reorganized

> Yes, guilt applies to me. I can't deny that in their factory I had to experience murderous agents of warfare being produced during peacetime. I can't deny how I was forced into silence by the allure of getting promoted and fear of the Gestapo. And I also can't deny that my brother and my father and tens of thousands from our country lie today under ruins because I didn't speak up. But does this make me the main person responsible? Those in charge, though, who made use of the poisonous gasses at their disposal, who explained to us that science didn't need to ask what it was for, these men are the innocent victims of our inventions? [trans. DH]

With these words the character of Dr. Scholz (Fritz Tillmann) in Kurt Maetzig's DER RAT DER GÖTTER [COUNCIL OF THE GODS] makes his confession, which is at the same time an accusation (1:13:30–1:14:09). Such a doubled function of 'guilt,' as an innocent guilt of knowing and omission on the one hand and an objective guilt of the perpetrators and initiators on the other, characterizes the basic rhetorical structure of this film as well as German post-war cinema in general. In this respect they initially seem – as is to be explained – to follow Karl Jaspers's distinctions of the *question of guilt*.[1] And yet the film is smitten with a curious alexithymia or emotional blindness: What does it mean for guilt to "apply" to him, that is, to hit him from outside and at the same time, using a marked "but" followed by a "though," to be rejected again as not his own guilt?

When Hannah Arendt entitled one of her central essays about the political significance of the crimes during the Nazi regime "Organized Guilt,"[2] it was meant to show that the political question of the relationship between the public and the individual after 1945 can be described as constantly reorganizing guilt. This occurred in the differentiations between accusatory objective guilt and the subjective sense of guilt, of affectively realizing responsibility, as well as in the constant shifts between individualistic and collectivist dimensions of guilt.

In the following I would like to use DER RAT DER GÖTTER to show what kinds of political effect enter through the staged evocation of feelings of guilt, of shame, rage, and other moral-ethical affects. What political and historical dynamics or contradictions are visible in the affective dramaturgies of guilt and the sense of guilt, of individual and collective feelings of guilt?

---

1 Karl Jaspers: *The Question of German Guilt* [1946], trans. E. B. Ashton. New York 1987.
2 Hannah Arendt: Organized Guilt and Universal Responsibility [1946]. In: id.: *Essays in Understanding. 1930–1954: Formation, Exile, and Totalitarianism.* New York 1994, 121–132.

https://doi.org/10.1515/9783110612110-003

Guilt was not reorganized for itself and for its own sake. It was much more about recreating the reality of a shared world of feelings, wishes, everyday structures of thinking and behaving, which were considered abused, corrupted, and devalued through the period of Nazi rule as much as they were considered completely untenable and emptied out through the experience of the end of the war. In this restructuring of sociality in view of the overwhelming degree of destruction, loss, and atrocities, in consideration of the absolute lack of secure historical, social, and political orientations, the relation to 'collective guilt,' to accusations of guilt and feelings of guilt was one of the few and at the same time highly embattled constants.

The persistence of the reference point of 'collective guilt' should not be confused with a consistency of the concept of its uses. Rather, it draws our attention to the various ways that guilt and feelings of guilt, accusations, apologies, and refusals to accept guilt were related to one another, what emotional dramaturgies were unleashed by 'collective guilt.' It can be demonstrated, both in the films as well as in the various discourses of political, theological, or cultural figures,[3] that this term itself often set in motion a reflection on responsibility and identity, producing completely contingent processes and alliances. 'Collective guilt' as a form of speech about norms, morality, and emotions has been effective as an *emotive* in William M. Reddy's sense,[4] since it oscillated unpredictably between a description of the state of the polity and the performative negotiation of this state. 'Collective guilt' is therefore particularly suitable in tracing how "terminological innovations not only draw attention to certain aspects of visible and non-visible reality, but become *creative*, that is, they generate a new dimension of reality that can be experienced psychically."[5]

The effectiveness of the concept that was made necessary by a new reality and that at the same time allowed it to emerge cannot be shown to be legible in any clear and direct way. This is a paradoxical situation, that the validity of a collective sense of guilt as a form of relation between individuals and a 'we' is only due to a history of evasion and repudiation in the first place. When looking into the feelings between the 'I' and the 'we' as part of aesthetic experience, the result will not lie in this or that decision for a certain meaning and affective implementation. Instead, the point is to outline the multiple contradictions, the

---

3 Cf. Jeffrey K. Olick: *In the House of the Hangman. The Agonies of German Defeat. 1943–1949.* Chicago / London 2005.

4 Cf. William M. Reddy: *The Navigation of Feeling. A Framework for the History of Emotions.* Cambridge 2008.

5 Maria-Sibylla Lotter: *Scham, Schuld, Verantwortung. Über die kulturellen Grundlagen der Moral.* Frankfurt a. M. 2012, 237 [trans. DH].

affective ambiguities and inconsistencies of the original constellation of a collective German responsibility and the "always precarious term 'guilt.'"[6]

The affective rhetorical structures of films, the aesthetic dis/continuities of cinema before and after 1945, as well as the relationship to the audiovisual documents of re-education and devastated landscapes should be analyzed as factors that have also contributed to the fact that the post-war period could become *the kind of past* that it is today. If we say, following Jürgen Habermas, that the crimes of National Socialism are not the impediment, but the *conditio sine qua non* of a German identity that can only be had as an 'unconventional' identity,[7] then this is the result of diverse processes of interpretation and remembrance, the foundations of which are laid here, but not in any way that predetermines how they will be constructed.[8] What we can analyze in the films of the first years of the post-war period is the genesis of a historical burden and of the specific temporal circumstances of an irreversibility of the collective sense of guilt.[9]

In this sense it is absolutely unavoidable that the films *must* be admonitions, reminders, reckonings, and at the same time also repressions, excuses, and monuments of self-pity. For they do not reflect any fully constituted political or psychic reality of post-way Germany. They offer images, metaphors, and affects from which the reality that we today call the post-war period could be formed, and which itself in turn is embedded in a wide variety of processes of memory in each present.

In the following I would first like to present the registers in which the question of guilt and the sense of guilt have been discursively worked out along general lines. I will mainly be referring to the influential text *The Question of German Guilt* by Karl Jaspers and to works by the social historian Jeffrey K. Olick on this as well as other positionings and counter positionings.[10] Following this I will analyze DER RAT DER GÖTTER as an example of the positions taken toward these registers of guilt. The film stands at the end of a transitional period; its production fell during the phase of the dual state formation and thus at the historical

---

6 Thomas Mann: Das Ende [1945]. In: id.: *Gesammelte Werke. Vol. XII: Reden und Aufsätze 4*. Frankfurt a. M. 1990, 944–950, here 946 [trans. DH].

7 Cf. Jürgen Habermas: Eine Art Schadensabwicklung. In: *Die Zeit* (11 July 1986).

8 On films as a form of experiencing historicity, see: Bernhard Groß: *Die Filme sind unter uns. Zur Geschichtlichkeit des frühen deutschen Nachkriegskinos. Trümmer-, Genre-, Dokumentarfilm*. Berlin 2015.

9 Cf. Olick: *In the House of the Hangman*, 105 and Jeffrey K. Olick: *The Politics of Regret. On Collective Memory and Historical Responsibility*. New York / London 2007, 143.

10 Cf. Olick: *In the House of the Hangman* and Olick: *The Politics of Regret*.

moment in which the immediate post-war period was converted, as a kind of ambiguous and often opaque memory filter, into a history of official state commemoration practices.[11] Using the film we can show how a particular cinematic relation to remembering Nazi Germany and the post-war period was crystallized during the transition from the Soviet Occupied Zone into the German Democratic Republic.

2.1 Resolving the Question of Guilt

The distinction between phenomena of guilt on the one hand and the specific relations to world and self involved in feelings of guilt on the other, as a methodological and heuristic distinction, was much more than an occasion for academic work on terminology in Germany after the Second World War. It points to a quite existential dimension, a need to 'resolve' German guilt objectively, that is, to illuminate it, to divide it into various forms of guilt, to make it possible to calculate it and to communicate it through judgments and operating instructions. Behind this lies the experience that a too general and not precisely defined accusation of guilt could always already be turned against itself. For 'collective guilt' was discredited as an improper equation of state and people, of Nazis and Germans as a continuation of National Socialist rhetoric[12] and was interpreted in the sense of the most extreme accusation of individual guilt and thus rejected.[13]

The need for resolution resulted from the dilemma that neither the crimes of war nor of genocide could be viewed, either in their quantity or in their quality, at the level of individual criminal misdeeds, and at the same time an undifferentiated accusation of guilt could be interpreted outright on the level of the worst, clearest form of guilt: Adolf Hitler as sole perpetrator. As we will see, however, this need for resolution gave rise to a new dilemma, namely the illusion that resolving the question would also resolve the guilt. Overcoming guilt thus becomes overcoming the question of guilt, as if correctly deploying the logical problem of the function of guilt would lead, objectively and on its own, to the first, second, and so forth derivations of this function and its corresponding consequences.

The link between undifferentiated accusations of collective guilt and self-righteous repudiation can therefore in no way be traced back solely to any

---

11 Cf. Olick: *In the House of the Hangman*, 6–11.
12 Cf. Olick: *In the House of the Hangman*, 55.
13 Cf. Olick: *In the House of the Hangman*, 196–198.

psycho-pathological reflex of the German people, but must include the Allied rhetoric of re-education.[14] The so-called atrocity films, and in particular the film DIE TODESMÜHLEN / DEATH MILLS (1946, Hanuš Burger and Billy Wilder) initially assumed that a simple parallel montage of parades and party conventions with the camps, that is, an "employment of atrocity imagery within a narrative of ordinary Germans' fanatical approbation of the Nazi regime,"[15] would entail a feeling of responsibility for the witness of horror that they screened.

Even if, taken from our viewpoint today, the images shown are unambiguously seen as testifying to the industrially organized genocide of European Jewry, at their first screenings they were illegible documents of anonymous horror directed at equally anonymous victims, and above all not associated with any wider framing narrative.[16]

What initially remained as an immediate effect from the atrocity films were shocking images and a head-on and at the same time vague accusation of guilt, a denunciation that hardly led to any realization of individual and collective responsibility. The attempt, through posters, films, and camp visits, to make it impossible for Germans to get away from their responsibility was relativized after barely one year – because the means used did not call forth the desired reactions and such a radical position seemed inopportune in the burgeoning competition between the occupying powers.

Even if the accusations were very quickly subdued again, Olick's work shows how much they marked the discourse of the post-war years, often running quite to the contrary of any original intentions.[17] The accusation of collective guilt was historically effective not due to its concrete declaration, but because of the different ways of reinterpreting it.[18] The accusation itself – not

---

14 Particularly the political left at the time harshly criticized the Allies' politics of re-education for having hindered the possibility of German work on memory. Cf. Olick: *In the House of the Hangman*, 11.

15 Susan L. Carruthers: Compulsory Viewing. Concentration Camp Film and German Re-Education. In: *Millennium. Journal of International Studies* (2001), Vol. 30, No. 3, 733–759, here 742.

16 Cf. Carruthers: *Compulsory Viewing*, 744. One might claim that the actual mode of perception of both the images from the camps or the Warsaw Ghetto and of the Nazi's self-staging consists in the déjà-vu, that is, in seeing them *again*, recognizing them *again*. One indication of the fact that these images are only visible at a second view can be seen in the reception histories and sustainability effects of DIE TODESMÜHLEN / DEATH MILLS compared, for instance, to NUIT ET BROUILLARD (NIGHT AND FOG, 1956, Alain Resnais) or MEIN KAMPF / DEN BLODIDA TIDEN (1960, Erwin Leiser), which have remained much stronger in the media memory.

17 Cf. Olick: *In the House of the Hangman*, 99–100.

18 Cf. Olick: *In the House of the Hangman*, 185.

what was being charged – developed into an emblem of German suffering in the post-war period.[19] So it became possible on the reverse side of the undifferentiated accusation to connect ostensible acknowledgments of guilt with self-serving analyses of the political, social, and cultural conditions of National Socialism. Questions of historical continuity and historical ruptures could constantly be played off one another in a way to exonerate and to impede any examination of individual guilt.[20]

Behind this dilemma, however, lies a truth about the nature of Nazi crimes and about individual collective guilt that was not well understood at the time. Hannah Arendt was one of the first to try to grasp this problem of understanding:

> In his play *The Last Days of Mankind*, about the last war, Karl Kraus rang down the curtain after Wilhelm II had cried, "I did not want this." And the horribly comic part of it was that this was the fact. When the curtain falls this time, we will have to listen to a whole chorus calling out, "We did not do this." And even though we shall no longer be able to appreciate the comic element, the horrible part of it will still be that this is the fact.[21]

This 'not having done anything' is quite simply the flip side of the collective rhetoric produced by Nazi propaganda itself. All the judicial and moral-philosophical terms available fail to reproduce the "boundaries dividing criminals from normal persons, the guilty from the innocent,"[22] which has become blurred:

> In systematic attempts to include everyone – and ultimately this means the whole world – into the crimes, that is, to generate a totality of guilt, everyone and no one is guilty at the same time. [...] Only in this reversal and suspension of perpetrator and victim, guilty and innocent, imagined as complete, does what constitutes the actual terror of National Socialism become totally real.[23]

In this respect the difficulties and misunderstandings of re-education appear in a new light, since they run up against an everyday experience in which the claim of morality and responsibility are dissolved, in which there could no longer be any taken-for-grantedness or any trust in one's own ability to judge.[24] The fact that they saw horrible and real crimes there on the screen can hardly

---

19 Cf. Olick: *In the House of the Hangman*, 13.

20 Cf. Olick: *In the House of the Hangman*, 233 and 331.

21 Arendt: *Organized Guilt and Universalized Responsibility*, 127.

22 Arendt: *Organized Guilt and Universalized Responsibility*, 125.

23 Alexander Meschnig: Totalität und Ende der Schuld. Nationalsozialismus und KZ-System. In: Gerburg Treusch-Dieter, Dietmar Kamper, Bernd Ternes (eds.): *Kursbuch 37. Schuld.* Tübingen 1999, 47–58, here 48.

24 Cf. Hannah Arendt: The Aftermath of Nazi Rule. In: *Commentary* (1950), Vol. 10, No. 4, 342–353, here 348.

be denied by anyone who saw DIE TODESMÜHLEN / DEATH MILLS at the cinema. What that is supposed to have to do with one's self and one's own responsibility or one's own sense of justice, however, was not readily accessible.[25] But even here it is the case that inferences to the life of the community are contained in these seemingly individual pathologies of the power of judgment: "For systematic mass murder [...] strains not only the imagination of human beings, but also the framework and categories of our political thought and action. [...] Where all are guilty, nobody in the last analysis can be judged."[26]

This is precisely the reflection behind Karl Jaspers's *The Question of German Guilt*, which in retrospect is the most effective attempt to differentiate at the time, and remains the most widely read even today. Namely, the book attempts to use clear categories and definitions to get to the point that everyone might have the courage to judge him or herself according to these criteria, and thus to feel a "co-responsibility"[27] that is necessary "for forming all political virtues that a civilized state of the future would need."[28]

Jaspers separates the guilt of the individual, which one would have to take responsibility for, either as 'criminal guilt' before the law, as 'moral guilt' exclusively before one's own conscience, or as 'metaphysical guilt' before God, from the collective 'political guilt' that one has to carry as a national subject, in the sense that hardships and prohibitions, the fact of the Allied occupation and demands for reparations would have to "be borne."[29] Jaspers therefore initially saw the role of the Nuremberg trials as to distinguish between the crimes of individuals and the crimes of the regime, less so that the legally guilty could be separated from the innocent, but that, through the absence of unconditional resistance, actual guilt could appear even more clearly as a question of accountability that no one could escape.[30]

The difficulty or the polyvalence of Jaspers's text lies in the fact that it is actually divided into two. On the first level the terminological distinctions amount to a strict separation between the public, objective dimension of legal guilt and political accountability on the one hand and the purely private, personal question of morality and responsibility for one's own actions and naked personhood on the other. This conceptual differentiation could be recombined

---

25 Cf. Arendt: *The Aftermath of Nazi Rule*, 349.

26 Arendt: *Organized Guilt and Universalized Responsibility*, 126.

27 Jaspers: *The Question of German Guilt*, 73.

28 Michael Schefczyk: *Verantwortung für historisches Unrecht. Eine philosophische Untersuchung.* Berlin / New York 2012, 10 [trans. DH].

29 Jaspers: *The Question of German Guilt*, 17, 20, and 24–25.

30 Cf. Jaspers: *The Question of German Guilt*, 38–42.

into a variety of arguments that could serve the assumption of guilt, but also the repudiation of any guilt.[31] The repudiation of collective thinking and thus of collective guilt beyond accountability at the national political level plays a central role in rationalizing the question of guilt.[32] Quite against his own intentions, Jaspers's text empowered those arguments that saw the question of responsibility as having been resolved by the Nuremberg trials. The combination of the *Question of German Guilt* and the speeches of the accused gave rise to a veritable "lexicon of exculpation"[33] for private and public purposes.

At a second level, however, a public appeal runs throughout the individual arguments in the *Question of German Guilt* that attempts to describe a bond of correct feeling that ultimately still turns out to be a feeling of collective guilt: "that in a way that is rationally not conceivable, which is even rationally refutable, I feel co-responsible for what Germans do and have done."[34] For Jaspers, this feeling seems to be the prerequisite to relate again to community in any meaningful way, which is not that of belonging to a people or of citizenship, but the new political community of the like-minded: "I feel close to those Germans who feel likewise – without becoming melodramatic about it – and farther from the ones whose soul seems to deny this link."[35] As a political text, it is about treating the sentence 'That is your guilt' – which can initially only be said in the area of factual execution of violence – so that the sentence: 'That is our guilt' can be publicly pronounced in the sense of moral responsibility.[36] The correct feelings become the condition of being able to say 'we' again.[37]

What Jaspers is aiming for, and what constantly gets lost in the debates about the distinctions of the four terms, is the fact that both the quality of the

---

31 Cf. Hannah Arendt and Heinrich Blücher: *Within Four Walls. The Correspondence Between Hannah Arendt and Heinrich Blücher, 1936–1968*, ed. Lotte Köhler. New York 2000, 179. On July 16, 1949 Blücher writes: "Still he [Jaspers, MG] can be purifying and illuminating for some, but he may also offer false comfort and false certainty for others." Jaspers himself, at any rate, was also clearly aware of this danger. Cf. Jaspers: *The Question of German Guilt*, 50; cf. also Olick: *In the House of the Hangman*, 312.

32 Cf. Jaspers: *The Question of German Guilt*, 24–26 and 50.

33 Olick: *In the House of the Hangman*, 115.

34 Jaspers: *The Question of German Guilt*, 74; cf. Olick: *In the House of the Hangman*, 289: "Jaspers' aim, put simply, was to make his compatriots – even those who had opposed the regime – *feel* guilty. By the same token, he wanted them to *feel* the appropriate *kind* of guilt and for the right reasons, and to do the right thing with these feelings."

35 Jaspers: *The Question of German Guilt*, 74.

36 Cf. Jaspers: *The Question of German Guilt*, 31.

37 Cf. Schefczyk: *Verantwortung für historisches Unrecht*, 10 and 120–121; cf. Olick: *In the House of the Hangman*, 283–290.

crime as well as the sheer quantity of the criminally guilty would not only have made it "nonsensical,"[38] but downright necessary to investigate collective guilt without falling into false collective thinking.[39] Heinrich Blücher, in his letters to Hannah Arendt, is therefore not entirely justified in his critique when he writes that "Jaspers' whole ethical purification-babble leads him to solidarity with the German National Community and even with the National Socialists, instead of solidarity with those who have been degraded."[40] For this is precisely the basis of co-responsibility: that Germans had decided, even without violating individual moral duties, for the community of the perpetrators and against the community of victims, "refusing absolute solidarity with the victims of the injustice."[41]

Where Blücher's critique is thoroughly applicable, however, is in its observation that there is a blind spot inscribed in Jaspers's way of posing the question of guilt, which is representative of the whole discourse of the immediate postwar period, namely the fact that the question of guilt as a "question we put to ourselves"[42] forgets the victims.

Many of the approaches dealing with German guilt from the time are met with the accusation that they serve "as a way to continue occupying themselves exclusively with themselves."[43] Inasmuch as the recognition of feelings of guilt were watered down by emphasizing categories and bodies of knowledge, the perpetrator-victim relationship was kept out of any reformulation of a shared identity.

The term collective guilt could always be understood as an empirical statement rather than a heuristic rule,[44] as the guilt of Germans rather than the guilt by Germans,[45] as the juridical charge of a people rather than as a feeling for the uncertainty of the moral situation. For this reason it is only on very first glance that it is surprising that the term was engrossed by perpetrators and followers – indeed in order to disavow it: "By overemphasizing the non-validity of this term, they demonstrate their own non-guiltiness to others and themselves."[46]

---

38 Jaspers: *The Question of German Guilt*, 34.

39 Cf. Jaspers: *The Question of German Guilt*, 50; cf. Olick: *In the House of the Hangman*, 313.

40 Arendt, Blücher: *Within Four Walls*, 84.

41 Schefczyk: *Verantwortung für historisches Unrecht*, 107 [trans. DH].

42 Jaspers: *The Question of German Guilt*, 22.

43 Arendt, Blücher: *Within Four Walls*, 84.

44 Cf. Schefczyk: *Verantwortung für historisches Unrecht*, 118.

45 Cf. Schefczyk: *Verantwortung für historisches Unrecht*, 174.

46 Meschnig: *Totalität und Ende der Schuld*, 56 [trans. DH].

This is why this concept was only used for a very short time by the victorious powers and practically not at all by the victims. One exception was Jean Améry, who decidedly based collective guilt precisely not on German self-questioning nor on any objectivity of the crimes.[47] He conceived it not as the mystic guilt of being German, but in the sense of a "vague statistical statement," which is the reverse of the victim's experience, which is "approximate and cannot be expressed in numbers"[48]: "It seemed to me as if I had experienced the atrocities as collective ones."[49]

This experience has a name in Améry: *ressentiment*. His description of this feeling immediately makes it clear how much it represents a counterpart to the sense of guilt. For as the sense of guilt intensifies in the aggrieved part, *ressentiment* intensifies in the culprit and both are characterized by a blocked temporality, by the scandal of irreversibility[50]:

> In pondering this question, it did not escape me that resentment is not only an unnatural but also a logically inconsistent condition. It nails every one of us onto the cross of his ruined past. Absurdly, it demands that the irreversible be turned around, that the event be undone. Resentment blocks the exit to the genuine human dimension, the future.[51]

This time-sense defends itself above all against the fact that it has been it too easy for the perpetrators to leave the past behind and to look to the future.[52] It demands a constant updating of the crimes, "by nailing the criminal to his deed"[53] to protest against the natural process of 'wound-healing.' *Ressentiment*, like the sense of guilt, aims for a "self-mistrust,"[54] for the experience of moral failure. A solidarity of Germans as co-perpetrators with their victims is based on the idea that "the German people would remain sensitive to the fact that they cannot allow a piece of their national history to be neutralized by time, but must integrate it."[55]

---

47 Cf. Jean Améry: Resentments [1966]. In: id.: *At the Mind's Limits. Contemplations by a Survivor or Auschwitz and its Realities*, trans. Sidney Rosenfeld, Stella P. Rosenfeld. Bloomington 1980, 62–81, here 70.

48 Améry: *Resentments*, 73.

49 Améry: *Resentments*, 65.

50 Cf. Vladimir Jankélévitch: *The Bad Conscience* [1951]. Chicago 2014, 39–41 and 54–58; cf. Olick: *The Politics of Regret*, 164.

51 Améry: *Resentments*, 68.

52 Cf. Améry: *Resentments*, 69.

53 Améry: *Resentments*, 72.

54 Améry: *Resentments*, 77.

55 Améry: *Resentments*, 78.

In his formulations and in the fact that Améry only published *At the Mind's Limits* (the German title *Jenseits von Schuld und Sühne* would translate as *Beyond Guilt and Atonement*) in 1966, something that has already been alluded to becomes clearer. It was a matter of time before the system of concentration and extermination camps, the atrocity of war and the extermination could be constituted as a historical burden that does not want to go away and to heal. Whether we position this time period from 1945 to the dual founding of states, to the Eichmann and Auschwitz trials, or to the Historian's Dispute of the 1980s, or whether we assume that this process is inconclusive per se, is another matter. At any rate it is a matter of processes of memory with their own duration and contingent dynamics, which creates the "field of history"[56] in the first place, on which can occur what Améry describes in the mode of wishing: "Two groups of people, the overpowered and those who overpowered them, would be joined in the desire that time be turned back and, with it, that history become moral."[57]

This field of moral history, according to this thesis, which arises from the interplay of *ressentiment* in Améry and the difficulties of the question of guilt in Jaspers, was not simply a given in the immediate postwar period. Time itself had to be registered as a factor in the relationships between perpetration, complicity, and victim. And the actual question would then not be where a sense of guilt was in effect in public discourse, in everyday experience, and in the forms of aesthetic experience in the years following 1945, but what affects were working in its place, what affects added up to the genesis of a historical collective sense of guilt on the part of the Germans, or what predominating affects initially blocked such a genesis. Every form of analysis is thus confronted with the unavoidable impurity of the emotional reactions that already begin with the immediate reaction to the evidence of the crimes themselves. Are disgust and revulsion in the face of the images of the camps a reaction to one's own involvement in the atrocities, or are they a rejection of the images themselves and of the accusation underlying them?[58]

A rage at the Nazi elite and their most evident supporters and beneficiaries can be ruled out in the sense of Hannah Arendt:

> The only conceivable alternative to the denazification program would have been a revolution – the outbreak of the German people's spontaneous wrath against all those they knew to be prominent members of the Nazi regime. Uncontrolled and bloody as such an uprising might have been, it certainly would have followed better standards of justice

---

56 Améry: *Resentments*, 143.

57 Améry: *Resentments*, 78.

58 Cf. Olick: *In the House of the Hangman*, 101.

than a paper procedure. But the revolution did not come to pass, and not primarily because it was difficult to organize under the eyes of four foreign armies. It is only too likely that not a single soldier, German or foreign, would have been needed to shield the real culprits from the wrath of the people. This wrath does not exist today, and apparently it has never existed.[59]

The opposite of missing rage is missing mourning, according to Mitscherlich's well-known argument, the impossible confession of having been affectively involved in the system of injustice.[60] "The real question for German society was one Allied soldiers had been asking as they marched through Germany: Where are all the Nazis?"[61] If one cannot admit to having been a Nazi, if one cannot admit to having decided for the complicity of withdrawing into the private and against solidarity with the persecuted, how should there ever be contrition and reversal?

One possible alternation would therefore be to ask to what degree it makes sense to assume a feeling of shame at first, such as Theodor Heuss attempted in a speech at the beginning of his presidency, in which he rejected collective guilt in the usual way:

> Because we lived in Germany, are we also guilty of this fiendish injustice? Am I? Are you? [...] The term "collective guilt" and its implications are an oversimplification, a distortion of the kind pounded home by the Nazis in talking about the Jews. In their eyes the mere fact that someone was a Jew automatically proved him guilty. But something like "collective shame" did grow up in that time and has remained with us. Hitler injured us in many ways, but that he drove us to the point of being ashamed of calling ourselves German in the same breath with him and his henchmen, that was the foulest blow of all.[62]

Here we can clearly see the blind spot that Jaspers also inscribed into the question of guilt: forgetting the victims. Anyone who looks into shame looks into what the extermination of the Jews and other crimes mean for the Germans, and not into what they mean for the relationship of the Germans to the victims. They ask what 'Hitler did to *us*,' into the loss of face, once again instituting, along with Ernst Jünger, Martin Heidegger, or Carl Schmitt, "the artificial realm of a heroic 'culture of shame.'"[63]

---

59 Arendt: *The Aftermath of Nazi Rule*, 349.

60 Cf. Alexander Mitscherlich, Margarete Mitscherlich: *The Inability to Mourn. Principles of Collective Behavior* [1967]. New York 1975.

61 Olick: *In the House of the Hangman*, 152.

62 Theodor Heuss: Mut zur Liebe [1949]. In: id.: *Die großen Reden. Der Staatsmann*. Tübingen 1965, 99–107, here 100–101 [trans. DH].

63 Helmut Lethen: *Cool Conduct. The Culture of Distance in Weimar Germany* [1994]. Berkeley 2002; cf. Olick: *In the House of the Hangman*, 297–320.

In addition, talking of collective shame is in a certain sense incoherent in itself. For shame is precisely not suited to a feeling of solidarity. Rather, it isolates and individualizes the persons' feeling from a community. Being ashamed of being German can only be done alone as an individual.[64] Collective shame destroys the relation to the victim as well as that to the perpetrator.

What remains where the sense of guilt, shame, and rage cancel each other out is an overwhelming self-pity. This is ultimately what characterizes the various public rhetorics as much as it does the common evaluation of German postwar cinema:

> What these films have in common is that they deal with the appearances of the fascist dictatorship as well as with the postwar period without delving into any comprehension of the contexts, portraying the politics that destroyed Germany other than as a faceless destiny. [...] Instead of causing silence with images, or recollecting that even shame and mourning could be given space, they constantly indulge in tame self-pity. [...] What these films have in common is also ultimately the tendency to draw a line under the past.[65]

There are two different interpretations of drawing this line under the past. The one variation assumes a conservative, "positivist-economic model of getting over the past,"[66] according to which decent people are allowed to show themselves as adjusted and amenable to the new order, and thus freed from responsibility. It is this line, drawn under the 'working through' as an 'overcoming' of the past to make it possible to continue biographical projects without trouble, for which Theodor W. Adorno later would only have sarcasm.[67] The other variation, which was associated with the hopes of the left and the official rhetoric of the GDR, was the idea that one embodied the line, that one became the radical historical break oneself. Both lines – that of respectability, humanity, and individuality and that of the purified collective of anti-fascist workers and farmers – can of course also be traced back to the relationship to the occupying forces in each case.[68]

---

64 Cf. Hilge Landweer: *Scham und Macht. Phänomenologische Untersuchungen zur Sozialität eines Gefühls*. Tübingen 1999, 50–52; cf. Christoph Demmerling and Hilge Landweer: *Philosophie der Gefühle. Von Achtung bis Zorn*. Stuttgart 2007, 219–220.

65 Klaus Kreimeier: Die Ökonomie der Gefühle. Aspekte des westdeutschen Nachkriegsfilms. In: Hilmar Hoffmann, Walter Schobert (eds.): *Zwischen Gestern und Morgen. Westdeutscher Nachkriegsfilm 1946–1962*. Frankfurt a. M. 1989, 8–32, here 14 [trans DH].

66 Kreimeier: *Die Ökonomie der Gefühle*, 11 [trans. DH].

67 Cf. Theodor W. Adorno: The Meaning of Working Through the Past [1959]. In: id.: *Interventions and Catchwords*, trans. Henry W. Pickford. New York 2005, 89–103.

68 Cf. Barton Byg: DEFA and the Traditions of International Cinema. In: Seán Allan, John Sandford (eds.): *DEFA. East German Cinema, 1946–1992*. New York / Oxford 1999, 22–41, here 23; cf. Robert R. Shandley: *Rubble Films. German Cinema in the Shadow of the Third Reich*. Philadelphia 2001, 17; cf. Kreimeier: *Die Ökonomie der Gefühle*, 10.

A critique of the poetics of drawing a line from the past and the incapacity of confessing guilt, however, should not be understood as a thorough condemnation of postwar cinema, as we find in some other works.[69] The attempts of the perpetrators to excuse themselves, the accusations of the Allies, and the *ressentiment* of the survivors as well as the appearances of self-pity and self-justification are just as relevant to the affect-economic network as are the feelings, seen as appropriate from today's viewpoint, of rage, of personal shame, and of the sense of guilt as a feeling of belonging to the accomplices and their descendants. The need to resolve guilt and to have unambiguous circumstances, the need for exoneration are thus not descriptions of facts, but are symptomatic of the – moral, political, and affective – uncertainties and contradictions of the postwar situation, and in part also serve the historical observers to understand and formulate their positions, their moral attitudes.[70]

The following is meant to be an attempt to show the temporal and affective logics in which the recognition and denial of responsibility, the individual moral feelings – as the sense of guilt or shame – and their interwovenness with a shared horizon of perceiving, feeling, and thinking, which has to be created anew, are thwarted or mutually realized. 'Shame' and 'the sense of guilt' do not designate a feeling, selectively realized at this or that moment of narration, but a script of perceptive, affective, and cognitive processes that emerges in the temporal structure of film, making it possible to have an aesthetic experience of complex relations to the world and the self. The leading hypothesis here goes that what the postwar films are actually offering in terms of identity and experience consists precisely in the tension between individual self-examination on the one hand and the desire for socially predetermined shared norms and evaluations of action on the other.

2.2 Der Rat der Götter: Fascism, Science, and Capital

For the DEFA films after 1948 in general and Der Rat der Götter in particular, the question of the poetological and rhetorical registers of 'collective guilt' and 'collective feelings of guilt' intensify in their problematic relationship to the

---

69 This tendency can be seen in particular in the contributions to Hilmar Hoffmann, Walter Schobert (eds.): *Zwischen Gestern und Morgen. Westdeutscher Nachkriegsfilm 1946–1962.* Frankfurt a. M. 1989; as well as in Wolfgang Becker, Norbert Schöll: *In jenen Tagen ... Wie der deutsche Nachkriegsfilm die Vergangenheit bewältigte.* Opladen 1995.
70 Cf. Olick: *The Politics of Regret*, 148.

ideal of a 'collective,' which constantly attempted to present itself as a 'national front of anti-fascism':

> The anti-fascism film of DEFA assumed an unbroken and fundamental narratability of past and present. This is the direct consequence of the requirement to explain history as an 'objective' and inevitably reasonable course. The experiences, influences, and traumas that cannot be integrated are reinterpreted or ignored as 'untypical' appearances. This results in a feeling of a certain historical distance to what happened.[71]

The self-conferred title of 'anti-fascism' allowed the Soviet Occupied Zone and later the GDR not only to take up concepts of 'people' ['*Volk*'] and 'culture,' which had become dubious by then, with relatively little problem,[72] but also to turn this potential against the west and to accuse it of "suppressing genuine national sentiment"[73] as a strategic element of its imperialism. The transition from a guilty collective into a national front against the 'warmongers' of monopoly capitalism seems predestined for a clearly constructed dramaturgy of feelings, which evokes an image of responsibility and the sense of guilt, only to transform it into a justified rage on the part of the 'working masses' against the actual culprits.

In Der Rat der Götter this is represented as follows: The film shows operations in and around a large chemical concern starting in 1933, going through the war and into the postwar period, that is, into its present. It is based on the implications of IG Farben for the war and extermination goals of National Socialism, which had been sufficiently documented in the Nuremburg Trials and in Richard Sasuly's book *IG Farben*: "Without IG Farben Hitler could never have gone to war."[74] This thesis is dialogically unfolded in all its aspects and blended with an educational novel about an average family.

This concern – which is indicated as IG Farben by a title frame at the beginning, but is never cited by name in the film itself – thus becomes a double metaphor. The first runs that National Socialist Germany had been a factory. There is virtually no representation of the exterior of this factory or of anything outside matters of the concern or its employees. Exceptions are the montage sequences spread out through the middle section of the film of documentary

---

71 Anne Barnert: *Die Antifaschismus-Thematik der DEFA. Eine kultur- und filmhistorische Analyse*. Marburg 2008, 166 [trans. DH].

72 Cf. Byg: *DEFA and the Traditions of International Cinema*, 23.

73 Anton Ackermann: Zum 5-jährigen Bestehen der DEFA. In: *Auf neuen Wegen – 5 Jahre fortschrittlicher deutscher Film*. (East) Berlin 1951, 5–8, here 8 [trans. DH].

74 Richard Sasuly: *IG Farben* [1947]. (East) Berlin 1952, 32 [trans. DH]; cf. Martin Brady: Discussion with Kurt Maetzig. In: Seán Allan, John Sandford (eds.): *DEFA. East German Cinema, 1946–1992*. New York / Oxford 1999, 77–92, here 77.

footage of war and destruction, but even these can be integrated into the metaphor, thus representing the product pallet, so to speak, of the factory. This metaphorical relation is the basis for the fact that the end of the film can be read as an image of national liberation.

The second metaphor shapes history as a mechanical process that can be penetrated by the natural sciences. Telling examples are the visual constructions in which workers organize and become components of a superior mechanical arrangement, or the way that individual characters are shown to be enmeshed in history through their literal entanglement in chemical laboratory apparatuses, conducts, and pipes.

The film's protagonist, the chemist Dr. Scholz, finds himself in a conflict between the identity concepts corresponding to the two metaphors. On one hand he is an employed scientist, that is, in the logic of the first metaphor he is a citizen that is misused by the concern's management, by capital as directed by the state. On the other hand is his identity as a family man, that is, as the child of a working class family and, in the logic of the second metaphor, as part of the intelligentsia associated by law with the proletariat, which has to play its role in class conflict. He is complicit, but learns in the process and enters into a new *compound* with the workers in order to destroy the bureaucratic-military machine of capital (which conveniently destroys itself – in the film). In the end he experiences exoneration by becoming a trailblazer of the peace front.

What is problematic about the relationship between guilt and collectivity expressed here, and this is my thesis, can be seen in the contradictions that arise between the ideologically overwrought rhetorical production and dissolution of guilt on the one hand and the affect-economic efficiency of its presentational modes and the stratification of temporalities on the other. The medial re-organization of guilt as a collective affect-economic process, that is, as a dramaturgy of incrimination and defense against guilt, of guilt and feelings of guilt, develops a dynamic of its own in the temporal unfolding of aesthetic experience, which can cause trouble for any propagandistic intentions.

The bad conscience of class consciousness

The rhetorical production of a purified collective in the DEFA films can be formulated succinctly in relation to DER RAT DER GÖTTER as follows: The question of guilt dissipates when the facts of the matter, the accusation, and the judgment are correctly understood from the perspective of the class question.

According to the Dimitrov Doctrine, formulated in 1935, war and genocide were the logical consequence of fascism as the logical consequence of the interests of capital.[75] This monocausal derivation begs the question of what it means that Wolfgang Becker and Norbert Schöll choose precisely this film as the only one that "attempts to explain National Socialism."[76] Would it not be necessary first to problematize what can count as an 'explanation' for National Socialism, which political, economic, historical, cultural, and social components have to be brought together in what concrete relations? In this respect the monocausal logic of Der Rat der Götter should be viewed as failing in its attempt to explain from the very beginning.

This close association between fascism and capital can already be seen in the film's arsenal of characters. "Except for one insignificant supporting character" – meaning 'Director von Decken' (Herwart Grosse), who overacts in his appearance, gestures, facial expressions and manner of speech – "there is no National Socialist in the film. Der Rat der Götter is thus an 'anti-fascist film' almost entirely without fascists."[77] But not only is the card-carrying National Socialist a solitary figure there, the *Wehrmacht* is also only embodied in one recognizable character, that of General Schirrwind (Helmuth Hinzelmann), and both become increasingly indistinguishable from the 'actual' representatives of the chemical concern over the course of the film. They are not so much mere marionettes as they are completely assimilated forces, which become the immanent elements of the system 'Council of the Gods.'

Such a preformed understanding corresponds to a dramaturgical economy that portrays an accumulation of class consciousness in the historical process, one that is established in such DEFA films as Die Buntkarierten (1949, Kurt Maetzig), Rotation (1949, Wolfgang Staudte) or Die Unbesiegbaren (1953, Arthur Pohl) in histories of cross-generational formation. Histories must repeat themselves in order to be able not to repeat themselves. In the sense of the poetics outlined above, drawing a line in a specifically socialist way, it is a matter of representing the postwar period as a potential – and in the west current – repetition of history that is impeded by changing consciousness and new relations of

---

75 Cf. Georgi Dimitrov: *The Fascist Offensive and the Tasks of the Communist International in the Fight for the Unity of the Working Class Against Fascism*. London 1935.

76 Becker, Schöll: *In jenen Tagen*, 35 [trans. DH].

77 Anne Kober: Antifaschismus im DDR-Film. Ein Fallbeispiel. Der Rat der Götter. In: Manfred Agathen, Eckhard Jesse, Ehrhart Neubert (eds.): *Der missbrauchte Antifaschismus. DDR Staatsdoktrin und Lebenslüge der deutschen Linken*. Freiburg i. Br. 2002, 202–220, here 207 [trans. DH].

ownership. At the same time this logic of repetition can be linked to a timeless stability of the correct standpoint:

> The German heroes of freedom from all times are on our side, whether they be the freedom heroes from the Peasants' Wars, the heroes among the Forty-Eighters, the German men and women in the workers' movement, or the martyrs of the resistance to Hitler. In the resistance, in this heroic community of fighters, in this community of suffering and dying among our people is founded the new liberal entity of the German people.[78]

Carrying on this repetitive structure of history not only means using 'anti-fascism' to install a suprahistorical, mythical interpretive model, but also means reducing the specificity of National Socialism in favor of a universal fascism.[79] Despecifying is in turn the prerequisite, not for explaining the relationship of the populace to National Socialism, but primarily for implementing its negation in the form of ignorance, naïveté, and seducibility. If one cannot "avert fate," then one can "maturely and *knowingly* endure" it, and one is then "prepared for the turnaround and the new era."[80]

In summary, from the perspective of a state doctrine of 'anti-fascism' the dramaturgy of German guilt goes as follows: German workers, the progressive-minded middle class, and the intelligentsia were not in complete possession of their progressive power due to a consciously manipulated media and socio-economic public sphere – their guilt is that of their powerlessness – and thanks to Germany's defeat in the war it became possible for them to rip the 'veil' off the circumstances, to recognize the truly guilty parties, and to join forces against them.

This is also the internal perspective of the film DER RAT DER GÖTTER. But can this so easily come undone as a temporal unfolding of an image of capital, science, and working class? What triggers my skepticism here is based on the openly pedagogical claim of the film.[81] The understanding of film as an educational effort is not a particular quality of DEFA films, but it does suggest a

---

78 Johannes R. Becher: *Deutsches Bekenntnis. Drei Reden zu Deutschlands Erneuerung.* Berlin 1945, 43 [trans. DH].

79 Cf. Barnert: *Die Antifaschismus-Thematik der DEFA*, 11.

80 Günter Agde: Position und Leistung des Spielfilmregisseurs Kurt Maetzig. In: id. (ed.): *Kurt Maetzig. Filmarbeit. Gespräche, Reden, Schriften.* (East) Berlin 1987, 413–494, here 434, [trans. DH, emphasis MG].

81 Cf. Kurt Maetzig: Probleme des realistischen Filmschaffens in der Deutschen Demokratischen Republik. In: *Auf neuen Wegen – 5 Jahre fortschrittlicher deutscher Film.* (East) Berlin 1951, 30–39, here 30 [trans. DH]: "Art is a social necessity. It is [...] a method of unifying people with society, a method of grasping reality. Herein lies the educational character of art. Art does not have the same educational duties as the school, as the lectern, as the newspaper, but those released by life itself, if you understand it right."

significant paradox, namely that "we were dealing with an audience that had experienced, or rather completed, a break in its civic disposition and morality."[82] The crux lies precisely in this casual 'or rather.' The film simultaneously assumes the learning process that it itself intends to portray, that it itself wants to be, as always already completed. This is exactly the circular reasoning in which the guilty conscience of class consciousness is encircled.

The issue here, then, is to show the temporal and affective logics in which moral emotion – as the sense of guilt or shame – and the shared scope of the collective both thwart and produce one another. To what degree is the purified collective itself a secondary treatment of the emotional process that can be described as an individually embodied 'collective sense of guilt?' How does the film produce the wish fulfillment of an objective, socially shared 'moral compass' by representing individual morality as insufficient in relation to a collective morality?

The affective logic of making a pact with the devil

The following will concern how the distinction between an objective 'guilt' and a 'collective sense of guilt' are medially organized as a process in the economy of affect. If we can describe the 'morality' of the sense of guilt – the complex script of perceptive, affective, and cognitive processes that unfold in the temporal structure of the film – as salvaging and reanimating a moral compass during the process of retrospectively realizing its failure, then one basic cultural model for such a script would be the pact with the devil. The fact that this plays a role in DER RAT DER GÖTTER only seems to be natural since – at least in Germany – wherever there is a scientist, Faust cannot be far away. The question is: who is selling his soul and to whom? The answer is obvious on the diegetic side: on the one hand the workers and the middle class are selling their souls to the false solutions of fascism, on the other the members of the Scholz Family are doing so to the chemical concern. Equally evident is the fact that they will each be allowed to win back their souls in the end, as class consciousness. The circumstances of life were bad, but the people were good. They were merely restricted in their power to resist by a lack of knowledge, which they transform through dreadful experience and indulgent lessons into historical insight.[83] The exceptions – the protagonist's brother, who could not be convinced from the start, and who only makes a short appearance then, and his sister Edith

---

82 Becker, Schöll: *In jenen Tagen*, 49 [trans. DH].

83 Cf. Becker, Schöll: *In jenen Tagen*, 109.

(Inge Keller), seduced by luster – either lose their lives in the war or remain loyal to the capitalist system.

But the following is at least as significant: The spectator also sells his soul, or rather is shown how he once sold his cinematic soul to the devil named UFA. The problem of expectation on the part of the spectators, who were contaminated by a certain film aesthetics and "used to the products of a jungle morality and a bottomless distortion of reality,"[84] runs like a leitmotiv through contemporary positions and critiques of cinema. Not to mention the entrenched automatism of filmmakers, like this widely cited polemic shows:

> They shoot the most primitive mediocrity. They make use of the most antiquated means of expression. They violate the most banal basic film rules. They disregard dramaturgical regularities. They convert the misery of our time into the most piteous construction of pathos. They take over the Nazi film patterns as if not the slightest thing had changed in the meantime.[85]

Among the 'solutions' for this grievance, including linking back to Weimar cinema or looking for new imaging matrices, for instance so-called 'socialist realism,' DER RAT DER GÖTTER represents a further variant, namely the strategically utilized, unmasking appropriation of the 'late UFA style.'[86] What is meant by this are those scenes in which the conspiracy of the industrialists – the self-proclaimed 'Council of the Gods' of the title – with the NSDAP, the Wehrmacht, and later the American cartel of Standard Oil is dialogically rubbed under our noses. They are kept in exactly those image types – bright and saturated, rather static than dynamic-vectorial or graphic-expressionistic – that one finds in this context referred to as 'late UFA style.' Spatial depth is discreetly illuminated in various medium shots, the backgrounds fill up the frame, unobtrusively ornate.[87]

There is, however, a minimal deviation from this stereotypical form that underscores the programmatic calculation once more. A moving camera is attached to the bodies of privy councilor Mauch and of his daughter, who has the Wehrmacht wrapped around her little finger, as the two forces that dominate the image and the other characters. At the large receptions or at intimate conversations

---

84 Ackermann: *Zum 5-jährigen Bestehen der DEFA*, 6 [trans. DH].

85 Wolfdietrich Schnurre: Rettung des deutschen Films. Eine Streitschrift [1950]. In: id.: *Kritiker*. Munich 2010, 269–314, here 269–270 [trans. DH].

86 Bernhard Groß has described such strategic appropriation of the UFA style, which attempts to structure past and present as modes of experience, using the example of ZWISCHEN GESTERN UND MORGEN. Cf. Bernhard Groß: Wahrnehmen – Observieren – 'Checken'. Geschichtlichkeit als ästhetische Erfahrung in ZWISCHEN GESTERN UND MORGEN. In: Hermann Kappelhoff, Bernhard Groß, Daniel Illger (eds.): *Demokratisierung der Wahrnehmung*. Berlin 2010, 115–134.

87 Cf. Groß: *Wahrnehmen – Observieren – 'Checken'*, 124.

it is always these two characters that pull the camera's gaze through the room, taking the choreography of the other characters along with them (e.g. 0:08:05–0:11:58 and 0:29:09–0:33:55). This coupling thus becomes the aesthetic experience of a historical connection between the film modality 'UFA' and the depiction of the origin of the war being in the interests of capital. It is, however, also effective in the sense of entangling the spectator's gaze, the spectator's sensation as a passive, moved object in the perceptual means that embody the historical forces. As spectators we are exactly as subordinated to them as is the singular individual, who is affected by the connections between politics and history.

Alongside the involvement of the individual spectator's gaze, which seems to exclude any form of critique, these visual spaces serve two other historically exonerating arguments. On the one hand they underscore the seductive, blinding potential of the regime itself, and not from any irrational collective madness, but as a promise of socio-economic advancement.[88] On the other, and in continuity with this, in a dance revue scene set in Switzerland (0:51:06–0:54:39), they present a contrast between the easygoing existence abroad, the salons of the elite, and the afflicted everyday life of the ordinary population.[89] The perceptual mode of exoneration simultaneously evokes the difference between 'us' and 'them.'

The 'pact with the devil' in Der Rat der Götter does not entail acquiescing to the cult of Hitler and racial ideology. It means accepting a simple, but in retrospect false solution for those problems and wishes for which socialism then represented the correct solution. While retreating to the private becomes the central topos of relieving guilt for the films from the western sector and the Federal Republic, in films like this it is precisely the wish to live 'unpolitically' that is the sin from which individuals have to be redeemed.[90]

The dramaturgy of the pact with the devil contains, alongside deception and self-deception, the corresponding element of the 'fall' or the 'collapse' of those making the pact, the disenchantment with the devil and the 'renunciation,' the 'revocation.' By appropriating the UFA style as a strategy to unmask it, the film performs the disenchantment of the 'council of the gods' by means of a gradual emptying and compressing of the image types associated with privy councilor Mauch and his sites of action. The spaces become increasingly shallower and more constricted, the backgrounds fall into disorder, the characters become more static, thus modulating perception over time, which is represented as a directly tangible deprivation of power, a retreat of fascination and a

---

88 Cf. Barnert: *Die Antifaschismus-Thematik der DEFA*, 329.
89 Cf. Becker, Schöll: *In jenen Tagen*, 131.
90 Cf. Barnert: *Die Antifaschismus-Thematik der DEFA*, 333.

literal extrication of the previously subjected spectator gaze. This visual aesthetic exorcism occurs in parallel to a transformation in the ways that the protagonist Dr. Scholz is staged. If over long phases of the film he had usually been constricted by the laboratory devices, the tightness of his family's private spaces, or by the dominance of the characters from the management of the concern, at the end of the film the dynamic of moving shots is now always exclusively linked with him (1:26:46–1:28:23). An 'unpolitical,' passively moved subject becomes an active, moving subject with 'political class consciousness':

> Scholz's transformation from an unpolitical and compliant tool to an active freedom fighter forms the central thread of the plot. The beginning and the end of Scholz's development are supposedly far apart from one another. Scholz's transformation is led by Maetzig and Wolf in a fairly simple, linear fashion. And yet the decisive factors that affect Scholz's changes are of such dramaturgical and historical weight that the linearity must logically follow.[91]

In its engagement with the historicity of the visual aesthetic qualities, the historical-political learning process portrayed by the film's plot becomes a learning process that itself runs through the cinema as a social practice and through the spectator as a perceiving being. This process, however, despite the interpretation cited here, is decisively not linear, but pervaded by repetitions, flashbacks, and anticipations.

Learning processes of the sense of guilt

This non-linearity can best be seen in the diegetic learning process that is shaped like a station drama from the early period of Expressionist theater.[92] This central sequence takes place between minute 39 and minute 49 of the film, after Dr. Scholz, despite the warnings of his uncle (Albert Garbe), the fatherly work leader, has assumed directorship of the factory's explosives division and immediately after 'Case B,' that is, the war, is initiated by the 'council of the gods.' The station drama that we go through with Dr. Scholz unfolds as a whole as audiovisual expressivity that turns a 'sense of guilt' into the object and into the somatic-synaesthetic mode of spectator feeling. In their interplay the stations form a pulsing rhythm of pressure and flight, activity and passivity, acceleration and deceleration.

---

91 Agde: *Position und Leistung des Spielfilmregisseurs Kurt Maetzig*, 436 [trans. DH].
92 This is also an indication that an understanding for the way media organizational patterns and their historical placement are assembled together is elementary for reconstructing the affect-economic function of post-war films.

The first station brings the metaphorics that systematically permeate the film (0:38:42–0:41:11) into the foreground. The German Reich is a factory, its population consists of materials and substances in a vast apparatus of lines and pipes through which they are passively guided. A malfunction in one of the apparatuses threatens to cause an accident and Dr. Scholz – who is at that moment giving board members von Decken and Hüttenrauch a tour of the factory – runs to help and prohibits anything worse from happening.

In the way that the connection works between perception and action, of hearing the alarm and the vapor coming out of the pipe, of seeing the signs, measuring devices, and valves on up to the movements and instructions, the film gives us an image of control on the one hand, an image of sensory-motor integration of perception, affection, and action, a Deleuzian movement-image in its pure form.[93] On the other hand this movement-image is embedded in a visual composition in which we can barely decide whether the character is in fact making his way through the factory or whether this is more like an illusion of control, whether this way through the guiding containers was not always preset, where any deviation would actually be impossible. The station ends with a figuration of perception and movement of a second order. The two *leading* employees of the concern, von Decken and Hüttenrauch, are placed into the image as the unmoved, perceiving, controlling counterpole to those who are being led. Their displaced dominance thus concludes the movement configuration of a 'just prohibited accident.' The film therefore presents a sensually marked shape to everyday life in the Third Reich: a constant emergency situation that does not allow for any possibility to act outside the most immediate sphere of influence and in which the individual knows that he is constantly under observation.

The second station (0:41:11–0:43:09) shows a cruel animal experiment as a synecdoche for the extermination of the Jews and other population groups, subversives, homosexuals, and the disabled. As if to preclude the thesis of a 'banality of evil,'[94] the station starts with a laboratory assistant carrying a whimpering puppy into the test chamber, which indicates its death. "Poor animal," she says [trans. DH], but she carries out her action without interruption, in a fluid movement until the end, obviously not *thinking* any more about it.

The object of the experiment is multiple, the scene functions in the overlapping of perception processes or rather in the successive bracketing of three triads

---

93 Cf. Gilles Deleuze: *Cinema I. The Movement-Image* [1983]. Minneapolis 1986.
94 Cf. Hannah Arendt: *Eichmann in Jerusalem. A Report on the Banality of Evil* [1963]. New York 2006; cf. Hannah Arendt: Some Questions on Moral Philosophy [1965]. In: id.; *Responsibility and Judgment.* New York 2003.

(like a Russian doll), each consisting of a dispositif of a gaze, a gazed upon, and somebody gazing:

The first triad consists of a pane of glass, the gazing Dr. Scholz, and the gazed upon, the wincing of the dying animal, which is shown through an insert that in fact documents such an experiment. This triad is bracketed by a second. The laboratory itself is now the context, Hüttenrauch and von Decken are the observers, Dr. Scholz is the object of their psychological experiment, the animals are their stimulus material. They observe how the wincing of the dying animal continues in the wincing in his face. And this in turn is bracketed in a third triad. The cinematic image makes something visible as a form to the spectator's gaze from the position of its historical present. We are the gazers, Dr. Scholz's powerlessness in the clutches of the two representatives of the regime is what there is to gaze upon. The wincing of the dying animal transforms into the wincing in Dr. Scholz's face and then becomes the diabolical winks shared between von Decken and Hüttenrauch.

For the spectator watching this nesting of a politically calculating reaction to a human reaction to a chemical-biological reaction, there develops an image of horror at a desperate situation. It all begins rather harmlessly. The laboratory is established in a steady succession of medium shots, and the characters are positioned in this space. Doors open and close (to the test chamber and to the laboratory room). When the threefold relation has been set up – we see Scholz from behind looking into the chamber, to the right and to the left Hüttenrauch and von Decken are looking at him – the frequency of cuts accelerates, the order "Gas!" is given, an unpleasant, high, sharply dissonant whistle begins and gets constantly louder. The shots become slower and slower, while short irregular, electronic-acoustic discordances accompany Scholz's facial and gestural reactions and finally the dying convulsions of a lamb and a small dog. While this pain-inducing soundtrack captures the event in an imposing presence, the shots that follow push it into an equally excruciatingly palpable distance. The camera looks through a window at Scholz, who is staring into the off space. Behind him, stacked up in a diagonal from front right to back left, are the other characters and the window to the experiment chamber. It is as if the film had suddenly jumped in time, switching into the visual mode of the rubble film. From *this* seeing there is no connection to action, and the space of the character's gaze becomes a temporal dimension aimed at a present the spectator, at the witnesses of the third triad. "But Dr. Scholz, you always did want to know the end result of your hydrazine research," von Decken says to him over his shoulder [trans. DH], referring to a temporally bracketed positioning of this scene between an open situation – the research, the experiment as the preliminary stage of reality – and an always already fulfilled reality of the gas chambers, a reality that cannot be reversed.

The last shot of this station shows Dr. Scholz stubbornly walking straight alongside a train track. Parallel to this a train crosses the image from back left to right front, that is, exactly in the direction that one shot previously had opened the temporal dimension to the spectator's historically retrospective gaze. White vapor rises from the locomotive and the factory smokestacks in the background, the whistling sound of the flowing gas sounds again. Is the train transporting poisonous gas? People? The following three stations revolve around the question of the visibility of the train and the invisibility of its contents: knowing and non-knowing, knowing and acting, knowing and speaking as a figuration of incommensurability, that is, equations that do not get solved, that do not find any common denominator.

On the one hand there are the unavoidable forms of evidence. The son Dieter says it directly: "Our factory helps to do away with the Jews and subhumans in the concentration camps" (0:43:09–0:44:26 [trans. DH]). And there is the physically visible cyclone gas cartridge with "package unit for Auschwitz" written on it, which Scholz directly bumps into when he 'takes a look around the factory,' as if he were a detective hot on the trail of a hidden reality (0:44:26–0:45:20 [trans. DH]). On the other hand, however, there are also the blockades, the paralyses, and the knowledge that this evidence is incommensurable with any idea of action. He can simply *do nothing* with his knowledge, with the gas cartridge, he cannot even communicate it. On the contrary, because of his knowledge he himself becomes isolated by the unconsciousness of the banal and the ordinary, which appears in the form of a flat bicycle tire (0:45:20–0:46:09).

What holds these three stations together in terms of their staging – the spoken word, the object 'cyclone gas cartridge,' and the ordinary – and links them to the previous station, the animal experiment, is the continuation of the gaze and movement directions of the character Dr. Scholz, as well as the directional vectors between him and the elements of evidence. The objects of evidence – his gaze, the train, the direction of Dieter's gaze when he speaks the truth out loud, the crates with Cyclone B – are always set into the image by a diagonal link between the depth of field and the foreground, which, as I have mentioned, partially indicates a temporal dimension, and which relates the foreground to the historical present of the spectator who is moved by the past. In contrast the gaze and movement vectors of the protagonist consist of a downward bending. He is constantly averting, unable to initiate any new movement. It is as if he were writhing on the tip of an arrow, which points – from the facts and objects that imply guilt – to him and to the spectators, and as if any renunciation would only produce a new diagonal, a new piece of incriminating evidence. What emerges from this is precisely the pulsation of harassment and flight that can be conceived as the expressive-synaesthetic mode of a sense of guilt.

The historico-political turn of this incommensurability of evidence and action that DER RAT DER GÖTTER undertakes finally becomes clearer through the unsettling effect of the sixth station (0:46:09–0:47:51). The uncle's calmness suddenly confronts the spectator with the situation that the learning process that one is supposed to be undergoing is pontificated as already fully accomplished. First he directly speaks out the metaphor that the German Reich is a factory: "Abroad it is well known. It's just that, once again, we Germans don't know anything. You see, Hans, it's like with our factory. The people that walk past outside can smell the stench five kilometers away, but those sitting inside no longer notice that it stinks at all." [Trans. D.H.] And then he converts this into an absolutely passive attitude of waiting it out, with which the harassing dimension of guilt is negated. He embodies a knowledge about what is coming or should come, an anticipated afterwards, which is blind to its own emotional processes that constitute it. Here there is a claim of the needlessness of what one might call the impulse of the sense of guilt: of acting *on the past*.

And it is precisely the scandal of irreversibility that then once again breaks through after all in the seventh and last station (0:47:51–0:48:41). The radio appears as the voice of conscience: "Did you also know that deadly experiments are being done on prisoners in Dachau with poisonous gas developed by German chemists?" [Trans. D.H.] The destruction of the radio is a desperate attempt to fend off the sense of guilt, making the voice go silent – provisionally a successful attempt, for the anger acted out provokes the reassuring knowledge of not really being guilty in the end.[95]

The interplay of the seven stations gives rise to claustrophobic images and movements of escape. This repeating dynamic, which seeks to provide sense evidence to the image while at the same time being a flight from that evidence, produces a bodily affection that represents a synaesthetic equivalent of the sense of guilt. And indeed as a 'knowledge about something' expressed as a feeling, that is, in another form of knowledge, which does not dwell in concepts and linguistic-discursive contents, but forms its contents as physical reactions and experiences. The various stations revolve in somatic activation around an 'object' of guilt, which is not given in any singular information or in any singular object. Rather, it designates the quality common to the animals that perish in pain, the gas cartridges, and the radio news. And they encircle a quite particular deictic function. The pure function of the 'listen and hear what you have

---

95 Cf. Patricia Greenspan: *Practical Guilt. Moral Dilemmas, Emotions, and Social Norms.* New York / Oxford 1995, 173.

done' becomes the mode of perception itself – without the 'what' and the 'do' getting isolated in the process.

Ultimately the film claims the efficacy of personal morality, an affective grounding of acting and thinking, while at the same time restricting it by suspending it as a figuration of powerlessness, only letting it dissipate into a suprapersonal morality in the film's final sequence, in which the protagonist becomes unified with the masses of working people. Here as well we can see that the claim that "linearity must take place quite logically"[96] goes astray. The dramaturgical and expressive function of the sense of guilt works precisely by shifting time, retrospection, and the work on irreversibility. For it is not the case that "his failure and the moral necessity of this responsibility is illuminated for Scholz with the sudden awareness of the concern's violations."[97] Quite to the contrary, it is obscured, becomes diffuse and deferred. After not being seen for a whole thirteen minutes before this approximately ten-minute-long sequence – the time in which his research is realized, more or less without him, in the war and the gas chambers – the protagonist once again disappears from the screen for ten minutes. The medium of film can also offer the mercy of internal exile.

What the film works out in this station drama is the contradiction between the effect of presences, the singular event, dispensing any spatio-temporal vector, of seeing a "package unit for Auschwitz," and an equally timeless ideological knowledge of dependencies that only recognizes this package as proof of the means and ways by which capital pursues its interests. This gap is filled up by the retrospection of the sense of guilt and in the hyperactivity of a retroactively guilty conscience certain scenes in the film can be read anew. For instance, it might also happen that some think that they had very nearly been gassed themselves. In the first encounter with the protagonist (0:02:07–0:04:36), we see him coughing and choking, flinging open a window while behind him rises the smoke of a chemical test series. "That stuff is demonic!" [Trans. D.H.] Here it becomes clear that the film is playing on a 'knowledge' of its spectators, which at the same time they have to learn in the first place in what follows.

In this opposition between a claim to certainty and the claim to conscience, we see exactly what the film seeks to negate on a different level, namely that there is a free-floating responsibility before any singular responsibility. The production of action-theory based causality and perpetration, questions of voluntariness, compulsion, accountability and so on are not the matrix of moral

---

96 Agde: *Position und Leistung des Spielfilmregisseurs Kurt Maetzig*, 436 [trans. DH].
97 Agde: *Position und Leistung des Spielfilmregisseurs Kurt Maetzig*, 436 [trans. DH].

categories, but secondary forms that are meant to provide the injured feelings, the fissures in the relation to the world, with a meaningful shape and symbolic legibility.[98] In the case of DER RAT DER GÖTTER it is the question of knowing and unknowing participation in the atrocities that is the focus of the ideological dissipation of responsibility. Life in National Socialism, its moral and political judgment are marked by a dividing line between a knowing and unknowing 'participation,' secretly retaining the humane without the quantity or quality of the deed in question having to play any role in the formulation of judgment.[99] It is, I would claim, exactly this dividing line that initially contradicts the sense of guilt, and that is introduced by the film, dramaturgically transferring the sense of guilt into other emotional domains, which are then compatible: shame about one's own ignorance and anger at the crimes of others.

The film takes to a paradoxical situation of not only showing a past "that does not stop inscribing itself, albeit not in the present of the action, but in the future of the historical events"[100]– as Thomas Elsaesser had written about Konrad Wolf's STERNE (1959). At the same time it also shows how a present gets inscribed in the past: not by seeking to undo the past, but by wishing to see the historical event as inevitable and suspended in itself.

This is nowhere clearer than in the relationship that the film assumes to the regularly introduced montage units from documentary footage. The music of Hanns Eisler always precedes the individual passes of armaments, the beginning of the war, retreat, destruction, and capitulation by one chapter, so during the armament section it already sounds like war, while it already sounds like defeat when the first division of tanks invades Poland. But whether this results in an "interpretation pointing to the future,"[101] as Maetzig himself thought, is open to doubt. That is, there is indeed a 'pointing interpretation,' but it does not point *to the future*, but *from the present* onto the images. They are transferred as images from their own temporality, which is open to interpretation, into an overdetermined situation that immobilizes them so that the ideological knowledge of dependencies unfolding in the narrative can nestle into them, blocking all ways back into the past except for one: "All of the economic decisions made by the board of IG Farben are immediately reduced to the political

---

98 Cf. Lotter: *Scham, Schuld, Verantwortung*, 211–214.

99 Cf. Becker, Schöll: *In jenen Tagen*, 50–51.

100 Thomas Elsaesser: Diagonale Erinnerung. Geschichte als Palimpsest in STERNE. In: Hermann Kappelhoff, Bernhard Groß, Daniel Illger (eds.): *Demokratisierung der Wahrnehmung*. Berlin 2010, 95–114, here 97 [trans. DH].

101 Maetzig: *Filmarbeit*, 31 [trans. DH].

events. In this way an impression of direct connection is conveyed to the spectator."[102]

The most telling example of this is certainly the first documentary sequence, which musically turns the visual documents of the armament into an act of war. It is introduced by a telephone call in which privy councilor Mauch announces that "the preparations for Case A are beginning." What this refers to is the armament program. This is followed by a cut to a document, one of Hitler's speeches, which seems to connect directly to the mission: "The goal has been set for us. German workers, begin!" [trans. DH] In this respect we could also object to an interpretation that posits that the documentary elements "increased the authenticity of the film and had a retrospective effect on the fictional story and the fictionalized figure."[103] It is much more the case that the 'story' has an effect on the documentary elements, incorporating them into the logic of their knowledge of dependencies, thus reducing armament, mass murder, and war, as well as reconstruction, to the business game of the concern shown in the film, and in doing so suppressing the particular constitutive elements of popular-national megalomania and racial ideology.

Trials of shame and anger

The only exception in which documentary images perpetuate a non-determined interpretive scope is the footage whose screening is diegetically framed. These are images from the liberated camps that are projected in a scene where the Nuremberg Trials are re-enacted (1:08:01–1:15:23) and that were partly also shown in TODESMÜHLEN / DEATH MILLS and other *re-education* films and here edited in. The focus – temporally as well as logically – is on footage of a cyclone delivery. Here the music stops. Instead we hear a faint, but ever growing murmur, one might call it the uneasiness of the contemporary cinema spectator, the presence of the cinematic perception, which suddenly breaks through to the soundtrack.

What exactly gets expressed by this uneasiness is unfolded as the film continues. Initially as to where we as spectators are positioned, namely not in the wide shots, in the seemingly objective surveillance looking in from the outside – like in most of the familiar visual documents of the Nuremberg Trials – but in an in-between space, along the axes of prosecuting attorneys and the bank of the

---

102 Kober: *Antifaschismus im DDR-Film*, 207 [trans. DH].
103 Agde: *Position und Leistung des Spielfilmregisseurs Kurt Maetzig*, 438 [trans. DH].

squirming accused as they try to make excuses. The staging then develops a centrifugal dynamic through the editing of figures searchingly looking around (1:10:05–1:11:50), a dynamic that atmospherically captures the entire visual space, exploding the axis of the accusatory gaze and the accused who are gazed at, a dynamic of gazes in all directions, from all directions, which can be described as the visibility of shame and disgrace become palpable – not only of these figures, but quite decidedly of the spectators's perception. The positioning of the camera in the following is increasingly unstable, wild pans alternate with fixed shots, an extreme low shot is suddenly replaced by an extreme top view.

In the middle of the atmosphere of shame Dr. Scholz now appears (1:11:50–1:15:23), although the term 'appears' is not appropriate here at all, for he does not turn up from some outside, nor does he enter through a door or the like, but neither is he already just there. His diegetic presence is completely withheld from us visually, and even the first shot where his presence is shown after his name is called, which only lasts two seconds, does not show him in close-up, but half hidden in the background, cramped into a doorjamb and partially hidden by court reporters. In other words: Dr. Scholz does not appear as a character, but embodies the shame. He emerges from the atmosphere of shame itself and draws the gazes toward himself. The shame here turns out to be a feeling that strives for transformation, "an unstable sensuality that desperately seeks metamorphosis into the expressive corporeality of some other emotion."[104] Scholz dissolves the atmosphere of shame since his speech, cited in the beginning, facilitates the affect-poetic double exoneration from a clear avowal of guilt and from the indignation aimed at the criminally guilty:

> For the infectious character of an atmosphere of shame perhaps even has consequences in terms of the aesthetics of effect [...]. Because the spectator is also compelled to experience this affect, the attempt at resolving through the guilt of a protagonist [...] is experienced by the audience as exonerating, and thus only to gladly adopted as a dramaturgical resolution.[105]

The dramaturgy of the film initially seems to come down to the Nuremberg Trials, but in fact these are only the endpoint of a first internal structure that is mirrored in the last half hour of the film. The film seeks to make its argument evident in the mirror structure, the argument that history must repeat itself in order not to repeat itself. What functions as therapeutic repetition in many postwar films – "a second shock always has to shake the returning soldier out

---

104 Jack Katz: *How Emotions Work*. Chicago 1999, 147; cf. Landweer: *Scham und Macht*.
105 Claudia Benthien: *Tribunal der Blicke. Kulturtheorien von Scham und Schuld und die Tragödie um 1800*. Cologne / Weimar / Vienna 2011, 230 [trans. DH].

of his lethargy, so that he believes in the miracle of reconstruction again"[106]–
has become a ritualized rhetorical weapon here. In one edition of the DEFA
newsreel Der Augenzeuge [The Eyewitness], which was run by Kurt Maetzig, on
the occasion of the elections for the Berlin City Council in December 1948,
which was being boycotted by the SED, we read:

> Then how did this history begin? First they came with their slogans, just like today. Then:
> In lockstep, march! [...] Then as now: Anti-Soviet agitation as the dumbing down of the
> masses.
>
> [...] But history does not repeat itself. What was possible in '33 cannot happen again
> in '48. Before '33 we were at odds and consciously divided by our class opponents. We
> were able to fight the calamity, but not to prevent it. Today the picture looks quite differ-
> ent. Today workers in all countries on Earth are working at increasing the peace front.
> Behind us workers not only stands the will to peace, but also the power to ensure it. All
> demagogues and war mongers, all armament hawks and heads of concerns will fail at
> this front of peace![107]

This is just one of a number of examples by which we can show how pertinent
this interpretive model of "then as now, but ..." was.

In the mirrored construction of temptation, disaster, and trial there are now
significant substitutions in Der Rat der Götter. It is not Scholz himself who enters a pact with the devil, but his son, by which the film, like certain other
DEFA productions, activates the character schema of cross-generational repetitions and differences for such an interpretive model. The devil is now the
American representative of Standard Oil (Willy Kleinau), who increasingly assumed the most active role in the discussions of the chemical concern. The
crime to be judged is the continued production of explosives after the war,
which triggers a disastrous explosion (1:28:23–1:33:46) and which is not represented as the past through documents and music. It is presented as a composition of presence, thus taking on a much larger weight in temporal quantity and
qualitative intensity than do the images of war time, the extermination camps,
or the experience of wreckage. And finally the judging authority is embodied
by the victims of the explosion, by the mass of workers and their relatives and
not by a corruptible jurisdiction (1:39:34–1:43:32). Central to this is the change
in the spectator's perspective, which is now no longer a self-judged object of

---

106 Thomas Brandlmeier: Von Hitler zu Adenauer. Deutsche Trümmerfilme. In: Hilmar
Hoffmann, Walter Schobert (eds.): *Zwischen Gestern und Morgen. Westdeutscher Nachkriegsfilm
1946–1962.* Frankfurt a. M. 1989, 33–61, here 46 [trans. DH].
107 Der Augenzeuge, No. 132 / 1948 (1948) [trans. DH]. Off-screen commentary on the entry:
"Wer die Wahl hat, hat die Qual – zum 5. Dezember 1948."

working out a given body of knowledge, but the subject of a judging knowledge. The 'attitude' shifts from accused to accusation.

At the latest with these substitutions it becomes clear what the film is excluding. At the very beginning it is insinuated that National Socialism was a phenomenon that might perhaps have had something to do with mobilizing the masses and the cult of the Führer, when, in a 28-second-long shot, Scholz and his uncle rummage around in the amorphous crowd of NSDAP supporters and counterdemonstrators (0:07:04–0:07:32). At any rate, this recognition of a particular appearance of publicness in the following is negated, since the masses only come into their own by organizing against the class enemy, in the trial before the gates of the destroyed factory. In the end the brief flash of a chaotic arrangement becomes a peaceful, sustained, and gestalt-like figuration of the mass of workers. When they appear as the nemesis, the incarnation of punitive justice, a space of action is created that did not exist before without them. Privy council Mauch, who had actually come to placate the masses, is visually excluded from this body and thus shipped back into the depths of history.

The offensive incrimination of the policy-makers is framed as an affect-dramaturgical station figuring the anger of the righteous, who experience their rise in the fact that they start from a singularity – from Scholz – and are taken up and shared by anonymous others.[108] If shame and its debilitating, individualizing tendency was still the affective mode of the first trial, here it has fled into a community: "Without any need for reflection, the individual in shame knows instantly and vividly that his or her integrity depends on being folded into membership in a transcending community."[109] The anger feeds on the transformation of diffuse accusations of guilt into a clear attribution of responsibility to privy council Mauch, as well as from the union of all present as being affected. Only the privy council's appearance concentrates the sentiments made up of indignation, desperation, and hope, the figuration of physical pain and commiseration of the individual characters: "The feeling of anger must have a personal object; there must be someone to be angry at. [...] While indignation can still be vague in the attribution of responsibility for the perceived injustice, in rage the opponent must already be identified."[110]

A central aspect of the final accusation is in part its rhetorical creation of a quasi tribal community at the level of language and imagery. For instance, the mass in front of the gate defends its *territory*, the factory, which has been

---

108 Cf. Demmerling, Landweer: *Philosophie der Gefühle*, 297.

109 Katz: *How Emotions Work*, 319.

110 Demmerling, Landweer: *Philosophie der Gefühle*, 305 [trans. DH].

utterly framed as a metaphor for Germany, for the fatherland. Over and over, Scholz's speech also appeals to family relations – "your husbands and sons" [trans. DH] – and the montage of close-ups and tight shots is less aimed at individuation than at the figuration of *similarity*, in which every face is only the expressive continuation of the other.[111]

In this operation, in which one fateful emanation of the process of history, that of fascism controlled by capital, is punished by another, the labor force, not only does the film construct an ending without a memory, but a temporal and historical deception. For the factory 'National Socialist Germany,' whose main products were war and genocide, is not destroyed from the outside by the Allied Powers. It destroys itself from the inside out, liberating itself when the truly guilty must now remain 'outside the gate.' The break with the past does not occur at the predetermined breaking point of the end of the war and liberation, it goes right through the postwar period, it is the break that then will be called the 'Cold War.'[112]

The knowledge of dependencies that led to evoking the guilty conscience over the course of the learning process is used here in order to make itself obsolete. "Cyclone for Auschwitz" and the camp documents are superseded by equating them with the factory explosion and thus with the German workers as victims of capital, by thus reducing them to "anti-Semitism as a special case of the anti-communist, anti-humanist nature of fascism."[113]

The feeling of responsibility that the film has arduously worked out is thus outright negated, disappearing in the blind spot of the peace front, or rather in the redefinition of responsibility, which no longer means that one has to answer to something, but is only aimed at "avoiding repeating past mistakes."[114]

---

111 Cf. J. Philippe Rushton: Genetic Similarity Theory, Ethnocentrism, and Group Selection. In: Irenäus Eibl-Eibesfeldt, Frank Kemp Salter (eds.): *Indoctrinability, Ideology, and Warfare*. New York / Oxford 1998, 369–388, here 371–372; cf. also Roger D. Masters: On the Evolution of Political Communities. The Paradox of Eastern and Western Europe in the 1980s. In: Irenäus Eibl-Eibesfeldt, Frank Kemp Salter (eds.): *Indoctrinability, Ideology, and Warfare*. New York / Oxford 1998, 453–478, here 457.

112 In a later interview, Maetzig claimed that the film was created parallel to the founding of the state, and 'only' took place in the period from 1944 to 1948, and that he could thus not be taking sides *for* the GDR and *against* the FRG. According to him the final montage is about an international peace movement, and not about taking a concrete position in the Cold War. Somewhat later in the same conversation, however, he says that for him the trial against the industry already marked the turning point to the Cold War and needed to be presented as such: Brady: *Discussion with Kurt Maetzig*, 78 and 87.

113 Agde: *Position und Leistung des Spielfilmregisseurs Kurt Maetzig*, 432 [trans. DH].

114 Agde: *Position und Leistung des Spielfilmregisseurs Kurt Maetzig*, 430 [trans. DH].

N2H4

So is the question of guilt 'resolved'? Did DER RAT DER GÖTTER separate the outrageous criminal guilt of the capitalists cleanly from the political guilt of everyone? Did it in fact encapsulate the question of moral and metaphysical guilt into pure individuals, rendering it socially irrelevant? There is an element of cinematic form that can be traced through the film and that causes me to doubt. The element is called 'hydrazine' – the colorless nitrogen compound N_2H_4, which stinks of ammonia and smokes on contact with air, the basis of the explosive agents and poison gasses that the narrative is about.

Why is this important? It gives us an idea of what is going on with the film's obsession with imaging its world and its characters smoking, steaming, and smoldering. Whether it is the small devices in the chemical laboratory, the large machines in the factory, the cigarette smoke in Mauch's salon, young Dieter's joke that transforms a glass of champagne into a small volcano at a private celebration or finally the columns of smoke in the background that visibly gush from the privy council's collar when he tries to restrain the outraged masses.

In the expulsion of the smoking devil by the cohesion of the masses as a peace front, the knowledge of dependencies is projected on the injured, diffuse feelings – on the loop of harassment and flight, on the infectious atmosphere of shame in the first trial – and claims a clear legibility of the same. What the film offers in terms of ideological identity, namely the class of workers and farmers, freed from any accusation, and the class-conscious intelligentsia, becomes – precisely *because* it *is* an offer of collective identity – thwarted by visible signs of an invisible force, a conflicting relation to the world, which is first realized in the spectator's perception.

The film permeates spectator perception with figurations that on the one hand cannot be understood, from today's viewpoint, as anything other than a metonymic relation to the smokestacks at the extermination camps. On the other hand they function on a more general level as the amalgamation of a series of oxymorons. The smoke is both an almost magical natural occurrence as well as a strictly technological-scientific phenomenon. It stands for a visibility of processes as well as for their obfuscation and concealment. It runs in precisely predetermined, sealed tracks and tubes, or can leak out at unpredictable spots. In other words: This smoke is the radical visualization of the interpenetration of knowing and not-knowing in a preconceived worldview of the cinema, in which guilt is shared by everyone.

In this respect, the ideological certainty turns out to be related to a collective emotionality in a double sense. A sense of belongingness arises through the affective reallocation of a collective emotionality in that this is related to a different 'we.' The 'we' of class struggle can only be conceived of as the reworking of a different, unspoken 'we,' as a reworking of the 'national community' ['*Volksgemeinschaft*'].

The 'national front of anti-fascism' is haunted by that feeling whose end it itself seeks to be. The guilty conscience of class consciousness is manifest in a dimension of collective emotionality. Before it can come to a matter of accusing the objectively guilty, one must go through one's own feelings of guilt and one's own shame in order to ascertain the non-guiltiness of one's own complicity: "A central cause of guilt feelings [...] is just the agent's need to reassure himself that he is *not* guilty. [...] The need to clear oneself of real or objective guilt can in this way generate guilt feelings."[115] What is expressed in the worker's dissociation from the 'council of the gods' – from those who do not or no longer belong to the 'we' – is the rejection of the collective sense of guilt, which one cannot shirk, which becomes all the more effective the more one seeks to reject accusations of guilt. While the reaction to the evoking of feelings of guilt ends narratively in an attempt at punishment, the failure of the first formal judgment in Nuremberg is expressed in an atmosphere of shame that in turn amounts to expelling the guilty from the community as not belonging to 'us,' therefore freeing oneself from liability.[116]

The motivating and plot-directing founding of the workers' front consists in avoiding a sense of guilt, in the attempt to get away from retrospection without having to apply oneself to recognizing or even restoring the integrity of the victims, without incorporating their perspectives or conceding the impossibility of such incorporation.[117]

In the film's affective dramaturgy the transformation of a sense of guilt into a sense of shame also entails a change in the concept of identity. On the one hand, in the transition from guilt to shame the belonging of the individual to a diffusely composed nation of perpetrators and tolerators is replaced by the stable, homogenized belonging to the purified class of workers.[118] On the other

---

115 Greenspan: *Practical Guilt*, 173.

116 Cf. Brian Lickel, Toni Schmader, Marchelle Barquissau: The Evocation of Moral Emotions in Intergroup Contexts. The Distinction Between Collective Guilt and Collective Shame. In: Nyla R. Branscombe, Bertjan Doosje (eds.): *Collective Guilt. International Perspectives*. Cambridge 2004, 35–55, here 47 and 50–51.

117 Cf. Sven Zebel, Bertjan Doosje, Russell Spears: It Depends on your Point-of-View. Implications of Perspective-Taking and National Identification for Dutch Collective Guilt. In: Nyla R. Branscombe, Bertjan Doosje (eds.): *Collective Guilt. International Perspectives*. Cambridge 2004, 148–168, here 155.

118 Cf. Lickel, Schmader, Barquissau: *The Evocation of Moral Emotions in Intergroup Contexts*, 44–47.

hand the way that belonging is understood and embodied at all undergoes a change. If a collective sense of guilt is based on perceiving social ties as the product of the interdependency of independent agents, so that violations to norms are always primarily conceived and sensed as violations of another person, in the sense of shame social ties are fundamental and essential for every individual, and the violation of norms is a violation of a diffuse, quasi natural order.[119] In this respect the replacement of feelings of guilt through the process of shame and anger is a political power shift, with which the need for conformity and order is clearly delineated as a basic affective structure of the emerging workers' and farmers' state. By converting a concept of social identity inherent to an affective attitude, DER RAT DER GÖTTER not only parallels the transformation of its protagonists from scientists to labor leaders. It generates "the formal anti-fascist unity of the new national people as a replacement for lost pan-German identity,"[120] as a replacement for the national community, which it itself claims not to exist, and which it indirectly confirms, precisely by giving it a new form.

2.3 Resolved Feelings

"We've got to take our responsibility somewhere,"[121] says one of the characters in Wolfgang Borchert's play *The Man Outside*. In the various attempts at resolving the question of guilt, both in philosophical and everyday political statements as well as in film and the other arts, this has always been one of the dominant basic motifs: After first sufficiently defining the differences and discussing guilt, then one no longer needs to judge oneself, no longer needs to experience this guilt affectively, no longer needs to ask about responsibility, but one can then charge the clearly guilty.

Writing about her visit to Germany five years after the end of the war, Hannah Arendt begins by depicting a general absence of feelings:

> But nowhere is this nightmare of destruction and horror less felt and less talked about than in Germany itself. A lack of response is evident everywhere, and it is difficult to say whether this signifies a half-conscious refusal to yield to grief or a genuine inability to feel. [...] This general lack of emotion, at any rate this apparent heartlessness, sometimes covered over

---

119 Cf. Landweer: *Scham und Macht*; cf. Ruth Benedict: *The Chrysanthemum and the Sword. Patterns of Japanese Culture* [1946]. London 1967; Greenspan: *Practical Guilt*, 134; and Jesse Prinz: *The Emotional Construction of Morals*. New York 2007, 307.
120 Brandlmeier: *Von Hitler zu Adenauer*, 45 [trans. DH].
121 Wolfgang Borchert: *The Man Outside* [1947], trans. David Porter. New York 1971, 103.

with cheap sentimentality, is only the most conspicuous outward symptom of a deep-rooted, stubborn, and at times vicious refusal to face and come to terms with what really happened.[122]

For Arendt the presumed resolution of feelings was not, for instance, a standard of individual collective 'healing,' but a way to purge the traces of crime and the destruction of the framework of moral value. For not every leaving-behind-oneself is desirable in terms of a politics of feeling: "to overcome bad feeling can also be to erase the signs of injustice."[123] Instead of overcoming feelings of guilt or shame, the only productive historical and political process would be that of integrating 'bad feelings' into the affective structure of the present and thus recognizing the experience of the victims.

The reasons that the contribution to German post-war cinema turned out to be rather disappointing for such a politics of guilty conscience are many and varied. There was simply no poetics, no modality of aesthetic experience that could be drawn upon in order to make this break in the historical identity of experience accessible. Instead, what coalesced was the flight into the privacy of impotence – "It is as though the Germans, denied the power to rule the world, had fallen in love with impotence as such"[124] – with a grammar of exculpation,[125] which alternated between various aesthetic and discursive registers. This grammar included, among other things, carefully avoiding thematizing anti-Semitism, thinking that all forms of suffering can be converted into one another, constantly and strictly distinguishing between "us" and "the Nazis," as if had been a matter of some odd form of invasion. Starting with the first German post-war film, DIE MÖRDER SIND UNTER UNS (THE MURDERERS ARE AMONG US, 1946, Wolfgang Staudte), on through films like IN JENEN TAGEN (SEVEN JOURNEYS, 1947, Helmut Käutner), EHE IM SCHATTEN (MARRIAGE IN THE SHADOWS, 1947, Kurt Maetzig),[126] one can find these evasive maneuvers almost everywhere.[127] Exceptions such as DER RUF (THE LAST ILLUSION, 1949, Josef von Báky) with Fritz Kortner or MORITURI (1948, Eugen York),[128] produced by Artur Brauner, only confirm the rule.

---

122 Arendt: *The Aftermath of Nazi Rule*, 342.

123 Sara Ahmed: *The Cultural Politics of Emotion*. New York 2004, 197.

124 Arendt: *The Aftermath of Nazi Rule*, 343.

125 Cf. Olick: *In the House of the Hangman*, 212.

126 Cf. Siegfried Kracauer: The Decent German. Film Portrait [1949]. In: Johannes von Moltke, Kristy Rawson (eds.): *Siegfried Kracauer's American Writings*. Berkeley / Los Angeles 2012, 157–161.

127 Cf. Shandley: *Rubble Films*, 181–192.

128 Cf. Groß: *Die Filme sind unter uns*, 375–381.

The problem that films like DER RAT DER GÖTTER cover up, elide, or in the best cases make palpable as their own misunderstanding is that 'one' is afflicted in such a way that is not resolved at the level of personal morality and accountability, that it is therefore not sufficient to verify the boundaries of personal culpability or to transfer personal-criminal guiltiness to others. The use of different affect rhetorics during the post-war period, from the accusations of collective guilt in the atrocity films and their fierce repudiation through the grammar of exculpation, to self-pity and genuine signs of the sense of guilt and the will to make amends, lay in treating the knowledge of the crimes as a specific kind of affective realization in the present.

If making amends – as motivation, temporal structure, and bodily experience – is the central criterion of the sense of guilt, then we can use German post-war cinema to study how a discourse of guilt and memory must fail if it does not manage to accept not only judging the guilt-inducing acts, but also and at the same time the responsibility for them.[129]

It is not a matter of forming an identity through guilt under the banner of fear and punishment, since this only results in rejection, the compulsion to justify, and thus the perpetuation of guilt as the negation of responsibility.[130] Rather, it is about getting to a feeling for a political community through the feelings of guilt, that is, by recognizing the experience of suffering and reinstating solidarity with the victims, which had been refused at the time, through the shared burden of responsibility. The fact that this did not occur, and what is more, that the surviving victims were the ones who suffered the most from feelings of guilt in the consequences of the totality of guilt organized by National Sociality Germany, that they and not the Germans were tormented by having betrayed solidarity with the dead "by not sharing or having shared the adversity,"[131] is "perhaps the greatest cynicism of history."[132]

---

129 Cf. Andreas Wildt: Die Moralspezifizität von Affekten und der Moralbegriff. In: Hinrich Fink-Eitel, Georg Lohmann (eds.): *Zur Philosophie der Gefühle*. Frankfurt a. M. 1993, 188–217, 210.

130 Cf. Claus H. Bachmann, Dietmar Kamper, Gerburg Treusch Dieter: Schuld und Geschichte – Aufs Spiel gesetzt. In: Gerburg Treusch-Dieter, Dietmar Kamper, Bernd Ternes (eds.): *Kursbuch 37. Schuld*. Tübingen 1999, 21–32, esp. 22, 27, and 30.

131 Wildt: *Die Moralspezifizität von Affekten und der Moralbegriff*, 214 [trans. DH].

132 Meschnig: *Totalität und Ende der Schuld*, 55 [trans. DH].

3 The Past: Hollywood Genre Poetics

If the convergence of political and historical processes and modalities of aesthetic experience forms the background to the issues raised in this work, then it might not at first seem an obvious move to turn to popular entertainment and genre cinema. But this step implies a theoretical understanding of genre cinema that will be presented and delved into in the following.[1] The goal is to work out how the experiential modalities of genre cinema are to be understood, namely, among other things, as a specific form and media practice in which a political community affectively relates back to itself. From this perspective, it should be plausible to determine how much this form of referral can take the shape of feelings of guilt.

Here I will be following the thesis that a particular way of thinking the political in genre cinema, one that positions every form of human community only in the concrete sensual dimension of a shared access to reality and a shared structure of recognizing self-articulation, is linked with a particular way of thinking about aesthetics, one that grounds the experience of art solely in a faculty of sensation equally accessible to all people. What Robert Burgoyne claims in relation to the history film in American cinema during the 1980s and 1990s can be extended to genre cinema in general. Behind every appearance, no matter how commercial and popular, there exists a dialogue between the new critical observation on the one hand and maintaining and passing down the central tropes of the political community on the other. This dialogue updates the fundamental breaks and power questions and articulates the basic fears, ambivalences, and hopes of this community.[2]

In order to work out the significance of genre poetics in a meaningful way, however, we must orient ourselves beyond the ideas of genre commonly found in many areas of film studies and everyday usage, which reduce genre to reproduced conventions and production cycles. As a starting point for this critique I will first turn to the theses of Stanley Cavell in order then to expand them to include an affect-poetic component on the basis of theories about melodrama.

---

1 The following theses and reflections are largely based on a collectively developed three-part lecture series, "Genre und Gemeinsinn," by Hermann Kappelhoff, Michael Lück and myself, held at the Free University in Berlin starting in the summer semester of 2013. Cf. Hermann Kappelhoff: *Front Lines of Community. Hollywood Between War and Democracy*. Berlin / Boston 2018.

2 Cf. Robert Burgoyne: *Film Nation. Hollywood Looks at U.S. History*. Minneapolis / London 1997, 1–15.

https://doi.org/10.1515/9783110612110-004

In *Pursuits of Happiness* Cavell explicitly rejects the idea of defining genres by specifying a large number of necessary or sufficient characteristics. A genre is not an object with characteristics that can be held up to a film as another object with characteristics like a stencil, comparing them and determining whether they match or not. What he suggests instead does not at first sound so very different from this:

> The idea is that the members of a genre share the inheritance of certain conditions, procedures and subjects and goals of composition, and that in primary art each member of such a genre represents a study of these conditions, something I think of as bearing the responsibility of the inheritance.[3]

In this sentence, however, there are two decisive aspects that I can only go into briefly here. At first Cavell makes clear that the relation of a genre film to the genre contains an *inherent* historicity. And it introduces an important shift: that the operations and themes that genre films share are not something that they simply 'have,' but that the films of a genre turn these operations and themes into their object. They are studies of their own conditions.

In Cavell genre refers to a process made up of movements of compensating for and negating such conditions, in which every film, every 'member' works on the conditions of the genre, adds new operations, or replaces and 'argues' that it partakes in this legacy despite or because of this. The films of a genre are not similar to one another because they refer to the same ideal model, but because they relate to one another. "I would mean not only that they look like on another or that one gets similar impressions from them; I would mean that they *are what they are* in view of one another."[4]

This belonging to one another is – and in this respect strictly connected with the judgment of taste according to Kant – governed by no concept and no law. There is no sum of characteristics, no grammar[5] that defines when which films can be counted as related, counted as a genre, except for the way that the films mutually put each other in perspective, expose each other to judgment, set an example: "a movie comes from other movies."[6] To be a genre film means

---

3 Stanley Cavell: *Pursuits of Happiness. The Hollywood Comedy of Remarriage*. Cambridge 1981, 28.

4 Cavell: *Pursuits of Happiness*, 29.

5 Cf. Stanley Cavell: The Politics of Interpretation (Politics as opposed to what?) In: id.: *Themes out of School. Effects and Causes*. Chicago 1984, 27–59, here 45: "The moral of ordinary language philosophy, and of the practice of art, is that grammar cannot dictate what you mean, what is up to you to say."

6 Cavell: *The World Viewed*, 7.

to be a film about the conditions of belonging to a genre. Every film reinvents the genre that it is part of.

Starting from this understanding, I will argue in the following that it is this process of mutual referential studies of their own conditions that makes it possible to grasp how genre films are constructed, converting subjective, private experiences into public ones,[7] and joining individually embodied experience with shared fantasies: "Showing us our fantasies, they express the inner agenda of a nation that conceives Utopian longings and commitments for itself."[8]

The degree to which it is also, and precisely, about failing in these utopias and self-commitments over and over again will be examined here in view of the sense of guilt, and by looking at one of the central genres of Hollywood cinema: the western. This genre is marked by the fact that it starts from a specific crisis situation of a community, then looking both inward and outward.[9] Beforehand, however, and based on this theoretical framing, I will have to sketch out genre cinema more thoroughly as a practice structured by different modes of aesthetic experience, one whose conditions can be defined largely by means of the shaping of affects and feelings.

3.1 Genre Poetics as Modalities of Aesthetic Experience

The thinking about the poetics of genre has its starting point with Aristotle, who understands poetics as the creation of social learning processes that comprehend the possibilities of being human in a variety of ways, and that is closely associated with a politics of feelings. With the term catharsis he introduces one of the most productive mysteries in the history of thinking about the arts. This term refers, independent of any concrete interpretation, to the central role of affect modulation for the various genres.[10]

Even though this is not the place to trace the systematic and historical lines of the *Poetics* through to the present, the reference here is particularly relevant because the common positions on film and genre tend to be determined by the interpretation of the *Poetics* based on the rules-based poetics of Horace and

---

7 A process that Cavell, following Emerson, calls "thinking." Cf. Stanley Cavell: *Cities of Words. Pedagogical Letters on a Register of the Moral Life.* Cambridge / London 2004, 29.

8 Cavell: *Pursuits of Happiness*, 18.

9 Cf. Burgoyne: *Film Nation*, 8.

10 Cf. Aristotle: *Poetics*, trans. George Whalley. Montreal 1997, 69; cf. Theo Girshausen: Katharsis. In: Erika Fischer-Lichte, Doris Kolesch, Matthias Warstat (eds.): *Metzler Lexikon Theatertheorie.* Stuttgart 2005, 163–170.

French Classicism.[11] The idea formulated there is that genres are separate entities that can be distinguished in a given order through fixed rules for the correspondences between aesthetic forms and the contents they represent.[12] This idea of a systematic and historically given order of genres and their strict maintenance is postulated as necessary for the cultural validity in each case and thus as fundamental for the poetics of rules in the early modern era and for their provisions how best to create works. It is in fact still in effect when the genres of Hollywood cinema are described as rules of mutually determining the contents of representation and of media forms and operations.[13] The concrete way that these rules are formulated in theories, however, no longer follows the concept of an ideal form, but an idea of prototypes and above all an idea of code agreement in the form of conventions.[14]

By such conventions, which are meant to regulate the relationship of a film to a genre, we then understand more or less simple lists of groups of characteristics, such as iconographies, stereotypical characters, and plot elements. These groups of characteristics are ultimately understood as the framing conditions for producing and understanding narratives. Here as well, however, there was a shift between classic rule-based poetics and the genre theory of popular cinema, for the applicability of the rule is no longer derived from the true and the beautiful, but 'only' means the psychologically efficient or commercially successful – in the ideal case each being identical with the other. Conventionality, according to the conviction that this all rests on, allows the film to convey narrative information quickly and unproblematically. This facilitation of cognitive understanding serves to satisfy basic universal needs and thus commercial success.[15] Here we see an aspect with which we can position the research approaches to genre as

---

11 Cf. Rick Altman: *Film / Genre*. London 1999, 1–12.

12 Cf. Horace: *Horace on Poetry. The 'Ars Poetica,'* ed. C. O. Brink. Cambridge 1971.

13 For a general overview that marks out the appropriate appreciation of the problems, I refer to the works of Rick Altman and Steve Neale; cf. Altman: *Film / Genre* and Steve Neale: *Genre and Hollywood*. New York 2000.

14 Cf. Thomas Sobchack: Genre Film. A Classical Experience [1975]. In: Barry K. Grant (ed.): *Film Genre Reader IV*. Austin 2012, 121–132, here 121. Other representatives of canonical positions on film genre as conventions are Andrew Tudor: Genre [1973]. In: Barry K. Grant (ed.): *Film Genre Reader IV*. Austin 2012, 3–11; cf. Edward Buscombe: The Idea of Genre in the American Cinema. In: Barry K. Grant (ed.): *Film Genre Reader IV*. Austin 2012, 12–26; cf. Noël Carroll: Film, Emotion, and Genre. In: Carl Plantinga, Greg M. Smith (eds.): *Passionate Views. Film, Cognition, and Emotion*. Baltimore 1999, 21–47.

15 Cf. Carroll: *Film, Emotion, and Genre*, 125. As an extreme example from the area of film theory based on evolutionary psychology, cf. Torben Grodal: *Embodied Visions. Evolution, Emotion, Culture and Film*. Oxford 2009.

a category of production economy in line with such taxonomic approaches. Both view genres (the one implicitly, the other explicitly) from a vantage point of economiziation, and always answer film analytical or cultural historical questions with variations on the relation between investment and return.

In this scenario, what falls short is above all the underlying understanding of genre as regulated by conventions. First, the term convention itself, in its usage in the social sciences, is unsuitable, since it is linked with a concept of the permitted and the forbidden, and presumes criteria for success or failure. That is to say: it imprints normative demands onto the poetic process.

Second, this approach entails a problematic concept of history. It constructs a transhistorical, timeless being,[16] and by setting up a primal form it forces any continuation to choose between conforming to it or of being a baroque appearance of decay. The fact that genre poetics never stops changing with every film thus becomes incomprehensible, giving rise to a history of genre without history.[17]

Third, and finally, thinking in conventions and rules leads, from a completely pragmatic point of view, to questions that are unsuited to describing the specific form of repetition of aesthetic structures that are meant with genres.[18] If we assume that a set of rules exists, a list of characteristics that determine whether films belong to a genre, we find ourselves at an impasse:

> They are defining a western on the basis of analyzing a body of films that cannot possibly be said to be westerns until after the analysis. [...] We are caught in a circle that first requires that the films be isolated, for which purpose a criterion is necessary, but the criterion is, in turn, meant to emerge from the empirically established common characteristics of the films.[19]

Behind these practical and ideological problems of thinking about conventions and corpora in current approaches to genre lies a terminological problem of understanding genres as objects with characteristics that are subject to rules according to which films would be produced and categorized as objects with corresponding characteristics. The taxonomical approach cannot work per se,

---

16 Very explicitly in Sobchack: *Genre Film. A Classical Experience*, 121–122.

17 Cf. Altman: *Film / Genre*, 19–22.

18 Cf. Altman: *Film / Genre*, 16–17.

19 Tudor: *Genre*, 5. The often proposed way out of this dilemma is not helpful, for either one constructs a cultural consensus (Tudor: *Genre*, 7: "Genre is what we collectively believe it to be.") or an awareness of genre (cf. Jörg Schweinitz: Genre und lebendiges Genrebewußtsein. In: *montage AV* (1994), Vol. 3, No. 2, 99–118) as an analytically impenetrable *black box*, which assimilates all theoretical and analytical problems, or one falls back on a simple examination of institutionalized discourses in industry and criticism (cf. Neale: *Genre and Hollywood*, 39–43).

because it has no standard on which to base what distinction makes a difference, what can be a genre characteristic in the first place, and whether a characteristic is necessary or sufficient in order to classify a film in this way or that.

This is not only a problem in historical theories. In current publications on film genres as well, a kind of two-world theory is dominant – despite any lip service paid to dealing with dynamics and open processes: here the world of ideas, classes, and terms, there the world of appearances. And in between the circular problem of inclusion and exclusion, of taxonomy and how to form a corpus.

At this point the main concern is to describe genre cinema at the level of the immanence of the dynamic of expressive audiovisual forms and as a system of recombining and interweaving such dynamics, and not as categorizing on the basis of rules and conventions. It should thus become possible to understand it as a form of cultural communication and generating meaning, which operates by shaping bodily sensations, by modulating the state of feelings. For this reason I am referring to the relevant works on the melodramatic mode by Peter Brooks, Christine Gledhill, and Hermann Kappelhoff, with whose help melodrama's cultural mode of disclosing the world is to be understood as a fundamental way that genre cinema works.

Following Gledhill I understand "the concept of modality as the sustaining medium in which the genre system operates."[20] Melodrama as a mode is thus not identical with the *women's film* or the *family melodrama*, but it is the form of meaning-making that lies at the basis of these and other genres, a "mode of conception and expression, as a certain system for making sense of experience, as a semantic field of force"[21] or in other words a "culturally conditioned mode of perception and aesthetic articulation."[22]

In the following I will briefly present an understanding of the melodramatic mode, showing how it can be distinguished in the individual modalities of genre in which the different forms of social experiences and conflicts are organized "in visceral, affective and morally explanatory terms."[23] For a more narrow description of the melodramatic mode we can initially start from Brooks's definition as the "mode of excess": "the postulation of a signified in excess of

---

20 Christine Gledhill: Rethinking Genre. In: Christine Gledhill, Linda Williams (eds.): *Reinventing Film Studies*. London 2000, 221–243, here 227.

21 Peter Brooks: *The Melodramatic Imagination. Balzac, Henry James, Melodrama, and the Mode of Excess* [1976]. New Haven / London 1995, xvii.

22 Gledhill: *Rethinking Genre*, 227.

23 Gledhill: *Rethinking Genre*, 229.

the possibilities of the signifier, which in turn produces an excessive signifier making large but unsubstantiable claims on meaning."[24]

The melodramatic narrative is not content to describe the banal surfaces of reality and to chronicle things as they are, reproducing what happens, what is said, and what kind of gestures are made. Things, speech acts, and gestures are 'put under pressure' to divulge an unrestricted and indefinite, emotional, moral meaning.[25] While Brooks initially presents this in relation to the novel as a successive dramatization of the reading process, it is in relation to the stage melodrama and to audiovisual forms that this form can be understood as a dramatization of the embodied process of perception in the time of its unfolding.[26] The spectator experiences the world as an affective process in which the surfaces of ordinary reality reveal themselves to be articulations of a dimension saturated by ethical forces.

Appearances are transformed in spectacular interactions and relationships between characters and objects. It is not so much the 'depth' of the meanings that plays a role here than the fact that the spectator qua spectacle and affective involvement comes into immediate contact with a world of moral conflicts.[27]

The term "moral occult,"[28] which Brooks introduces for this, is not unproblematic, since it initially implies a mere appearance of decay in the sacred order. But strictly speaking it means nothing more and nothing less than the drama of occultizing, that is, the concealment of the moral as something non-sensual in sensual reality. That is to say, it means the precarious perceptibility of the good and the bad. In this sense the melodramatic mode can be taken as a cultural practice that works on a fundamental problem of ordinary experience. Namely the question of how to recognize the claim to morality and articulate moral problems. How to identify ethical imperatives? And the answer to this mode of experience is: by directly linking morality and feeling, by affectively assessing social and moral conflicts, and, in the process of unfolding the conflicts, of evoking feelings of compassion and admiration, of anger, of disgust, and of outrage or of shame and guilt. It is not at all about a moral dilemma as a thought experiment,

---

24 Brooks: *The Melodramatic Imagination*, 199.

25 Cf. Brooks: *The Melodramatic Imagination*, 1.

26 Cf. Hermann Kappelhoff: Artificial emotions. Melodramatic practices of shared interiority. In: Rüdiger Campe, Julia Weber (eds.): *Rethinking Emotion. Interiority and Exteriority in Premodern, Modern, and Contemporary Thought*. Berlin / Boston, 2014, 264–288.

27 Cf. Brooks: *The Melodramatic Imagination*; cf. Gledhill: *Rethinking Genre*, 232–234 and Augustin Zarzosa: Melodrama and the Modes of the World. In: *Discourse* (2010), Vol. 32, No. 2, 236–255, here 239.

28 Brooks: *The Melodramatic Imagination*, 5.

but about morality's difficulty to make itself recognizable, of showing the good, innocent, and virtuous: "making the world morally legible."[29]

A central indicator of the visibility of virtue is the capacity to suffer by the individual, physical body, which is enduring mental pain. The melodramatic mode interrogates structures of being together, forms of the social in the sign of its radical contingency toward whether and how they cause suffering: "The realm of melodrama is not a world inhabited by things whose essence threatens to escape us; it is a world in which ideas inflict suffering."[30] On the one hand this names the melodramatic mode as a general constant under the strategies of dramatizing experience, and on the other it points to the historical emergence of a particular form in which the melodrama appears as a dominant form in cultural meaning-making, with which the culture of western modernity shows itself to be a perception of the world that can no longer derive the ethical and moral imperative from anything other than from this suffering:

> The origins of melodrama can be accurately located within the context of the French Revolution and its aftermath. This is the epistemological moment which it illustrates and to which it contributes [...]. It comes into being in a world where the traditional imperatives of truth and ethics have been violently thrown into question, yet where the promulgation of truth and ethics, their instauration as a way of life, is of immediate, daily, political concern.[31]

The melodramatic mode itself, or the appearance of certain melodramatic forms, can therefore be seen as a historical event.[32] For what distinguishes it and other modes is the potential to form specific modalities of aesthetic experience and intersections of poetics in historical constellations, while at the same time making these historical constellations mutually referential in their differences and repetitions.

This is why the feelings in the melodramatic genre are not the feelings of individual psychology, but artificial, aesthetic feelings as historically emergent relations to the world and forms of meaning-making, which would not exist at all in their specific historical constellations without concrete forms and aesthetic operations. Without the sentimental novel, without the Gothic novel, without the family melodrama and action movies, what we get in these complex process forms of feelings would simply not exist.

---

29 Brooks: *The Melodramatic Imagination*, 42.
30 Zarzosa: *Melodrama and the Modes of the World*, 242–243.
31 Brooks: *The Melodramatic Imagination*, 14–15.
32 Cf. Stanley Cavell: *Contesting Tears. The Hollywood Melodrama of the Unknown Woman.* Chicago 1996, 42.

Independent of questions of concrete, individual content, the melodramatic mode is a way of experiencing for which we can claim a primacy of the shaping of affective sensation by dynamic rhythm and surface structures. These appeal to the spectator to realize moral entities and social ideas in his or her own body as affective supports – they are thus radically secular, historical, and gendered, creating specific socio-historical showcases for examining the human capacity to suffer.[33] According to Gledhill there can be no singular genre of "melodrama" because this mode per se blurs boundaries, thus incorporating other modes and registers of cultural production. The realization of social and moral fields of conflict as affective supports then also designates the level at which the differentiations and connections of individual genres can be described as complex ramifications of the melodramatic mode: "Thus action and sentiment, pathos and spectacle, presumed today to appeal to differently gendered audiences, are drawn into a composite aesthetic and dramatic modality, capable of different emphases and generic offshoots."[34]

The distinction between individual genres therefore does not run between different iconographies, stereotypes, and corpora, but between different visual forms and temporal structures.[35] In this sense not only are genre modalities of the melodramatic mode "different versions of reality,"[36] but so are the other modes of aesthetic experience, in particular the comic or the tragic mode. These different versions of reality are distinguished by other structures and effects in each case, and thus stand in a diachronous as well as a synchronous relationship to one another.

Genres are different forms of generating perceiving, feeling, and thinking in physical-material processes, and are thus shaping ordinary, historical, social, political, gendered, etc. relationships and conflicts. They do this by creating various complex structures of space and time, which should be understood as modulations and dramatizations of the reception process. And these perceptive structures of "narrative and physical rhythms"[37] designate the level at which something like genre hybridizing can grasped as a meaningful concept

---

33 Cf. Gledhill: *Rethinking Genre*, 228–234. For Gledhill it is also decisive at this point that the class-specific forms of proletariat and bourgeois entertainment were brought together in the nineteenth century, giving rise to something like a modern mass public.

34 Gledhill: *Rethinking Genre*, 230.

35 An exemplary attempt to systematize such a form of distinction is Linda Williams's term *body genres*; cf. Linda Williams: Film Bodies. Gender, Genre, and Excess [1991]. In: Barry K. Grant (ed.): *Film Genre Reader IV*. Austin 2012, 159–177.

36 Brooks: *The Melodramatic Imagination*, 203.

37 Cavell: *The World Viewed*, 31.

in the first place, both in terms of film analysis and of cultural studies, for ultimately no genre film is restricted to a single mode of expression, but always already shapes its affect dramaturgy through the interaction of different modes and affect dynamics, therefore constructing alignments in the historical space of the poetics of genre.[38]

3.2 Genre Poetics and the Sense of Guilt

What connections exist then between the affective dynamics, the temporal structures of individual genre modalities of the melodramatic mode, and the sense of guilt as a particular temporal shape and physical dynamics? My thesis in this work is that feelings of guilt play a possible but not necessarily constitutive role for the conditions of all genres, but represent an affective modality of the studies of these conditions. In other words: they are part of the affective poetics of a film, where the process of compensating and negating the "procedures and subjects and goals of composition"[39] takes place in the form of a morally evaluative revision.

The experiences of suffering that are staged in the melodramatic mode do not merely signify the collisions of interest and problems found in a given society, but are constitutive as moral conflicts and above all as political ones. They directly concern questions of the use of violence in the emergence and preservation of the society, of the intimate connection between terror and civilization, of the fragility of civil orders and the threat to them by internal power conflicts and violence, they concern the endless processes of inclusions and exclusions, of having and not-having, of duties and desires. The affective dynamics of such fundamental conflicts are relevant wherever there is no possibility to resolve them by appealing to a higher level, and wherever it is in fact no longer about solutions for practical conflicts, but about the protesting experience of suffering as the sole possible but always only temporary proof of a moral and ethical imperative.

Such an affective-political conception of the circumstances of genre poetics and the established social breaking points decidedly positions itself outside a tradition that judges according to a dichotomy of 'ritual' and 'ideological'

---

38 Cf. Matthias Grotkopp, Hermann Kappelhoff: Film Genre and Modality. The Incestuous Nature of Genre Exemplified by the War Film. In: Sébastien Lefait, Philippe Ortoli (eds.): *In Praise of Cinematic Bastardy*. Newcastle upon Tyne 2012, 29–39.
39 Cavell: *Pursuits of Happiness*, 28.

functioning.[40] My intention at this point is not to explain whether the dramatizing and moralizing of 'social contradictions' in genre cinema manipulatively exploits the real needs of spectators and impedes them from dealing with the problems in real life, and that the films would thus act in the interests of those who profit from these contradictions.[41] But it is also not my intention here to celebrate genre films naively as the free and fantasy-laden self-expression of a culture in which the audience sees its ideas and values reflected.[42]

The conflicts, contradictions, and problems that are reflected here do not get resolved in one or the other direction, but become available in each case as unresolved and constitutive for any political community. In this sense expressive modes and genre modalities are the register in which the community relates to itself: "society talking to itself."[43] The fact that the conditions and expressive modes can be viewed at a more fundamental level, as the given social conflicts, can in part be substantiated by the specific creation of historicity and legacy. The genre structures that generate meaning are always already repetitions and temporary re-constructions, which behave toward one another in the larger coherence of the genre system. They construct historicity in a way that they, as current views of the world, always also refer to other views in a continuing process of compensation and negation of expressive forms, thus creating the alignments of a shared history. And this history, which is ultimately my thesis, can in part be seen as a feeling that makes it possible to experience the bond to the contexts of violence and conflicts, the unfulfilled hopes and promises that gave rise to a political community, and which characterize them both outwardly and inwardly, to experience them as a sense of guilt: "Even within the area of mass culture, there always exists a current of opposition, seeking to express by whatever means are available to it that sense of desperation and inevitable failure which optimism itself helps to create."[44]

Genres have become crystallized in their historical becoming as the various forms in which films refer to one another as aesthetic forms. They propose the

---

40 Cf. Altman: *Film / Genre*, 26–28 and Neale: *Genre and Hollywood*, 220–230.

41 For an extreme variation, cf. Judith Hess-Wright: Genre Films and the Status Quo [1974]. In: Barry K. Grant (ed.): *Film Genre Reader IV*. Austin 2012, 60–68.

42 For example, cf. John G. Cawelti: *Adventure, Mystery, and Romance. Formula Stories as Art and Popular Culture*. Chicago 1976.

43 Gledhill: *Rethinking Genre*, 238. According to Gledhill modes articulate social questions as aesthetic ones and the other way around, conducting a continuous exchange between cultural conflicts and fictional worlds.

44 Robert Warshow: The Gangster as Tragic Hero [1948]. In: *The Immediate Experience. Movies, Comics, Theatre and other Aspects of Popular Culture*. Cambridge / London 2001, 97–103, here 98–99.

world of perceptions in a historically situated community in such a way that it becomes visible to itself. They constitute a complex process of forming, consolidating, and expanding feelings of belonging, which can in no way be referred back to any absolute concept or absolute origin. In Rorty's sense[45] this process can only be understood as the radical contingency of any political community, and is never realized except in the shaping of individual experiences in historical developed, changeable presents.

The way that society speaks to itself in genre is by modulating a holistic feeling for the shared relation to the self and to the world. That is, genre modalities are part of a historically contingent political reality, whose internal and external contexts of violence they articulate, thus formulating the possibility for other forms of living together. By referring to and recombining expressive modalities, genres help to bring forth a social cohesion as mode of experience: be it the gangster film as the revision of the pursuit of happiness under the sign of urbanity,[46] be it the science fiction film as a technical-historical transfer of the certainty of individual mortality to the human species,[47] or be it the experience of the historicity of gender relations in family melodramas and in the *comedy of remarriage*.[48]

From this viewpoint, the sense of guilt would not be a supplement to be added to the existing register of feelings in a genre, but the affective effect of a new perspective, of a new feeling. It is the common past, present, and future materialized in the expressive forms that are *now* sensed as laden with guilt. It is the feelings of belonging, shared by the individual spectators, that is *now* modulated as a guilty conscience. Genre poetics makes it possible to grasp just such changes in affective relations as shifts and continuities in experiential modes of the community. This relation certainly becomes particularly clear in two genres, the western and the war film, where "the relation of the individual to the political community is grounded in a mythologizing recourse to historical events, to the talk of the birth and rebirth of the nation by overcoming injustice, violence, and the terror of war."[49]

The melodramatic forms of staging the western starting in the 1960s, which will be at issue in the following discussion of LITTLE BIG MAN, can be understood in this sense as redistributions of affective and moral attitudes in view of the

---

45 Cf. Richard Rorty: *Contingency, Irony, and Solidarity*. Cambridge 1998.
46 Cf. Warshow: *The Gangster as Tragic Hero*.
47 Cf. Susan Sontag: The Imagination of Disaster [1965]. In: id.: *Against Interpretation and Other Essays*. New York 1966, 209–225.
48 Cf. Cavell: *Pursuits of Happiness* and Cavell: *Contesting Tears*.
49 Kappelhoff: *Front Lines of Community*, 125.

social upheavals in the USA at the time, and as new perspectives on the sense of history in view of the experiences of the Vietnam War. The violence of processes of exclusion and cruelty toward the others in one's own past – not only as a historical fact, but as a law of motion of the community's imagination in genre poetics, which is why LITTLE BIG MAN leaves the Vietnam War as a reference far behind itself – is transposed as a feeling of guilt into a feeling of new solidarity or new moral identity. Old concepts and expressive forms of history and nation are staged in such a way that they are experienced, and thus discarded, as causing suffering and in contradiction to the community's self-image. Following Robert Burgoyne, we can describe such a redistribution of moral identity in the register of the sense of guilt as an experience of internal non-identity, that is, of an identity that is neither generated from any abstract idea nor from any ethnic origin, but from the frictional energy of inclusive and exclusive relations and the feelings that emerge from them:

> Social identity, as conceived in these films, originates neither from "above," in alignment with the nation-state, nor from below, with ethnicity or race, but rather from "across," through horizontal relations whose antagonistic and transitive character is best represented in terms of "inside" and "outside." [...] identity is constructed in relations of opposition and, occasionally, imitation "from across."[50]

Bringing in an 'outside' by realizing a guilty conscience and the failure of solidarity associated with it is both a critique and a reinvigoration of a promise to just this solidarity of a political community. Precisely such feelings of guilt and the internal non-identity thus refer to the degree to which history and the community have been emancipated from metaphysical or totalitarian contexts, and are generated over and over again, now qua genre poetics as experience.

The feelings of guilt, shame, and rage, as well as those of pride and admiration in the expressive modalities of genre, designate those breaks and lines of conflict that arise when the community perceives itself as changing, and change the register of perception, of feelings, and of expressivity themselves, becoming the object of modulation through aesthetic processes. It is therefore not only an altered description (Rorty) or an altered narrative (Burgoyne) that arises when, during the decisive moments and refigurations of history, the boundary zones are shifted into the center of the community,[51] but in fact an altered network of the modes of experience and feelings for the shared world.

For this reason, it is not solely a matter of the sense of guilt for this of that historical event during the settling of the West or in the wars of the American

---

50 Burgoyne: *Film Nation*, 3.
51 Cf. Burgoyne: *Film Nation*, 12.

nation. Rather, these are the reference points, the source for an altered feeling for the community, a feeling for the history of a lost innocence. What needs to be demonstrated in the following is how films relate to shifts in the community's affect economy by reconfiguring genre poetics, and shape these shifts as forms of aesthetic experience. I will need to analyze the poetic calculation that aims, in the altered relation, at a shared past and simultaneously at an altered mode of political legitimation in the present:

> Political legitimation depends just as much on collective memory as it ever has, but this collective memory is now often one disgusted with itself, a matter of "learning the lessons" of history more than of fulfilling its promise or remaining faithful to its legacy.[52]

3.3 Little Big Man: The Dysfunctionality of the Western

Like few other genres in Hollywood cinema, the western is associated with a particular idea of 'promise.' It consists in the simple formulation that one can identify with the landscape, with the wilderness, infusing them with a dynamic frontier of cultivation and the creation of order. The classical western story, but not the history that it seeks to originate, ends before this process will have destroyed the wilderness as a promise of freedom and an object of desire. One characteristic of this dynamic movement is the claim of the necessity of violence at the moment of founding the order, and at the same time the necessity of masking or justifying the role of violence.[53]

The relationship of necessary violence to necessary masking of violence is valid both for the internal as well as for the external relations of white society. Inwardly, the dilemma of the revolver hero in SHANE (1953, George Stevens) or THE MAN WHO SHOT LIBERTY VALENCE (1962, John Ford) consists in the fact that the use of open physical violence can indeed suspend the natural law of the strongest, but does not create the peace of a community:

> Power may prevent chaos, but it is impotent to establish the order of community; powerlessness may attract destruction, but accepting the limitation of one's individual power can attract higher power to one's aid. And a stern moral is drawn: justice, to be

---

52 Olick: *The Politics of Regret*, 122.

53 Cf. Stanley Cavell: The Incessance and the Absence of the Political. In: Andrew Norris (ed.): *The Claim to Community. Essays on Stanley Cavell and Political Philosophy*. Stanford 2006, 263–317, here 310; cf. John G. Cawelti: *The Six Gun Mystique*. Bowling Green 1971, 14 and Richard Slotkin: *Gunfighter Nation. The Myth of the Frontier in Twentieth-Century America*. New York 1992, and passim.

done, must be seen to be done; but justice, to be established, must not be seen to be established.[54]

Outwardly, in turn, the myth of "regeneration through violence"[55] overwrites the process of displacing the others, that is, the indigenous population, as a side effect of the unavoidable movement dynamic and permanent transformation that means 'America.' As such the western is

> the elaboration of the communal fantasy of the bringing of law to a land, having to serve at the same time as the veiling of the fact that the land was not previously void of human order, but that the new bringers or supplicants of law have voided that order.[56]

What is central for the affective dynamics of the western genre is ultimately the fundamental transitoriness as one of its conditions, as is embodied and studied in one of the most famous examples in the structural element of the stagecoach. The community of passengers in STAGECOACH (1939, John Ford) is constituted in the movement and the spatial restriction in contrast to the breadth of the landscape, always dissipating, immediately becoming stratified whenever the coach arrives and stops somewhere.[57] The starting and ending points of the journey are identical, what counts is merely the possibility of being able to set off again.

The affective registers of the genre feed on such moments of the interim, of contingent loyalties, of feelings of friendship and commitment, as well as of the melodramatic experiences of suffering and sensations of justice and injustice. Added to this come the registers of staging violence, which encompasses on the one hand horror and powerlessness – the pathos of the weaker – and on the other thrill and action. With these dynamics and patterns the western shapes an affective image of history – not as a glorifying and falsifying narrative of a common past, but as a concept of those forces, temporalities, and processual forms that produce history and identity in the first place.

At first glance the frontier, as the dominant interpretive scheme of an implicit "theory of cause-and-effect and therefore a theory of history,"[58] seems to be self-coherent and clear in its ideological function. In Richard Slotkin's formulation it describes a process of becoming history through external, physical expansion on the basis of a temporary separation followed by a regeneration: "The Myth represented the redemption of American spirit or fortune as something to

---

54 Cavell: *The World Viewed*, 58.

55 Slotkin: *Gunfighter Nation*, 10–12.

56 Cavell: *The Incessance and the Absence of the Political*, 310.

57 Cf. Slotkin: *Gunfighter Nation*, 309–311.

58 Slotkin: *Gunfighter Nation*, 6.

be achieved by playing through a scenario of separation, temporary regression to a more primitive or 'natural' state and *regeneration through violence.*"[59]

The decisive point is that the lines of conflict and breaking points of this myth are not resolved completely harmoniously, so that it is multiform in itself and in constant revision. The reason for this is above all that the interplay between a fundamental transitivity and a concept "of a world divided by significant and signifying borders"[60] necessarily leads to a permanent ambivalence between contradictory attributions and movement dynamics, which at the same time always assert the dream of a break with the past *and* the expansive continuity of the civilization.[61] These demarcations and the acts of violence and states of violence that they are based on become available on the one hand for a multitude of mechanisms of inclusion and exclusion – wilderness and civilization, east and west, monopolistic big business and progressive-democratic small-time settlers and small-scale entrepreneurs, city and country, cultures of violence and Christian charity, etc.[62] On the other hand these mechanisms are not at all homogenous, but time and again come into conflict with one another, thus making the fundamental operations of violent demarcations and trespassings and the suffering and guilt created by them visible. The problem of violence as the catalyst for a (re-)creation of the community is that of all catalysts. They are simply not used up in the reactions that they cause.

The internal polymorphism of the frontier myth can be seen, for instance, in John G. Cawelti, who shows that the different traditions of the west are in conflict with one another and thus provide the material for melodramatic conflicts and redistribution of values.[63] At the same time they are mutually complementary justificatory schemes for the exploitation, dispossession, and eradication of the original inhabitants of North America. This violent expulsion only represents one facet on which I would like to concentrate in particular in the following, since it represents the most striking and most fundamental form of violent inclusions and exclusions in the western genre: the relationship of the frontier to the Native Americans. I should clarify from the beginning that this will at no point be about the representation or misrepresentation of the Native Americans in the Indians of

---

59 Slotkin: *Gunfighter Nation*, 12.

60 Slotkin: *Gunfighter Nation*, 351.

61 Cf. John G. Cawelti: The Frontier and the Native American. In: Joshua C. Taylor: *America as Art*. Washington D. C. 1976, 135–183, here 141.

62 Cf. Slotkin: *Gunfighter Nation*, 351.

63 Cf. Cawelti: *The Frontier and the Native American.*

the western genre.[64] Even if it is legitimate to formulate an appropriate and objective representation as a desirable, moral, and aesthetic standard, it is also evident that the study of the western "will reveal little about Native American people of the past or present, but a lot about the evolution of white American attitudes and values."[65]

In its basic myths the west is always simultaneously the place where the civilization of the east coast does not quite reach yet but will be established, and the place where a quite different, religiously renewed form of community is introduced. While for the one the original inhabitants are only a bother and an obstacle to progress, to the other they are both a fascinating and threatening counterpart. For the individual, however, the west is also the possibility of completely realizing oneself anew in relation to society – be it through a new relationship to nature, be it through the promise of sudden immeasurable wealth.

For the frontier as a site of self-invention, the Indian is not only a "positive symbol for whatever natural virtues were being projected onto the frontier,"[66] but at the same time is equipped with a higher insight, which also contains an insight into the inevitability of his own disappearance. At the same time, his violent expulsion can be reduced to a mere attendant phenomenon, which can always be blamed on the few who pursue the wish for fortune too ruthlessly and greedily. As the victim of the few and the guardian of lost treasures, then, he acquires public sympathy for himself because he allows the white society to forget the actual bloody conflicts and the continuing injustice and instead to nostalgically enjoy mourning the irrecoverable glory and magic of the Vanishing American.

It is significant that these schemes of justification for repression and elimination can – at least potentially – thwart one another, and the individual forms of the frontier myth shape inner ambivalences and moral conflicts as the fundamental crisis formation of a community. This takes place in particular wherever the process of an identity "from across" (Burgoyne) becomes visible, and, through processes of disturbance and of affective shifting, a fundamental ambivalence of violence and guilt is inscribed in this.

---

64 I decided to use to the term "Indians" rather than "Native Americans" in the following to describe the characters in the films, thus making it clear that there will be no attempt whatsoever to relate the representations in the westerns to a historical lived reality, even if this means accepting that the historical subsumption of these lived realities cannot be revised under the ideological, mythological, and symbolic distortions of the hegemonic perspective in this terminology. Cf. Cawelti: *The Frontier and the Native American*, 137.

65 Michael Hilger: *From Savage to Nobleman. Images of Native Americans in Film*. Lanham 1995, 2.

66 Michael V. Moses: Savage Nations. Native Americans and the Western. In: Jennifer L. McMahon, B. Steve Csaki (eds.): *The Philosophy of the Western*. Lexington 2010, 261–290.

"So our slaughtered beauty mocks us ..."

The film Little Big Man will serve as the object here since it clearly has the intention not only to shape a possible revision of the frontier myth, but in fact to turn the transmutability of the conditions of the genre so that they become impossible conditions, morally and affectively unbearable. What it allows us to experience, painfully, is not the contradiction between the different justifications and movement dynamics of the frontier, but the fact of the constant drawing of borders.

In doing so Little Big Man joins up with several lines of tradition in the genre all at once. These are, on the one hand, John Ford's cavalry films and their ambivalence between a critique of the illusion of an equitable legal discourse between whites and Native Americans and its simultaneous confirmation.[67] In particular, Fort Apache (1948, John Ford) ultimately transfers the image of a wild independence into a concept of the Indians as the simple people, stricken by circumstances and the corrupt elite.[68]

Another line of tradition that Little Big Man very directly refers to is that of 'going native,' which has served, ever since James Fenimore Cooper's *Leatherstocking Tales* (1823–1841), to imagine new communal forms, and as the same time always already to mourn them as impossible: from the lastness of the *Last of the Mohicans*, via the romance, destined for failure, between the white man and the red woman in Broken Arrow (1950, Delmer Daves) as a metaphor for the unattainable peace between the races, to the formation of the new, environmentally conscious white couple, with the blessing of the doomed natives, in Dances with Wolves (1990, Kevin Costner).

Little Big Man transfers these and other visual forms and temporal structures into an affect-dramaturgical course between melodramatic ways of staging and a mode of satire with which the experience of suffering is confronted with a perception of randomness, with the arbitrariness and groundlessness of its causes.[69] While on the one hand – in relation to the Indians – there is an appeal to the spectators' moral feelings, on the other hand the historical self-positioning of white society, its own standpoint, is ridiculed through absurdities and through the undermining of the ideals that it has produced of itself. This clarifies two strategies of efficiency, which belong to the potential of genre cinema to deliver,

---

67 Cf. Michael J. Shapiro: The Demise of 'International Relations'. America's Western Palimpsest. In: *Geopolitics* (2005), Vol. 10, No. 2, 222–243.

68 Cf. Moses: *Savage Nations*, 271.

69 On satire, cf. Northrop Frye: *Anatomy of Criticism. Four Essays*. Princeton 1957, 223–239.

even in the negation of its procedures and compositional patterns, still valid information about the state and the self-image of a community. Melodramatic reassessments and mechanisms of justifying and masking violence, as well as the satirical disorganization of the social image represented, make available decisive shifts in the affective balance of this community. The contingency and instability of the one mode of depiction is what makes the moralizing, the affective taking-sides as the effective intention of the other, meaningful in the first place.

With Little Big Man we are dealing with one of those westerns in and with which the whole genre is meant and available for inspection. It can be inspected as the form that produced an image of American history from out of the North American landscape and the people that move westwards in it, and that evokes the satisfying feeling of still being part of the continuing settling of the west. The film is based on the novel of the same name by Thomas Berger from 1964,[70] and the film translates the relationship between farce and historiography into the relationship between farce and film history. Both film and book gain a perspective through a framing story in which the 121-year-old Jack Crabb (Dustin Hoffman) tells his life story as oscillating between two cultures, the white and the Cheyenne:

> It was Crabb's quite extraordinary fate to be captured by the Cheyennes at the age of ten, raised by them as a brave, rescued by the whites at the age of fifteen, and then to spend the next twenty years surviving two marriages, bankruptcy, sometime careers as an Indian scout and con artist, alcoholism, a brief period as a suicidal hermit, and, finally, General Custer's ill-timed decision to push on into the territory of the Little Big Horn.
>
> The film has the circular form of encounters with friends or relatives that Jack has somehow lost earlier along the way. [...] Most important, however, are the re-encounters with his Cheyenne family, presided over by the ancient chief, Old Lodge Skins (Chief Dan George), through whose eyes Jack Crabb watches the virtual extinction of "human beings," which is what the Cheyennes call themselves.[71]

The medium of the framing story, however, is more than just a narrative gimmick. It points to the time of its emergence as a breaking point, as a moment of realizing a conclusive loss. Little Big Man came out in the cinemas at Christmastime in 1970, and at the same time Stanley Cavell was writing about an end of myths as a natural state of the cinema:

> Every American city has someone in it who remembers when part of it was still land. In the world of the Western there is only land, dotted here and there with shelters and now and

---

70 Cf. Thomas Berger: *Little Big Man* [1964]. London 1999.
71 Vincent Canby: Movie Review. Little Big Man. In: *New York Times* (15 December 1970).

then with a dash of fronts that men there call a city. The gorgeous, suspended skies achieved in the works of, say, John Ford, are as vacant as the land. When the Indians are gone, they will take with them whatever gods inhabited those places, leaving the beautiful names we do not understand (Iroquois, Shenandoah, Mississippi, Cheyenne) in place of those places we will not understand. So our slaughtered beauty mocks us, and gods become legends.[72]

The loss that is supposed to be in discussion here does not only mean the disappearance of the Indians, but of the possible futures that should have been maintained in the western. The discrepancy between the present and the landscape as a historical promise is only one facet of the disillusionment. In fact, the film is about revising the "epistemological foundation upon which we have constructed American history,"[73] not only through the satirical contents that it takes from the novel, but in how it works directly on the audiovisual patterns, expressive forms, and temporal structures of the western genre.

In this respect it is indeed correct to point out that the film conforms to the *zeitgeist* of countercultures, sexual revolutions, civil rights and anti-war movements.[74] But as prefabricated attributions, these references seem to me to obscure both the view to the details of the audiovisual staging as well as the more fundamental meaning of the genre modalities: "The film, much more than the novel, is a search for identity."[75] Only by starting from an analysis of the film as an interrogation of moral identity can these contemporary historical references be meaningfully worked out, and the political and social processes of power and violence of the present be meaningfully related to an image of history.

For ultimately the revaluation of the idea of history contained in the myth of the western is not only a discursive operation, but must also be understood as an affective experience: pride or shame, rage or guilt – when it comes down to it, the pathos of belonging, in view of the violence that is carried out in one's name, develops moral appeal.

---

72 Cavell: *The World Viewed*, 59–60.

73 W. Bryan Rommel-Ruiz: *American History Goes to the Movies. Hollywood and the American Experience*. New York 2011, 119.

74 Cf. Margo Kasdan, Susan Tavernetti: Native Americans in a Revisionist Western. LITTLE BIG MAN (1970). In: Peter C. Rollins, John E. O'Connor (eds.): *Hollywood's Indian. The Portrayal of the Native American in Film*. Lexington 1998, 121–136, here 125; cf. Moses: *Savage Nations*, 274–275.

75 Jacquelyn Kilpatrick: *Celluloid Indians. Native Americans and Film*. Lincoln / London 1999, 85.

Dramaturgy of violence and (stereo-)types of genres

Perhaps the most important and obvious dramaturgical structural element of the film is the constant shifts in the belonging of the protagonist as Jack Crabb or as Little Big Man, adopted son of Chief Old Lodge Skins, to the two cultures of the whites and the Cheyenne. These shifts, however, do not simply occur. Every time that the boundaries of belonging are newly drawn around this character, it is a violent encounter between whites and Indians. The fact that it is occasionally "two movies in one,"[76] whose concepts of values, politics, morality, ownership and community forms not simply come together, but only collide from act of violence to act of violence, is not the film's weakness, as some commentators[77] seem to suggest, but precisely the experience that LITTLE BIG MAN is about: that the forms of imagining American history cannot conceive of any other transition between social forms than that of a perpetual state of war.

The myth of "regeneration through violence"[78] is continuously reproduced only so that a "redemption of American spirit or fortune"[79] does not arise at any point in time. The film thus makes a fundamental operation of the genre visible and thwarts the claim that it would be possible to derive power and legitimacy from violence, which, according to Hannah Arendt, who I draw on here to keep these two terms distinct from one another, is not permissible: "It is insufficient to say that power and violence are not the same. Power and violence are opposites, where the one rules absolutely, the other is absent."[80]

For Arendt, "power springs up whenever people get together and act in concert"[81] and stems from the appeal to a common past. Violence, in contrast, is an instrumental medium and "can be justifiable, but it never will be legitimate."[82] The epistemological operation of LITTLE BIG MAN is to show that the mode of the western claims at this point an equation[83] or causal derivation. The film thus allows us to see how the classic western imagines the transformation of violence, justifiable because motivated by self-defense and protection of the

---

76 Dan Georgakas: They Have not Spoken. American Indians in Film. In: Gretchen M. Bataille, Charles L. P. Silet (eds.): *The Pretend Indians. Images of Native Americans in the Movies.* Ames 1980, 134–142, here 140.

77 Cf. Georgakas: *They Have not Spoken*; cf. Kilpatrick: *Celluloid Indians*, 84–94.

78 Slotkin: *Gunfighter Nation*, 12.

79 Slotkin: *Gunfighter Nation*, 12.

80 Arendt: *On Violence*, 56.

81 Arendt: *On Violence*, 52.

82 Arendt: *On Violence*, 52.

83 Cf. Arendt: *On Violence*, 52: "The current equation of violence with power rests on government's being understood as domination of man over man by means of violence."

weak, into legitimate power, which founds the community and is founded by the community. It does this by using repetitions, duration, and excess of the representation of violence, not only to demonstrate its insufficient justification, but also its absolute inappropriateness for regulating how to live together. It shows that "what can never grow out of [the barrel of a gun] is power."[84] This opens up for inspection what *frontier* means in the mythology. It no longer designates the space in which America has not yet been formed, but where it should be, a space whose violent conquering and civilizing is legitimated by the community that is meant to arise there. Instead there is only a front.

This revision of the founding formula can be seen directly in the way the film is staged, or in its revisions of specific ways of staging. One scene in particular presents this in a quite exemplary way. In it a stagecoach is held up (0:49:23–0:52:30) and this point in the film directly refers to a scene from STAGECOACH (1:09:15–1:17:42), but at the same time it deprives the western of a visual idea that characterizes John Ford's westerns in general and STAGECOACH in particular. I mean the image of the landscape and the skies above it, in which the heroic vector of moving westward is inscribed, with all the trappings of settlements and civilization that rush in with the cloud of dust raised by the stagecoach. In the exalted expansiveness of this image, settlement and civilization are sensed as a project that can never run up against its borders, neither in space nor in time.

LITTLE BIG MAN does indeed repeat the tumultuous mixtures made up of gestures of heroism, cowardice, and piety in the interior of the stagecoach as well as certain actions that are unmistakably referencing STAGECOACH, in particular the jump from the stagecoach and from horseback to horseback to the foremost horse in the six-horse team. But the movement of the stagecoach itself is deprived of the specific relationship to the landscape. No pan to a wide shot shows us – which happens twice in STAGECOACH – the lurking Indians with a fanfare signaling ethnicity. In fact, the framing of LITTLE BIG MAN is marked by extreme closeness and fragmentation: a chaotic bundle of human bodies, horse bodies, parts of the stagecoach, and pieces of luggage flying about. This battle takes place outside the categories of the territorial, causing the heroism of the movement and its potential to be a civilizing force to get lost.

Another face of the revision of the expressive modes of the western genre can be seen in the audiovisual reversal of a scene from another film by John Ford, in this case THE SEARCHERS (1956). Classic captivity narratives have always been linked with anticipated or suggested violence, particularly toward women.

---

84 Arendt: *On Violence*, 53.

Ford's sound film westerns – from Stagecoach and Drums along the Mohawk (1939) to Cheyenne Autumn – play with the racist and sexualized fantasies of fear and lust, at the same time attempting to look critically at the projections of these fantasies on the Indians as "the source of much of the worst violence on the frontier:"[85] "Ford shows how graphically and powerfully racist fears fill in the undefined spaces in an ambiguous situation."[86] What Little Big Man does right at the beginning (0:03:01–0:07:16) is, first, to bring the bloody corpse out of the darkness of the imagination – where it was hidden in The Searchers – and into the foreground of the image. While the covered wagon smolders in the background and the title appears, the foreground shows a chaise longue with Bordeaux red upholstering on which a bloody corpse is draped, tastefully arranged in form and color. And second, the film turns the face, whose expression makes what happens legible to us, morally and emotionally, from John Wayne's into the face of a Cheyenne.[87] Any impulse of legitimizing violence through racist and sexual fears thus comes to nothing from the very beginning.

I will come back at a later point to the treatment of a further expressive pattern of the genre, embodied in the appearances of the cavalry in Ford and in particular in the Custer biopic They Died with their Boots on (1941, Raoul Walsh).

This eversion or refusal of the dynamic patterns of the classical western genre also entails suspending the roles embedded in these patterns as forms of acting and as forms of identification. This already starts with the choice of the lead actor: not 'The Duke' John Wayne, but the nice young man who has just graduated.[88] The film takes the contrast in Berger's novel, between Dustin

---

85 Ken Nolley: The Representation of Conquest. John Ford and the Hollywood Indian, 1939–1964. In: Peter C. Rollins, John E. O'Connor (eds.): *Hollywood's Indian. The Portrayal of the Native American in Film.* Lexington 1998, 73–90, here 87.

86 Nolley: *The Representation of Conquest*, 87.

87 Here as well, the evaluations that measure the film by the ambivalences in the novel go awry. In the novel, in fact, the Cheyenne carry out the massacre that leads the protagonists into their tents. Cf. Hilger: *From Savage to Nobleman*, 180; cf. John W. Turner: Little Big Man. The Novel and the Film. In: Gretchen M. Bataille, Charles L. P. Silet (eds.): *The Pretend Indians. Images of Native Americans in the Movies.* Ames 1980, 156–162, here 159. Instead, the point is that the film creates its own ambivalences through a direct relationship to film history aimed at concrete forms.

88 "Hoffman was widely identified as a personification of the youth culture of the '60s after his performance in The Graduate (1966) [sic!] and he had been featured in a 1967 [sic!] *Life* article ("Dusty and the Duke") as an alternative to the John Wayne model of American heroism." (Slotkin: *Gunfighter Nation*, 630.) In one scene this connection is made explicit by framing Jack's encounter with his former foster mother (Faye Dunaway) in the bordello exactly like a shot from The Graduate (1967, Mike Nichols), where the character of Ben (Dustin Hoffman) is received in the bedroom by Mrs. Robinson (Anne Bancroft).

Hoffman's stable identity as Little Big Man and the way that he, as Jack Crabb, stumbles from one role into the other in the society of the whites, as a structural element: "In the Indian world his identity remains consistent, but in the white world he tries on personalities and lifestyles like one tries on costumes."[89] This search for a white identity is doomed to fail, since the social roles that he is trying on are in fact not personality formats, but only costumes.

But it is not just that the society of the whites – "goal-oriented, hypocritical, and exploitative"[90]– cannot offer any meaningful identities, as a whole it also no longer produces a microcosm of any sort, any social network. It is a social form in which the plurality of individualities only comes into its own in the form of reciprocal betrayal. While at certain points the novel seems to be about encounters with more or less encoded historical figures, from Wild Bill Hickok and Wyatt Earp to Walt Whitman, the film is about the types and stereotypes of the genre that Jack tries out and the way white sociality appears as a 'dysfunctional assemblage' that is in need of explanation.[91]

In order to explain the significance of this operation, it is useful to come back to Stanley Cavell's definition of *type*. Namely, for Cavell, the types of classical genre cinema are not a matter of simple stereotypes and similarities: "For what makes someone a type is not his similarity with other members of that type but his striking separateness from other people."[92] Instead they are a matter of forms in which individuality and sociality are reconciled: "particular *ways* of inhabiting a social role."[93]

In the history of the genre the staging of individual socialities – along a constant oscillation of characters between stereotypical character types as similarities, mere façades, and costuming and the specific, particular realizations of these in each case – describes the changing positionings of the spectator in relation to the possibilities and limits of becoming and recognizing individuality. Films as art and forms of thinking are references to the possibility of political community and individual self-development, they are:

> about the arbitrariness and the inevitability of labels, and hence about the human need
> for society and the equal human need to escape it, and hence about human privacy and

---

89 Kilpatrick: *Celluloid Indians*, 85.

90 Kasdan, Tavernetti: *Native Americans in a Revisionist Western*, 128.

91 Cf. Moses: *Savage Nations*, 273. Incidentally, this is why the film at the same time 'fails' as the picaresque novel that it purports to be, since society no longer appears as a stratified, homogenous fabric, which the hero could somehow then go through, and since this society is always trickier than any rogue could ever be.

92 Cavell: *The World Viewed*, 33.

93 Cavell: *The World Viewed*.

unknownness. They are about the search for society, or community, outside, or within, society at large.[94]

The western genre is therefore not about simply recognizing the role of the settler, the gunslinger, the killer, the hooker with a heart of gold and so on, and of integrating them into a fixed social and narrative structure through ready-made labels. Since these types also always contain a fleeting dimension through "inflections of demeanor and disposition,"[95] which eludes being fixed by stereotyping and social role models, the films politically refer to the possibilities of accentuating oneself as individuality within a plurality of eccentric self-images.[96]

Little Big Man does not allow Dustin Hoffman's individuality and the social roles that his character slips into to come together. Although he does play the gunfighter, he does not embody it, the affinity between individual autonomy and lawlessness[97] is completely lost on him. The humor that the film develops from this, when he grabs at his weapon in absurdly overdecorated costumes, squinting his eyes and jumping back in fear at every little movement and noise (0:39:59–0:44:58), is not that of a caricature that acts out its object all the more clearly by distorting it in its specific qualities. It is much more a mixture of humiliation and ridiculousness that sets in because this cultural coding, and thus the image of the community that it brings with it, simply no longer match the physical reality and individuality of the character. This then distinguishes the film fundamentally from parodies such as Support your Local Sheriff! (1969, Burt Kennedy) or Cat Ballou (1965, Elliot Silverstein), in which even the most improbable or reluctant hero generally in the end – in his own quite particular way – fulfills his role and defends the community.

At the very latest when Jack, dead drunk, waltzes into the morass (1:39:09–1:40:27 and 1:48:04–1:49:30), when the make-up on the face of his former foster mother and now prostitute (Faye Dunaway) forms a pale blue puff of decay (1:42:44–1:48:04), and when we once again encounter the conman who not only disposes of his soul, but also of body parts in hope of quick riches (1:48:04–1:49:30), it becomes clear that the film amounts to a judgment of disgust and revulsion at this white society. As Jack Crabb, Dustin Hoffman goes through the various traditions of the cultural mythology of the frontier, not only acting out their contradictions, but transforming them all in such a way that they now appear as masking the one singular mythology: the dream of

---

94 Cavell: *The World Viewed*, 176.

95 Cavell: *The World Viewed*, 35.

96 Cf. Cavell: *The World Viewed*, 34–35.

97 Cf. Cavell: *The World Viewed*, 176.

secret treasures, of America as a goldmine. Selfishness and greed therefore seem to be the true expression of the American dream and the pursuit of happiness.[98]

Past and present of the massacre

In the presentation so far of the diverse revaluations of the visual forms and characters of the genre, the question of the register of feeling in these revisions can be answered most clearly by means of a comic-satirical note. Things look somewhat different if we put these revaluations in relation to the structural, dramaturgical function of violence. In the constant staging of collisions between whites and Indians, which always lead to new boundaries of belonging being drawn around Jack Crabb / Little Big Man, there is a clear increase in intensity, the highpoint of which simultaneously signifies a radical new perspective on the image of the cavalry in the genre. The cavalry is described as a paradigm of American identity that has become radically dysfunctional and the source of irresponsible suffering.

The subject is the scene in which a historical reference and a reference to the present of the film, 100 years later, come into alignment with one another in an uncanny way – the massacres of the Washita River (November 1868) and of My Lai (March 1968) and other acts of cruelty on the part of American soldiers in Vietnam that had just become public. After Little Big Man has founded a patchwork family with four women and an adopted child, his main wife Sunshine (Aimée Eccles) has borne him a son and the tribe has settled in a wintery landscape – "for once, we were in a safe place, given to us by treaty" – they are attacked by the cavalry around Custer, which ruthlessly slaughters everyone. Little Big Man and Old Lodge Skins pass through the chaos undisturbed, but are forced to look on helplessly as women, children, and eventually Sunshine are killed by the soldiers (1:26:10–1:33:52).

Here, what has always represented the embodiment of the threatened self, of civilization and what still represents the bridge from the legitimation of violence to the legitimation of power – namely women and children that cannot defend themselves – is clearly assigned to the side of the culturally other.[99] In addition we as spectators are put into a curious tension made up of direct proximity to being affected and a judging distance to the event itself, with which

---

98 Cf. Cawelti: *The Frontier and the Native American*, 179–180.
99 Cf. Nolley: *The Representation of Conquest*, 80.

the scene, as I will explain more precisely, shapes the expressive and temporal structure of a sense of guilt. In part, however, this scene is haunted by the familiar images and sounds of the genre. The memory of a positive identification with the cavalry as they storm in, which clearly no longer functions in its own present, is made painfully present.

Such a link between the past and the present, however, is no genuine invention of this film, but marks the public perception of the war in Vietnam. The enemy territory was "Indian country"[100] and to get from Redskins to Reds as an image of the enemy, only a single syllable needed to be dropped. THE BIG PICTURE. A NATION BUILDS UNDER FIRE (1967, Harry Middleton), a propaganda film by the Department of Armed Forces Information & Education of the U.S. Defense Ministry features John Wayne as a guest moderator in a South Vietnamese village as a mirror image of the peaceful settler in the American western, and he in turn, in THE GREEN BERETS (1968, John Wayne, Ray Kellogg), Hollywood's only heroic-optimistic attempt to produce a classical war film about the war in progress, had the soldiers defending their fort 'Dodge City' from the attacking 'savages'.[101]

As Richard Slotkin elaborately details in *Gunfighter Nation*, this led to the fact that even contemporary reporting on war crimes in Vietnam were marked by a plainly inverted usage of the representational patterns of the western. Slotkin describes the presentation of image and text in Life Magazine's reporting[102] on the massacre of My Lai as a "'cinematic' way of telling the story,"[103] reasoning:

> The inversion of the normal war-movie / Western scenario is now complete. Instead of rescuing the woman/child from rape and slaughter, the Americans commit rape – in fact, child-rape – and murder amid the burning buildings of the "settlement." We are back in the symbolic terrain of the captivity myth – the terrain of Mary Rowlandson [author of one of the first captivity reports to become famous, MG] and Ethan Edwards [the protagonist played by John Wayne in Ford's THE SEARCHERS, MG] – only now *we* are the "savages."[104]

For Slotkin, what is decisive for the affective effect of this inversion – and my thesis is that this is also the case for the staging of the massacre in LITTLE BIG MAN – is that we as recipients cannot simply switch sides with the reversal of

---

100 Daniel Hallin: *The "Uncensored War". The Media and Vietnam.* New York / Oxford 1986, 142–143.

101 Cf. Hermann Kappelhoff, Christian Pischel, Eileen Rositzka and Cilli Pogodda: The Green Berets. Der Vietnamkriegsfilm als Herausforderung der klassischen Genrepoetik. In: Thomas Morsch (ed.): *Genre und Serie.* Munich 2015, 75–110.

102 Cf. Hal Wingo, Roland L. Haeberle: The Massacre at Mylai. In: *Life Magazine* (5 December 1969), 36–45.

103 Slotkin: *Gunfighter Nation,* 584.

104 Slotkin: *Gunfighter Nation,* 586.

the attribution of victim and perpetrator. Instead the representations aim for a feeling of implying the one seeing in what is being seen: "The cognitive play that this quasi-cinematic narrative invites seems designed to make us *feel* that complicity."[105] In its constant alternation between unfounded cruelty on the one hand and the judging assessment of this cruelty on the other, the representation aims for a play in the powers of imagination with the demonic potential of one's own civilization, which remains deliberately unresolved.[106]

Now it is just such an oscillation between an observing, judging distance and an unbearable proximity, an implication in the positions of the spectators, victims, and perpetrators at once, that structures the relevant scene from LITTLE BIG MAN and gives it the affective tinge of a sense of guilt in the alternation between being made passive and the move to escape. Significantly, this includes the fact that the individual modes of staging and affects combined here in this almost eight-minute-long scene are not resolved in a uniform sentiment, but that the successful rescue is at the same time a hopeless failure.

At the level of audiovisual composition, and in particular of camera work, it is about a deliberate alternation between shots from an extreme distance, extreme telephoto optics, and very brief close shots, often fragmentary and permeated with blurring movements. Only at a very few points is there something like a range of action established for the characters, who are either sedate viewers or anonymous bodies that flash for split seconds, who ride and shoot or run and are struck.

Little Big Man's despairing view into the off space at the beginning of the scene is simply not linked in any coherent space with the extreme telephoto shots of a dreamlike, hazy winter landscape, which show spectral riders on horseback (1:26:40–1:26:58). The following long shots and telephoto shots are accompanied by an eerie march music that very gradually becomes louder, initially showing the army's movement toward the Cheyenne's camp as a physically unstoppable force (1:26:58–1:27:54). They ride and ride and ride, then suddenly they are in the midst of tipis felling Indians. In particular those views from the long shots that show the camp at the river from the other shore have an impressive foreground of branches and tree limbs, making this positioning particularly palpable as one of powerless distance. It is the position that Little Big Man will assume at the end of the scene when he has to look on and see his Indian wife Sunshine and their child being killed.

The entry of the cavalry into the camp is shaped as an explosive perceptual event by the sudden change to chaotic, rapidly edited views (1:27:54–1:28:28),

---

105 Slotkin: *Gunfighter Nation*, 584.
106 Cf. Slotkin: *Gunfighter Nation*, 586.

against which Little Big Man only has a single answer. He and Old Lodge Skins withdraw into the tent where the old chief calmly lights a pipe, while Little Big Man wildly thrashes about and we see no more of the violence (1:28:28–1:29:37). While Little Big Man attempts to convince the chief to flee – by explaining to him that a dream had granted him invisibility – the soundtrack and the military music also changes and is replaced by Indian war cries, accompanied by the whistling of bullets.

The following section adds to the scene a level of voice-over commentary by the old Jack Crabb, which is characteristic for many passages in the film (1:29:37–1:30:51). While Little Big Man and Old Lodge Skins run through the wildly edited scenes of carnage, now once again accompanied by the eerie music, the spectators are placed into an impossible relation to the events that they simultaneously perceive as far away and past and as utterly near and present. What follows is an alternation between close shots of Little Big Man and tele-objective shots showing General Custer, which resemble the previously shown wide shots and tele-shots showing the cavalry storming in (1:30:51–1:31:19). In its audiovisual conventionality, a conversation between Custer and his lieutenant with its extremely racist rhetoric creates a decelerating moment that seems even more disturbing in contrast to the dominant poles here of wide shots and quickly edited fragments (1:31:19–1:31:49).

The following montage is then the climax of the entire film (1:31:49–1:33:15). Soldiers on ponies shoot and strike Indians rushing out of burning tipis. On the soundtrack the howls of animals blend with the screams of women and children. Hardly any single shot lasts longer than two seconds. The moments of fear, confusion, and horror, which so far have only been alluded to and then retracted, break out unimpeded. At a certain point (1:32:16) two axes of movement and vision crystallize from out of this chaos, which are edited in together: Sunshine running away from a mounted soldier, the child in her arms, and Little Big Man's desperate screams and gestures. Each of their movements is initially aligned to the other in its direction, both beginning by stumbling, from right to left and from back to front in the image. Then, however, they are disconnected again, with him calling out, on all fours in the snow, while she is shot down over and over again from new perspectives, gets up again and is hit once more. Between the shots the soundtrack then thins out, and with the last gunshots, in complete silence, brief images of Sunshine collapsing while holding the bloody bundle close to her alternate with shots of Little Big Man, also collapsed on the ground and writhing.

The scene ends with the gradual return of the sounds of the military band over images of retreating soldiers and dead Indians – children, the aged, and women. The last shots show the musicians standing in rank and file, in the extreme tele-objective shots that are so characteristic for this scene, making a blurry, ghostly appearance through the swathes of haze, smoke, and heat.

If we put these chronologically itemized observations together, we can recognize how much the retrospective character of the sense of guilt is inscribed in this scene. Excessive repetitions alternate with deceleration – the episode in the tipi, Custer briefing his officers – and at the same time there is an increase in the evocations of fear and confusion, sympathy and finally pain and powerlessness. Over the entire temporal unfolding the scene corresponds to the experience of irreversibility. The worst has always already happened, it is tormenting, but there is no way to change it. In the tele shots and wide shots as well as in the unconnected fragmentary details, every form of coordinated activity and temporal flow is blocked. Even the staging of the bodies and the movements of the characters constantly fluctuate between undirected activation, an impulse to flee, and the total passivation of the protagonists, who can now only slump down into themselves. We want to look away, to close our eyes and ears, but it imposes itself on us over and over again.

The effect of the music here is of particular interest, not only because it contributes so significantly to the inevitability of the events with its constant repetition and propulsive rhythm. It is in fact an Irish drinking and dance song, *Garryowen*, which Custer had personally chosen as the battle hymn of the 7th Cavalry. Using this song the film flips one of the central representational tropes of the western genre on its head:

> Music, which is typically used to guide emotional responses in the audience, maintains this Eurocentric emphasis in the positive emotional resonance Westerns give to folk songs, military tunes, and traditional hymns. Indian music, when it is suggested, is as limited as Indian speech and almost invariably associated with war, stereotypically invoking a sense of threat and suspense.[107]

The decisive point is that the film does not simply switch sides, does not simply assume the Indian perspective, redefining the events of the action and the affective tone from there. Instead the emotional register of the ethnocentric white perspective is radically altered. It is now their *own* symbols and signs that radiate menace. This cultural complicity simultaneously contains the debilitating powerlessness of not being able to hold onto one's own past: "The 'voice' of the music brings up feelings of swelling pride at odds with the reality of what the soldiers are doing to the village. The result is eerily disconcerting inner speech."[108]

---

107 Nolley: *The Representation of Conquest*, 82.
108 Kilpatrick: *Celluloid Indians*, 93.

It is not merely the drastic representation of slaughtered women and children that makes this scene notable, but also the dull feeling that this might have some sort of causal relationship with other images and sounds of the genre and the operations of mythology.[109] In particular, these are the images and sounds from They Died with their Boots on – although this relation, and this also goes for other references in the film, is clearly more diffuse than the category of citation could accommodate, for it is ultimately about the meaning-making function of forms in a cultural field. One could at the same time refer this scene to a passage in The Searchers that also combines massacres of Indians, this specific piece of music and a wintry scenery with a very similar color palette – but which has the trauma of white women as its closure.

In They Died with their Boots on the power of music, the simultaneously energetic and joyful motif in a montage sequence in the middle of the film, is the decisive binding agent for the emergence of the 7th Cavalry as a body with a shared identity. In constantly increasing, enlarging ensembles – from solo singing with piano accompaniment to large brass bands – *Garryowen* first underscores the formation of this military unit, until they eventually parade before the eyes of the public, made up of proud women and representatives of the East, benevolent trappers, the pioneers of the frontier. Following this, still borne by the same motif, now somewhat faster and intermingled with other familiar motifs such as the trumpet signal of the advance and drumming connoted as Indian, a montage sequence realizes what the text on screen promises: "And so was born the immortal 7th U.S. Cavalry which cleared the plains for a ruthlessly advancing civilization that spelled doom to the red race."

Little Big Man manages to invoke the visual repertoire and the frivolous gestures, with which the complications of history are pushed aside here, from this and many other films, and indeed as a gut instinct: 'I know this music, I know these images, but something is different.' The dramaturgy of feelings works as a kind of dysfunctionality detector, and in just this capacity it justifies the effect of this scene. It intervenes directly in the self-image of a community.

This is also why the question of whether this scene is either about My Lai *or* Washita, either the Indian Wars *or* Vietnam, is the wrong question.[110] Precisely because no one can escape the connection to Vietnam, it is all the more significant that Little Big Man works at recognizing this bloodbath, tracing it back to the characters, basic narrative models, and the visual structures of the genre mythology. It uses identification models and affective operations to expose

---

109 Cf. Slotkin: *Gunfighter Nation*, 613.
110 For a contrasting position, cf. Kilpatrick: *Celluloid Indians*, 93.

them as false conclusions and pitfalls. It confronts the attractiveness of the self-images generated by the mythology with the historical guilt that these self-images have caused and continue to cause. It is precisely about short circuiting the link between historical and imaginary image of the cavalry and the contemporary images of geopolitical and military might.[111]

Due to the interconnection of historical and contemporary images of the military, it is also important to relate the parallels that LITTLE BIG MAN draws between Washita and My Lai to the internal logic of the dramaturgical role of violence. It is at once an escalation and a memory of other scenes in the film that cannot be reduced to the Vietnam metaphor. There is a scene very early in the film, for instance, in which the Cheyenne appear too late at the site of a massacre (0:17:07–0:18:40) and decide "We must have a war on these cowards and teach them a lesson." This scene, however, ends in a slapstick insert in which the warfare of the Indians and that of the whites is contrasted (0:20:02–0:22:01). The second time that women and children are explicitly killed by the army we are literally on the wrong side of events, with Jack Crabb as a scout, namely on the side of the army (1:04:00–1:10:17). Although he immediately steps out of line from the violence, he fails to reveal himself to the Indians as one of 'them,' to get to the right side.

As a whole, we can speak of an affect-dramaturgical escalation in the staging of the massacres, which consists not only in the quantitative and qualitative escalation of the explicit representation of violence. Rather, this escalation eventually transposes the relationship of the sad horror over powerlessness and rage into a feeling of painful guilt, which is inscribed in the spectator position as a position that is implied in the events and at the same time eludes them. The feeling of the spectator is the feeling of an always-coming-too-late, always finding-oneself-on-the-wrong-side, unawares.

At this point it is clear why the film has incorporated these conspicuous repetitive loops. Just as feelings of guilt have something to do with the fact that we endlessly represent events to ourselves, playing them through, working away at them, so LITTLE BIG MAN also works away: at white society, at the

---

111 One might compare the famous scene of the helicopter attack in APOCALYPSE NOW (1979, Francis Ford Coppola), which not only deals with the inheritance of the cavalry by the squadron of helicopters in terms of its contents – as had already been done affirmatively in THE GREEN BERETS – but also, in terms of form, by using the same uncanny break, underscored by music as psychological warfare, of an inexorable advance in the explosion of violence and destruction. Even the extreme telephoto shots of a shallow, glimmering backdrop of smoke and fire are almost identical in both films, only that in one it is horses whisking through the foreground of the image, and in the other it is helicopters.

massacres, at the character of 'Custer' as the embodiment of the military, and at the military as an image of community.[112]

An impetus thus arises in the relationship that the film develops in the repetitions on the cavalry, an impetus that – from out of guilt – contains something like a fulfillment fantasy of the wish for compensation with the slaughter at Little Big Horn (1:51:18–2:03:35). This is important since – as Hannah Arendt writes in *On Violence* – the self-accusation 'We are all guilty' in itself does not yet contain anything about action or change. It is, however, an intermediate step, we are moved, concerned, appealed to. Only in the rage and indignation over injustice does a more concrete political dimension of human affectivity develop.[113] But this fulfillment fantasy is not without internal contradictions, for in Custer's violent punishment the film reinstalls the regenerative function of violence in the mythology of the frontier: "It implies that its violence is an essential and necessary part of the process through which American society was established and through which its democratic values are defended and enforced."[114]

By attributing those values and virtues that produced the self-description in classical Hollywood to the Indians, and by at the same time playing through the threat to and rescue of these values in the acts of violence and counter-violence, Little Big Man dysfunctionalizes the classical western genre while at the same time confirming it in the end: "To recover one's proper role in the myth of regenerative violence we must actually or implicitly identify with the enemy and see him as an embodiment of those virtues we once claimed as our own."[115]

At any rate, we would be misunderstanding both the function of mythology as well as the intended impact of the film as an intervention in the affective economy of American society if we interpreted this identification as an actually assumable position and political agenda.[116] As a modulation of the affective registers of genre, of the evocation of the ties of friendship and community, of feelings of justice and injustice towards a feeling of shared historical guilt, the film is precisely concerned with assuming an affective and moral attitude of disidentification in relation to the role of historical self-images that persists into the present in the justification of violence that cannot be legitimized.

---

112 Cf. Slotkin: *Gunfighter Nation*, 292.
113 Cf. Arendt: *On Violence*, 63–65.
114 Slotkin: *Gunfighter Nation*, 352.
115 Slotkin: *Gunfighter Nation*, 591.
116 Cf. Slotkin: *Gunfighter Nation*.

A feeling for one's own history

If LITTLE BIG MAN is about the disturbing inscription of a perspective of the other, it is initially obvious that with these Cheyenne, who call themselves 'human beings,' with the stress on the first syllable, it is not about a concrete historical group, but about the embodiment of an idea of another form of the social. One of the basic maxims of the western genre remains intact here as well. The only good Indian is a metaphorical Indian. It is this distortion that creates a projection surface for the self-attribution of a white national identity from the invisible real-historical way of life of the Native Americans in their particularity – be it in the demarcation, as a counter-image or as a mirror, as a prism or in the form of mutual outbidding, in which every noble savage finds his white man, who can be just a bit more noble and just a bit more savage.[117]

In the end the Chief Old Lodge Skins decides: "It is a good day to die." And when Little Big Man asks him why, he answers: "Because there's no other way to deal with the white man." In the novel we read at an earlier point:

> Whatever else you can say about the white man, it must be admitted that you cannot get rid of him. He is in never-ending supply. There has always been only a limited number of Human Beings, because we are intended to be special and superior. Obviously not everybody can be a Human Being. To make this so, there must be a great many inferior people. To my mind, this is the function of white men in the world. Therefore we must survive, because without us the world would make no sense.[118]

And as if it wanted to take this last sense at its word, the film, in contrast to the novel, does not allow the chief to die on his own volition. In the novel his last words still formulate the utopia of a universal Indianness:

> Even if my people must eventually pass from the face of the earth, they will live on in whatever men are fierce and strong. So that when women see a man who is proud and brave and vengeful, even if he has a white face, they will cry: 'That is a Human Being!'[119]

One might claim that in 1970 this is no longer conceivable and that it is Little Big Man's / Jack Crabb's insistent presence that prohibits exactly this peaceful

---

117 Cf. Nolley: *The Representation of Conquest*, 88 and Rommel-Ruiz: *American History Goes to the Movies*, 120–123; cf. Kilpatrick: *Celluloid Indians*, 67; cf. Slotkin: *Gunfighter Nation*, 19 and 630. One might only think of AVATAR (James Cameron, 2009) to bring the continuing attractiveness of the latter model up to the present.

118 Berger: *Little Big Man*, 157.

119 Berger: *Little Big Man*, 419.

acceptance of one's own disappearance. In Vine Deloria's words: "But the Indian survives because whites have many unanswered questions about who they are."[120]

In his comparative critique of the film and the novel, which is against the film from the beginning, John W. Turner writes:

> In the novel, Berger captures this ironic sense of the Indian defeated even in victory by concluding Jack's narrative of the battle with the death of Old Lodge Skins. [...] More than simply the death of one man, the death of the old chief symbolizes the death of a mode of life.
>
> Penn's comic ending, therefore, not only undermines the dignity of Old Lodge Skins, but also raises questions about Penn's historicism. To a great extent, Penn seems to resist the historical implications of the conflict on the Plains. By opting for a sentimental ending, Penn undermines the effectiveness of his cinematic achievement in the Washita scene [...].
>
> As a result, the movie lacks the closure that its story demands. Having entered the arena of history, Penn obligates himself to a narrative structure that rests on the opposition between the past and the present.[121]

The point is that what is broken down here, but not recognized as a consequence of how it functions in its genre poetics, is what the film is in fact not trying to be: a historically precise, judging representation of the Indian Wars of the second half of the nineteenth century and a eulogy to a lost way of life. It is not about history as a collection of events, but about the forms and processes in which this history is conceived. It is about the rules of the game in the 'arena of history.' This is why the film operates both in the melodramatic as well as the satirical mode. In recourse to these and other expressive systems, it is an attempt to revise the sentimental form of the western genre. And this revision precisely does not want to achieve any kind of 'closure' but to make it possible to perceive how the violence of history contributes to shaping one's own present.[122] By leaving 'its' Indian alive, the film insists on the possibility of a new conception of the community through the imaginary contact with what one has annihilated. The prospect of a better life, a more open and more peaceful social form for the whites survives with the image of the Native Americans, and this is directly linked with a cultural sense of guilt as a specific feeling for one's own history.[123] While the living on of the old chief contains the hope that the white man's dominance is a temporary mistake, a fata morgana

---

120 Vine Deloria: Foreword / American Fantasy. In: Gretchen M. Bataille, Charles L. P. Silet (eds.): *The Pretend Indians. Images of Native Americans in the Movies.* Ames 1980, ix–xvi, here xiv.
121 Turner: *Little Big Man*, 161.
122 Cf. Ahmed: *Cultural Politics of Emotion*, 200.
123 Cf. Maurine T. Schwarz: Collective Guilt, Conservation, and Other Postmodern Messages in Contemporary Westerns. In: *American Indian Culture and Research Journal* (2002), Vol. 26, No. 1, 83–105, here 86–87, 92, and 95.

in the becoming of another society, this hope remains inscribed with the awareness that the becoming of every social form is tied to violence and guilt.

After the 'regeneration through violence' is revised through the dysfunctionality of its actual application in the western genre and attained again, this maxim is no longer useful as a historical explanation. Instead it remains there as what actually needs explaining time and again. In the film's framing story the interviewer of the old Jack Crabb expects a western as an explanation for the slaughter at Little Big Horn. He does indeed get a western – or something similar to a western – but no explanation. LITTLE BIG MAN does not replace the myth with an idea of historical veracity, but with the inner variety and ambivalence of the myth, its destructiveness, in which there are now always two sides of the frontier, two sides of violence.

The wish that one feels to prohibit the massacre and abuse does not alter the past, but it does alter what this past will have meant. And this change is now palpable as a shift in the set of values and in the modalities of aesthetic experience, in the dynamic patterns of the genre. In this sense it is about the affective reference to a certain mode of historicity, for which identity always emerges from the experience of internal non-identity, and for which history is precisely not suitable as something that one simply proudly finds oneself in, but in which one always loses one's innocence anew.[124]

If the western designates the way that America sees itself historically and spectators experience themselves as part of a historical national character, then LITTLE BIG MAN shows how this way of establishing oneself as a historical project led to catastrophic consequences. An implicit theory of history that looks for progress, self-preservation, and self-discovery through conquering and reallocating territories, and that was highly functional from the Mayflower to the landing in Normandy, gets lost with the Vietnam War. As a value system and expressive form of a national culture, the mythology of the western is destroyed precisely by the fact that the official politics of the Nixon administration believed to be maintaining the mythology uninterrupted, while films like LITTLE BIG MAN sought to rescue the mythology by dysfunctionalizing it.[125] They rework the genre as a cultural model and pursue a specific genealogy of morality in order to unsettle the false confidence in the valence of values, and to conceive of the possibility of better values.[126] The right feelings can help to understand that one has misunderstood oneself.

---

124 Cf. Burgoyne: *Film Nation*, 1–12.
125 Cf. Slotkin: *Gunfighter Nation*, 623.
126 Cf. Prinz: *The Emotional Construction of Morals*, 217.

4 The Future: Global Responsibility and the Rhetoric of Climate Change

On January 10, 2013 the Haus der Kulturen der Welt [HKW] in Berlin began a two-year series of exhibitions and events entitled *The Anthropocene Project*. The series is based on the observation raised by a wide variety of academic disciplines that the human species has changed the planet in a way that can only be appropriately understood as a new geological age:

> Nature as we know it is a concept that belongs to the past. No longer a force separate from and ambivalent to human activity, nature is not an obstacle nor a harmonious other. Humanity forms nature. Humanity and nature are one, embedded from within the recent geological record.[1]

The aim of the term Anthropocene – not invented, but highly influenced by the Dutch chemist and Nobel prizewinner Paul J. Crutzen[2]– is not merely to designate changes that can be measured by the natural sciences, nor to name a 'catastrophe' that could be derived from this, but to fundamentally change how we describe the self and the world.

The focus – conceptually and in terms of attention economics – is most assuredly man-made climate change.[3] On the one hand it is deeply rooted in ordinary local practices due to the energy-intensive lifestyle of the western world. On the other hand, and at the same time, it concerns globalized political decision-making processes. In addition – more than just another scientific 'scenario' – it entails a multitude of 'stories of catastrophe.' Every consideration of climate change – scientific, political, journalistic, or artistic – includes the idea of always also having to thematize its highly problematic representability[4] and

---

1 Bernd M. Scherer, Kathrin Klingan: Introduction. In: *The Anthropocene Project. An Opening*. Program for the event at the Haus der Kulturen der Welt. Berlin 10–13 January 2013, 2–7, here 2.

2 Paul J. Crutzen, Eugene F. Stoermer: The 'Anthropocene'. In: *IGBP Newsletter* (2000), No. 41, 17–18; cf. also Jan Zalasiewicz, Mark Williams, Alan Smith, Tiffany L. Barry, Angela L. Coe, Paul R. Bown, Patrick Brenchley, David Cantrill, Andrew Gale, Philip Gibbard, F. John Gregory, Mark W. Hounslow, Andrew C. Kerr, Paul Pearson, Robert Knox, John Powell, Colin Waters, John Marshall, Michael Oates, Peter Rawson, Philip Stone: Are We Now Living in the Anthropocene? In: *GSA Today* (2008), Vol. 18, No. 2, 4–8.

3 From a natural sciences perspective, the justification for a man-made geological era are climate change but also increased radioactivity, the change of the Earth's surface due to mining and agriculture, and chemical changes in the air, water, and soil.

4 Cf. Julie Doyle: Seeing the Climate? The Problematic Status of Visual Evidence in Climate Change Campaigning. In: Sidney Dobrin, Sean Morey (eds.): *Ecosee. Image, Rhetoric, and*

https://doi.org/10.1515/9783110612110-005

its cultural-historical and media-theoretical requirements. Any attempt at establishing, understanding, arguing climate change, or at drawing on it as a basis for action or judgment, is based on complex ideas of humanity, nature, time, and history, of the power to act and causality, which – according to the Anthropocene thesis – require a radical readjustment: "What image of humanity takes shape if nature appears to us in the image of man, *as if it were human?*"[5]

Assuming this necessity of a new perspective, the four-day opening event of the Anthropocene Project asked into whether the Anthropocene is now a 'cosmology' or a 'doomsday scenario,' whether it is 'luxury or necessity,' whether it is 'just,' 'new,' or even 'beautiful.' None of the keynotes, dialogues, and discussions, however, posed the question of how the Anthropocene 'feels,' whether it causes fear or rage, whether we feel shame or guilt, for instance, whether there is reason for disgust or pity, whether there is cause for hope.

This omission is certainly not by chance. Indeed, it represents, so to speak, the blind spot between the two discursive forms that define the field: the idea of a positive reasoning in the natural sciences on the one hand and the related idea of rationality in the line of reasoning in ethical and moral reflections as a basis for political decisions on the other.

In contrast, the task would be to demonstrate how linguistic and symbolic forms used to operate in science and the wider public are themselves grounded in affect. For on the one hand we can assert that thinking in the natural sciences, and even more so political thinking, also cannot be separated from sensorimotor and emotional 'circuits' as embodied processes.[6] On the other hand, the step from science to the public sphere, exactly where it aims to initiate or change behavior, does not proceed without emotional forms of appeal and narratives.[7]

Nature. New York 2009, 279–298; cf. Birgit Schneider: Ein Darstellungsproblem des klimatischen Wandels? Zur Analyse und Kritik wissenschaftlicher Expertenbilder und ihren Grenzen. In: *Kritische Berichte. Zeitschrift für Kunst- und Kulturwissenschaften* (2010), Vol. 38, No. 3, 80–90; Michael D. Mastanedra, Stephen H. Schneider: Vorbereitungen für den Klimawandel. In: Paul J. Crutzen, Mike Davis, Michael D. Mastrandrea, Stephen H. Schneider, Peter Sloterdijk (eds.): *Das Raumschiff Erde hat keinen Notausgang.* Frankfurt a. M. 2011, 11–59.

5 Scherer, Klingan: *Introduction,* 3.

6 Cf. George Lakoff, Mark Johnson: *Philosophy in the Flesh. The Embodied Mind and Its Challenge to Western Thought.* New York 1999; cf. Raymond W. Gibbs: *Embodiment and Cognitive Science.* New York 2006.

7 Cf. George Lakoff: Why it Matters How We Frame the Environment. In: *Environmental Communication* (2010), Vol. 4, No. 1, 70–81; cf. Stephen Daniels, Georgina H. Endfield (eds.):

Within the context of the Anthropocene Project at the HKW, questions of framing and narrativizing were indeed addressed, but they were nonetheless always raised at the level of knowledge formation, which ignores the affective potential of narrating. The following will thus turn to long-format documentary films to reconstruct the contribution of emotions in the 'reality' of the Anthropocene. Full-length films for the cinema seem on the one hand to be an exception, since their quantitative share in cultural and media forms that are dedicated to climate change, compared to reporting in newspapers and magazines, in trade journals, radio features, and television documentaries, etc. is relatively slight. On the other hand, the audiovisual formats produced for the cinema are exactly those cultural spheres that can bring feelings up to the surface of discourse. Furthermore, films in the cinema, due to their wider exposure, are well suited to represent a significant scale type for the public exchange of ideas: "Feature-length films can acquire a distributed media presence, acting as focal points for public discourse about science."[8]

The amalgamation of public attention can certainly be shown most clearly in the film that serves as a standard and a reference point for the hybrid genre of climate change films: AN INCONVENIENT TRUTH (2006, Davis Guggenheim), based on lectures and the book of the same name by Al Gore, former U.S. vice-president and presidential candidate. One has to speak of a hybrid genre here because films such as THE AGE OF STUPID (2009, Franny Armstrong), THE GREAT WARMING (2006, Michael Taylor), or THE 11TH HOUR (2007, Leila and Nadia Connors) blur the per se not particularly clearly drawn borders between the documentary film, the propaganda film, and the instructional or utility film. This hybridization should be understood as an attempt to activate the plural relations to a shared world, to culturally and socially shared forms of knowledge, thought, belief, perception, and emotion. Some of the examples such as LE SYNDROME DE TITANIC (2009, Nicolas Hulot and Jean-Albert Lièvre), tend toward being essay films, others to classical natural reports, such as the BBC's two-part ARE WE CHANGING PLANET EARTH? and CAN WE SAVE PLANET EARTH? (2006, Nicolas Brown and Stephen Cooter).

For all the differences in their poetological compositions, the common denominator of these climate change films is a) that they attempt to create sensual and conceptual evidence of the causes, processes, and dangers of ecological destruction and global climate change and b) that they couple this

---

Journal of Historical Geography (2009), Vol. 35, No. 2 (Special Issue. Narratives of Climate Change), 215–404.

8 Felicity Mellor: The Politics of Accuracy in Judging Global Warming Films. In: *Environmental Communication* (2009), Vol. 3, No. 2, 134–150, here 136.

creation of evidence with a medial treatment of emotions, which aims to change attitudes and everyday ways of acting in their audiences. How these films work on the conditions of communicating climate change, as well as how they clearly define their political intention to convince, can be useful to the fundamental question of audiovisual rhetoric in media studies, both analytically and theoretically.

To this end I will first establish the necessity of relying on the idea of rhetoric, and of developing film analytical perspectives from it. Following this I will turn to the exemplary case of AN INCONVENIENT TRUTH, making the claim that it is directly based on the fundaments and calculations of ancient rhetoric. The premise is that the film combines an affective address to the spectator with the work of (environmental) political persuasion. The target of this address ranges from global political agreements to everyday decisions about energy-saving lightbulbs. And it contains a warning about the dangers of ignoring it. An idea of concern and responsibility in the shape of an anticipated sense of guilt will thus be examined as a central component of the directorial and dramaturgical strategies of AN INCONVENIENT TRUTH.

4.1 Rhetoric in the Anthropocene

From a naïve standpoint, one might point out that being aware of the greenhouse effect and the exhaust fumes produced by human beings does not require any sophisticated art of mediation and persuasion, if only the numbers and calculations are properly established. But the hockey-stick[9] is the hockey-stick is the hockey-stick: The history of the environmental movement(s) shows, that ecology in the strict sense of the natural sciences as such contains no impetus to political action.[10] If, following the work of Joachim Radkau, we ask what the interchange between science, climate models, and political and media publics looked like in the environmental movements, it becomes clear that 'nature' could only become the 'environment' by going through struggles for the elementary quality of life,

---

9 This is the term used for the famous temperature curve by the team surrounding paleo-climatologist Michael Mann, first published in: Michael E. Mann, Raymond S. Bradley, Malcom K. Hughes: Global-Scale Temperature Patterns and Climate Forcing Over the Past Six Centuries. In: *Nature* (1998), Vol. 392, No. 6678, 779–787. Cf. Birgit Schneider: Die Kurve als Evidenzerzeuger des klimatischen Wandels am Beispiel des 'Hockey-Stick-Graphen.' In: Karin Harrasser, Helmut Lethen, Elisabeth Timm (eds.): *Zeitschrift für Kulturwissenschaften* (2009), No. 1, 41–55.
10 Cf. Joachim Radkau: *The Age of Ecology*. Cambridge 2014.

that "only because the issue at stake was not a law of nature but human well-being or even survival did environmentalism acquire a political potential."[11] And at least since Rachel Carson's successful anti-DDT book *Silent Spring* (1962), these struggles were not just carried out at the level of model building, but at the level of narratives, scenarios, and the substantiation of facts in situations that are accessible to an embodied activity of the imagination.

The necessity of a rhetoric of climate change, however, can also be derived from the meaning of emotions. Indeed, they motivate indispensable aspects of individual and collective decision-making processes. Furthermore, it can be argued that persuasion of the 'rightness' of facts and arguments is an affective process, and that assent goes along with affective agreement. In other words, if films want to persuade us to change our lives, then this persuasion needs a platform of commonality, which they themselves must establish in the first place. This is why they necessarily refer to a spectrum of affectively shared values and norms, shared images, and narratives, working on producing individual and collective self-attributions so that they emotionally appear in contradiction to inaction and in line with environmentally friendly thinking and action.

We therefore must assume that the normative basis on which the films formulate their concern is not given without presuppositions, and must ask quite specifically where the 'importance' of the individual arguments and problems comes from. For cognitive schemata and linguistic spaces of resonance, for emotions and for visual forms and thus for embodied film perception, it does not go without question whether action is motivated, for instance, by the duty to conserve divine creation or by compassion for an endangered world of plants and animals, whether the political duty draws on compassion with far off affected population groups or with concern for the sustainability of one's own livelihood or even the existence of one's children or grandchildren. It is in no way a matter of setting values between rational and irrational, altruistic and egotistical motivations, but of recognizing the irrational and the egotistical as well, and of taking account of them in the central role they play for questions of argumentation and address.

Ultimately rhetoric is justified as an analytical method since it can be used to describe the persuasion, the creation of 'importance' and 'commonality' not simply as the state of things, but as processual forms, as "transformations of the emotional space."[12] Rhetoric allows us to understand the patriotic talk in AN INCONVENIENT TRUTH, the telling of stories, and the expressive tropes and

---

11 Radkau: *The Age of Ecology*, 99.
12 Hilge Landweer: Normativität, Moral und Gefühle. In: id. (ed.): *Gefühle. Struktur und Funktion*. Berlin 2007, 237–254, here 252 [trans. DH].

figures in the climate change films, as forms that produce evidence and that turn 'facts' into something like 'opinions.' Rhetoric as an instrument of description makes the films understandable as processes that shape the affect-dramaturgical journey through fear, insecurity, and anticipated guilt up to a sense of clarity and consistency.

Then what is rhetoric or where does it take place? Turning to Aristotle we can understand it as an art without an object of its own and without its own expertise, as the "means of discovering the possible means of persuasion in reference to any subject whatever."[13] In its ancient conception, rhetoric means the art of 'speaking well' in both the technological as well as the moral-ethical sense.[14] Hans Blumenberg, however, allows for a more general understanding of rhetoric as the absolute necessity of giving form and symbolizing in the construction of meaning and communication. This is derived anthropologically from a human relation to reality, which always works indirectly through forms of representation and metaphor, and from the fact that morality and reason are only given as an enduring provisional arrangement.[15] Such a justification of rhetoric – whether conceived in relation to intersubjective forms as in Blumenberg, to the institutionalized situation of speech in Aristotle and other ancient rhetorics,[16] or to the interaction in situations in the living environment such as in Hilge Landweer[17]– it is about critiquing a false idea of rationality as well as an affective and physical grounding of morality and action.

An expanded conception of rhetoric thus not only encompasses the diverse techniques of persuasive speech, but the fact that a formation unfolding in space and time is constitutive for every act of communicating, perceiving, and understanding. For:

> Real reason is: mostly unconscious (98 %); requires emotion; uses the "logic" of frames, metaphors, and narratives; is physical (in brain circuitry); and varies considerably, as

---

13 Aristotle: *The "Art" of Rhetoric*, trans. John Henry Freese. London 1926, 15.

14 Cf. Heinrich Lausberg: *Handbook of Literary Rhetoric. A Foundation for Literary Study*. Leiden 1998, 17–23.

15 Cf. Hans Blumenberg: An Anthropological Approach to the Contemporary Significance of Rhetoric. In: Kenneth Baynes, James Bohman, Thomas McCarthy (eds.): *After Philosophy. End or Transformation*. Cambridge 1987, 429–438.

16 These speech institutions include in particular speech before the law, advisory speech in political decisions, praise or reproof of individual persons, cf. Martin Vöhler: Zwischen Pathos und Reflexion. Bewegte Erfahrungen in der antiken Rhetorik. In: Anke Hennig, Brigitte Obermayr, Antje Wessels, Marie-Christin Wilm (eds.): *Bewegte Erfahrungen. Zwischen Emotionalität und Ästhetik*. Zürich 2008, 17–26, here 19.

17 Cf. Landweer: *Normativität, Moral und Gefühle*.

frames vary. And since the brain is set up to run a body, ideas and language can't directly fit the world but rather must go through the body.[18]

In particular for 'objects' such as Nature, Humanity, Time, History, etc. the operation of naming reaches its limits and becomes detached through metaphoricity. Rhetoric is not something that first had to be added to how we communicate the facts and the risks of man-made climate change. In view of the situation that these facts and risks are not 'things' that one can point a finger at, they need rhetoric as the "technique for coming to terms in the provisional state prior to all definitive truths and ethics. Rhetoric creates institutions where evident truths are lacking."[19]

In this respect many presentations, reports, texts, and films are at risk of leaving behind a gaping hole between calculation, that is, the measurable facts of the ecology of the natural sciences and the variable computations and models that are extrapolated from it, and fabulation, that is, the scenarios that tell and envision what this means for human beings. We act as if the pressure to act sprang from scientific facts, forgetting that numbers and graphics do not tell us 'what to do.' Behind an attitude that trusts solely in scientific exactness lies the idea that opinions are per se something unfounded, instead of seeing them as an attitude "for which the reasons are diffuse and not regulated by method,"[20] based not on theoretically confirmed reasons and agreements, but on provisional ones. Such an attitude makes orientation in action impossible exactly where it is most urgently desired, namely in view of the undefined and the undefinable. If in contrast we recognize and make explicit the rhetorical situation in which the facts are framed in each case, we can no longer conceal the fact that we are then also targeting opinion when we are citing seemingly 'naked' facts and evidence.

In view of a compulsion to act, the aim of rhetorical operations is to overcome the permanent provisional state of the human being's deficient truths, creating there moral and political institutions where final evidence is always lacking. These do not serve to veil and manipulate facts, they are not the opposite of truth – that would be the lie[21]– but serve to work out which issues are even at stake, and how it relates to the issues. They unfold and disclose situations.[22]

---

18 Lakoff: *Why it Matters How We Frame the Environment*, 72.

19 Blumenberg: *An Anthropological Approach to the Contemporary Significance of Rhetoric*, 435.

20 Blumenberg: *An Anthropological Approach to the Contemporary Significance of Rhetoric*, 448.

21 Cf. Arendt: *Wahrheit und Politik*; cf. Mellor: *The Politics of Accuracy in Judging Global Warming Films*.

22 Cf. Landweer: *Normativität, Moral und Gefühle*, 238–240.

And these rhetorical situations, in which as a rule there is "no certainty and there is room for doubt,"[23] do not simply consist of facts and issues 'about' which we speak, but of those speaking and those spoken to, and consist in part of reciprocal positioning: "What are the shared implicit ideas that form the groundwork for what is said?"[24] In this sense, rhetoric does not aim for conversion, but for "ensuring [...] non-contradiction,"[25] and for a recognition on the part of the one spoken to that the situation being unfolded is his or her own. This is why, in the discussion about the 'reality' of climate change and the consequences that follow for politics, economics, and the ordinary life of ordinary people, it is not a matter of facts in and of themselves, but of the place of these facts in a self-description that is constantly being reformed.[26]

The rhetorical situation therefore concerns not only the description of the issues, but also always attributions of self and other: Who is speaking to whom? What is appropriate here? And it operates with forms, metaphors, and feelings that anchor and ground norms in the commonly shared world. In this respect, any rationality of the argumentation does not lie in refraining from feelings, but in disclosing ambivalences and contradictory nuances, in working out an insecurity of feelings and the moral norm to establish feelings as the basis for norms and actions.[27] When climate change films evoke a feeling of anticipated guilt, they are not grounding or defining any 'new' norm or morality, but rather a new perspective on the existing validity of norms into a 'clear and clearly felt' liability and responsibility for plants and animals, people who live far away, and future generations.

If rhetoric means how people deal with the transformation of facts and opinions, how they deal with the compulsion to act in view of a lack of evidence, then it has a very particular entitlement with regard to climate change. Indeed, we are dealing here with an object that is characterized by a fundamental representational problem. The temporal and spatial expansion of climate change is completely inaccessible due to a complex interaction of the aftereffects of long past, present, and possible future activities, due to its global expansion, and due to unpredictable feedback phenomena, exceeding any possibility of ordinary perception.

---

23 Aristoteles: *The "Art" of Rhetoric*, 17.

24 Landweer: *Normativität, Moral und Gefühle*, 238 [trans. DH].

25 Blumenberg: *An Anthropological Approach to the Contemporary Significance of Rhetoric*, 442.

26 Cf. Blumenberg: *An Anthropological Approach to the Contemporary Significance of Rhetoric*, 435–436.

27 Cf. Landweer: *Normativität, Moral und Gefühle*, 248 and passim.

The 'being' of global climate change is on the one hand an accumulation of a vast array of statistical values and measurements, of computations and variables. These data designate physical and chemical processes whose spatio-temporal dimensions can hardly be grasped. On the other hand, global climate change is also the realization of these processes, which can still only be understood mathematically, in gradual shifts of climatic and biospheric parameters, which remain just as inaccessible to individual experience. And it is the realization of these processes in extraordinary events whose attribution to one another is unstable, and which can only be conceived outside their particular singularities with great difficulty: hurricanes, floods, droughts.

We should not be deceived, however, by the fact that this representational problem is usually only thematized as a problem in translating science for laypeople and political policy makers. Even within the empirical sciences and their positivistic epistemology this represents a radical paradigm change. The focus of climate research is no longer on observable, countable, and measureable facts, but predictions and hypotheses whose telos lies in the fact that even those who made them themselves hope that they do not come true. Research on global warming thus moves outside the modern discourse of knowledge production – and, instead of claiming and legitimating this outside as its own logic, climate research becomes vulnerable and dubious due to this discourse of the necessary falsifiability of scientific assertions.[28]

There are two dominant forms of synthesis as a reaction to the representational and epistemic difficulties of climate change. The first aims to foreground the rhetorical situation and to join the engaged individual as a speaker to the ideal image of the one spoken to. Whether it is the photographer James Balog in CHASING ICE (2012, Jeff Orlowski), the politician Al Gore, or the well-known television presenter David Attenborough. The other form of synthesizing climate discourse works in the direction of forming and symbolizing as modes of producing evidence. The computational model, such as is represented in the extensive and well-illustrated reports by the IPCC (Intergovernmental Panel on

---

28 Julie Doyle, for instance, has emphatically argued, in relation to photography, how the temporality of photographic depiction undercuts climate-political warnings of a possible future in such a way that the one and only thing remaining of the indexical verification of what is depicted of 'climate change' is the indicating gesture of taking a photography, that is, the input of the photographer as a witnessing figure. For the representation and communication of climate change in the practice of environmental activism, this means that it has become critical due to a primacy of visual communication, iconography, and the provision of evidence through visible effects: cf. Doyle: *Seeing the Climate?*

Climate Change)[29] functions as a matrix for mutually confirming graphics, curves, or animations – which, for instance, always represent an ever reddening globe. Neither generates affective and moral meaningfulness through individually ensured facts, nor through the quantifiable prognoses of damage: "They show nothing less than a concern for the whole. For this reason, climate images are also *political images* from the very beginning."[30]

4.2 Analysis of Audiovisual Rhetoric

The general necessity of rhetoric in the social communication about climate change can now be applied more specifically with regard to films as affect dramaturgies and expressive visual forms. A central step in this analysis will be to trace spectator experience, at the level of the film as well as at the level of the individual sequence, as an experience of evidence of what is being spoken about and shown. A brief example from AN INCONVENIENT TRUTH can be used here to show how the rhythm and expressive movement quality of the images generate their own dynamic, their own meaning, in an interplay with semantics and the rhythm of the spoken word, which goes beyond merely illustrating the content of the words.

The example is a clip from a sequence in which the principle, technological solvability of the problem is at issue (01:19:56–01:20:27). Initially we see Al Gore speaking before an audience, in the background is a huge graphic showing the possible technologies of cutting down on CO_2 – "We have everything we need, save perhaps political will." Then Gore gets louder, rousing his audience as the camera switches to a close up – "But you know what? In America, political will is a renewable resource." – and then as the audience begins applauding the camera cuts to a wide shot with a slightly ascending crane pan. In the next close up – "We have the ability to do this!" – a video projection begins in the background, a blurry wave-like movement that synaesthetically matches the applause that has broken out. This is followed by a short montage of black-and-white footage underscored by the following words: "Each one of us is a cause of global warming. But each of us can make choices to change that ..." An aerial shot of an extremely geometric suburban settlement is followed by three brief

---

29 Cf. Intergovernmental Panel on Climate Change: *Climate Change Report (IPCC). Synthesis report. Longer report – adopted 1 November 2014*. Geneva 2014. http://www.ipcc.ch/report/ar5/syr/ (last accessed: 12 September 2016).
30 Schneider: *Ein Darstellungsproblem des klimatischen Wandels?*, 84 [trans. DH].

shots filmed with an extreme telephoto lens, showing an intersection glimmering in the heat, a crowd of people, and a traffic jam on a five-lane highway. After this montage the image briefly goes to black on the word 'change' before other images appear, now in color, as Al Gore continues speaking: "… with the things we buy, the electricity we use, the cars we drive." Every phrase corresponds to a shot, at first another aerial shot of a broad solar field, then a steep view from below of an elevated electric train driving by a white skyscraper and blue skies in the background, and finally a time lapse shot of a giant, revolving solar panel in front of a vast landscape. All three shots are marked by radiating blue tones and a circular motion, of the camera itself in the first and second shots, of the rotating objects in the second and third. On the words "We can make choices to bring our individual carbon emissions …" we see a pan that follows a hybrid car from Toyota driving through a green-auburn landscape and a telephoto shot with similar coloring showing a random crowd of Asian people on bicycles. The sentence ends on "… to zero" and the montage ends with a fixed wide shot on a group of windmills stretching far out into the horizon in a rich green landscape against a blue sky. Taken together, the words and images create a new, increased sense that would not have come from either the one or the other alone. It is about nothing less than a revolution. Individual decisions are 'turns,' 'revolving and rotating,' which together 'change the world' and turn an urban constriction, a bland stasis in bleak black-and-white into a colorful world that is futuristic and natural at the same time. In addition, the montage promises that the changes get to a goal, achieving peace once again through 'zero emissions,' ending in a wide-open horizon.

The task of analyzing audiovisual rhetoric would be to show, as in this example, how language and the dynamic of audiovisual movement mutually structure one another in order to affect the spectator so that he or she takes on cognitive and moral attitudes, perceiving certain persons, objects, and issues as to be desired or rejected. As a technology of suggestion, audiovisual rhetoric cannot, nor should it be contrasted to a rational logic of language, as tends to be the case in certain works, such as those of Gesche Joost: "An argument is built quite differently in film than in a speech, it makes use of the suggestive power of images, working with visual evidence, whereas the verbal argument is more based on rational deduction."[31]

Not only is this strict alternative between rational and suggestive argumentation fundamentally wrong, such a separation and attribution also ignores the

---

31 Gesche Joost: *Bild-Sprache. Die audio-visuelle Rhetorik des Films.* Bielefeld 2008, 25 [trans. DH].

logical operations of the image and the suggestive power of the word. The specificity of audiovisual rhetoric should be derived much more from hypotheses about how images of expressive movement lead to modes of embodied experience so that the spoken word is perceived and realized in a different way (and in reverse) or how specific forms of providing evidence and deducing are formed by this.

Such a direction starts from the observation that great significance was intended for the gestural physical application of a speaking person already in ancient rhetorics[32] and that the gestural is a prominent object of examination in contemporary research questions in linguistics as well, as a physical behavior unfolding in time.[33] To put it more succinctly, to what degree can moving images also be understood as a behaving 'body' of a speaking person?[34]

A complete, systematically worked out, and integral approach to an audiovisual rhetoric is still something desirable in the current research landscape, something that can also not be achieved in the brevity of this chapter. Usually what has been examined are either special partial areas, such as the question of audiovisual figures and tropes, or intended effects, such as in advertising or political propaganda.[35] Here I will attempt to join the two sides together, analyzing concrete temporal structuring of image, sound, and word as affecting spectators and evaluating them in the context of their intended social effects.

Of the two mutually complementary analytical perspectives, which are both derived from the main features of ancient rhetoric, the first aims to produce a shared scope of values and moral and emotional significance by unfolding the rhetorical situation between speaking position, object, and addressee, while the second targets the forming and shaping processes as producing processes of understanding. The latter does not merely refer to the translation of figures and tropes from language into analogous audiovisual structures or to 'understanding' tropes due to images or a reversed decoding of visual

---

32 Cf. Völer: *Zwischen Pathos und Reflexion*, 23–25.

33 Cf. Cornelia Müller: *Metaphors Dead and Alive, Sleeping and Waking. A Dynamic View.* Chicago 2008; cf. Alan Cienki, Cornelia Müller (eds.): *Metaphor and Gesture.* Amsterdam / Philadelphia 2008.

34 This in no way means the passive transfer of literary and linguistic rhetorics to audiovisual presentations, but it does point to a wider question: What are the commonalities and particularities in each case of embodied constellations of perception in audiovisual media and in linguistic and gestural face-to-face communication as two media forms of shaping affective and cognitive processes? Cf. Cornelia Müller, Hermann Kappelhoff: *Cinematic Metaphor. Experience – Affectivity – Temporality.* Berlin / Boston 2018.

35 Cf. Joost: *Bild-Sprache*, 34–49.

sequences through language.[36] It is a matter of the common denominator between verbal language and audiovisual expressivity. Both the tropes and the figures of linguistic rhetoric can be understood as elements of temporal structure, and thus join up with the analysis of the temporal unfolding of images and sounds.[37]

The first analytical perspective is based on the model of Aristotle, according to whom forms of address in each case correspond at the same time to components of the rhetorical situation: "Now the proofs furnished by the speech are of three kinds. The first depends upon the moral character of the speaker, the second upon putting the hearer in to a certain frame of mind, the third upon the speech itself, in so far as it proves or seems to prove."[38]

What can initially be established is that all three means are directly aimed at the audience, at those who are to be persuaded. The decisive thought at this point is that successful rhetoric not only requires managing somehow, at some time, to bring all three proofs – *lógos* (argument / reason) or *prâgma* (thing), *êthos* (character), and *páthos* (emotion), or in their Latin version *docere* (to instruct), *delectare* (to please), and *movere* (to move)[39]– into effect, but that it depends on placing these forms of address in relation to one another dramaturgically so that they appear as inseparably bound to one another. Persuasive speech can only be conceived as a self-contained process that integrates all three levels.

---

36 Cf. Joost: *Bild-Sprache*, 40.

37 The two formal principles of linguistic rhetoric – tropes as forms of semantic manipulation in the sense of an improper speech and figures as manipulation of word order as well as the relation between sentence structures (cf. Lausberg: *Handbook of Literary Rhetoric*, 248–271 and 271–334) – can neither simply be adopted nor should a self-contained systematics of audiovisual figures be developed as an equivalent. (Joost suggests a division into five categories, which remain extremely heterogeneous within themselves, cf. Joost: *Bild-Sprache*, 151–154). But I would like to take up a theoretically grounded distinction to the degree that I identify figures, as a rule, as clearly delimited, closed forms in audiovisual forms, while tropes such as metaphor – especially as they are understood in cognitive linguistics – only unfold dynamically over the course of the film, relating to one another or developing from the transfer of a semantic or perceptual dynamic from one modality to the other; cf. Cornelia Müller, Susanne Tag: The Dynamics of Metaphor. Foregrounding and Activating Metaphoricity in Conversational Interaction. In: *Cognitive Semiotics* (2010), No. 6, 85–120; cf. Cornelia Müller, Christina Schmitt: Audio-visual Metaphors of the Financial Crisis. Meaning Making and the Flow of Experience. In: *Revista Brasileira de Linguística Aplicada / Brazilian Journal of Applied Linguistics* (2015), Vol. 15, No. 2 (Special Issue. Metaphor and Metonymy in Social Practices), 311–341; cf. Müller, Kappelhoff: *Cinematic Metaphor*.

38 Aristotle: *The "Art" of Rhetoric*, 17.

39 Cf. Lausberg: *Handbook of Literary Rhetoric*, 113–118.

The first means of persuasion, *lógos* or *docere*, initially seems to favor the level of language in film – the report, verbal naming, and deductions. We should, however, strictly distinguish between those theories that focus on a thinking proper to images and those, like Gesche Joost, who take a position that reduces the image to its representational function:

> Overall I assume that argumentative structures can be traced back to a latent, existing pattern and require the understanding of an intellectual background. Emphasizing the image thus does not mean that argumentative deductions are conveyed only qua visual evidence, but that the argumentation process follows a scheme of logical linkage, which makes use of the *evidence* for argumentative purposes.[40]

The audiovisual level would thus only contribute to the *lógos* when its clarity and undoubtedness cannot themselves be explicitly argumentative, but only replace explicit argumentational steps in language. In contrast, it should first be pointed out that the coming-to-bear of the 'language pattern' is only achieved in the first place through the audiovisual presentation. In other words: if thinking and understanding cannot be divorced from processes that proceed temporally, then – for all the admitted primacy of verbal language in many factually existing audiovisual formats – we cannot assume any theoretical priority between word and moving image. Therefore I am drawing on approaches that assume that the sequence of images can have an inherent argumentative quality.[41] Second, precisely in the case of climate change we cannot get around taking into account the possibility of an independent logical quality of diagrams and other visual representational forms, and from there also redefining the relationship of the argumentative potential of image and language.

While the difficulty of the audiovisual analysis of the *lógos* thus lies in the hasty identification of argument and word, the danger of the analysis of the second means of persuasion, that of *êthos* or *delectare*, is that it gets reduced to a process of identifying with the empirical speaker or protagonist.[42] This is above all the case when the Aristotelian character requirements of good

---

40 Joost: *Bild-Sprache*, 103 [trans. DH].

41 Cf. the paradigmatic positions of Eisenstein and Deleuze: Sergei M. Eisenstein: The Fourth Dimension in Cinema [1929]. In: id.: *Sergei Eisenstein. Selected Works, Volume 1, Writings, 1922–1934*, ed. Richard Taylor. London 1988, 181–194 and Gilles Deleuze: *Cinema I. The Movement-Image* [1983]. Minneapolis 1986 and also Gilles Deleuze: *Cinema II. The Time-Image* [1985]. Minneapolis 1989; cf. Raymond Bellour: Thinking, Recounting. The Cinema of Gilles Deleuze. In: *Discourse. Journal for Theoretical Studies in Media and Culture*, Vol. 20, No. 3, 56–75.

42 Gesche Joost, for instance, falls into this fallacy. After quite correctly separating the "orator" as a structural phenomenon from the empirical person (cf. Joost: *Bild-Sprache*, 86–93),

sense, virtue, and goodwill[43] are understood as characteristics of a natural person. The Latin version of *delectare*, that is, of pleasing, however, shows how this can be conceptualized differently in terms of media studies, namely as a particular form of affective effect on the side of the addressee, a gentle, constant "emotional bridge [...] *between* the speaker and the audience,"[44] which can be reconstructed as a function to be analyzed, as a formally applied structuring of the film. As relevant indications here in Latin rhetorics we can name the diversification of forms of expression and the introduction of humor.[45]

From the standpoint of film studies, which can look back at a long theoretical tradition of the moving image as an emotional machine, the role of *páthos* or *movere* in audiovisual rhetoric is seemingly self-explanatory. Nonetheless, here as well the analytical perspective must also be clearly marked out, for it is not a matter of emotions as the result of cognitive judgments about things and people. It is also not only about introducing what can be designated, in relation to its denotative contents, as particularly moving, shocking, or otherwise "strong images,"[46] nor is it about topoi that claim an extra-cinematic being as especially emotionalizing. Neither is it only about feelings represented by characters' gestures or facial expressions, or the capacity of the film to dispense stimuli at a purely physiological level that are then realized by the spectator as simple reflexes. On the contrary, we should assume a media specific process of emotionalizing spectators, which, following Hermann Kappelhoff's approach, is based on the film-analytical concept of the expressive movement as well as on a (neo)phenomenological understanding of embodiment.

I assume here that the decisive level of *páthos* or *movere* does not concern the emotional appeals that can be observed individually, but the complex feeling of agreement that unfolds through these. I understand this complex feeling of affectively grounding a value-community as the basis for sensing certain issues with specific feelings like disgust, rage, shame, or guilt, that is, as the basis for experiencing one's own sociality and being-in-relation in one's own body as a painful of pleasurable partisanship:

> Spectator feeling corresponds neither to an individual unity of affect nor to the summary succession of different, discrete emotions; it is much more tied to the continuous

---

she reintroduces a reduced idea of identification with characters as the structure of the *êthos* (cf. Joost: *Bild-Sprache*, 111–121).

43 Cf. Aristotle: *The "Art" of Rhetoric*, 171.

44 Lausberg: *Handbook of Literary Rhetoric*, 114 [emphasis MG].

45 Cf. Lausberg: *Handbook of Literary Rhetoric*, 114–115.

46 Joost: *Bild-Sprache*, 109 [trans. DH]; cf. Lausberg: *Handbook of Literary Rhetoric*, 116.

modeling of a complex emotion that unfolds over the course of the film (a mood, an atmosphere), which is grounded in aesthetic pleasure.[47]

At the same time we should emphasize that influencing spectators' feelings by modeling their perceptual sensation in this way does not detract them from reasoning. While there is indeed a general preconception that quickly positions feelings as something downstream from argumentation that is presumed in the listener in order to appeal to it, on closer inspection they can in fact be made relevant in communication, through their relation to objects and matters of fact, their function in disclosing the world and values. In the reciprocal unfolding of *lógos*, *êthos*, and *páthos* feelings can be credibly justified, feelings can be represented as legitimate or illegitimate: "Speakers attempt to explain why they feel what they feel and, in a more normative way, why everyone should feel what they feel."[48]

As will be shown in the analysis of AN INCONVENIENT TRUTH, the decisive point at which the heuristic separation of the three means of persuasion is once again combined is that of forming identity and belonging: the community of those who feel that the reasonable reasons for feeling this way or that are legitimate and credible, the community of those who see the evidence of human-induced climate change as legitimate reasons to feel fear, to be angry at certain agents, and to feel guilty themselves – and from this to develop motivation for specific actions.

Analyzing audiovisual rhetoric is one way to describe the fundamental dimension of the multimodal, affectively based construction of meaning through temporally structured processes.[49] Building on this, cultural work on certain recurring forms of such constructions of meaning can be analyzed, as has been done for various areas of communication in recent decades, preferentially in relation to the object of the metaphor.

Two theoretical presuppositions about audiovisual rhetoric must be added to this. The rhetorical creation to be analyzed can and should not be viewed as something to be added on to non-rhetorical material "as a deviation from ground zero."[50] Instead, within the always already temporally structured and formed moving images, certain recurring, formulaic patterns should be shown and described with regard to their affective and persuasive effects. And precisely with respect to audiovisual metaphors and other topoi, it is important not simply to understand them as translations of previous tropes from language into audiovisual

---

47 Kappelhoff, Bakels: *Zuschauergefühl*, 86 [trans. DH].

48 Raphaël Micheli: Emotions as Objects of Argumentative Constructions. In: *Argumentation* (2010), Vol. 24, No. 1, 1–17, here 13; cf. also Landweer: *Normativität, Moral und Gefühle*.

49 Cf. Kappelhoff, Müller: *Embodied Meaning Construction*.

50 Joost: *Bild-Sprache*, 148 [trans. DH].

illustrations, or to inquire into them only by understanding tropes from language based on corresponding images and visual contents, or by understanding visual tropes based on their illustration in language. This amounts to reconsidering:

> the relationship between logos and the imagination. The realm of the imagination could no longer be regarded solely as the substrate for transformations into conceptuality – on the assumption that each element could be processed and converted in turn, so to speak, until the supply of images was used up – but as a catalytic sphere from which the universe of concepts continually renews itself, without thereby converting and exhausting this founding reserve.[51]

Just as we can reconstruct the poetics of narrative film forms through the logic of a law of the particular world that unfolds over the course of the film, we can also show the fundamental principles of the temporal unfolding of image, sound, and language for non-fictional forms.[52] These principles in turn determine consistent metaphorical tropes, the supply of images, and general outlines, channeling "what can offer itself up for experience in the first place."[53]

Climate change films, according to the hypothesis that I am following here, work on giving the spectator a certain experience, which can be described as the affective experience of being embedded in collective contexts of causation, suffering, and compensation. By arranging the rhetorical situation and by unfolding physically experienced processes of creating meaning and sense over time, the films shape a construction of identity – be it national, be it an idea of world citizenship – which is linked with moral evidence.

In the following I will show how films shape the time of watching as the time of reconstructing understanding and of assuming responsibility. How do they turn 'facts' into something like 'opinions' through 'persuasive speech'? How do they convey the impression of understanding and consenting to the spectator as an aesthetically experienced whole?

The terminological chain of nature, environment, and Earth signifies the relation between a humanly shared world and a morally relevant counterpart, which at the same time is part of this common world. In their history as terms, these are already extremely heterogeneous in themselves, because there is no conceptual bracket that keeps together nature as an object of the sciences, of research into natural laws and the idea of nature as an organism, as a pure

---

51 Hans Blumenberg: *Paradigms for a Metaphorology* [1960], trans. Robert Savage. Ithica 2010, 4.
52 Cf. Kappelhoff, Müller: *Embodied Meaning Construction*; Kappelhoff: *Die vierte Dimension des Bewegungsbildes.*
53 Blumenberg: *Paradigms for a Metaphorology*, 63.

quality and open space for human self-realization.[54] The polyvalence of the term nature does not lead straight "to the modern concern for nature."[55] There is thus a fundamental fluctuation that prevails in the climate change films between a wide variety of 'natures,' which ultimately also entails implicit and completely divergent ideas of the human being as an agent between cultural entity and natural product.[56]

The aim of introducing the term Anthropocene is not only to gain a new understanding of nature, as if this would already be achieving something. For the fact that nature is no longer boundlessly superior to human beings in the Anthropocene is only one side of the coin. Unfortunately, we must learn by the same token that it is therefore also no longer boundlessly resilient. There are bounds now, but we do not know where they lie.[57] Our task is "a new realization of the factually existing limitations of human beings."[58] And since this realization means traversing the limits in a certain way, it is important that this traversal only take place in the imagination and in speculation, and not in the irreversible processes of the technicalization of the world.[59]

The metaphor of "Spaceship Earth"[60] is one such imaginative attempt to realize these limits and to rehabilitate a geocentric and anthropomorphic worldview: the Earth understood as the home for humanity, whose finiteness would be made into an elementary component of its political, scientific, and technological plans.[61] According to Barbara Ward and Buckminster Fuller,

---

54 Cf. Radkau: *The Age of Ecology*, 11–13.

55 Radkau: *The Age of Ecology*, 12. For Radkau this is reflected in the heterogeneous sources and particularities of environmental protection, from the fight against water and air pollution and animal and forestry conservation on to nuclear risks. Only since the end of the Cold War have these extremely varied topics temporarily given way to a new *grand récit* in climate change.

56 Cf. Ruth Groh, Dieter Groh: *Die Außenwelt der Innenwelt. Zur Kulturgeschichte der Natur.* Vol. II. Frankfurt a. M. 1996, 91; cf. also Ruth Groh, Dieter Groh: *Weltbild und Naturaneignung. Zur Kulturgeschichte der Natur.* Vol. II. Frankfurt a. M. 1991.

57 Cf. Peter Sloterdijk: *How big is 'big'?* http://www.collegium-international.org/index.php/en/contributions/127-how-big-is-big (last accessed: 13 March 2018).

58 Hannah Arendt: The Archimedean Point [1969]. In: id.: *Thinking without a Banister. Essays in Understanding 1953–1975.* New York 2018, 406–418, here 417.

59 Cf. Arendt: *The Archimedean Point.*

60 This metaphor was developed by Buckminster Fuller and shortly thereafter taken up by Barbara Ward. It was recently updated by Peter Sloterdijk and others. Cf. Barbara Ward: *Spaceship Earth.* New York 1966; cf. Sloterdijk: *How big is 'big'?*; cf. Buckminster Fuller: *Operating Manual for Spaceship Earth.* Carbondale / Edwardsville 1969.

61 Cf. Hannah Arendt: The Conquest of Space and the Stature of Man [1968]. In: *Between Past and Future. Eight Exercises in Political Thought.* New York 2006, 260–274, here 273.

since the beginning of industrialization we live on a hybrid planet, the 'Earth' is no longer a natural variable, but a construct.[62] The Earth is no longer the 'outside' of an infinite nature, but an interior, and this interior not only has a 'memory,' it also provides feedback.[63] In order to manage, to navigate this post-natural world, another technology will be necessary, a technology that continues "natural production principles at an artificial level."[64] This, incidentally, would bring humanity, irony of history, back to Aristotle's concept of technology, according to which we "must imagine the artificial structure as a product of nature"[65]– only that this is now based on reciprocity.

The idea of Spaceship Earth has become a visual form, not least through the photograph called *Blue Marble*, which was taken on December 7, 1972 by the Apollo 17 Mission.[66] The idea of the Earth in this image has itself become a hybrid, mediating between the sense of distance and technological fantasies of control, and an awareness for the fragile physical character of the Earth.[67] One might say that the application of a variety of metaphors, tropes, and figures of nature, environment, and Earth lies in producing this fragility as an embodied attitude on the side of the spectator. Even if we establish that there is no solidly established register for the Anthropocene as a new form of history – what kinds of action, what agents, what categories of means and ends count?[68]– it is still beyond doubt that this will not work without moral rigor and layers of imagination. Without a concept of the Earth as a hybrid human-nature spaceship, as something innocent, sensitive, and fragile, there can be no concern, no fear of loss, and no motivation to act.

---

62 Cf. Sloterdijk: *How big is 'big'?*

63 Cf. Sloterdijk: *How big is 'big'?*

64 Sloterdijk: *How big is 'big'?*

65 Hans Blumenberg; Imitation of Nature. Toward a Prehistory of the Idea of the Creative Being. In: *Qui Parle* (2000), Vol. 1, No. 12, 17–54, here 41.

66 Cf. Horst Bredekamp: Blue Marble. Der Blaue Planet. In: Christoph Markschies, Ingeborg Reichle, Jochen Brüning, Peter Deuflhard (eds.): *Atlas der Weltbilder*. Berlin 2011, 367–375. For Bredekamp the reason for the deliberate technological sheen of the assumption is also: the orientation to the customs of cartography, the aesthetics and symbolism of the form, of the "circular lighting of a dark square" (Bredekamp: *Blue Marble. Der Blaue Planet*, 368 [trans. DH]).

67 Cf. Bredekamp: *Blue Marble. Der Blaue Planet*, 370; cf. Horst Bredekamp: Der Mensch als Mörder der Natur. Das 'Iudicium Iovis' von Paulus Niavis und die Leibmetaphorik. In: Heimo Reinitzer (ed.): *All Geschöpf ist Zung' und Mund*. Hamburg 1984, 261–283.

68 Cf. Bruno Latour: *Politics of Nature. How to Bring the Sciences Into Democracy*. Cambridge 2004, 154–161, and passim.

If we follow these reflections and observations, we can clearly derive the role of an 'anticipated guilt' as a hinge between the evidence from the natural sciences, the consequences calculated, and the impetus to act. We must experience solidarity with the physicality of the Earth and with the future passengers in the moment of their potential injury and their possible recovery as a pressure that weighs down on us and can only be relieved through correct action. The sense of guilt as an affect of the irreversibility of time must be projected into the future, the unconscious flow of the present must be interrupted, so that there can even be something like a future.

The films, therefore, operate – not only in relation to the physical process of climate change – with complex temporalities: the cause lies in the past, which cannot be changed, and the present, but the consequences lie in the future, which runs along the narrow edge between necessarily possible and simultaneously not unavoidable. Even in relation to ethical-moral valuation, the interaction of various time references and speeds is relevant here. I propose viewing the anticipated sense of guilt – and not inevitable, essentially tragic guilt – as a possible affect-dramaturgical form with which to shape just this complex perspective on time and the capacity to act. The specific temporality of the sense of guilt would then be turned upside down by anticipating it. For the actual area of concentration of the sense of guilt is not in future, but in the already committed, irreversible damage to another,[69] and it appears with a temporal delay:

> Guilt as a phenomenon has a very clear temporal unfolding. The moment of the guilt feeling occurs after that moment in which the action that is the source of the guilt feeling has been committed. [...] In order to make this relationship between the two moments intelligible we have to introduce an element of reconstruction which ties together the two moments. The reconstruction concerns a re-evaluation of the action that was committed in the moment of negligence. [...] What the act of reconstruction accomplishes is a changing of the "innocent" situation into a moment of negligence, which is revealed in and through the moment of guilt.[70]

The anticipated sense of guilt in the discourse of climate change aims completely to rework this temporal unfolding, to re-evaluate the seeming 'innocence' of contemporary behavior.

---

69 Cf. Demmerling, Landweer: *Philosophie der Gefühle*, 222–223.
70 Gunnar Karlsson, Lennart G. Sjöberg: The Experiences of Guilt and Shame. A Phenomenological-Psychological Study. In: *Human Studies* (2009), Vol. 32, No. 3, 335–355, here 339.

4.3 An Inconvenient Truth: A Patriotic Speech

Any examination of the cinematic treatment of climate change cannot get around two particular films: Roland Emmerich's The Day After Tomorrow (2004), "the first major disaster movie of the post-9/11 era,"[71] and Al Gore and Davis Guggenheim's An Inconvenient Truth. While the first contributed to turning the relationship of humanity to nature into a reference point for the popular imagination, a wave that certainly reached its highpoint with James Cameron's Avatar (2009), the latter has contributed, unlike any other film, to turning climate consciousness and environmental problems into an object for the kind of documentary films shown in cinemas, and the elevated public awareness associated with this.

The fact that An Inconvenient Truth not only won the Oscar for Best Documentary in 2007, but earned Al Gore and the International Panel on Climate Change the Nobel Peace Prize in December 2007, positions it as distinguished and exemplary both within the media industry as well as in the wider public: "These awards position Gore's environmental rhetoric as internationally authorized and in certain ways globally sanctioned as praiseworthy."[72] The doubled distinction, even if the official award winner at the Oscars was the film's director Davis Guggenheim, made it difficult afterwards to distinguish between the achievement of the film and of the person Al Gore:

> We all owe him a huge debt of gratitude for his singular, Nobel Peace Prize-winning effort to alert the world to the disruptive potential of climate change through his documentary An Inconvenient Truth, at a time when many, many people wanted to just ignore it – and they still do. Never has one man done more to wake up the world to a serious problem than Al Gore has.[73]

As much as one might argue over the superlatives that this praise ends up with, this opinion is representative for the recognition of the central role of Gore and his film for the discourse on climate change, both as a reference point within media treatment of it as well as for the standards and stereotypes of ways of representing influenced by it. It is therefore no surprise that the interest of so-

---

71 Stephen Keane: *Disaster Movies. The Cinema of Catastrophe.* New York / Chichester 2001, 95.

72 Laura Johnson: (Environmental) Rhetorics of Tempered Apocalypticism in An Inconvenient Truth. In: *Rhetoric Review* (2009), Vol. 28, No. 1, 29–46, here 29.

73 Thomas L. Friedman: *Hot, Flat, and Crowded. Why We Need a Green Revolution – And How It Can Renew America.* New York 2008, 114.

called climate skeptics is concentrated on discrediting the representational means of this *one* film.[74]

The appearance of the orator

This strong symbiosis between the film and the public persona Al Gore can not only be traced back to facts and concomitant circumstances outside the film, or to press about the film fixated on personality, it is an elementary component of the staging strategies of the film itself.[75] In the following I would like to show how the film AN INCONVENIENT TRUTH generates an artificial character named 'Al Gore' as *auctoritas* and as the hero of a puritan jeremiad,[76] and how this character – in the sense of the understanding of *êthos* and *delectare* from ancient rhetoric – not only holds together the various forms of address in the film, but also bundles together the different traditions that have formed in the discourse about the environment and climate.

This bundling can be seen most clearly in the appearance of the character 'Gore' at the beginning of the film. Here it turns out that this is no staging of a pre-existing person speaking to us, but that this speaker himself only emerges in the first place through a reciprocal affecting of language and audiovisuality, through the bundling of forms of discourse, and through the temporal unfolding of a spectator position in the cinematic composition.

It begins with a unit of expressive movement in which voice and image are clearly merged with one another. Shots of a peaceful riverbank in the warm, late afternoon light of summer are accompanied by an off-screen voice, the

74 A particularly telling example here would be the legal controversy that arose in 2007 over using AN INCONVENIENT TRUTH in schools in Great Britain, which, not coincidentally, also coincided with the attempt to establish THE GREAT GLOBAL WARMING SWINDLE (2007, Martin Durkin) as a cinematic 'response' to Al Gore. Cf. Jonathan Leake: Please, Sir! Gore's Got Warming Wrong. In: *The Sunday Times* (14 October 2007); cf. Mellor: *The Politics of Accuracy in Judging Global Warming Films.*

75 Cf. Johnson: *(Environmental) Rhetorics of Tempered Apocalypticism in AN INCONVENIENT TRUTH*, 37.

76 Cf. Thomas Rosteck, Thomas S. Frentz: Myth and Multiple Readings in Environmental Rhetoric. The Case of AN INCONVENIENT TRUTH. In: *Quarterly Journal of Speech* (2009), Vol. 95, No. 1, 1–19; cf. Richard Hamblyn: The Whistleblower and the Canary. Rhetorical Constructions of Climate Change. In: *Journal of Historical Geography* (2009), Vol. 35, No. 2, 223–236.

voice of Al Gore speaking slowly, with deliberate pauses, soft piano chords punctuate his speech:

> You look at that river gently flowing by. You notice the leaves rustling with the wind. You hear the birds; you hear the tree frogs. In the distance you hear a cow. You feel the grass. The mud gives a little bit on the river bank. It's quiet; it's peaceful. And all of a sudden, it's a gear shift inside you. And it's like taking a deep breath and going: "Oh yeah, I forgot about this." (0:00:34–0:01:20)

Along with these calls to an embodied power of the imagination, a simulated sensuality of the landscape being experienced here – we *see* and *hear*, we *feel* the grass and the consistency of the earth – the images are framed by a constant, subtle movement of the camera, which does not convey the sense data individually evoked by the words (we do not hear any cow in the distance), but that shape the described qualities of this language as a sensation. A slow pan to the right accompanies the 'gently flowing by' of the river, what is acoustically imagined is synaesthetically represented by the flickering of the light reflecting from the water to the undersides of the leaves. A slow pan back to the left rounds off this figure, insisting on the words "taking a deep breath and going ..." to the river, as if the camera were following the call to breathe deeply. A metaphor about remembering and forgetting is being set up, which will only be completely realized over the course of the film, played through in a variety of facets, namely the metaphor of 'time as a river.'

Our seeing and hearing merge in this unit of expressive movement into an imagination of nature as a spiritual resource. Significantly then, the first 50 seconds of the film link the following arguments with a very specifically American aesthetics, philosophy, and politics of nature, namely a desire to realize, in views of the American landscape, the "spiritual content [...] that landscape could provide."[77]

In Ralph Waldo Emerson and Henry David Thoreau the contemplative view to the landscape then also becomes paradigmatic for the renunciation of European philosophy as a system in favor of the fragment, of closeness and baseness, of the everyday as the starting point to fine tune their own philosophy.[78]

> In the woods we return to reason and faith. [...] Standing on the bare ground, – my head bathed by the blithe air and uplifted into infinite space, – all mean egotism vanishes. [...]

---

77 Joshua C. Taylor: *America as Art*. Washington D. C. 1976, 107. This moral aesthetics of landscape, with the detour through landscape conservation as one of the oldest and most effective strands of the environmental movements, continues to work in the current shaping of the power to imagine climate change. Cf. Taylor: *America as Art*, 130.
78 Cf. Stanley Cavell: *The Senses of Walden*. Chicago 1981, 141–152, and passim.

> In the tranquil landscape, and especially in the distant line of the horizon, man beholds somewhat as beautiful as his own nature.[79]

The film thus invites us to perceive the beauty of a peaceful landscape,[80] to stand on the 'bare ground.' AN INCONVENIENT TRUTH also rises up from this ground into 'infinite space,' showing us, first on a computer screen, then as a motif filling up the entire movie screen, the Earth is a photograph taken from outer space, into which the camera slowly zooms. The picture of the Earth marks the beginning of the lecture as a narrative report (0:01:20–0:01:40): "This is the first picture of the Earth from space that any of us ever saw. It was taken on Christmas Eve 1968, during the Apollo 8 mission." It therefore begins with the question 'what will be spoken about,' which is visually linked immediately to the question 'who is being spoken to?' Four brief shots show parts of a audience that seems to be extremely spellbound. In each shot there are only 3 to 6 people that can seen at any given time, sitting in a relatively dark room with their faces illuminated from the front. This brevity contributes the impression of a mixed, but on average quite young, educated, and academic looking audience.

This beginning, however, is only the semblance of a beginning. In the middle of the second sentence it fades out and another speech fragment with a totally changed tonality fades in. The following three shots (0:01:40–0:01:47) now show a completely different audience, clearly Asian looking faces in a new setting. This fragment of speech is then once again faded out and a diffuse composition rich in orchestral timbre now takes over the soundtrack, as the image jumps to the lighting of yet another room, showing us the speaker, Al Gore, from behind as he bows to his applauding audience. The orchestral sounds and the moving hand camera that films Gore from behind as he is constantly surrounded by a wide variety of people in the following, blend spaces and times into an impressionistic merger, into a simultaneously intimate and public co-presence of speaker and listeners (0:01:47–0:02:06). The fact that this man has something to say is initially clarified to us by nothing other than the fact that people are listening to what he has to say.

In the following shot, however, this authority becomes a specific quality of the character as an inherent numinous power. What ensues is the 'actual' appearance of Al Gore on stage as the speaker (0:02:06–0:02:22). He is shown again from behind, followed by a slightly shaky hand camera. His purposeful

---

79 Ralph Waldo Emerson: Nature [1836]. In: id.: *Nature and Selected Essays.* New York 1982, 35–82, here 39.

80 Later in the film, however, this landscape significantly turns out not to be untouched, but a cultural landscape completely shaped by people: the Gore family farm.

movement; the backlighting in the otherwise dark, narrow hall, which turns his body into a glowing silhouette, giving out short flashes through the movement; a voice over a loudspeaker that sounds as if it were coming from far away, announcing "Ladies and gentlemen: Al Gore" – all this forms the appearance as one of a classic hero of Hollywood cinema, a Rocky of environmental politics. And in order to attenuate this overblown presentation this is followed by a turn, the valence of which cannot be overestimated for the *êthos* of the speaker. He indicates humor, self-mockery, and modesty by introducing himself with the words: "I am Al Gore. I used to be the next President of the United States of America." This paradoxical formulation is met with laughter and applause from the audience. Even when he objects "I don't find that particularly funny," he lowers his head smiling, signaling modesty.

After this initial appearance, which itself is multiple, comes another facet, another appearance of the character Al Gore. Accompanied by the wafting orchestral composition, six shots show him to be a "visible personification of that affective media loop"[81] (0:02:22–0:02:40). People cheering on the roadside, Gore at his podium, coming out of Air Force One waving, enthusiastically being greeted with his wife, etc. The archival footage from the life of a statesman gradually becomes more abstract and defamiliarized, for it is filmed from a television screen, as is clear from a bluish tinge and stripes running from bottom to top, and the camera zooms in so close to the screen in the end that the last shot is an extreme close-up of Gore, marked by the horizontal stripes of a television screen. His gaze in the last shot is focused far away to the right, by which the film transitions to the next decisive aspect of the character, his quality as a 'visionary.'

The third unit of expressive movement in the opening scene – after the image of nature and the multiple appearances of Al Gore – is now showing the privileged relationship between Al Gore and 'this story' (0:02:40–0:04:11). He is sitting in the back of a limousine, a laptop open on his lap, his voice speaks from off screen: "I've been trying to tell this story for a long time and I feel as if I've failed to get the message across." In the background an unspecified suburban backdrop rushes by from right to left. Gore in close up, shown slightly from below, looks out pensively from the car toward the right, tree tops fly by unclearly in the background, and the film now edits this gaze into the off-screen space with a parallel tracking shot to a dirty-blackened ice landscape that seems to be melting, with many small icebergs drifting toward it. This edit uses the fact that the speed of this shot corresponds very precisely to the speed of the background that whisked by in the previous shot, allowing this fragile

---

81 Brian Massumi: *Politics of Affect*. Cambridge 2015, 33.

landscape to appear as a point-of-view shot. Even while riding in a car through American suburbia, Al Gore has a clear view of the fate of the planet.

The music then becomes more intense, more dissonant, and a high and unpleasant, quivering sound, which will be purposefully used later in the film, turns the following shots of melting blocks of ice, dried up desert landscapes, smoking chimneys, and a burning scrubland into a threatening backdrop. Once again a close up – "I was in politics for a long time. I'm proud of my service." – links this image with a menace that is increased once again. Blurry and shaky shots of a storm, presumably Hurricane Katrina, at one point underscored with a brief alarming sequence of sounds mixing metallic scraping with indistinct screams of people. While we can now hear a radio interview on the soundtrack with Ray Nagin, the mayor of New Orleans at the time that Hurricane Katrina flooded the city, what we see is another stage of the functional defining of the character Al Gore as a mediator (0:03:21–0:04:12). In the following shots, he is associated with the destruction of the environment and the destructive force of nature not only through the structure of the gaze, but also through the act of arranging media witnesses. Over and over a screen with news footage forms the background of an extreme close up, we see detail shots of Gore's computer screen, on which he is preparing a keynote presentation (that is, the presentation that we are about to see as spectators of the film).

Over the course of the third unit of expressive movement the spatiality of the image has increasingly transformed into a medial, two-dimensional surface. Of the movement through space, be it during the various station of the 'appearance,' be it the tracking shot along the melting ice, the only thing left now is a pure, intensity of surface movement, which is seen in the last shot of the opening sequence as a reflection of light and shadow on the car window behind which Gore is sitting, as the title of the film comes onto the image (0:04:00–0:04:12). From now on the film develops along the basic structure of a lecture in front of an audience, which is shown as continuous with recurring, reacting faces. This lecture situation is kept so unspecific that it can cover all possible speaking situations and relationships between speakers and listeners: the classroom (there are frequent references to Al Gore as a schoolboy), the genre of public slide show presentation by scientists or world travelers, the polis, and "the mythical town hall of primitive democracy."[82]

The opening sequence of AN INCONVENIENT TRUTH goes to great pains to present the speaking position of Al Gore as a figure, as an artificial construct.

---

82 Jonathan Kahana: *Intelligence Work. The Politics of American Documentary*. New York 2008, 31.

For the topic of the film is not immediately given, but is initially only schematically present, only getting its contours in the following course of the film. To this point it has only been an 'it.' An 'it' that was forgotten, a "story" or "message," an 'it' that should be recognized and acknowledged. And at the same time 'it' contains "the moral imperative to make big changes." But where does this imperative come from? What moral norms are at stake here, and where and how are they constituted? The film begins by representing the norm of a spiritual quality proper to nature, to be founded as a sense experience in the world of the spectator. On this basis it develops a concrete guideline for its spectators, giving them a model in the images of the attentive and almost reverentially listening audience, and it develops Al Gore as a versatile point of contact and relay station for all possible discursive forms about climate change.

The emphasis on the *êthos*, on "Who is speaking?" in the opening sequence provides us with a clue to the rhetorical structure of the film and to the rhetorical situation as An Inconvenient Truth presents it. For the figure of the speaker is positioned so strongly and dominantly in relation to the spectator position because the latter is still unclear as the subject of concern, fear, or guilt, and has to be produced in the first place by the film. The film will be revealed in the end as a patriotic speech, which is already hinted at here by the symbols of the state that Al Gore is embedded in, or that are tellingly placed into the background. But this patriotic speech is aimed at an understanding of the American nation as a part of the world population, which is not yet contained in the current patriotic discourse and which the film attempts to generate as an affective attitude and a moral stance. And it generates this by starting from a new, scientifically informed viewpoint on the issue, which gets its relevance as a moral message through the commitment and credibility of the one who brings this information to the people in such a way that those who are listening to him, heeding him, form the core of a new understanding of community.

Lógos

The 'truth' that the film carries in its title, and that is meant to be backed scientifically, become plausible, precisely in the first half of An Inconvenient Truth through the history of the origins of the facts presented, an operation that has to do with the original concept of *evidentia* in Latin rhetoric, which is:

> the vividly detailed depiction of a broadly conceived whole object [...] through the enumeration of (real or invented) observable details. [...] The simultaneity of the details

> which determines the static character of the object as a whole is the eyewitness's experience of simultaneousness; the speaker places himself and his audience in the position of the eyewitness.[83]

The fact of rising carbon dioxide levels in the air is thus combined with the vivid depiction of carrying out the first measurements and the biographical encounter between the speaker and the originator of this series of tests. The constantly thinning ice caps in the Arctic and Antarctic are primed by details, such as the names of the participating scientists, friends of Al Gore, and their personal observations.

There is a different argumentative function to the animation sequence at the beginning of the film, which is kept simple (0:08:31–0:09:35). It is not the greenhouse effect represented here, but the simplicity of this process, its quality as premise, as an unassailable assumption: "That brings up the basic science of global warming and I'm not going to spend a lot of time on this because you know it well." This process thus corresponds to the idea of the enthymeme as one of the most important means in Aristotle's *Rhetoric*, namely not explicitly to formulate certain steps of argumentation, particularly of premises, but to leave them implicit as the opinions shared by the listeners, so that "we suppose anything to have been demonstrated".[84] In Aristotle it becomes clear that for rhetoric the true and the seemingly true, the proven and the seemingly proven can be traced back to the same forms and the same cognitive capacities. For the spectators of AN INCONVENIENT TRUTH it thus means that at the moment when they perceive the perceptual simplicity of the process, they simultaneously accept it as an appropriate description, particularly since space is taken for a counter argument in the 'alternative' explanation that follows. Every possible objection is shown and outdone by the satirical animation sequence in the style of Matt Groening's TV series THE SIMPSONS, and thus deflated and ridiculed in advance.

The majority of the film's argumentation afterwards refers to the evidence that climatic changes are taking place, that these are associated with greenhouse gasses, and that they have a wide variety of effects on nature and humanity. Only at two points is there any explicit engagement with the fact that concrete human activity is the cause of these changes. The first is purely verbal in the presentation of the fundamental schema of the greenhouse effect (0:07:35–0:09:35) and the second is embedded in a very general reflection

---

83 Lausberg: *Handbook of Literary Rhetoric*, 359.
84 Aristotle: *The "Art" of Rhetoric*, 9.

about technology and population growth as factors that have turned the human species into a force of nature (1:00:59–1:06:43).

This departure from locating climate change in everyday, individual, or collective behavior is thus both cause and effect for a quite specific quality of the film's poetics, namely the trust in graphs as a key medium of scientificity:

> The film establishes the graph as a compelling form of public knowledge and reckoning, shown singly, with animated lines, or in combination with other visual forms such as world maps and scenic and aerial landscape images, particularly those which show the insignia of climate change, from shrinking lakes to collapsing ice walls. Panoramic in scope, running the length of the lecture stage, the graphs plot various indices of climate change over various timescales, their local topography of peaks and troughs telling an over-riding story.[85]

The decisive point at this stage is in fact that it is not a matter of the evidence of the individual graph, that not every curve and every bar graph claims something on its own, but that a kind of 'history of progress' is in fact being spun from graph to graph. A 'highlight' of this history is surely the moment when Al Gore's body markedly becomes a part of the graph, his body becomes the cursor on the screen as a graphic display, and he has to be lifted up in order to be able to show the prognosis for the state of CO_2 concentration (0:21:42–0:23:40).[86]

But it is not only visually that the orator is part of the graphics as a seemingly neutral form of knowledge. At one point, for instance, the camera rolls horizontally from left to right over a bar graph of average annual temperatures (0:27:00–0:27:16), while we hear Gore's voice speaking with a monotonous modulated voice: "These are actual measurements of atmospheric temperatures since our Civil War. Any given year it looks like it's going down ..." Precisely at the moment when he says "... but the overall trend is extremely clear ..." the direction the camera is moving changes from horizontal to diagonal going up on the right, accelerating its motion with words that are particularly strongly emphasized, also prosodically: "... and in recent years, it's uninterrupted and it is intensifying."

Al Gore's body and voice being turned into a graph is only one aspect that makes it clear here how much the credibility of the figure speaking in this film

---

85 Stephen Daniels, Georgina H. Endfield: Narratives of Climate Change. Introduction. In: *Journal of Historical Geography* (2009), Vol. 35, No. 2 (Special Issue. Narratives of Climate Change), 215–222, here 221.

86 There is a variation on this deictic function in the second half of the BBC documentary The Truth about Climate Change (0:53), in which Sir David Attenborough and a scientist walk along a graph projected on the floor of a large hall, taking the verbal metaphor "to walk somebody through something" at its word.

is becoming the central reference value for the rhetorical structure. His own life story and the argumentation are closely linked, the representation of scientific facts is tied to the narrative of the learning processes of the speaker himself. And this is constantly related to the audience, whose presence is emphasized time and again, listening attentively, laughing, applauding.

Êthos

There are very few media figures that fulfill the characteristics of cleverness, virtue, and goodwill through their pure presence, through their persona as does Sir David Attenborough, who, in the first five minutes of the BBC documentary ARE WE CHANGING PLANET EARTH? puts himself into relation to the evidence of his earlier nature reports, so that the title not only seems to mean the changing of the planet, but also a revision, a reworking of his own, epic, thirteen-part series LIFE ON EARTH (1979). The credibility of his character is created through the use of his own body alone, both in the jungle as well as at his desk, as the image of the wise old man.

In the case of AN INCONVENIENT TRUTH the production of credibility takes on two different basic forms as 'putting oneself in play.' The one concerns the open ways of dealing with the film's own rhetoricity, the other the narrative construction with which the facts and Al Gore's biography are linked together. Precisely the first shows how much *êthos* is to be conceived on the side of the spectator as a felt pleasure, which arises through an evaluation of 'honesty:' "A key issue is the honesty of the film, not in terms of the filmmaker's motivations but in terms of how open the film is in its rhetorical claims."[87] So the audience's laughter in the scene already mentioned, in which Gore stands on the rising platform in order to be able to follow the course of the CO_2 curve with his body, serves as the simultaneous recognition of this measure as a staging and at the same time of this odd appropriateness of this extreme measure in light of extreme data.[88]

Using humor and alternation, this and other scenes work on constructing the *delectare*, the pleasing as a gentle, perpetual affect-bridge between the film and the spectators: be it through self-irony, be it through verbal jibes against so-called climate skeptics, or for instance through ridiculing a graph from the first Bush government, which opposes the planets and a stack of gold bars on a

---

87 Mellor: *The Politics of Accuracy in Judging Global Warming Films*, 143.
88 Cf. Mellor: *The Politics of Accuracy in Judging Global Warming Films*, 145.

scale (1:13:53–1:15:22). The insertion of the humorous cartoon and other satirical moments in the film has the function of being able, like a 'court jester,' to constantly speak truths, directly and bluntly, since they appear as an apparent hyperbole.

What is at least as openly exhibited – and for some commentators reason enough to devalue the film as a whole as pure self-representation[89]– is the fact that a personalized narrative is dedicated to the figure of Al Gore, which is very closely linked with the representation of scientific facts and the environmental messages. The structure of this link, however, as Thomas Rosteck and Thomas S. Frentz have shown, assumes a very special mytho-poetic form: "a narrative form of personal transformation [...] going from innocence through trials to wisdom."[90] In its form An Inconvenient Truth corresponds more or less exactly to the monomythical hero story according to Joseph Campbell:

> A hero ventures forth from the world of common day into a region of supernatural wonder: fabulous forces are there encountered and a decisive victory is won: the hero comes back from this mysterious adventure with the power to bestow boons on his fellow men.[91]

Science appears as a "region of supernatural wonder," from which Al Gore returns to give his spectators his 'blessing,' which here takes the form of curves and graphs. The various stations of Gore's worldwide trip and the worldwide collection of data and measurements are not stops on a journey in space and time. Rather, they are stations on an inner journey. They are – like his private and political crises – transformations, revelations. The first disappointments on the political level and his son's serious accident (0:23:51–0:27:00), the questionable electoral defeat in 2000 (0:32:52–0:35:17), as well as his sister's death from cancer (1:06:43–1:09:12) become moments of contemplation, both in content and form, by interrupting the lecture, moments that always at the same time turn out to be new insight and newly gained decisiveness. The strength that the figure Al Gore brings with him from his battles makes him not only a credible speaker – as the attentive audience in the film wordlessly but unanimously 'announces' – but at the same time humanizes what is spoken, humanizes the scientific figures and data.

The orator draws his credibility, however, also in another way, for he frames himself in this position as an 'exception,' that is, as someone who stands at the margin of society, since he assumes that his message is not

---

89 Cf. Rosteck, Frentz: *Myth and Multiple Readings in Environmental Rhetoric*, 3 and 17–18, also 17.

90 Rosteck, Frentz: *Myth and Multiple Readings in Environmental Rhetoric*, 4.

91 Joseph Campbell: *The Hero with a Thousand Faces*. New York 1949, 30.

welcome, that it isn't flattering.[92] It is precisely this speaker position that entered the North American rhetorical tradition as the genre of the jeremiad, the politico-religious preaching of impending destruction and approaching redemption:

> As a literary term, jeremiad is applied to any work which, with a magniloquence like that of the Old Testament prophet (although it may be in secular rather than religious terms), accounts for the misfortunes of an era as a just penalty for great social and moral evils, but usually holds open the possibility for changes that will bring a happier future.[93]

The jeremiad also aims at the entirety of a polity and in this sense it only follows that the euphoric promise of salvation at the end of the film takes the form of an utterly patriotic pathos. It is thus necessary also to put the 'apocalyptic rhetoric' of AN INCONVENIENT TRUTH in relation to a fundamental political mood of fear and concern, which has much more to do with the political era post 9/11 than with climate change alone.[94] Such a chiasmus is also suggested by the film itself when it has the rising sea level flooding Manhattan and the World Trade Center Memorial (0:57:58–0:58:46).

Contrary to the myth of the hero as a literary genre, one problem the film has to deal with is that the heroic mission is not already fulfilled with the end of the film itself, but that this end can only be the promise of a going-into-fulfillment of rescue. The narrative conclusion of the film AN INCONVENIENT TRUTH takes place in the movie theater, which in a certain sense is represented in the film itself by the images of the audience.

Páthos

The basis of the film's affective structure is, as we can conclude from what we have said so far, that of a multiple transfer of attributions of being affected. The orator's private tragedies, the threats envisioned for animals and the environment, for the future of humanity, the responsibility of national and international communities in the here and now – all these levels are wrapped up in the spectator's experience and interrelated. The film's audiovisual composition – and this begins with the first images and sounds in the film, the images, directed

---

92 Cf. Rosteck, Frentz: *Myth and Multiple Readings in Environmental Rhetoric*, 12–13.

93 (Art.) Jeremiad. In: M. H. Abrams: *A Glossary of Literary Terms*. Boston 1999, 138–139, here 138.

94 Cf. Rosteck, Frentz: *Myth and Multiple Readings in Environmental Rhetoric*, 12; cf. Johnson: *(Environmental) Rhetorics of Tempered Apocalypticism in AN INCONVENIENT TRUTH*, 42.

outward, of the speaker's self-affectation in view of nature as a spiritual resource – forms a body of speech in a sense that is absolutely not metaphorical, which is experienced by the spectators as a permanent translation machine and ultimately aims at a translation into individual, embodied attitudes.

This rhetorical strategy of transferal can be seen most clearly when the 'talk' turns to Hurricane Katrina (0:30:31–0:32:10): "And of course, the consequences were so horrendous, there are no words to describe it." At this statement the image slowly moves back from a satellite image of the whirlwind. This figure of *dubitatio* or *aporiesis*, which plays an "oratorical helplessness,"[95] a speechlessness, is continued in a verbal *aposiopese*, a break in the speech drenched in affect, but that as an audiovisual form does everything but break. On the contrary, it is ratcheted up in a montage set to somber guitar riffs, projecting on the screen the "indescribable" inner images evoked by language. Images from the flooded streets and from the overcrowded emergency accommodations in the Superdrome, which on the one hand use digital artifacts to refer to their quality as concrete media documents, and on the other hand unfold these documents using slow motion and color distortions as a memory of the suffering caused by the disaster that is shared through media. When speech returns, the line of transmitting affective consternation continues, first from the speaker to the remembering and commiserating spectators, and then realized in the questioning appeal to a national community. While a zoom into a photograph of New Orleans taken from the air continues in an almost apocalyptic lighting mood in a back view to Al Gore, as he reflects in a voice-over: "Something new for America, huh? But how in God's name could that happen ... here?" And the answer to this question is given by returning to the presentation that follows, and is implicitly decoded as a way to read his own message: We didn't listen to the scientists' warnings. What's 'new' for America can be described as an experience of loss, one of lost innocence, mourning for a lost, innocent, collective ego, inserted into the general tenor of a lost world:

> The dominant change Gore presents is loss, constructing change as dangerous [...] Gore's lamentation underscores a view of the global environment as irrevocably changed. In the sense that you can't go home again (though you may revisit the family farm to the tune of sentimental music).[96]

This form of loss is present throughout An Inconvenient Truth, from the first images of nature – "I forgot about this." – through the private and political

---

95 Lausberg: *Handbook of Literary Rhetoric*, 343.
96 Johnson: *(Environmental) Rhetorics of Tempered Apocalypticism in An Inconvenient Truth*, 31–32.

defeats of the figure of Al Gore, up to the decisive turn in the final scene as a temporal fiction, a message from a precarious future. At the same time the film's work of mourning consists in once again ending up at a power to act from this loss, projecting the lost innocence from the past into a future where it can be regained.

The film's first hour is initially about a constant alternation between the topos of climate change as a fact, usually treated with graphics and other visual forms, and the topos of the examples of negative consequences, usually more heavily charged with affect, aiming at fear or compassion. Wherever climate change concerns human beings, fear more often plays a decisive role, or better yet, trepidation, for at no point does the film go for shock effects. When it is a matter of the consequences for animals, however, pity is evoked. An animation sequence shows a polar bear at sea, gasping for breath, the last ice floe breaks under his paws and the wide expanse of the sea emphasizes his vulnerability, his desolation (0:43:28–0:44:00).

A very instructive example for the evocation of fearful expectation through expressive movement dynamics in relation to the consequences for human beings is the scene about the extent of rising sea levels (0:56:52–0:58:45). For the expanding masses of water animated into the satellite footage from Florida, San Francisco, the Netherlands, Shanghai, Bangladesh etc. are not mere visualizations of a before-and-after comparison of 'states,' but are very precisely animated in the speed of their expansion as a sinister being, as an expanding malicious shadow, as an inexorable danger 'attacking' the mainland. This speed may correspond to a deeply rooted fear-inducing perception scheme, but it is certain that it also very precisely corresponds to a reference from media history, which can be considered a cultural paradigm for representing an encroaching danger. In Frank Capra's series of propaganda films from the Second World War WHY WE FIGHT (1942–1945) it is exactly the same speed with which the expanding claims to power and military conquest of the Axis powers is illustrated. The comparison with terrorism, which Al Gore sets up by showing the prognosis for flooding in Manhattan and to the World Trade Center Memorial Site, therefore only articulates something that was already present from the beginning as an expressive dynamic. The consequences of climate change, in terms of their political and moral significance, can be equated with the threat from fascism in the past or terrorism in the present, and should thus be treated as such.

Particularly in the second third of the film, the question of morality is initially tied quite directly to such representations of the immediate effects of climate change. In the last third is it linked to the experience of loss and projected fears of loss, appearing as an alternation between outrage over the conspiracies of a political-industrial complex against the climate and science on the one hand, and feelings of anticipated guilt on the other.

The doubled encoding of the issues being treated here – experience the effects as fear *and* as pity, sensing the political dimension as outrage *and* as guilt – is thus a quite fundamental factor in stabilizing the norm of a duty in relation to the climate. This norm, and the criteria introduced by the film, are taken on and consolidated precisely through the fact that they are experienced in contexts that are in each case related to the self and to the outside.[97] Only the transfer of personal, individual struggles to the common, global responsibility turns climate change into a question of justice, a question of the sense of justice.[98]

To finish this section and to go into the question of anticipated guilt, it is necessary to reconstruct the affective dramaturgy of the last approximately 20 minutes of the film step by step. From the parable of tobacco farming and his sister's death from cancer, with which the affective tonality of the sense of guilt is brought into the film, through the unfolding of outrage, the appeal to patriotic pride and hope, up to the temporal fiction of the closing scene.

The parable of the family's tobacco farming and the sister's death from cancer (1:06:43–1:09:12) is not the first scene in which Al Gore's personal loss or personal fear of loss is projected onto climate change. Equally impressive and explicit is the association drawn between the son's serious accident and the endangering of the climate (0:23:51–0:27:00). At first glance in both cases it is primarily the verbal-linguistic association that connects it with the 'actual' topic of the film, as seen at the end of the tobacco scene: "It's just human nature to take time to connect the dots. I know that. But I also know that there can be a day of reckoning, when you wish you had connected the dots more quickly."

Audiovisually this scene is built around a plurality of pasts whose connection is presented, by means of visual and narrative flow that is constantly breaking off in repetitive loops, as a slowly forming feeling of painful loss. It is first the rich colors of the 8mm footage, images of a childlike-innocent form of haptic exploration of the world on the farm; second it is the black-and-white film footage from the tobacco harvest, which associate this memory with a larger, objective process; and third it is the two black-and-white photographs

---

97 Cf. Landweer: *Normativität, Moral und Gefühle*, 241–248; cf. Hilge Landweer: Der Sinn für Angemessenheit als Quelle von Normativität in Ethik und Ästhetik. In: Kerstin Andermann, Undine Eberlein (eds.): *Gefühle als Atmosphären. Neue Phänomenologie und philosophische Emotionstheorie*. Berlin 2011, 57–78, here 59–66.

98 Cf. Johnson: *(Environmental) Rhetorics of Tempered Apocalypticism in An Inconvenient Truth*, 36–37.

that show the sister as a young woman with Al Gore as a child in the wider circle of the family, and which are used to commemorate the dead. These three references to the past are now placed into relation to footage of Al Gore from the present.

During the beginning of the scene, as the seemingly innocent association of childhood and tobacco is initially presented (1:06:43–1:07:05), the remembering voice breaks off and we see Gore in the present in a barn, speaking of the fact that one could have known better, without the context already being clear at that point (1:07:05–1:07:25). Following this the film also seemingly breaks this line of commenting from the present and Gore's off-screen voice now talks about the two photographs of which we gradually learn are of his older sister (1:07:25–1:07:58). In the second photograph the barn appears in the background of the image, which is also prominently featured in the first memory image and in the present-day footage, and the logic of breaking is justified here in the broken life: "She died of lung cancer."

Beginning with Al Gore in the present, driving on the grounds of the farm, the sequence of these references to the past is now reversed. We first see the black-and-white footage, which goes from the tobacco harvest from the romance of childhood into a cool assembly line work and finally to the vivid colors of 8mm footage of the farm and the barn (1:07:58–01:08:39). All of this is permeated with a melancholy mood of belatedness, the wish to shift the dilapidation of the shed, that is apparent in the footage from the present, into the past. The scene ends again with Al Gore in the present, in the barn, standing at the lower edge of the image, overwhelmed by the ramshackle structure of the shed threatening to collapse above him (1:08:39–1:09:14): The hand-held camera imitates the shots and movements that exuded their own charm at the beginning of the scene as 'innocent' 8mm images, but which now end in disenchantment, gradually losing their own dynamic and ending in a standstill. This is intensified on the soundtrack by the introduction of a whirring-piercing noise at high frequencies. The feeling of guilt ascribed to the figure of Al Gore in relation to his sister is realized for the spectator as a crushing attempt, to revise the innocence and naivety of the earlier images, stopping the movement because it comes too late.

Following this the film jumps from the blocked temporality of the sense of guilt and returns to its 'actual' topic, proposing a further affect-dramaturgical interface. And indeed, it turns to the shocking fact that and how the representation of scientific consensus was falsified for economic and political opportunism. This is initially – now once again at the level of the slide-show presentation – more or less simply stated (1:09:13–1:10:50), but afterwards there develops an idea of staging like that of a paranoia thriller in a Hollywood film from the 1970s.

It begins with a conversation that stages Gore at the telephone and at the computer as the center of a research team (1:10:50–1:11:48) and continues with archival footage of a congressional hearing (1:11:48–1:12:20). Then a yellowed newspaper is faded in, once again arousing the association with the representational language of extensive research. The following shots, while the music becomes somewhat calmer, show Gore in a dark room, suggesting secrecy and tireless work. His commentary from off screen very openly links this atmosphere of persecution and disclosure with the film that the spectators are seeing: "I've seen scientists, who were persecuted, ridiculed, deprived of jobs, income, simply because the facts they discovered led them to an inconvenient truth that they insisted on telling." It is this staging of Gore as the advocate of the immobilized, suppressed discoverers of inconvenient truths that is mobilized into a feeling of outrage in the scenes that follow.

The final appeal of the film can be divided into several steps that build on one another. While the first scenes aim at the solubility of the problem, at the possibility of acting at all, the following aim as what we, along with Hans Blumenberg, could call the "ensuring [...] non-contradiction."[99] It is quite simply about representing the principle compulsion to act and the proposed options to act – however unspecific they may be – so that they are in accord with the system of cultural self-descriptions. After the scene described above of 'transformation,' of changing the world through individual decisions, the whole problematic is narrowed into the question of political will (1:21:24–1:22:35): "Are we capable of rising above ourselves and above history?" The interesting thing about this 'we' is that it suggests a completely changing belongingness. Initially it means the community of speaker and audience in the here and now. At the word "we" he points his finger down at the ground where Al Gore is standing, before then raising the hand upwards, supporting the metaphor of "rising above ourselves" as bodily growing, growing beyond ourselves. In the following this 'we' then clearly means a patriotic 'we' of the American nation, and then this nation and various extraordinary individuals continually become a synecdoche for humanity as a whole:

We established freedom and self-determination in the United States, then in France and then all over the world. The same year Lincoln freed America's slaves, Russia freed its serfs. [...] The entire world defeated fascism. [...] The world supported Nelson Mandela's victory in tearing down the apartheid system. [...] We landed on the moon, the very

---

99 Blumenberg: *An Anthropological Approach to the Contemporary Significance of Rhetoric*, 442.

example of what's possible when we are at our best. We worked together to bring down Communism.

The chain individual-America-world can therefore not be dissolved into components, but means the one in the other, means a shared space of feeling and judging. Each of the stations enumerated by Gore is thus accompanied by historical visual documents, whose unquestioned familiarity marks them as medially shared icons of historicity and moral consensuality. A large number of them, however, have something else in common, for they represent images of historical self-correction, which always also follows from an elementary injustice, an agony. They only give rise to pride because they have ended a guilt, recognized an agony, acknowledged a just concern, albeit somewhat late. And they are always repeatable in themselves, they were suitable for imitation. The revolution in America was repeated in France, after Gandhi came the Civil Rights Movement, etc. This first conclusion of the film, mainly to be understood as a patriotic pep talk through the increasing, almost overwhelming prosody in Al Gore's voice, is then dissolved by a decelerating moment that compare climate change with the hole in the ozone layer (1:22:35–1:23:08).

The film's last scene (1:23:08–1:25:57) once again takes up and reverses the logic of the beginning, which ran from an image of nature, past the shaping of the character of Al Gore, to a series of images of the planet. In both cases, although with different goals, Al Gore literally appears to be the mediating figure between a cosmic perspective and a human one, between science and questions of morality.

It begins with images of the Earth as a vulnerable body and of their increase, Earth as a small pixel within an overwhelming panorama of galactic structures (1:23:08–1:24:29). A tinkling piano music underscores the words that are spoken in a reflective tone and solemn tempo.

> You see that pale blue dot? That's us. Everything that has ever happened in all of human history has happened on that … pixel: all the triumphs and all the tragedies, all the wars, all the famines, all the major advances. It's our only home. And that is what is at stake: our ability to live on planet Earth, to have a future as a civilization.

The film cuts once again to iconic images of the Earth, first *Earthrise*, then *Blue Marble*: "I believe this is a moral issue." From this tonality and reflectivity, we jump again into a summary of Al Gore as a mediating figure (1:24:29–1:25:07). A close-up of his laptop, a brief shot in which he enters a building, then the hand-held shot that has already been seen at the beginning of the film, heroically showing him in back light back stage on the way onto stage. A black-and-white photograph, which shows him as a silhouette in front of a rather abstract composition of a satellite image, from which there is a slow zoom out, interrupts this brief impulse to motion again. A window to the future has opened and through this window we first see a melting iceberg, destroyed tropics, and finally again the river landscape from the beginning of the film (1:25:07–1:25:57).

The fact that the last images of the film (1:25:17–1:25:57) once again show the same peaceful, nostalgic river landscape as the first images is more than just a question of formal closure, even if this is certainly an important factor for the rhetorical effectiveness of the film as a whole. It is much more the affect-poetical consequence of a complex metaphoricity of these images of the river that unfolds over the course of the film as the idea of time as a river, of the river of time in connection with the temporality of the sense of guilt as the feeling of painful irreversibility.

At first the river stands for a state of physical and mental peace – through the even rhythm of the editing, the slow pans, the tinkling piano – as well as for a certain form of constancy and durability (0:00:34–0:01:20). At the end of the scene, which is about his son's serious accident, the image of the river becomes a medium in whose movement things are remembered and preserved or forgotten and perished (0:24:42–0:27:00). It becomes an image of becoming and elapsing: "The possibility of losing what was most precious to me. [...] I felt that we could really lose it. That what we take for granted might not be here for our children."

The connection becomes even clearer when for the first time it is about the Gore family farm (0:38:54–0:40:07). The topic of loss, of nostalgia, and of mourning, lost innocence is emphasized by the materiality of the 8mm footage. The slightly unsettled camera movements underscore another new facet, for time as such becomes unsettled, the relationship between past, present, and future is disturbed on a directly sensual level. Something has happened, and so normality and the regularity of the flow are lost:[100]

> The places where people live were chosen because of the climate pattern that has been pretty much the same on earth since the end of the last ice age, 11,000 years ago. Here on this farm, the patterns are changing. And it seems gradual in the course of a human lifetime, but in the course of time as defined by this river, it's happening very, very quickly.

At the same time the metaphor here becomes a catachresis, a fracture, in which it is bent back through language to the concrete river and its sense of time, a

---

100 Cf. Hans Blumenberg: *Quellen, Ströme, Eisberge*, ed. Ulrich von Bülow, Dorit Krusche. Frankfurt a. M. 2012, 154.

sense of time that is maintained in the last shot, in which the river seems first to stop, and then even to be frozen.

What does this disturbance of the river consist in? It consists in the river of time also being the flow of history: "The stream of time becomes a transport route, one that can only be taken in one direction, in which those who come before have to leave something, to transmit something, to those who come afterwards."[101] And we have altered and endangered this flow itself. And this leads to the knowledge that the most important thing that this river transports is itself, the river. For we do not know who or what will receive the consequences of the present beyond the bend. The end of the film amounts precisely to the rights of those who come later, to an anticipated feeling of guilt with regard to them. Our moral feelings and our political stances must learn not only to drift, but to swim downstream and upstream (1:25:17–1:25:57): "Future generations may well have occasion to ask themselves: 'What were our parents thinking? Why didn't they wake up when they had a chance?' We have to hear that question, from them, now."

The film itself seeks to be the disclosure of these voices, seeks to filter them out of the repetitive, unpleasantly whirring noise. Just as unspoiled nature is no such thing, but a cultural landscape formed by human beings, the mourned loss is a promise, a consolation. The anticipated feeling of guilt is already suspended in the hopeful message itself, the changes and destruction that haunt us today are the warnings that prohibit our demise.

The duration of the film as the duration of a persuasion

According to its title, the film is trying to persuade its spectators of AN INCONVENIENT TRUTH.

> *Licentia* is a bold, insulting reproach to the audience, insisting only on the truth, involving the risk of turning the audience against the speaking party; the speaker expects the audience to be able to cope with an unpleasant, objective truth; and he even hopes by this means to gain more sympathy, as he implies in a manner flattering to the audience.[102]

The film performs an effort of persuasion in a double respect. It aims at convincing as a process, as a persuading through the temporal unfolding of arguments and emotional stances. But is also aims at a commitment from its

---

101 Blumenberg: *Quellen, Ströme, Eisberge*, 140 [trans. DH].
102 Lausberg: *Handbook of Literary Rhetoric*, 337.

audience, it tries to be the expression of a conviction that they already have and that it wants to solidify:

> Further, *licentia* may also be applied cunningly, in such a way that the (so-called) truth that has been presented is quite in agreement with the opinion of the audience, so that, precisely through the form of *licentia*, the audience is indeed confirmed in its complacency and, as a result, shows the speaker sympathy.[103]

At no point does the film generate a concrete accusation to the audience of having behaved wrongly in the *past*. The losses and consequences of climate change registered so far with mourning and pity are the consequences of the conscious manipulation by others and of his, Al Gore's, inability to impart the message.

The affect dramaturgy of the film is thus strongly directed at outrage toward climate skeptics that flares up time and again. It is a dramaturgy of an alternation between vigorously delivered scientific findings and powerlessness, scenes of resignation, of retreat, which then become a new beginning over and over again. In this movement, in this escalation of a conviction, the spectators are part of the film's message.[104]

The audience's self-identification as activists is generated by a feeling of anticipated guilt. We are *now not yet* guilty, for our lack of knowledge is still innocent, only scientists and a few privileged persons such as Al Gore could already have had insights into the future. Sheets of ice breaking up and Hurricane Katrina are not punishments, but warnings to listen to science now or else in fact to be morally responsible for the consequences.

The basic settings that Al Gore repeats verbally over and over again, that this is a 'moral issue' and that failing to act would be 'unethical,' are conveyed by means of his *êthos* and by an idea of scientific integrity as a meta-norm standing above all others. The anticipated guilt concerns a breach of this norm. In the film itself the individual concrete, everyday, or political forms of causation and the possible avoidance of the catastrophe play a marginal role, precisely because the norm of scientificity itself is the focus.

It is this meta-norm with which An Inconvenient Truth ensures, for instance, the question of bipartisanship, so intractable in the American political system, in order to bridge the gap between Democrats and Republicans, which is pointedly the case in relation to environmental protection. Precisely this

---

103 Lausberg: *Handbook of Literary Rhetoric*, 337.
104 Cf. Johnson: *(Environmental) Rhetorics of Tempered Apocalypticism in An Inconvenient Truth*, 43.

meta-norm turns the film into a patriotic speech, encouraging a new beginning as reconstituting a situation that had gone out of balance. Under this reframing, any previous political fight becomes irrelevant to the situation today. While so-called dyed-in-the-wool Democrats are supposed to like the message, since it fits their own program, the value system represented, precisely in relation to the image of nature and Al Gore's private tragedies, is aimed at a conservative world view of family, at the divine mandate to maintain and protect creation, and at the USA's place as a trailblazer for humanity.

In the end, the figure of Al Gore simultaneously serves as a medium and a representative, since he both conveys the facts and actuates the affective attitudes, and in a counter move represents an exonerating position for the spectator with respect to the responsibility for the already occurring losses, damages, and disasters. The film is not only an argumentative presentation of climate change as a fact, but also an argument for the fact that scientific facts have a history and that to understand issues one always also needs a good teacher. The message of the affect dramaturgy of the film, built on *êthos* and an anticipated sense of guilt, is the following: We only learn from the right models and these have so far been kept from us. Starting now, however, we belong to those in the know. Starting now there's no longer any excuse.

4.4 Catastrophe and Control

AN INCONVENIENT TRUTH ends with illustrations of the planet Earth, which exhibit its vulnerability, its fragility. The same goes for almost all engaged films on climate change, such as THE AGE OF STUPID, THE 11TH HOUR, THE TRUTH ABOUT CLIMATE CHANGE, and LE SYNDROME DE TITANIC. These images of the Earth as a vulnerable body on a dark background of the universe attempt to make it possible for the spectator to grasp how humans have overstepped their power. The film has to take this path, for there is no prohibition, inscribed in nature, written down somewhere, announced by some authority, that we would have transgressed. It is much more the knowledge that we might have gone too far that gives rise to the prohibition in the first place. It is only the feeling of the Earth's vulnerability, of a destabilization of our own taken-for-grantedness, that makes us aware of our own responsibility and the standards of our individual and collective action. What is important here is that arousing a sense for global responsibility is not simply a matter of appealing to individual psychological attitudes. The films work at constituting a subject position that treats areas of responsibility and dispositions toward action as pertinent, a position whose temporal and spatial dimensions far exceed the scope and duration of its own life:

> Our reasons for acting on climate change are not (or at least not primarily) that doing so will be good (or at least not bad) *for us*; they are deeper and more morally serious than that. [...] To dither when one might prevent moderate harms to oneself by taking modest precautionary action is folly to be sure, but its moral import is limited. By contrast, to engage in willful self-deception and moral corruption when the lives of future generations, the world's poor, and even the basic fabric of life on the planet is at stake is a much more serious business.[105]

The flip side of the imagination, temporalities, and also affect dramaturgies of the anticipated guilt implied here is the attempt once again to rescue the reach of human action by emphasizing its fragility and contingency, by destabilizing the boundaries between technology and nature, everyday life and history. Only someone who affirms a certain amount of control and free self-determination among interdependent agents can feel guilty and responsible at all in the sense described here. And thus the loss of control that is sensed becomes a collective self-assurance.

Climate change films generally avoid formulating accusations of guilt as direct attacks on their spectators' self-image, for these attacks would trigger a strong defense mechanism, which would immediately reject the entire message with anger and hostility. It is the feelings of guilt generated by a temporal enfolding of the perception of a wounded counterpart, of the planet, of animals, or of future generations, that make it possible to change attitudes, indeed precisely when the possibilities of alleviating guilt through particular actions are communicated along with this at the same time.[106]

---

105 Stephen M. Gardimer: *A Perfect Moral Storm. The Ethical Tragedy of Climate Change.* New York 2011, 11.

106 Cf. Daniel J. O'Keefe: Guilt as a Mechanism of Persuasion. In: James P. Dillard, Michael Pfau (eds.): *The Persuasion Handbook. Developments in Theory and Practice.* London 2002, 329–344, here 331; cf. Marissa Jiménez, Kenneth C. C. Yang: How Guilt Level Affects Green Advertising Effectiveness? In: *Journal of Creative Communications* (2008), Vol. 3, No. 3, 231–254, here 248; cf. Monique M. Turner, Jill C. Underhill: Motivating Emergency Preparedness Behaviors. The Differential Effects of Guilt Appeals and Actually Anticipating Guilty Feelings. In: *Communication Quarterly* (2012), Vol. 60, No. 4, 545–559, here 546; cf. also Mark A. Ferguson, Nyla R. Branscombe: Collective Guilt Mediates the Effect of Beliefs about Global Warming on Willingness to Engage in Mitigation Behavior. In: *Journal of Environmental Psychology* (2010), Vol. 30, 135–142; cf. Lisa L. Massi Lindsey: Anticipated Guilt as Behavioral Motivation. An Examination of Appeals to Help Unknown Others Through Bone Marrow Donation. In: *Human Communication Research* (2005), Vol. 31, No. 4, 453–481.

Some studies attempt to supplement this by examining the effects of encouraging positive self-images and by emphasizing increased well-being due to sustainable

The anticipated sense of guilt is now sensed as the threat of future painful experiences on the basis of a not yet fulfilled duty. It also gets its motivating power from its own temporal dynamic structure, for it initially interrupts the flow of the present, interrupting and avoiding further harmful action.[107]

When the films seek to convince us to change our lives, then they overwhelm us not with incontrovertible, overwhelming evidence, but instead create a platform of communality in their temporal unfolding. They necessarily refer to shared values and norms, to shared images and narratives, working at representing these as self-attributions and relating them to climate change so that they appear to be in conflict with not acting and in accord with acting.

In the alternation of anticipated reparation and impending doom, in the alternation between the various levels of political, historical, and ordinary action we have the experience of constantly jumping from one narrative into another, and the history in which we as spectators think, feel, and perceive becomes increasingly mobile, increasingly more speculative.

In this respect the anticipated sense of guilt, just like the politics of historical guilt,[108] is an element of the modern understanding of time, and both are part of the affective signature of the modern era, of the perceptibility of historical structural change as an event[109] and of the present as an enduring state of transition and crisis, in Adorno's terms, of history as a permanent catastrophe.[110] The paradox here is that it is precisely the causal, spatial, and temporal dimensions and complexities of climate change that completely elude this perception paradigm of modernity and of catastrophe. For what 'catastrophe' signalizes is immediate, drastic, qualitative change and the clear separation of a before and after, between which the catastrophe operates as a pure event, as a potency without a meaning of its own.[111]

---

behavior: Víctor C. Verdugo: The Positive Psychology of Sustainability. In: *Environment, Development, Sustainability* (2012), Vol. 14, No. 5, 651–666.

107 Cf. Jens Agerström, Fredrik Björklund, Rickard Carlsson: Emotions in Time. Moral Emotions Appear more Intense with Temporal Distance. In: *Social Cognition* (2012), Vol. 30, No. 2, 181–198, here 196; cf. David M. Amodio, Patricia G. Devine, Eddie Harmon-Jones: A Dynamic Model of Guilt. Implications for Motivation and Self-Regulation in the Context of Prejudice. In: *Psychological Science* (2007), Vol. 18, No. 6, 524–530, here 525.

108 Cf. Jeffrey K. Olick: *The Politics of Regret. On Collective Memory and Historical Responsibility*. New York / London 2007.

109 Cf. Reinhart Koselleck: Wie neu ist die Neuzeit? In: *Historische Zeitschrift* (1990), Vol. 251, No. 3, 539–553.

110 Cf. Theodor W. Adorno: *Negative Dialectics* [1966]. New York 1973, 320.

111 Cf. Olaf Briese, Timo Günther: Katastrophe. Terminologische Vergangenheit, Gegenwart und Zukunft. In: *Archiv für Begriffsgeschichte* (2009), Vol. 51, 155–195.

The designation of climate catastrophe is thus actually nonsensical as a perceptual category to ordinary, individual people, and the affective interruptions of irreversibility, the paradoxical movement of making reparations for what has not yet fully come, are attempts to do justice to it at the level of a feeling for global responsibility. If we can control the future less than ever, then we must make it our duty to control this lack of control somehow, and to prepare ourselves and behave appropriately.[112] For it is not by means of "panic fear but intellectually mediated concern"[113] that we can make sense of the threat that is simultaneously concretely defined and abstract and diffuse in terms of time and space.

The fact that the actually evident powerful potential of a politics of climate and bio-technology has not yet been effectuated ultimately also lies with an inactivity of our reigning understanding of how to conceive danger and risk, according to which the concern for the hypothetical future has to be presented as a reaction to an acutely menacing catastrophe. For environmental protection unfortunately seems to be powerful and in the position to coincide with other, especially economic interest positions exclusively when the necessities of life seem to be endangered in the here and now, and when the catastrophe is a quite direct threat, and less when it is 'only' about concern for a still completely undefined future, which can only be calculated to a limited degree.[114]

The technological and intellectual conditions of climate change, the affective temporality of modernity, thus seems to be in conflict with realizing the necessary changes in action:

> In this way globalization paradoxically works against its own underlying trend: By asserting one expansion after another across the board it compels across-the-board restrictions. By seeking to generalize affluence it discovers that in the final instance globally only the opposite is practicable, namely frugality for all.
>
> [...] We will be expected to choose between the ethics of fireworks and the ethics of asceticism. [...] The citizens of rich nations will without exception not only feel that struggle of the Titans within themselves, but will also make public by their private consumer decisions on what side they stand.[115]

The patriotic talk in AN INCONVENIENT TRUTH and the affect dramaturgy of anticipated guilt aim precisely at necessarily having to decide before a quite different

---

112 Cf. Elena Esposito: Die offene Zukunft der Sorgekultur. In: Lorenz Engell, Bernhard Siegert, Joseph Vogl (eds.): *Gefahrensinn. Archiv für Mediengeschichte*. Munich 2009, 107–114, here 112.
113 Radkau: *The Age of Ecology*, 402.
114 Cf. Radkau: *The Age of Ecology*, 17.
115 Sloterdijk: *How big is 'big'?*

class of necessities no longer allows for any free decisions, before we become 'victims of comfort':

> No rocket's gonna fly that high,
> There's no escaping the enemy, It's you & I,
> We've poisoned up the water,
> We're chokin' on the air,
> Let's stop before it gets too late,
> Or is it already too late?
> Is it already too late?
>
> I'm just a victim of comfort,
> I got no one else to blame,
> I'm just a victim of comfort,
> A cryin' shame.[116]

---

116 Keb' Mo': Victims of Comfort. In: id.: *Keb' Mo'*. Epic 1994, No. 4.

5 Conclusion: The Cinema's Guilty Conscience

Victims of Comfort of the consumer society, the Germans at the time of National Socialism – and this not only means the cheering masses, but those that lived their everyday lives in peace – the conquerors of the Wild West and their descendants: What they all share is "the collective experience that something that they actually didn't sense as bad, ended in horror."[1] That experience, of feeling something different *now*, of mistrustfully resituating one's own moral reality, is what I have attempted to describe as a particular affective appearance of temporality and historicity. The feeling of guilt does not uncover something in the past, the present, or the future, which would then be objectively already there as guilt. Rather, it represents a shift in our relationship to the world and to the other, it is a qualitative shift of our sensibility.

As an intrusion into the value content of time, the sense of guilt is thus extremely paradoxical, since first it makes the irreversibility of what happened painfully present, and second it is the feeling that refers us to the fact that the authority of feelings and the subjective judgments by which we orient ourselves in moral reality can lead us astray, guiding us into false communities and leading us to infringe on solidarities.

The media evocation of a collective sense of guilt should therefore not have been investigated for its relation to a denotation of reality, but primarily for its effects[2]: How does it provoke the question of what we might have done to deserve this pain, this burden, this interruption in the flow of time?[3] How does it shape the exercise in the painful recognition of our separation from one another, and of the always possible inconsistency of the ego?[4]

> The human beings we know, hence the human institutions we participate in, are, with certain exceptions, as such infected with unreality. And there are no instances of the human, in some realer or higher state, in some other realm. We are what, here and now, is what there is of the human, and we are, or it is, lacking; we are not what we are meant to be, not what the human expects of itself.[5]

---

1 Wolfgang Müller: Die 'German Angst'. Nirgendwo in der Welt ist die ökologische Diskussion so emotional aufgeladen wie in Deutschland. Eine historische Reflexion zwei Jahre nach Fukushima. In: *Die Zeit* (14 March 2013) [trans. DH].
2 Cf. Sara Ahmed: *The Cultural Politics of Emotion*. New York 2004, 14.
3 Cf. Patricia Greenspan: *Practical Guilt. Moral Dilemmas, Emotions, and Social Norms*. New York / Oxford 1995, 229, fn. 36.
4 Cf. Greenspan: *Practical Guilt*, 129–136.
5 Stanley Cavell: *Cities of Words. Pedagogical Letters on a Register of the Moral Life*. Cambridge / London 2004, 210.

https://doi.org/10.1515/9783110612110-006

The films that I have analyzed under these premises are thus not works that tell their spectators 'something about feelings of guilt.' They produce feelings of guilt and other affects as intersubjective forms of experience, creating them as possibilities, relationships, and standpoints to embody between 'I' and 'we.' In this respect they are part of a politics of feelings, if we understand this not as institutions and laws of statehood and of social management, but as an idea of community in the sense of Hannah Arendt, Richard Rorty, and Stanley Cavell, as a work-in-progress and a constantly shifting horizon of inclusions and exclusions without origin and without any target to reach: "The political is much more the site at which a society operates on itself and its history, and which impels the autonomous shapes of its coexistence."[6]

The political dimension of a collective sense of guilt ultimately stands – even if there may be early event forms of interruption, of traumatization, and of loss of innocence – in a close connection with a realm of historical experience *after* the break in civilization. Politics and community no longer take place in a coherent, stable space of operational guidelines and social, cultural practices as the nation was previously imagined,[7] but only in the question, posed to memory, of how it can possibly continue at all. The politics of contrition, regret, guilt, and exculpation is "part of broad transformations tied up with the decline, rather than the triumph, of the nation-state."[8]

Add to this the fact that these contexts of meaning and ideals of community cannot be separated from concrete media forms and practices. Guilt and responsibility are not simply what is represented in the films, which would then be turned into feelings by the spectators, for the films shape experiences of being affectively concerned with guilt and responsibility. This is why it was eminently important in the individual chapters of this work to leave a lot of space for representing the discursive, poetic, or rhetorical logics of the films themselves, in whose frames feelings and affect dramaturgies are visible in the first place as operational forms and can be understood as specific sensibilities, affective relationships to the self and the world, which are produced by the films. Only against the backdrop of the contemporary discussion of guilt could DER RAT DER GÖTTER [COUNCIL OF THE GODS] be read as the affect dramaturgy of a grammar of exoneration from guilt as a charge against the 'objectively' guilty.

---

6 Joseph Vogl: Einleitung. In: id. (ed.): *Gemeinschaften. Positionen zu einer Philosophie des Politischen*. Frankfurt a. M. 1994, 7–27, here 21 [trans. DH].

7 Cf. Benedict Anderson: *Imagined Communities. Reflections on the Origin and Spread of Nationalism* [1983]. London / New York 2006, 26.

8 Jeffrey K. Olick: *The Politics of Regret. On Collective Memory and Historical Responsibility*. New York / London 2007, 137.

It could be shown how the historicity of Hollywood's genre poetics made it possible to experience the dimension of historical violence and hubris as something that continued to be in effect in the affective structure of the present. Finally, it became possible to trace which rhetorical strategies and principles of audiovisual form could be accessed in order to produce climate change as a shared situation in which a feeling of guilt is staged in anticipation, so that "failure to act incurs a cost in discomfort."[9] Comfort becomes discomfort. What feels good or what did feel good can end up radically bad.

Such an affective structuring of temporality could even be detached in a certain sense from the singular events of world history as a historically emergent form of experience. In the cultural practice of sentimental enjoyment in the mode of melodrama and in the aesthetics of suspense, the thriller, and horror, feelings of guilt are not only the object of representation, but their cultivation as forms of self-relation and as a model of cultural identity. The affect poetics of entertainment cinema are constantly reworkings of the fact that we sometimes simply cannot bear one another. They lead us in temporal relations of tension and balancing acts between the actually preferable values, solidarity, and the acknowledgement of the limitedness and the ordinariness of life and our asocial desires to get out of the contingency and imperfection of human relations and to demand the extra-ordinary. They shape the painful, unpleasant experience of wanting something, seeing something, or wanting to see something that we can then actually not want (any longer), turning even this experience into a form of self-pleasure.[10]

In a film like SHUTTER ISLAND, in which history and narration meet in the obviousness of contingency and contradictoriness, the question of historicity intersects with the cultural practice of this mode of taking pleasure in the constant revision of the standpoints of judgment. The film works on a perceiving, feeling, and thinking that is always already tied to the history of the cinema, for which 'in truth' everything could also be completely different, where this 'truth' means moral evidence and not just facts. The sense of guilt drives the affective critique of the world as appearance, behind which it presumes a hidden dimension of motifs and its own logic of the event, without ever landing at

---

9 Greenspan: *Practical Guilt*, 74.

10 Precisely the introduction of a critical, distanced reflection on this structure itself, according to Christine Wheatley, is an indication of Haneke's didactic calculations; cf. Catherine Wheatley: *Michael Haneke's Cinema. The Ethic of the Image*. New York / Oxford 2009. In contradiction to her assessment, however, I would nonetheless insist that even this experience of self-evaluation represents a form of aesthetic pleasure, which has merely changed poetological register.

any end point in an endless regression of speculations and revisions. The object of the sense of guilt is not the loss of innocence, positioned in a specific past, but the fact that history and community mean *always already* losing one's innocence, always already risking the failure of the moral compass.[11]

If the sense of guilt is a form that structures a relationship between past, present, and future, thus producing a specific temporality of history, then – and I would like to close with this excursus – we can also tell the history of cinema in this manner. At least we can interpret Jean-Luc Godard's Histoire(s) du Cinéma (1998) in such a way. Cinema has misjudged itself, it has betrayed its own historicity as an aesthetics of the co-presence of multiplicity and thus betrayed its own status as witness.[12] The crimes of the twentieth century cannot be separated from a failure of cinema, for while it constantly anticipated them it never understood this anticipation, and since it has been incapable of at least being present at the sites of these crimes. The connection between violence and tears in the movie theaters and between 'real tears' and 'real blood' is that of a missed solidarity between imagination and reality.[13] Ever since then the history of the cinema has been a history of retrospectively realizing missed opportunities, a history of absolute polyvalence, in which every image refers to this failure, to this guilt of the cinema.[14]

For cinema also knows the 'second guilt,' in the cinema too forgetting annihilation is part of annihilation. The aesthetics of montage in Godard is the attempt to counteract this forgetting, not as work on remembering something, but by giving the memory "a visual form of haunting, a musicality of knowledge."[15] The images that Histoire(s) du Cinéma shows us are snatched away from what they remind us of. They are not so much memories of this or that as they are memories of memory, of the time of historicity.[16] The fact that we as spectators are constantly confronted with this, that the images disappear again

---

11 Cf. Michael Lück: Mystery, Crime, Thriller. Vom Sog dunkler Vergangenheit im Hollywood-Kino der 2000er Jahre. In: Jennifer Henke, Magdalena Krakowski, Benjamin Moldenhauer, Oliver Schmidt (eds): *Hollywood Reloaded. Genrewandel und Medienerfahrung der Jahrtausendwende.* Marburg 2013, 171–189.

12 Cf. Jacques Rancière: A Fable without a Moral. Godard, Cinema, (Hi)stories [2001]. In: id.: *Film Fables.* London 2006, 171–188; cf. Jean-Luc Godard, Youssef Ishaghpour: *Archéologie du cinéma et mémoire du siècle.* Tours 2000, 64.

13 Cf. Jean-Luc Godard: *Histoire(s) du Cinéma. Vol. I(a): Toutes les histoires.* Paris 1998, 108–115.

14 Cf. Rancière: *A Fable without a Moral,* 187–188; cf. Georges Didi-Huberman: *Images in Spite of All* [2004]. Chicago 2008, 126.

15 Didi-Huberman: *Images in Spite of All,* 138.

16 Cf. Godard, Ishaghpour: *Archéologie du cinéma et mémoire du siècle,* 18.

in the montage before we have apprehended or comprehended them, and that they turn up over and over again over the course of the more than four-hour-long film, that the HISTOIRE(S) also constantly remind themselves of themselves, is central for the film's affect-poetic effectiveness. Between despairing and hoping, between irreversible disappearance and the possibility of return, between horror and nostalgic recognition, every image is part of a flow rushing forward and at the same is an interruption, an opening through which "the resistance of the present between the past and the future is eliminated, and these, magically fused, descend together on the head of the sinner."[17]

In an often cited note, Walter Benjamin described the work of turning memory into thinking as follows: "History decays into images, not into stories."[18] This means, above all, that the writing of history consists in administering decay, in creative destruction, and not in the production of continuities and comprehensive historical processes as entireties. Just before this citation we read: "An object of history is that through which knowledge is constituted as the object's rescue."[19] Also in Godard, this rescue, which returns in Siegfried Kracauer as the "redemption of physical reality,"[20] does not mean the rescue of what is shown and depicted, but 'knowledge,' the rescue of wanting to understand, the rescue of the experiential dimension of images and sounds: "It is not about exculpating the actors of history or the actors of cinema but, rather, about opening sight itself to a start-up of knowledge and to an orientation of ethical choice."[21]

In HISTOIRE(S) DU CINÉMA the sense of guilt and compensation are directly aimed at seeing, hearing, and remembering. The aesthetic of the montage is an attempt to reproduce the capacity of the cinema to "rescue the honor of the real."[22] For this potential is not ontologically given, but a question of aesthetic practice, which can only be claimed, struggled for, defended, and enforced on the concrete level of images. It is a question of historical and political practice, and thus is itself in need of rescue.[23] In Godard the technique of montage

---

17 Walter Benjamin: Painting, or Signs and Marks [1917]. In: id.: *Selected Writings I: 1913–1926.* Cambridge 1996, 83–86, here 84; cf. Didi-Huberman: *Images in Spite of All*, 169–171.

18 Walter Benjamin: *The Arcades Project* [1928–1940], trans. Howard Eiland, Kevin McLaughlin. Cambridge 1999, 476.

19 Benjamin: *The Arcades Project*, 476.

20 Siegfried Kracauer: *Theory of Film. The Redemption of Physical Reality* [1960]. Princeton 1990.

21 Didi-Huberman: *Images in Spite of All*, 179.

22 Godard: *Histoire(s) du Cinéma. Vol. I(a)*, 88 [trans. DH].

23 Cf. Jacques Aumont: *Amnésies. Fictions du cinéma d'après Jean-Luc Godard.* Paris 1999, 42; cf. Godard, Ishaghpour: *Archéologie du cinéma et mémoire du siècle.*

becomes an ideal operation in which images hold judgment over images,[24] that is, they test for a feeling for the possibility of a shared world without the aid of any abstract concept.

Precisely with images of horror and annihilation, the cinema has to prove itself as an ethical-moral practice by putting us as seeing persons into relation to events that do not 'tolerate witnesses' wherever they occur in actual fact.[25] What is meant here are not only those images in which the gruesome, the destructive, and the annihilated are depicted, wherein lies also a danger of the senses being blunted.[26] Instead it is a matter of images that show horror and annihilation as that for whose sake it is necessary to see and to remember, that is, to "redeem horror from its invisibility"[27]: "Their secret telos was not some superficial, appellative function that pointed toward a course of concrete action, but instead their enshrining in memory."[28]

One of the functions of memory is to bring the images of horror, the bodies of those murdered, the invisible, together with images that the cinema makes of living and loving beings, to show that their coexistence in history is also part of the (hi)story of cinema. In Godard this culminates in the statement that without the cinema he would have had no idea that he had a history.[29] This nexus between historical facts and images is not one of mirroring or depiction. It is a task that consists in the fact that images, as something that people make and produce, should at the same time become something that makes it possible to remember the world, and to change it, as what happens in the form of action and speech among people:

> In order to be what the world is always meant to be, a home for men during their life on earth, the human artifice must be a place fit for action and speech, for activities not only entirely useless for the necessities of life but of an entirely different nature from the manifold activities of fabrication by which the world itself and all things in it are produced.[30]

---

24 Cf. Jean-Luc Godard: Jean-Luc Godard rencontre Régis Debray [1995]. In: Alain Bergala (ed.): *Jean-Luc Godard par Jean-Luc Godard. Vol. II: 1984–1998*. Paris 1998, 423–431, here 430; cf. Aumont: *Amnésies*, 123.

25 Cf. Siegfried Kracauer: Das Grauen im Film [1940]. In: ders.: *Werke. Vol. VI.3: Kleine Schriften zum Film 1932–1961*. Frankfurt a. M. 2004, 312–314, here 313.

26 Cf. Kracauer: *Das Grauen im Film*, 313.

27 Kracauer: *Theory of Film*, 306 [trans. DH].

28 Gertrud Koch: *Siegfried Kracauer. An Introduction*, trans. Jeremy Gaines. Princeton 2000, 109.

29 Cf. Jean-Luc Godard: *Histoire(s) du Cinéma. Vol. II(a): Seul le cinema*. Paris 1998, 39.

30 Hannah Arendt: *The Human Condition*. Chicago 1958, 173–174.

In this sense the cinema cites both physical reality and human activity, and it cites itself, citing all of this in court.[31] Cinema indicts the connection between our desire for happiness, beauty, and complete expression and the violence and annihilation in history. It indicts the gap "between the need for happiness and the ruthless caprice of physical reality"[32] and brings to mind "in fear and trembling [...] of what man is capable."[33] The cinema is in a position to show – for instance where the simplest of all ordinary, unambitious do-gooders, Chaplin's tramp, transforms into Hitler in THE GREAT DICTATOR (Charles Chaplin, 1940) – that horror is at home in the interior of the humanity of the twentieth century, that is, in the interior of the cinema itself.[34]

Our history has "really never quite lost a certain odour of blood and torture."[35] Images never cease proclaiming horror and annihilation. Living and surviving today means bearing the burden of responsibility for the excluded and the solidarity that has always already failed. Despair seems appropriate. But exactly this imperative to despair, the pain of the guilty conscience, is at the same time already the possibility of recovering the upright gait, for it would be much worse not to despair, not to be able to suffer, that is, to forget.[36] In Godard the cinema, the arts are surprisingly also constantly becoming a permanent restart,[37] not as a blank page, but as the question of what can now be begun with this legacy, with this history, with this responsibility. And so the guilty conscience realizes that our moral fate is at stake in every act.[38] The despair in the sense of guilt is immanently related to an implicit promise of happiness – and in reverse: *Le bonheur n'est pas gai.*

---

31 Cf. Jean-Luc Godard: Le bon plaisir de Jean-Luc Godard [1995]. In: Alain Bergala (ed.): *Jean-Luc Godard par Jean-Luc* Godard. Vol. II: 1984–1998, ed. Alain Bergala. Paris 1998, 305–322, here 312. Cf. Aumont: *Amnésies*, 60.

32 Hans Blumenberg: *Shipwreck with Spectator. Paradigm of a Metaphor for Existence* [1979], trans. Steven Rendall. Cambridge 1997, 26.

33 Hannah Arendt: Organized Guilt and Universal Responsibility [1946]. In: id.: *Essays in Understanding. 1930–1954: Formation, Exile, and Totalitarianism.* New York 1994, 121–132, here 132.

34 Cf. Godard, Ishaghpour: *Archéologie du cinéma et mémoire du siècle*, 70.

35 Friedrich Nietzsche: *On the Genealogy of Morality* [1887]. Cambridge 2016, 43.

36 Cf. Vladimir Jankélévitch: *The Bad Conscience* [1951]. Chicago 2014, 113–117 and 127–131.

37 Cf. Godard, Ishaghpour: *Archéologie du cinéma et mémoire du siècle*, 87–88.

38 Cf. Jankélévitch: *The Bad Conscience*, 27; cf. Cavell: *Cities of Words*, 11.

Bibliography

Abrams, Meyer H. / Harpham, Geoffrey G.: *A Glossary of Literary Terms*. Boston 1999.

Ackermann, Anton: Zum 5-jährigen Bestehen der DEFA. In: *Auf neuen Wegen – 5 Jahre fortschrittlicher deutscher Film*. (East) Berlin 1951, 5–8.

Adorno, Theodor W.: The Meaning of Working Through the Past [1959]. In: id.: *Interventions and Catchwords*, trans. Henry W. Pickford. New York 2005, 89–103.

Adorno, Theodor W.: *Negative Dialectics* [1966]. New York 1973.

Agde, Günter: Position und Leistung des Spielfilmregisseurs Kurt Maetzig. In: id. (ed.): Kurt Maetzig: *Filmarbeit. Gespräche, Reden, Schriften*. (East) Berlin 1987, 413–494.

Agerström, Jens / Björklund, Fredrik / Carlsson, Rickard: Emotions in Time. Moral Emotions Appear More Intense with Temporal Distance. In: *Social Cognition* (2012), Vol. 30, No. 2, 181–198.

Ahmed, Sara: *The Cultural Politics of Emotion*. New York 2004.

Altman, Rick: *Film / Genre*. London 1999.

Améry, Jean: Resentments [1966]. In: id.: *At the Mind's Limits. Contemplations by a Survivor or Auschwitz and its Realities*, trans. Sidney Rosenfeld, Stella P. Rosenfeld. Bloomington 1980, 62–81.

Amodio, David M. / Devine, Patricia G. / Harmon-Jones, Eddie: A Dynamic Model of Guilt. Implications for Motivation and Self-Regulation in the Context of Prejudice. In: *Psychological Science* (2007), Vol. 18, No. 6, 524–530.

Anderson, Benedict: *Imagined Communities. Reflections on the Origin and Spread of Nationalism* [1983]. London / New York 2006.

Arendt, Hannah: Organized Guilt and Universal Responsibility [1946]. In: id.: *Essays in Understanding. 1930–1954: Formation, Exile, and Totalitarianism*. New York 1994, 121–132.

Arendt, Hannah: The Aftermath of Nazi Rule. In: *Commentary* (1950), Vol. 10, No. 4, 342–353.

Arendt, Hannah: *The Human Condition*. Chicago 1958.

Arendt, Hannah: *Eichmann in Jerusalem. A Report on the Banality of Evil* [1963]. New York 2006.

Arendt, Hannah: Some Questions on Moral Philosophy [1965]. In: id.: *Responsibility and Judgment*, ed. Jerome Kohn. New York 2003, 49–146.

Arendt, Hannah: The Conquest of Space and the Stature of Man [1968]. In: id.: *Between Past and Future. Eight Exercises in Political Thought*. New York 2006, 260–274.

Arendt, Hannah: Hannah Arendt: *On Violence*. New York 1969.

Arendt, Hannah: Truth and Politics [1969]. In: id.: *Between Past and Future. Eight Exercises in Political Thought*. New York 2006, 223–259.

Arendt, Hannah: The Archimedean Point [1969]. In: id.: *Thinking without a Banister. Essays in Understanding 1953–1975*. New York 2018, 406–418.

Arendt, Hannah: *Lectures on Kant's Political Philosophy* [1982], ed. Ronald Beiner. Chicago 1992.

Arendt, Hannah: *Was ist Politik? Fragmente aus dem Nachlaß*, ed. Ursula Lud. Munich 1993.

Arendt, Hannah / Blücher, Heinrich: *Within Four Walls. The Correspondence Between Hannah Arendt and Heinrich Blücher 1936–1968*, ed. Lotte Köhler. New York 2000.

Arendt, Hannah: *The Promise of Politics*, ed. Jerome Kohn. New York 2005.

Aristotle: *The "Art" of Rhetoric*, trans. John Henry Freese. London 1926.

Aristotle: *Poetics*, trans. George Whalley. Montreal 1997.

https://doi.org/10.1515/9783110612110-007

Aristotle: *Nicomachean Ethics*. Indianapolis 2014.

Arnold, Magda: *Emotion and Personality*. New York 1960.

Aumont, Jacques: *Amnésies. Fictions du cinéma d'après Jean-Luc Godard*. Paris 1999.

Bachmann, Claus H. / Kamper, Dietmar / Treusch-Dieter, Gerburg: Schuld und Geschichte – Aufs Spiel gesetzt. In: Gerburg Treusch-Dieter, Dietmar Kamper, Bernd Ternes (eds.): *Kursbuch 37. Schuld*. Tübingen 1999, 21–32.

Bagnoli, Carla (ed.): *Morality and the Emotions*. Oxford 2011.

Balázs, Béla: Visible Man or the Culture of Film [1924]. In: id.: *Early Film Theory. Visible Man and The Spirit of Film*. New York 2010, 1–90.

Barker, Jennifer: *The Tactile Eye. Touch and the Cinematic Experience*. Berkeley 2009.

Barnert, Anne: *Die Antifaschismus-Thematik der DEFA. Eine kultur- und filmhistorische Analyse*. Marburg 2008.

Barrett, Lisa Feldman / Bar, Moshe: See it with Feeling. Affective Predictions during Object Perceptions. In: *Philosophical Transactions of the Royal Society* (2009), Vol. 364, 1325–1334.

Becher, Johannes R.: *Deutsches Bekenntnis. Drei Reden zu Deutschlands Erneuerung*. Berlin 1945.

Becker, Wolfgang / Schöll, Norbert: *In jenen Tagen … Wie der deutsche Nachkriegsfilm die Vergangenheit bewältigte*. Opladen 1995.

Bellour, Raymond: Thinking, Recounting. The Cinema of Gilles Deleuze. In: *Discourse. Journal for Theoretical Studies in Media and Culture* (1998), Vol. 20, No. 3, 56–75.

Bellour, Raymond: Le Dépli des Émotions. In: *Trafic* (2002), Vol. 42, 93–128.

Bellour, Raymond: *Le Corps du Cinéma. Hypnoses, Émotions, Animalités*. Paris 2009.

Bellour, Raymond: Going to the Cinema with Guattari and Stern. In: Eric Alliez, Andrew Goffey (eds.): *The Guattari Effect*. London 2011, 220–234.

Benedict, Ruth: *The Chrysanthemum and the Sword. Patterns of Japanese Culture* [1946]. London 1967.

Benjamin, Walter: Painting, or Signs and Marks [1917]. In: id.: *Selected Writings 1: 1913–1926*. Cambridge 1996, 83–86.

Benjamin, Walter: *The Origin of German Tragic Drama* [1928]. London 1998.

Benjamin, Walter: *The Arcades Project* [1928–1940], trans. Howard Eiland, Kevin McLaughlin. Cambridge 1999.

Benthien, Claudia: *Tribunal der Blicke. Kulturtheorien von Scham und Schuld und die Tragödie um 1800*. Cologne / Weimar / Vienna 2011.

Benthien, Claudia: Antikes 'Schuldbewußtsein' und psychoanalytische Mythologie. In: Claudia Benthien, Hartmut Böhme, Inge Stephan (eds.): *Freud und Antike*. Göttingen 2011, 241–267.

Berger, Thomas: *Little Big Man* [1964]. London 1999.

Birkenhauer, Theresia: Tragödie. Arbeit an der Demokratie. Auslotung eines Abstandes. In: *Theater der Zeit* (2004), No. 11, 27–28.

Blumenberg, Hans: *Paradigms for a Metaphorology* [1960], trans. Robert Savage. Ithica 2010.

Blumenberg, Hans: *Shipwreck with Spectator. Paradigm of a Metaphor for Existence* [1979], trans. Steven Rendall. Cambridge 1997.

Blumenberg, Hans: An Anthropological Approach to the Contemporary Significance of Rhetoric. In: Kenneth Baynes, James Bohman, Thomas McCarthy (eds.): *After Philosophy. End or Transformation*. Cambridge 1987, 429–438.

Blumenberg, Hans: Imitation of Nature. Toward a Prehistory of the Idea of the Creative Being. In: *Qui Parle* (2000), Vol. 1, No. 12, 17–54.

Blumenberg, Hans: *Quellen, Ströme, Eisberge*, ed. Ulrich von Bülow, Dorit Krusche. Frankfurt a. M. 2012.

Wolfgang Borchert: *The Man Outside* [1947], trans. David Porter. New York 1971.

Brady, Martin: Discussion with Kurt Maetzig. In: Seán Allan, John Sandford (eds.): *DEFA. East German Cinema, 1946–1992*. New York / Oxford 1999, 77–92.

Brandlmeier, Thomas: Von Hitler zu Adenauer. Deutsche Trümmerfilme. In: Hilmar Hoffmann, Walter Schobert (eds.): *Zwischen Gestern und Morgen. Westdeutscher Nachkriegsfilm 1946–1962*. Frankfurt a. M. 1989, 33–61.

Bredekamp, Horst: Der Mensch als Mörder der Natur. Das 'Iudicium Iovis' von Paulus Niavis und die Leibmetaphorik. In: Heimo Reinitzer (ed.): *All Geschöpf ist Zung' und Mund*. Hamburg 1984, 261–283.

Bredekamp, Horst: Blue Marble. Der Blaue Planet. In: Christoph Markschies, Ingeborg Reichle, Jochen Brüning, Peter Deuflhard (eds.): *Atlas der Weltbilder*. Berlin 2011, 367–375.

Brewer, William F. / Lichtenstein, Edward H.: Stories Are to Entertain. A Structural-Affect Theory of Stories. In: *Journal of Pragmatics* (1982), Vol. 6, 473–486.

Briese, Olaf / Günther, Timo: Katastrophe. Terminologische Vergangenheit, Gegenwart und Zukunft. In: *Archiv für Begriffsgeschichte* (2009), Vol. 51, 155–195.

Brooks, Peter: *The Melodramatic Imagination. Balzac, Henry James, Melodrama, and the Mode of Excess* [1976]. New Haven / London 1995.

Burgoyne, Robert: *Film Nation. Hollywood Looks at U.S. History*. Minneapolis / London 1997.

Buscombe, Edward: The Idea of Genre in the American Cinema. In: Barry K. Grant (ed.): *Film Genre Reader IV*. Austin 2012, 12–26.

Byg, Barton: DEFA and the Traditions of International Cinema. In: Seán Allan, John Sandford (eds.): *DEFA. East German Cinema, 1946–1992*. New York / Oxford 1999, 22–41.

Campbell, Joseph: *The Hero with a Thousand Faces*. New York 1949.

Canby, Vincent: Movie Review. LITTLE BIG MAN. In: *New York Times* (15 December 1970).

Carroll, Noël: *The Philosophy of Horror or Paradoxes of the Heart*. New York 1990.

Carroll, Noël: Film, Emotion, and Genre. In: Carl Plantinga, Greg M. Smith (eds.): *Passionate Views: Film, Cognition, and Emotion*. Baltimore 1999, 21–47.

Carroll, Noël: Art, Narrative & Emotion. In: id.: *Beyond Aesthetics. Philosophical Essays*. Cambridge 2001, 215–235.

Carroll, Noël: Art, Narrative, and Moral Understanding. In: id.: *Beyond Aesthetics. Philosophical Essays*. Cambridge 2001, 270–293.

Carroll, Noël: Aesthetic Experience. A Question of Content. In: id.: *Art in Three Dimensions*. Oxford / New York 2010, 77–108.

Carroll, Noël: Art and Mood. In: id.: *Art in Three Dimensions*. Oxford / New York 2010, 301–328.

Carruthers, Susan L.: Compulsory Viewing. Concentration Camp Film and German Re-Education. In: *Millennium. Journal of International Studies* (2001), Vol. 30, No. 3, 733–759.

Casetti, Francesco: *The Lumière Galaxy. Seven Keywords for the Cinema to come*. New York 2015.

Cavell, Stanley: Aesthetic Problems of Modern Philosophy [1976]. In: id.: *Must We Mean What We Say?* Cambridge 2002, 73–96.

Cavell, Stanley: *The World Viewed. Reflections on the Ontology of Film* [1971]. Cambridge / London 1979.

Cavell, Stanley: *The Claim of Reason. Wittgenstein, Skepticism, Morality, and Tragedy* [1979]. New York / Oxford 1999.

Cavell, Stanley: *Pursuits of Happiness. The Hollywood Comedy of Remarriage.* Cambridge / London 1981.

Cavell, Stanley: *The Senses of Walden* [1972]. Chicago 1981.

Cavell, Stanley: The Politics of Interpretation (Politics as opposed to what?) In: id.: *Themes out of School. Effects and Causes.* Chicago / London 1984, 27–59.

Cavell, Stanley: What Becomes of Things on Film. In: id: *Themes out of School. Effects and Causes.* Chicago / London 1984, 173–183.

Cavell, Stanley: What Photography Calls Thinking [1985]. In: William Rothman (ed.): *Cavell on Film.* Albany 2005, 115–133.

Cavell, Stanley: *Contesting Tears. The Hollywood Melodrama of the Unknown Woman.* Chicago / London 1996.

Cavell, Stanley: *Cities of Words. Pedagogical Letters on a Register of the Moral Life.* Cambridge / London 2004.

Cavell, Stanley: Performative and Passionate Utterance. In: id.: *Philosophy the Day after Tomorrow.* Cambridge / London 2005, 155–191.

Cavell, Stanley: The Incessance and the Absence of the Political. In: Andrew Norris (ed.): *The Claim to Community. Essays on Stanley Cavell and Political Philosophy.* Stanford 2006, 263–317.

Cawelti, John G.: *The Six Gun Mystique.* Bowling Green 1971.

Cawelti, John G.: *Adventure, Mystery, and Romance. Formula Stories as Art and Popular Culture.* Chicago 1976.

Cawelti, John G.: The Frontier and the Native American. In: Joshua C. Taylor: *America as Art.* Washington D. C. 1976, 135–183.

Cienki, Alan / Müller, Cornelia (eds.): *Metaphor and Gesture.* Amsterdam / Philadelphia 2008.

Colli, Giorgio: Afterword. In: Friedrich Nietzsche: *The complete works of Friedrich Nietzsche. Vol. VIII: Beyond Good and Evil / On the Genealogy of Morality.* Stanford 2014, 423–430.

Coplan, Amy: Feeling without Thinking. Lessons from the Ancients on Emotion and Virtue-Acquisition. In: *Metaphilosophy* (2010), Vol. 41, No. 1/2, 132–151.

Crutzen, Paul J. / Stoermer, Eugene F.: The 'Anthropocene'. In: *IGBP Newsletter* (2000), No. 41, 17–18.

Crutzen, Paul J. / Mastrandrea, Michael D. / Schneider, Stephen H. / Davis, Mike / Sloterdijk, Peter (eds.): *Das Raumschiff Erde hat keinen Notausgang.* Frankfurt a. M. 2011.

D'Aloia, Adriano: Edith Stein geht ins Kino. Empathie als Filmtheorie. In: *montage AV* (2010), Vol. 19, No. 1, 79–100.

Damasio, Antonio R.: *Descartes' Error. Emotion, Reason and the Human Brain.* New York 2006.

Damasio, Antonio R.: *Looking for Spinoza. Joy, Sorrow and the Feeling Brain.* Orlando 2003.

Daney, Serge: Le travelling de Kapo. In: *Trafic* (1992), No. 4, 5–19.

Daniels, Stephen / Endfield, Georgina H. (eds.): *Journal of Historical Geography* (2009), Vol. 35, No. 2 (Special Issue. Narratives of Climate Change), 215–404.

Daniels, Stephen / Endfield, Georgina H.: Narratives of Climate Change. Introduction. In: *Journal of Historical Geography* (2009), Vol. 35, No. 2 (Special Issue. Narratives of Climate Change), 215–222.

Deigh, John: *Emotions, Values, and the Law.* Oxford 2008.

Deleuze, Gilles: *Expressionism in Philosophy. Spinoza* [1968]. New York 1992.

Deleuze, Gilles: *Francis Bacon. The Logic of Sensation* [1981]. London 2003.

Deleuze, Gilles: Painting Sets Writing Ablaze [1981]. In: id.: *Two Regimes of Madness. Texts and Interviews 1975–1995*. New York 2006, 181–187.

Deleuze, Gilles: *Cinema I. The Movement-Image* [1983]. Minneapolis 1986.

Deleuze, Gilles: Cinema-1, Premiere [1983]. In: id.: *Two Regimes of Madness. Texts and Interviews 1975–1995*. New York 2006, 210–212.

Deleuze, Gilles: Portrait of the Philosopher as a Moviegoer [1983]. In: id.: *Two Regimes of Madness: Texts and Interviews 1975–1995*. New York 2006, 213–221.

Deleuze, Gilles: *Cinema II. The Time-Image* [1985]. Minneapolis 1989.

Deleuze, Gilles / Guattari, Félix: *Anti-Oedipus. Capitalism and Schizophrenia* [1972]. Minneapolis 1983.

Deleuze, Gilles / Guattari, Félix: *A Thousand Plateaus. Capitalism and Schizophrenia* [1980], trans. Brian Massumi. Minneapolis 1987.

Deleuze, Gilles / Guattari, Félix: *What is Philosophy?* [1991], trans. Graham Burchell, Hugh Tomlinson. London 1994.

Deloria, Vine: Foreword / American Fantasy. In: Gretchen M. Bataille, Charles L. P. Silet (eds.): *The Pretend Indians. Images of Native Americans in the Movies*. Ames 1980, ix–xvi.

Delumeau, Jean: *Sin and Fear. The Emergence of a Western Guilt Culture, 13th–18th Centuries* [1983]. New York 1990.

Demmerling, Christoph / Landweer, Hilge: *Philosophie der Gefühle. Von Achtung bis Zorn*. Stuttgart 2007.

Demmerling, Christoph / Landweer, Hilge: Hume. Natur und soziale Gestalt der Affekte. In: Hilge Landweer, Ursula Renz (eds.): *Klassische Emotionstheorien. Von Platon bis Wittgenstein*. Berlin 2008, 395–412.

Dewey, John: The Theory of Emotion I. Emotional Attitudes. In: *The Psychological Review* (1894), Vol. 1, No. 6, 553–569.

Dewey, John: The Theory of Emotion II. The Significance of Emotions. In: *The Psychological Review* (1895), Vol. 2, No. 1, 13–32.

Dewey, John: *The Middle Works, 1899–1924, Vol. IX: 1916. Democracy and Education*. Carbondale 2008.

Dewey, John: *Reconstruction in Philosophy* [1919]. New York 1920.

Dewey, John: *Art as Experience* [1934]. New York 1980.

Diderot, Denis: Conversation of a Father with His Children [1771]. In: id.: *This Is Not a Story and Other Stories*. London 1993, 126–160.

Didi-Huberman, Georges: *Images in Spite of All* [2004]. Chicago 2008.

Dimitrov, Georgi: *The Fascist Offensive and the Tasks of the Communist International in the Fight for the Unity of the Working Class Against Fascism*. London 1935.

Döring, Sabine (ed.): *Philosophie der Gefühle*. Frankfurt a. M. 2009.

Döring, Sabine: Allgemeine Einleitung. Philosophie der Gefühle heute. In id. (ed.): *Philosophie der Gefühle*. Frankfurt a. M. 2009, 12–65.

Doyle, Julie: Seeing the Climate? The Problematic Status of Visual Evidence in Climate Change Campaigning. In: Sidney Dobrin, Sean Morey (eds.): *Ecosee. Image, Rhetoric, and Nature*. New York 2009, 279–298.

Eisenstein, Sergei M.: The Montage of Film Attractions [1924]. In: id.: *Selected Works. Vol. I: Writings, 1922–1934*, ed. Richard Taylor. London 1988, 39–58.

Eisenstein, Sergei M.: The Fourth Dimension in Cinema [1929]. In: id.: *Selected Works. Vol. I: Writings, 1922–1934*, ed. Richard Taylor. London 1988, 181–194.

Eisenstein, Sergei M.: Organic Unity and Pathos in the Composition of Potemkin [1939]. In: id.: *Problems of Film Direction*. Honolulu 2004, 1–9.

Eisenstein, Sergei M.: Perspectives [1929]. In: id.: *Selected Works. Vol. I: Writings, 1922–1934*, ed. Richard Taylor. London 1988, 151–160.

Elsaesser, Thomas: Diagonale Erinnerung. Geschichte als Palimpsest in Sterne. In: Hermann Kappelhoff, Bernand Groß, Daniel Illger (eds.): *Demokratisierung der Wahrnehmung*. Berlin 2010, 95–114.

Emerson, Ralph W.: Nature [1836]. In: id.: *Nature and Selected Essays*. New York 1982, 35–82.

Esposito, Elena: Die offene Zukunft der Sorgekultur. In: Lorenz Engell, Bernhard Siegert, Joseph Vogl (eds.): *Gefahrensinn. Archiv für Mediengeschichte*. Munich 2009, 107–114.

Faulkner, William: *Requiem for a Nun* [1951]. New York 2011.

Feagin, Susan L: Empathizing as Simulating. In: Amy Coplan, Peter Goldie (eds.): *Empathy. Philosophical and Psychological Perspectives*. Oxford 2011, 149–161.

Ferguson, Mark A. / Branscombe, Nyla R.: Collective Guilt Mediates the Effect of Beliefs about Global Warming on Willingness to Engage in Mitigation Behavior. In: *Journal of Environmental Psychology* (2010), Vol. 30, 135–142.

Freud, Sigmund: Mourning and Melancholia [1917]. In: *On Murder, Mourning and Melancholia*. London 2005, 201–218.

Freud, Sigmund: *Civilization and Its Discontents* [1930]. New York 1989.

Frevert, Ute: *Emotions in History. Lost and Found*. Budapest / New York 2011.

Friedman, Thomas L.: *Hot, Flat, and Crowded. Why We Need a Green Revolution – And How It Can Renew America*. New York 2008.

Früchtl, Josef: *Ästhetische Erfahrung und moralisches Urteil. Eine Rehabilitierung*. Frankfurt a. M. 1996.

Frye, Northrop: *Anatomy of Criticism. Four Essays*. Princeton 1957.

Fuller, Buckminster: *Operating Manual for Spaceship Earth*. Carbondale / Edwardsville 1969.

Gardiner, Stephen M.: *A Perfect Moral Storm. The Ethical Tragedy of Climate Change*. New York 2011.

Garrett, Aaron V.: Leidenschaften und Moral Sense. In: Hilge Landweer, Ursula Renz (eds.): *Klassische Emotionstheorien. Von Platon bis Wittgenstein*. Berlin 2008, 373–391.

Georgakas, Dan: They Have not Spoken. American Indians in Film. In: Gretchen M. Bataille, Charles L. P. Silet (eds.): *The Pretend Indians. Images of Native Americans in the Movies*. Ames 1980, 134–142.

Gibbs, Raymond W.: *Embodiment and Cognitive Science*. New York 2006.

Giordano, Ralph: *Die zweite Schuld – oder Von der Last Deutscher zu sein*. Hamburg 1987.

Girshausen, Theo: Katharsis. In: Erika Fischer-Lichte, Doris Kolesch, Matthias Warstat (eds.): *Metzler Lexikon Theatertheorie*. Stuttgart 2005, 163–170.

Gledhill, Christine: Rethinking Genre. In: id., Linda Williams (eds.): *Reinventing Film Studies*. London 2000, 221–243.

Godard, Jean-Luc: *Histoire(s) du Cinéma. Vol. I(a): Toutes les histoires*. Paris 1998.

Godard, Jean-Luc: *Histoire(s) du Cinéma. Vol. II(a): Seul le cinema*. Paris 1998.

Godard, Jean-Luc: Le bon plaisir de Jean-Luc Godard [1995]. In: Alain Bergala (ed.): *Jean-Luc Godard par Jean-Luc Godard. Vol. II: 1984–1998*. Paris 1998, 305–322.

Godard, Jean-Luc: Jean-Luc Godard rencontre Régis Debray [1995]. In: Alain Bergala (ed.): *Jean-Luc Godard par Jean-Luc Godard. Vol. II: 1984–1998*. Paris 1998, 423–431.

Godard, Jean-Luc / Ishaghpour, Youssef: *Archéologie du cinéma et mémoire du siècle*. Tours 2000.

Goldie, Peter: *The Emotions. A Philosophical Exploration*. Oxford 2000.

Greenspan, Patricia: *Practical Guilt. Moral Dilemmas, Emotions, and Social Norms*. New York / Oxford 1995.

Grodal, Torben: *Moving Pictures. A New Theory of Genres, Feelings and Cognition*. Oxford 1997.

Grodal, Torben: Emotions, Cognitions, and Narrative Patterns in Films. In: Carl Plantinga, Greg M. Smith (eds.): *Passionate Views: Film, Cognition, and Emotion*. Baltimore 1999, 127–145.

Grodal, Torben: *Embodied Visions. Evolution, Emotion, Culture and Film*. Oxford 2009.

Groh, Ruth / Groh, Dieter: *Weltbild und Naturaneignung. Zur Kulturgeschichte der Natur. Vol. I*. Frankfurt a. M. 1991.

Groh, Ruth / Groh, Dieter: *Die Außenwelt der Innenwelt. Zur Kulturgeschichte der Natur. Vol. II*. Frankfurt a. M. 1996.

Groß, Bernhard: Wahrnehmen – Observieren – 'Checken'. Geschichtlichkeit als ästhetische Erfahrung in ZWISCHEN GESTERN UND MORGEN. In: Hermann Kappelhoff, Bernhard Groß, Daniel Illger (eds.): *Demokratisierung der Wahrnehmung*. Berlin 2010, 115–134.

Groß, Bernhard: *Die Filme sind unter uns. Zur Geschichtlichkeit des frühen deutschen Nachkriegskinos. Trümmer-, Genre-, Dokumentarfilm*. Berlin 2015.

Grotkopp, Matthias / Kappelhoff, Hermann: Film Genre and Modality. The Incestuous Nature of Genre Exemplified by the War Film. In: Sébastien Lefait, Philippe Ortoli (eds.): *In Praise of Cinematic Bastardy*. Newcastle upon Tyne 2012, 29–39.

Günzel, Stephan: Herrenmoral – Sklavenmoral. In: Henning Ottmann (ed.): *Nietzsche Handbuch. Leben – Werk – Wirkung*. Stuttgart / Weimar 2011, 253–255.

Habermas, Jürgen: Eine Art Schadensabwicklung. In: *Die Zeit* (11 July 1986).

Haidt, Jonathan: The Moral Emotions. In: Richard Davidson, Klaus Scherer, Hill Goldsmith (eds.): *Handbook of Affective Sciences*. Oxford 2003, 852–870.

Hallin, Daniel: *The "Uncensored War". The Media and Vietnam*. New York / Oxford 1986.

Hamblyn, Richard: The Whistleblower and the Canary. Rhetorical Constructions of Climate Change. In: *Journal of Historical Geography* (2009), Vol. 35, No. 2, 223–236.

Hammer, Espen: *Stanley Cavell. Skepticism, Subjectivity, and the Ordinary*. Cambridge 2002.

Helm, Bennett: *Emotional Reason. Deliberation, Motivation, and the Nature of Value*. Cambridge 2001.

Henrich, Joseph / Heine, Stephen J. / Norenzayan, Ara: The Weirdest People in the World? In: *Behavioral and Brain Sciences* (2010), Vol. 33, 61–135.

Heuss, Theodor: Mut zur Liebe [1949]. In: id.: *Die großen Reden. Der Staatsmann*. Tübingen 1965, 99–107.

Hilger, Michael: *From Savage to Nobleman. Images of Native Americans in Film*. Lanham / London 1995.

Horace: *Horace on Poetry. The 'Ars Poetica'*, ed. C. O. Brink. Cambridge 1971.

Hume, David: *A Treatise of Human Nature* [1739], ed. David Fate Norton, Mary J. Norton. Oxford 2000.

Intergovernmental Panel on Climate Change: *Climate Change Report (IPCC). Synthesis report. Longer report – adopted 1 November 2014*. Geneva 2014. http://www.ipcc.ch/report/ar5/syr/ (last accessed: 12 September 2016).

James, William: What Is an Emotion? In: *Mind* (1884), Vol. 9, No. 34, 188–205.

Jancovich, Marc / Reboll, Antonio Lázaro / Stringer, Julian / Willis, Andy (eds.): *Defining Cult Movies. The cultural politics of oppositional taste*. Manchester 2004.

Jankélévitch, Vladimir: *The Bad Conscience* [1951]. Chicago 2014.

Jaspers, Karl: *The Question of German Guilt* [1946], trans. E. B. Ashton. New York 1987.

Jiménez, Marissa / Yang, Kenneth C. C.: How Guilt Level Affects Green Advertising Effectiveness? In: *Journal of Creative Communications* (2008), Vol. 3, No. 3, 231–254.

Johnson, Laura: (Environmental) Rhetorics of Tempered Apocalypticism in AN INCONVENIENT TRUTH. In: *Rhetoric Review* (2009), Vol. 28, No. 1, 29–46.

Joost, Gesche: *Bild-Sprache. Die audio-visuelle Rhetorik des Films*. Bielefeld 2008.

Kahana, Jonathan: *Intelligence Work. The Politics of American Documentary*. New York 2008.

Kant, Immanuel: *Groundwork of the Metaphysics of Morals* [1785 / 1786]. Cambridge 1998.

Kant, Immanuel: *Critique of Practical Reason* [1788]. Cambridge 1997.

Kant, Immanuel: *Critique of Judgment* [1790]. Cambridge 1987.

Kant, Immanuel: *The Metaphysics of Morals* [1797]. Cambridge 1991.

Kant, Immanuel: *Anthropology from a Pragmatic Point of View* [1798 / 1800]. Cambridge 2006.

Kappelhoff, Hermann: *Matrix der Gefühle. Das Kino, das Melodrama und das Theater der Empfindsamkeit*. Berlin 2004.

Kappelhoff, Hermann: Politik der Gefühle. Veit Harlan, Detlef Sierck und das Melorama des NS-Kinos. In: Harro Segeberg (ed.): *Mediale Mobilmachung I. Das Dritte Reich und der Film*. Munich 2004, 248–265.

Kappelhoff, Hermann: Die vierte Dimension des Bewegungsbildes. Das filmische Bild im Übergang zwischen individueller Leiblichkeit und kultureller Fantasie. In: Anne Bartsch, Jens Eder, Kathrin Fahlenbrach (eds.): *Audiovisuelle Emotionen. Emotionsdarstellung und Emotionsvermittlung durch audiovisuelle Medienangebote*. Cologne 2007, 297–311.

Kappelhoff, Hermann: *The Politics and Poetics of Cinematic Realism* [2008]. New York 2015.

Kappelhoff, Hermann / Bakels, Jan-Hendrik: Das Zuschauergefühl. Möglichkeiten qualitativer Medienanalyse. In: *Zeitschrift für Medienwissenschaft* (2011), Vol. 5, No. 2, 78–96.

Kappelhoff, Hermann / Müller, Cornelia: Embodied Meaning Construction. Multimodal Metaphor and Expressive Movement in Speech, Gesture, and Feature Film. In: *Metaphor and the Social World* (2011), Vol. 1, No. 2, 121–153.

Kappelhoff, Hermann: Artificial emotions. Melodramatic practices of shared interiority. In: Rüdiger Campe, Julia Weber (eds.): *Rethinking Emotion. Interiority and Exteriority in Premodern, Modern, and Contemporary Thought*. Berlin / Boston, 2014, 264–288.

Kappelhoff, Hermann / Pischel, Christian / Rositzka, Eileen / Pogodda, Cilli: The Green Berets. Der Vietnamkriegsfilm als Herausforderung der klassischen Genrepoetik. In: Thomas Morsch (ed.): *Genre und Serie*. Munich 2015, 75–110.

Kappelhoff, Hermann: *Front Lines of Community. Hollywood Between War and Democracy*. Berlin / Boston 2018.

Karlsson, Gunnar / Sjöberg, Lennart G.: The Experiences of Guilt and Shame. A Phenomenological-Psychological Study. In: *Human Studies* (2009), Vol. 32, No. 3, 335–355.

Kasdan, Margo / Tavernetti, Susan: Native Americans in a Revisionist Western: LITTLE BIG MAN (1970). In: Peter C. Rollins, John E. O'Connor (eds.): *Hollywood's Indian. The Portrayal of the Native American in Film*. Lexington 1998, 121–136.

Katz, Jack: *How Emotions Work*. Chicago 1999.

Keane, Stephen: *Disaster Movies. The Cinema of Catastrophe*. New York / Chichester 2001.

Kerger, Henry: Moral. In: Henning Ottmann (ed.): *Nietzsche Handbuch. Leben – Werk – Wirkung*. Stuttgart / Weimar 2011, 284–286.

Kierkegaard, Søren: *The Concept of Anxiety* [1844]. Princeton 1980.

Kierkegaard, Søren: The Sickness unto Death [1849]. In: id.: *Fear and Trembling and The Sickness unto Death*. Princeton 2013, 235–478.

Kilpatrick, Jacquelyn: *Celluloid Indians. Native Americans and Film*. Lincoln / London 1999.

Klibansky, Raymond / Panofsky, Erwin / Saxl, Fritz: *Saturn and Melancholy. Studies in the History of Natural* Philosophy, *Religion and Art*. New York 1964.

Kober, Anne: Antifaschismus im DDR-Film. Ein Fallbeispiel: Der Rat der Götter. In: Manfred Agathen, Eckhard Jesse, Ehrhart Neubert (eds.): *Der missbrauchte Antifaschismus. DDR Staatsdoktrin und Lebenslüge der deutschen Linken*. Freiburg i. Br. 2002, 202–220.

Koch, Gertrud: Siegfried Kracauer. *An Introduction* [1996], trans. Jeremy Gaines. Princeton 2000.

Koch, Gertrud: Zu Tränen gerührt. Zur Erschütterung im Kino. In: Klaus Herding, Bernhard Stumpfhaus (eds.): *Pathos, Affekt, Gefühl. Die Emotionen in den Künsten*. Berlin 2004, 562–574.

Koselleck, Reinhart: Wie neu ist die Neuzeit? In: *Historische Zeitschrift* (1990), Vol. 251, No. 3, 539–553.

Kracauer, Siegfried: *Theory of Film. The Redemption of Physical Reality* [1960]. Princeton 1990.

Kracauer, Siegfried: *History. The Last Things Before the Last* [1969]. New York 1995.

Kracauer, Siegfried: Das Grauen im Film [1940]. In: id.: Werke. Vol. VI,3: *Kleine Schriften zum Film 1932–1961*. Frankfurt a. M. 2004, 312–314.

Kracauer, Siegfried: The Decent German. Film Portrait [1949]. In: Johannes von Moltke, Kristy Rawson (eds.): *Siegfried Kracauer's American Writings*. Berkeley / Los Angeles 2012, 157–161.

Kreimeier, Klaus: Die Ökonomie der Gefühle. Aspekte des westdeutschen Nachkriegsfilms. In: Hilmar Hoffmann, Walter Schobert (eds.): *Zwischen Gestern und Morgen. Westdeutscher Nachkriegsfilm 1946–1962*. Frankfurt a. M. 1989, 8–32.

Laarmann, Matthias: Schuld. II. 2. Neues Testament und Patristik. In: Joachim Ritter, Karlfried Gründer (eds.): *Historisches Wörterbuch der Philosophie*. Vol. VIII. Darmstadt 1995, 1448–1450.

Laine, Tarja: *Shame and Desire. Emotion, Intersubjectivity, Cinema*. Brussels 2007.

Laine, Tarja: *Feeling Cinema. Emotional Dynamics in Film Studies*. New York 2011.

Lakoff, George: Why it Matters How We Frame the Environment. In: *Environmental Communication* (2010), Vol. 4, No. 1, 70–81.

Lakoff, George / Johnson, Mark: *Philosophy in the Flesh. The Embodied Mind and Its Challenge to Western Thought*. New York 1999.

Landweer, Hilge: *Scham und Macht. Phänomenologische Untersuchungen zur Sozialität eines Gefühls*. Tübingen 1999.

Landweer, Hilge: Normativität, Moral und Gefühle. In: id. (ed.): *Gefühle. Struktur und Funktion*. Berlin 2007, 237–254.

Landweer, Hilge: Die Macht der Erinnerung. Gewissensgefühle in Khaled Hosseinis Drachenläufer. In: Ingrid Kasten (ed.): *Machtvolle Gefühle*. Berlin 2010, 297–311.

Landweer, Hilge: Der Sinn für Angemessenheit als Quelle von Normativität in Ethik und Ästhetik. In: Kerstin Andermann, Undine Eberlein (eds.): *Gefühle als Atmosphären. Neue Phänomenologie und philosophische Emotionstheorie*. Berlin 2011, 57–78.

Laugier, Sandra: Wittgenstein and Cavell. Anthropology, Skepticism, and Politics. In: Andrew Norris (ed.): *The Claim to Community. Essays on Stanley Cavell and Political Philosophy*. Stanford 2006, 19–37.

Lausberg, Heinrich: *Handbook of Literary Rhetoric. A Foundation for Literary Study*. Leiden 1998.

Latour, Bruno: *Politics of Nature. How to Bring the Sciences into Democracy*. Cambridge 2004.

Lazarus, Richard: *Emotion and Adaptation*. New York 1991.

Leake, Jonathan: Please, Sir! Gore's Got Warming Wrong. In: *The Sunday Times* (14 October 2007).

LeDoux, Joseph: *The Emotional Brain. The Mysterious Underpinnings of Emotional Life*. New York 1996.

Lethen, Helmut: *Cool Conduct. The Culture of Distance in Weimar Germany* [1994]. Berkeley 2002.

Lickel, Brian / Schmader, Toni / Barquissau, Marchelle: The Evocation of Moral Emotions in Intergroup Contexts. The Distinction Between Collective Guilt and Collective Shame. In: Nyla R. Branscombe, Bertjan Doosje (eds.): *Collective Guilt. International Perspectives*. Cambridge 2004, 35–55.

Lindsey, Lisa L. Massi / Ah Jun, Kimo / Hill, Jennifer B.: Anticipated Guilt as Behavioral Motivation. An Examination of Appeals to Help Unknown Others Through Bone Marrow Donation. In: *Human Communication Research* (2005), Vol. 31, No. 4, 453–481.

Lipps, Theodor: *Ästhetik, Psychologie des Schönen und der Kunst I. Grundlegung der Ästhetik*. Hamburg 1903.

Lotter, Maria-Sibylla: *Scham, Schuld, Verantwortung. Über die kulturellen Grundlagen der Moral*. Frankfurt a. M. 2012.

Lück, Michael: Mystery, Crime, Thriller. Vom Sog dunkler Vergangenheit im Hollywood-Kino der 2000er Jahre. In: Jennifer Henke, Magdalena Krakowski, Benjamin Moldenhauer, Oliver Schmidt (eds.): *Hollywood Reloaded. Genrewandel und Medienerfahrung der Jahrtausendwende*. Marburg 2013, 171–189.

Maetzig, Kurt: Probleme des realistischen Filmschaffens in der Deutschen Demokratischen Republik. In: id.: *Auf neuen Wegen. 5 Jahre fortschrittlicher deutscher Film*. (East) Berlin 1951, 30–39.

Maetzig, Kurt: *Filmarbeit. Gespräche, Reden, Schriften*, ed. Günter Agde. (East) Berlin 1987.

Mann, Michael E. / Bradley, Raymond S. / Hughes, Malcom K.: Global-Scale Temperature Patterns and Climate Forcing Over the Past Six Centuries. In: *Nature* (1998), Vol. 392, No. 6678, 779–787.

Mann, Thomas: Das Ende [1945]. In: id.: *Gesammelte Werke. Vol. XII: Reden und Aufsätze 4*. Frankfurt a. M. 1990, 944–950.

Marks, Laura: *The Skin of the Film. Intercultural Cinema, Embodiment, and the Senses*. Durham 2000.

Massumi, Brian: Navigating Movements. Interview by Mary Zournazi. In: id.: *Politics of Affect*. Cambridge 2015, 1–46.

Massumi, Brian: Of Microperception and Micropolitics. Interview by Joel McKim. In: id.: *Politics of Affect*. Cambridge 2015, 47–82.

Massumi, Brian: *Politics of Affect*. Cambridge 2015.

Massumi, Brian: *Ontopower. War, Powers, and the State of Perception*. Durham 2015.

Mastanedra, Michael D. / Schneider, Stephen H.: Vorbereitungen für den Klimawandel. In: Paul J. Crutzen, Mike Davis, Michael D. Mastrandrea, Stephen H. Schneider, Peter Sloterdijk (eds.): *Das Raumschiff Erde hat keinen Notausgang*. Frankfurt a. M. 2011, 11–59.

Masters, Roger D.: On the Evolution of Political Communities. The Paradox of Eastern and Western Europe in the 1980s. In: Irenäus Eibl-Eibesfeldt, Frank Kemp Salter (eds.): *Indoctrinability, Ideology, and Warfare*. New York / Oxford 1998, 453–478.

Matravers, Derek: *Art and Emotion*. Oxford 1998.

Mellmann, Katja: Gefühlsübertragung? Zur Psychologie emotionaler Textwirkungen. In: Ingrid Kasten (ed.): *Machtvolle Gefühle*. Berlin 2010, 107–119.

Mellor, Felicity: The Politics of Accuracy in Judging Global Warming Films. In: *Environmental Communication* (2009), Vol. 3, No. 2, 134–150.

Merleau-Ponty, Maurice: *Phenomenology of Perception* [1945]. London 2002.

Merleau-Ponty, Maurice: *The Primacy of Perception* [1946]. Evanston 1964.

Merleau-Ponty, Maurice: The Film and the New Psychology [1947]. In: id.: *Sense and Non-Sense*. Evanston 1964, 48–59.

Meschnig, Alexander: Totalität und Ende der Schuld. Nationalsozialismus und KZ-System. In: Gerburg Treusch-Dieter, Dietmar Kamper, Bernd Ternes (eds.): *Kursbuch 37. Schuld*. Tübingen 1999, 47–58.

Meyerhold, Vsevolod: Biomechanics [1922]. In: id.: *Meyerhold on Theatre*. London / New York 1998, 197–203.

Meteyard, Lotte / Vigliocco, Gabriella: The Role of Sensory and Motor Information in Semantic Representation. A Review. In: Paco Calvo, Toni Gomila (eds.): *Handbook of Cognitive Science. An Embodied Approach*. Amsterdam / Oxford / San Diego 2008, 293–312.

Meyer-Sickendiek, Burkhard: *Affektpoetik. Eine Kulturgeschichte literarischer Emotionen*. Würzburg 2005.

Micheli, Raphaël: Emotions as Objects of Argumentative Constructions. In: *Argumentation* (2010), Vol. 24, No. 1, 1–17.

Michotte van den Berck, Albert: The Character of 'Reality' of Cinematographic Projections [1948]. In: Georges Thinès, Alan Costall, George Butterworth (eds.): *Michotte's Experimental Phenomenology of Perception*. Abingdon 2013, 197–208.

Michotte van den Berck, Albert: The Emotional Involvement of the Spectator in the Action Represented in a Film. Toward a Theory [1953]. In: Georges Thinès, Alan Costall, George Butterworth (eds.): *Michotte's Experimental Phenomenology of Perception*. Abingdon 2013, 209–218.

Mitscherlich, Alexander / Mitscherlich, Margarete: *The Inability to Mourn. Principles of Collective Behavior* [1967]. New York 1975.

Mo', Keb': Victims of Comfort. In: id.: *Keb' Mo'*. Epic 1994. Nr. 4.

Morin, Edgar: *The Cinema, or the Imaginary Man* [1956]. Minneapolis 2005.

Morris, Herbert (ed.): *Guilt and Shame*. Belmont 1971.

Morris, Herbert: Nonmoral Guilt. In: Ferdinand Schoeman (ed.): *Responsibility, Character, and the Emotions. New Essays in Moral Psychology*. Cambridge 1987, 220–240.

Morsch, Thomas: *Medienästhetik des Films. Verkörperte Wahrnehmung und ästhetische Erfahrung im Kino*. Munich 2011.

Moses, Michael V.: Savage Nations. Native Americans and the Western. In: Jennifer L. McMahon, B. Steve Csaki (eds.): *The Philosophy of the Western*. Lexington 2010, 261–290.

Müller, Cornelia: *Metaphors Dead and Alive, Sleeping and Waking. A Dynamic View*. Chicago 2008.

Müller, Cornelia / Tag, Susanne: The Dynamics of Metaphor. Foregrounding and Activating Metaphoricity in Conversational Interaction. In: *Cognitive Semiotics* (2010), Vol. 6, 85–120.

Müller, Cornelia / Christina Schmitt: Audio-visual Metaphors of the Financial Crisis. Meaning Making and the Flow of Experience. In: *Revista Brasileira de Linguística Aplicada /*

Brazilian Journal of Applied Linguistics (2015), Vol. 15, No. 2, Special Issue: Raymond W. Gibbs Jr., Luciane Corrêa Ferreira (eds.): *Metaphor and Metonymy in Social Practices*, 311–341.

Müller, Wolfgang: Die 'German Angst'. Nirgendwo in der Welt ist die ökologische Diskussion so emotional aufgeladen wie in Deutschland. Eine historische Reflexion zwei Jahre nach Fukushima. In: *Die Zeit* (14 March 2013).

Münsterberg, Hugo: *The Photoplay. A Psychological Study*. New York / London 1916.

Musil, Robert: *The Man Without Qualities. Vol. II* [1932]. New York 1995.

Neale, Steve: *Genre and Hollywood*. New York 2000.

Nietzsche, Friedrich: *Beyond Good and Evil. Prelude to a Philosophy of the Future* [1886], ed. Rolf-Peter Horstmann, Judith Norman, trans. Judith Norman. Cambridge 2002.

Nietzsche, Friedrich: *On the Genealogy of Morality* [1887]. Cambridge 2016.

Nolley, Ken: The Representation of Conquest. John Ford and the Hollywood Indian. 1939–1964. In: Peter C. Rollins, John E. O'Connor (eds.): *Hollywood's Indian. The Portrayal of the Native American in Film*. Lexington 1998, 73–90.

Norris, Andrew: Introduction. Stanley Cavell and the Claim to Community. In: id. (ed.): The *Claim to Community. Essays on Stanley Cavell and Political Philosophy*. Stanford 2006, 1–18.

Norris, Andrew: Political Revisions. Stanley Cavell and Political Philosophy. In: id. (ed.): *The Claim to Community. Essays on Stanley Cavell and Political Philosophy*. Stanford 2006, 80–97.

Nussbaum, Martha: *The Fragility of Goodness. Luck and Ethics in Greek* Tragedy *and* Philosophy. Cambridge 1986.

Nussbaum, Martha: *Love's Knowledge. Essays on Philosophy and Literature*. Oxford 1990.

Nussbaum, Martha: *Poetic Justice. The Literary Imagination and Public Life*. Boston 1995.

Nussbaum, Martha: *Upheavals of Thought. The Intelligence of Emotions*. Cambridge 2001.

Nussbaum, Martha: *Hiding from Humanity. Disgust, Shame, and the Law*. Princeton 2004.

Nussbaum, Martha: Emotions as Judgments of Value and Importance. In: Robert C. Solomon (ed.): *Thinking About Feeling. Contemporary Philosophers on Emotions*. New York 2004, 183–199.

Olick, Jeffrey K.: *In the House of the Hangman. The Agonies of German Defeat*. 1943–1949. Chicago / London 2005.

Olick, Jeffrey K.: *The Politics of Regret. On Collective Memory and Historical Responsibility*. New York / London 2007.

O'Keefe, Daniel J.: Guilt as a Mechanism of Persuasion. In: James Price Dillard, Michael Pfau (eds.): *The Persuasion Handbook. Developments in Theory and Practice*. London 2002, 329–344.

Ottmann, Henning (ed.): *Nietzsche Handbuch. Leben – Werk – Wirkung*. Stuttgart / Weimar 2011.

Peirce, Charles S.: Lectures on Pragmatism [1903]. In: id.: *Collected Papers. Vol. V: Pragmatism and Pragmaticism*, ed. Charles Hartshorne, Paul Weiss. Cambridge 1934, 14–212.

Piers, Gerhart / Singer, Milton B.: *Shame and Guilt. A Psychoanalytic and a Cultural Study* [1953]. New York 1971.

Plantinga, Carl: Synästhetische Affekte. Szenarios von Schuld und Scham in Hitchcocks Filmen. In: Anne Bartsch, Jens Eder, Kathrin Fahlenbrach (eds.): *Audiovisuelle Emotionen*.

Emotionsdarstellung und Emotionsvermittlung durch audiovisuelle Medienangebote. Cologne 2007, 350–361.

Plantinga, Carl: *Moving Viewers. American Film and the Spectator's Experience.* Berkeley 2009.

Plessner, Helmuth: *Levels of Organic Life and the Human. An Introduction to Philosophical Anthropology* [1929], trans. Millay Hyatt. New York 2019.

Plessner, Helmuth: Die Deutung des mimischen Ausdrucks. Ein Beitrag zur Lehre vom Bewußtsein des anderen Ichs [1925]. In: id.: *Gesammelte Schriften. Vol. VII: Ausdruck und menschliche Natur.* Frankfurt a. M. 1982, 67–130.

Plessner, Helmuth: *Laughing and Crying. A Study of the Limits of Human Behaviour* [1941]. Evanston 1970.

Plessner, Helmuth: Zur Hermeneutik nichtsprachlichen Ausdrucks [1967]. In: id.: *Gesammelte Schriften. Vol. VII: Ausdruck und menschliche Natur.* Frankfurt a. M. 1982, 459–477.

Prinz, Jesse: *Gut Reactions. A Perceptual Theory of Emotion.* New York 2004.

Prinz, Jesse: *The Emotional Construction of Morals.* New York 2007.

Prinz, Jesse: Is Empathy Necessary for Morality? In: Amy Coplan, Peter Goldie (eds.): *Empathy. Philosophical and Psychological Perspectives.* Oxford 2011, 211–229.

Pudovkin, Vsevolod: *Selected Essays*, ed. Richard Taylor. Chicago 2006.

Pugmire, David: Emotion and Emotion Science. In: *European Journal of Analytic Philosophy* (2006), Vol. 2, No. 1, 7–27.

Radkau, Joachim: *The Age of Ecology* [2011]. Cambridge 2014.

Rancière, Jacques: A Fable without a Moral. Godard, Cinema, (Hi)stories [2001]. In: id.: *Film Fables.* London 2006, 171–188.

Rapp, Christoph: Aristoteles. Bausteine für eine Theorie der Emotionen. In: Hilge Landweer, Ursula Renz (eds.): *Klassische Emotionstheorien. Von Platon bis Wittgenstein.* Berlin 2008, 47–67.

Reddy, William M.: *The Navigation of Feeling. A Framework for the History of Emotions.* Cambridge 2008.

Ricœur, Paul: *Fallible Man* [1960], trans. Charles A. Kelbley. New York 1986.

Ritter, Martin: Schuld II. 1. Hebräische Bibel und Frühjudentum. In: Joachim Ritter, Karlfried Gründer (eds.): *Historisches Wörterbuch der Philosophie. Vol. VIII.* Darmstadt 1995, 1446–1447.

Rivette, Jacques: *On Abjection.* URL: http://www.dvdbeaver.com/rivette/ok/abjection.html (last accessed: 8 May 2020).

Robinson, Jenefer: *Deeper Than Reason. Emotion and its Role in Literature, Music, and Art.* Oxford 2005.

Robnik, Drehli: Körper-Erfahrung und Film-Phänomenologie. In: Jürgen Felix (ed.): *Moderne Film Theorie.* Mainz 2002, 246–280.

Röttger-Rössler, Birgitt: Emotion und Kultur. Einige Grundfragen. In: *Zeitschrift für Ethnologie* (2002), Vol. 127, No. 2, 147–162.

Rommel-Ruiz, W. Bryan: *American History Goes to the Movies. Hollywood and the American Experience.* New York / London 2011.

Rorty, Amélie O. (ed.): *Explaining Emotions.* Berkeley 1980.

Rorty, Amélie O. (ed.): *Essays on Aristotle's Ethics.* Berkeley 1980.

Rorty, Richard: Solidarity or Objectivity? In: id.: *Objectivity, Relativism, and Truth. Philosophical Papers.* Cambridge 1991, 21–34.

Rorty, Richard: *Contingency, Irony, and Solidarity.* Cambridge 1998.

Rorty, Richard: *Achieving our Country. Leftist Thought in Twentieth-Century America*. Cambridge 1999.

Rorty, Richard: Erwiderung auf Hauke Brunkhorst. In: Thomas Schäfer, Udo Tietz, Rüdiger Zill (eds.): *Hinter den Spiegeln. Beiträge zur Philosophie Richard Rortys mit Erwiderungen von Richard Rorty*. Frankfurt a. M. 2001, 162–165.

Roskamm, Wilhelm: Mitleid. In: Henning Ottmann (ed.): *Nietzsche Handbuch. Leben – Werk – Wirkung*. Stuttgart / Weimar 2011, 283–284.

Rosteck, Thomas / Frentz, Thomas S.: Myth and Multiple Readings in Environmental Rhetoric. The Case of An Inconvenient Truth. In: *Quarterly Journal of Speech* (2009), Vol. 95, No. 1, 1–19.

Rushton, J. Philippe: Genetic Similarity Theory, Ethnocentrism, and Group Selection. In: Irenäus Eibl-Eibesfeldt, Frank Kemp Salter (eds.): *Indoctrinability, Ideology, and Warfare*. New York / Oxford 1998, 369–388.

Sartre, Jean-Paul: *Being and Nothingness* [1943]. New York 1993.

Sasuly, Richard: *IG Farben* [1947]. (East) Berlin 1952.

Schaal, Gary S. / Heidenreich, Felix: Zur Rolle von Emotionen in der Demokratie. In: *Aus Politik und Zeitgeschichte* (2013), Vol. 63, No. 32/33, 3–11.

Schäfer, Thomas / Tietz, Udo / Zill, Rüdiger (eds.): *Hinter den Spiegeln. Beiträge zur Philosophie Richard Rortys mit Erwiderungen von Richard Rorty*. Frankfurt a. M. 2001.

Scheer, Monique: Are Emotions a Kind of Practice (and Is that What Makes Them Have a History)? A Bourdieuian Approach to Understanding Emotion. In: *History and Theory* (2012), Vol. 51, No. 2, 193–220.

Schefczyk, Michael: *Verantwortung für historisches Unrecht. Eine philosophische Untersuchung*. Berlin / New York 2012.

Scheler, Max: Repentance and Rebirth [1917]. In: id.: *On the Eternal in Man*. London 1960, 33–66.

Scherer, Bernd M. / Klingan, Kathrin: Einführung. In: *Das Anthropozän-Projekt. Eine Eröffnung. Programmheft zur Veranstaltung im Haus der Kulturen der Welt*. Berlin 10–13 January 2013, 2–7.

Scherer, Klaus: What Are Emotions? And How Can They Be Measured? In: *Social Science Information* (2005), Vol. 44, No. 4, 693–727.

Schiller, Friedrich / Goethe, Johann W. von: *Correspondence Between Schiller and Goethe from 1794 to 1805*, ed. George H. Calvert. New York 1845.

Schmale, Holger: Ein Präsident, der gerne mehr tun würde. Gauck bekennt das Vergessen als zweite deutsche Schuld. Reparationsforderungen wird er in Berlin ansprechen. In: *Berliner Zeitung* (8 March 2014).

Schmitz, Hermann: Der Leib im Spiegel der Kunst. In: id.: *System der Philosophie*. Vol. II,1. Bonn 1966.

Schmitz, Hermann: Der Gefühlsraum. In: id.: *System der Philosophie*. Vol. III,2. Bonn 1969.

Schmitz, Hermann: *New Phenomenology. A Brief Introduction* [2009]. Milan 2019.

Schmitz, Hermann: *Das Reich der Normen*. Freiburg i. Br. 2012.

Schneider, Birgit / Nocke, Thomas: Image Politics of Climate Change. Introduction. In: id. (eds.): *Image Politics of Climate Change. Visualizations, Imaginations, Documentations*. Bielefeld 2014, 9–26.

Schramm, Holger / Wirth, Werner: Exploring the Paradox of Sad-Film Enjoyment. The Role of Multiple Appraisals and Meta-Appraisals. In: *Poetics* (2010), Vol. 38, No. 3, 319–335.

Schnurre, Wolfdietrich: Rettung des deutschen Films. Eine Streitschrift [1950]. In: id.: *Kritiker*. Munich 2010, 269–314.

Schwarte, Ludger: *Vom Urteilen. Gesetzlosigkeit, Geschmack, Gerechtigkeit*. Berlin 2012.

Schwarz, Maurine T.: Collective Guilt, Conservation, and Other Postmodern Messages in Contemporary Westerns. In: *American Indian Culture and Research Journal* (2002), Vol. 26, No. 1, 83–105.

Schweinitz, Jörg: Genre und lebendiges Genrebewußtsein. In: *montage AV* (1994), Vol. 3, No. 2, 99–118.

Shandley, Robert R.: *Rubble Films. German Cinema in the Shadow of the Third Reich*. Philadelphia 2001.

Shapiro, Michael J.: The Demise of 'International Relations'. America's Western Palimpsest. In: *Geopolitics* (2005), Vol. 10, No. 2, 222–243.

Shaviro, Steven: *The Cinematic Body*. Minneapolis 1993.

Sheets-Johnstone, Maxine: Getting to the Heart of Emotions and Consciousness. In: Paco Calvo, Toni Gomila (eds.): *Handbook of Cognitive Science. An Embodied Approach*. Amsterdam / Oxford / San Diego 2008, 453–465.

Slaby, Jan: Emotionaler Weltbezug. Ein Strukturschema im Anschluss an Heidegger. In: Hilge Landweer (ed.): *Gefühle. Struktur und Funktion*. Berlin 2007, 93–11.

Slaby, Jan: Affective Intentionality and the Feeling Body. In: *Phenomenology and the Cognitive Sciences* (2008), Vol. 7, No. 4, 429–444.

Slaby, Jan: Möglichkeitsraum und Möglichkeitssinn. Bausteine einer phänomenologischen Gefühlstheorie. In: Kerstin Andermann, Undine Eberlein (eds.): *Gefühle als Atmosphären. Neue Phänomenologie und philosophische Emotionstheorie*. Berlin 2011, 125–138.

Sloterdijk, Peter: *How big is 'big'?* http://www.collegium-international.org/index.php/en/con tributions/127-how-big-is-big (13 May 2018).

Slotkin, Richard: *Gunfighter Nation. The Myth of the Frontier in Twentieth-Century America*. New York 1992.

Smith, Adam: *The Theory of Moral Sentiments* [1759]. Cambridge 2002.

Smith, Greg M.: *Film Structure and the Emotion System*. Cambridge 2003.

Smith, Murray: *Engaging Characters. Fiction, Emotion, and the Cinema*. Oxford 1995.

Sobchack, Thomas: Genre Film. A Classical Experience [1975]. In: Barry K. Grant (ed.): *Film Genre Reader IV*. Austin 2012, 121–132.

Sobchack, Vivian: *The Address of the Eye. A Phenomenology of Film Experience*. Princeton 1992.

Sobchack, Vivian: What My Fingers Knew. The Cinesthetic Subject, or Vision in the Flesh. In: id.: *Carnal Thoughts. Embodiment and Moving Image Culture*. Berkeley / Los Angeles / London 2004, 53–84.

Solomon, Robert C.: *The Passions. Emotions and the Meaning of Life*. Indianapolis / Cambridge 1976.

Solomon, Robert C.: *True to Our Feelings. What Our Emotions Are Really Telling Us*. Oxford 2006.

Sondermann, Maria A.: Einführung. In: Edith Stein: *Gesamtausgabe. Vol. V: Zum Problem der Einfühlung*, ed. Maria A. Sondermann. Freiburg 2008, xi–xxvi.

Sontag, Susan: The Imagination of Disaster [1965]. In: id.: *Against Interpretation and Other Essays*. New York 1966, 209–225.

Sousa, Ronald de: *The Rationality of Emotion*. Cambridge 1987.

Stein, Edith: *On the Problem of Empathy* [1917]. Washington D. C. 1989.

Stern, Daniel: *The Interpersonal World of the Infant*. New York 1985.
Stern, Daniel: *Forms of Vitality. Exploring Dynamic Experience in Psychology, the Arts,* Psychotherapy, *and* Development. Oxford 2010.
Strub, Christian: Sympathie, moralisches Urteil und Interesselosigkeit. In: Hilge Landweer, Ursula Renz (eds.): *Klassische Emotionstheorien. Von Platon bis Wittgenstein*. Berlin 2008, 415–434.
Tan, Ed S.: Film-Induced Affect as a Witness Emotion. In: *Poetics* (1995), Vol. 23, No. 1/2, 7–32.
Tan, Ed S.: *Emotion and the Structure of Narrative Film. Film As An Emotion Machine*. Mahwah 1996.
Tappolet, Christine: Emotionen und die Wahrnehmung von Werten. In: Sabine A. Döring (ed.): *Philosophie der Gefühle*. Frankfurt a. M. 2009, 439–461.
Taylor, Gabriele: *Pride, Shame, and Guilt. Emotions of Self-Assessment*. Oxford 1985.
Taylor, Joshua C.: *America as Art*. Washington D. C. 1976.
Tedjasukmana, Chris: Wie schlecht sind die schlechten Gefühle im Kino? Politische Emotionen, negative Affekte und ästhetische Erfahrung. In: *montage AV* (2012), Vol. 21, No. 2, 11–27.
Tomkins, Silvan: *Shame and Its Sisters. A Silvan Tomkins Reader*, ed. Eve Sedgwick, Frank Adam. Durham 1995.
Tracy, Jessica / Tangney, June Price / Fischer, Kurt W. (eds.): *The Self-Conscious Emotions. The Psychology of Shame, Guilt, Embarrassment, and Pride*. New York 1995.
Tudor, Andrew: Genre [1973]. In: Barry K. Grant (ed.): *Film Genre Reader IV*. Austin 2012, 3–11.
Turner, John W.: Little Big Man. The Novel and the Film. In: Gretchen M. Bataille, Charles L. P. Silet (eds.): *The Pretend Indians. Images of Native Americans in the Movies*. Ames 1980, 156–162.
Turner, Monique M. / Underhill, Jill C.: Motivating Emergency Preparedness Behaviors. The Differential Effects of Guilt Appeals and Actually Anticipating Guilty Feelings. In: *Communication Quarterly* (2012), Vol. 60, No. 4, 545–559.
Vaage, Margrethe B.: Fiction Film and the Varieties of Empathic Engagement. In: *Midwest Studies in Philosophy* (2010), Vol. 34, No. 1, 158–179.
Verdugo, Victor C.: The Positive Psychology of Sustainability. In: *Environment, Development, Sustainability* (2012), Vol. 14, No. 5, 651–666.
Vertov, Dziga: *Kino-Eye. The Writings of Dziga Vertov*, ed. Annette Michelson. Los Angeles / Berkeley 1984.
Vetlesen, Arne J.: *Perception, Empathy, and Judgment. An Inquiry into the Preconditions of Moral Performance*. University Park 1994.
Vöhler, Martin: Zwischen Pathos und Reflexion. Bewegte Erfahrungen in der antiken Rhetorik. In: Anke Hennig, Brigitte Obermayr, Antje Wessels, Marie-Christin Wilm (eds.): *Bewegte Erfahrungen. Zwischen Emotionalität und Ästhetik*. Zürich 2008, 17–26.
Vogl, Joseph: Einleitung. In: id. (ed.): *Gemeinschaften. Positionen zu einer Philosophie des Politischen*. Frankfurt a. M. 1994, 7–27.
Voss, Christiane: *Narrative Emotionen. Eine Untersuchung über Möglichkeiten und Grenzen philosophischer Emotionstheorien*. Berlin 2004.
Voss, Christiane: Narration, Emotion und kinematografische Illusion aus philosophischer Sicht. In: Anne Bartsch, Jens Eder, Kathrin Fahlenbrach (eds.): *Audiovisuelle Emotionen. Emotionsdarstellung und Emotionsvermittlung durch audiovisuelle Medienangebote*. Cologne 2007, 312–329.

Walsh, Lynda: 'Tricks', Hockey Sticks, and the Myth of Natural Inscription. How the Visual Rhetoric of Climate gate Conflated Climate with Character. In: Birgit Schneider, Thomas Nocke (eds.): *Image Politics of Climate Change. Visualizations, Imaginations, Documentations*. Bielefeld 2014, 81–104.

Ward, Barbara: *Spaceship Earth*. New York 1966.

Warshow, Robert: The Gangster as Tragic Hero [1948]. In: id.: *The Immediate Experience. Movies, Comics, Theatre and other Aspects of Popular Culture*. Cambridge / London 2001, 97–103.

Wheatley, Catherine: *Michael Haneke's Cinema. The Ethic of the Image*. New York / Oxford 2009.

Wied, Minet de / Zillmann, Dolf / Ordman, Virginia: The Role of Empathic Distress in the Enjoyment of Cinematic Tragedy. In: *Poetics* (1995), Vol. 23, No. 1/2, 91–106.

Wildt, Andreas: Die Moralspezifizität von Affekten und der Moralbegriff. In: Hinrich Fink-Eitel, Georg Lohmann (eds.): *Zur Philosophie der Gefühle*. Frankfurt a. M. 1993, 188–217.

Williams, Bernard: *Shame and Necessity*. Berkeley 2008.

Williams, Linda: Film Bodies. Gender, Genre, and Excess [1991]. In: Barry K. Grant (ed.): *Film Genre Reader IV*. Austin 2012, 159–177.

Wilson, Margaret: Six Views of Embodied Cognition. In: *Psychonomic Bulletin & Review* (2002), Vol. 9, No. 4, 625–636.

Wingo, Hal / Haeberle, Roland L.: The Massacre at Mylai. In: *Life Magazine* (5 December 1969).

Wissenschaftlicher Beirat der Bundesregierung Globale Umweltveränderungen: *Welt im Wandel. Sicherheitsrisiko Klimawandel*. Berlin / Heidelberg 2008.

Wittgenstein, Ludwig: *Philosophical Investigations* [1953], trans. G. E. M. Anscombe. Oxford 1958.

Wright, Judith H.: Genre Films and the Status Quo [1974]. In: Barry K. Grant (ed.): *Film Genre Reader IV*. Austin 2012, 60–68.

Wurmser, Léon: *The Mask of Shame*. Baltimore 1981.

Wuss, Peter: Konflikt und Emotion im Filmerleben. In: Matthias Brütsch, Vinzenz Hediger, Ursula von Keitz, Alexandra Schneider, Margrit Tröhler (eds.): *Kinogefühle. Emotionalität und Film*. Marburg 2005, 205–224.

Yacavone, Daniel: *Film Worlds. A Philosophical Aesthetics of Cinema*. New York 2015.

Yanal, Robert J.: *Paradoxes of Emotion and Fiction*. University Park 1999.

Zalasiewicz, Jan / Williams, Mark / Smith, Alan / Barry, Tiffany L. / Coe, Angela L. / Bown, Paul R. / Brenchley, Patrick / Cantrill, David / Gale, Andrew / Gibbard, Philip / Gregory, F. John / Hounslow, Mark W. / Kerr, Andrew C. / Pearson, Paul / Knox, Robert / Powell, John / Waters, Colin / Marshall, John / Oates, Michael / Rawson, Peter / Stone, Philip: Are We Now Living in the Anthropocene? In: *GSA Today* (2008), Vol. 18, No. 2, 4–8.

Zarzosa, Augustin: Melodrama and the Modes of the World. In: *Discourse* (2010), Vol. 32, No. 2, 236–255.

Zebel, Sven / Doosje, Bertjan / Spears, Russell: It Depends on your Point-of-View. Implications of Perspective-Taking and National Identification for Dutch Collective Guilt. In: Nyla R. Branscombe, Bertjan Doosje (eds.): *Collective Guilt. International Perspectives*. Cambridge 2004, 148–168.

Filmography

THE 11TH HOUR. Directors: Leila Connors, Nadia Connors. USA 2007.

APOCALYPSE NOW. Director: Francis Ford Coppola. USA 1979.

ARE WE CHANGING PLANET EARTH? Directors: Nicolas Brown, Stephen Cooter. UK 2006.

DER AUGENZEUGE [THE EYEWITNESS], No. 132. Director: Kurt Maetzig. D 1948.

AVATAR. Director: James Cameron. USA 2009.

THE BIG PICTURE. A NATION BUILDS UNDER FIRE. Director: Harry Middleton. USA 1967.

BROKEN ARROW. Director: Delmer Daves. USA 1950.

DIE BUNTKARIERTEN [THE GIRLS IN GINGHAM]. Director: Kurt Maetzig. D 1949.

CAN WE SAVE PLANET EARTH? Directors: Nicolas Brown, Stephen Cooter. UK 2006.

CAT BALLOU. Director: Elliot Silverstein. USA 1965.

CHASING ICE. Director: Jeff Orlowski. USA 2012.

CHEYENNE AUTUMN. Director: John Ford. USA 1964.

DANCES WITH WOLVES. Director: Kevin Costner. USA / UK 1990.

DRUMS ALONG THE MOHAWK. Director: John Ford. USA 1939.

EHE IM SCHATTEN [MARRIAGE IN THE SHADOWS]. Director: Kurt Maetzig. D 1947.

THE DAY AFTER TOMORROW. Director: Roland Emmerich. USA 2004.

FORT APACHE. Director: John Ford. USA 1948.

THE GRADUATE. Director: Mike Nichols. USA 1967.

THE GREAT GLOBAL WARMING SWINDLE. Director: Martin Durkin. UK 2007.

THE GREAT WARMING. Director: Michael Taylor. USA / CAN 2006.

THE GREEN BERETS. Directors: Ray Kellogg, John Wayne. USA 1968.

HISTOIRE(S) DU CINÉMA. Director: Jean-Luc Godard. F 1998.

AN INCONVENIENT TRUTH. Director: Davis Guggenheim. USA 2006.

IN JENEN TAGEN [SEVEN JOURNEYS]. Director: Helmut Käutner. D 1947.

JUD SÜß. Director: Veit Harlan. D 1940.

KAPÒ [KAPO]. Director: Gillo Pontecorvo. I / F / YU 1960.

LIFE ON EARTH. Director: David Attenborough. UK 1979.

LITTLE BIG MAN. Director: Arthur Penn. USA 1970.

THE MAN WHO SHOT LIBERTY VALENCE. Director: John Ford. USA 1962.

MEIN KAMPF / DEN BLODIDA TIDEN. Director: Erwin Leiser. D / SWE 1960.

DIE MÖRDER SIND UNTER UNS [THE MURDERERS ARE AMONG US]. Director: Wolfgang Staudte. D 1946.

MORITURI. Director: Eugen York. D 1948.

NUIT ET BROUILLARD [NIGHT AND FOG]. Director: Alain Resnais. F 1956.

DER RAT DER GÖTTER [COUNCIL OF THE GODS]. Director: Kurt Maetzig. DDR 1950.

ROTATION. Director: Wolfgang Staudte. D 1949.

DER RUF [THE LAST ILLUSION]. Director: Josef von Báky. D 1949.

THE SEARCHERS. Director: John Ford. USA 1956.

SHANE. Director: George Stevens. USA 1953.

SHUTTER ISLAND. Director: Martin Scorsese. USA 2010.

THE SIMPSONS. Director: Matt Groening. USA 1989–.

STAGECOACH. Director: John Ford. USA 1939.

SUPPORT YOUR LOCAL SHERIFF! Director: Burt Kennedy. USA 1969.

STERNE. Director: Konrad Wolf. DDR / BG 1959.

LE SYNDROME DE TITANIC. Directors: Nicolas Hulot, Jean-Albert Lièvre. F 2009.

https://doi.org/10.1515/9783110612110-008

THEY DIED WITH THEIR BOOTS ON. Director: Raoul Walsh. USA 1941.

TRIUMPH DES WILLENS [TRIUMPH OF THE WILL]. Director: Leni Riefenstahl. D 1935.

DIE TODESMÜHLEN / DEATH MILLS. Directors: Hanuš Burger, Billy Wilder. D 1946.

DIE UNBESIEGBAREN. Director: Arthur Pohl. DDR 1953.

UNFORGIVEN. Director: Clint Eastwood. USA 1992.

WHY WE FIGHT. Directors: Frank Capra, Anatol Litvak. USA 1942–1945.

ZWISCHEN GESTERN UND MORGEN [BETWEEN YESTERDAY AND TOMORROW]. Director: Harald Braun. D 1947.

https://doi.org/10.1515/9783110612110-009

Film Index

https://doi.org/10.1515/9783110612110-010